ADVANCE PRAISE FC

QUALITATIVE RES:
AN INTRODUCTIO.

MW01491662

"In this exceptional text, deMarrais, Roulston, and Copple masterfully weave their combined decades of expertise into a solid foundation of qualitative research. Graduate students and other newcomers to qualitative inquiry will appreciate the authors' inviting, clear, and accessible writing. Readers will learn about various ways of qualitative thinking, ethical reasoning, engaging theoretical frameworks and perspectives, and collecting and analyzing data: each of the necessary skills to embark on their own scholarship. Additionally, readers will find an abundance of activities, resources for further reading, and real-world examples from dissertations and extant literature. It is clear that the authors—who are superstars in the field—have perfected their approach to introducing readers to qualitative inquiry. I highly recommend *Qualitative Research Design and Methods: An Introduction* for anyone who is hoping to learn more about qualitative research!"

Leia K. Cain, Ph.D.
Assistant Professor of Evaluation, Statistics, and Methodology
Coordinator, Qualitative Research Methods in Education Graduate Certificate
Department of Educational Leadership and Policy Studies
University of Tennessee

"deMarrais, Roulston, and Copple have created an accessible, experiential, and enjoyable guide for novice qualitative researchers that not only introduces the aesthetics and pragmatics of creating quality studies, but also inspires readers to produce meaningful works of inquiry with passion. The critical quality differentiating this introductory portal from others is the author's commitment to explain carefully why qualitative research is more important than ever to understand, question, and change our world. In doing so, the authors skillfully alert beginning researchers to the challenges they will face and the responsibilities they will need to embrace to conduct ethical and effective research."

Ronald J. Chenail, Ph.D.
Provost and Executive Vice President for Academic Affairs
Professor of Family Therapy
Nova Southeastern University

"*Qualitative Research Design and Methods: An Introduction* (2024) is a beautiful creation from three of our most revered members of the qualitative research community. This book provides exactly the kind of grounding novice qualitative researchers can immediately benefit from—complete with learning objectives for each chapter, engaging examples, and activities to help guide learners through the process of designing and carrying out qualitative inquiry projects."

Thalia M. Mulvihill, Ph.D.
Professor of Social Foundations of Education and Higher Education
Teachers College
Ball State University

"As someone who trains and teaches novice qualitative researchers, I have noted the need for an accessible, comprehensive, and appropriately critical introduction to qualitative methods. *Qualitative Research Design and Methods* is that book. deMarrais, Roulston, and Copple offer a pedagogical approach throughout, with learning objectives, reading questions, concise charts and infographics, clear explanations that engage with the "why" along with the "how" of qualitative methods, and both historical and interdisciplinary examples—all while emphasizing ethical, social justice-oriented methodological practices. This book is an important and long overdue resource for the field and for researchers at any stage."

Stephanie Anne Shelton, Ph.D.
Director of Diversity, College of Education
Associate Professor, Qualitative Research
Educational Studies in Psychology, Research Methodology, and Counseling
The University of Alabama

"The authors bring decades of experience in teaching and conducting qualitative research to offer an accessible, theoretically grounded, and practically oriented guide to designing and conducting qualitative studies with ethical relationships at the forefront. Sensitive to the epistemologically diverse, interdisciplinary, and ever-changing nature of the field of qualitative inquiry, the authors share multiple perspectives and examples and offer ideas and questions, rather than recipes to follow. Through such inclusive writing and questions, the authors invite readers into dialogue and learning that is situationally can culturally responsive and responsible to the people and spaces in which the reader designs and conducts their own studies. Furthermore, the book includes invitations for considering and embracing international and global perspectives, rare in other methodology textbooks."

Audra Skukauskaitė, Ph.D.
Professor, University of Central Florida

QUALITATIVE RESEARCH DESIGN AND METHODS

QUALITATIVE RESEARCH METHODOLOGIES: TRADITIONS, DESIGNS, AND PEDAGOGIES

EDITED BY KATHLEEN DEMARRAIS, MELISSA FREEMAN, JORI HALL, AND KATHRYN ROULSTON

The *Qualitative Research Methodologies: Traditions, Designs, and Pedagogies* series is designed to encourage qualitative researchers to look both backward and forward in the field of qualitative inquiry. We invite authors to submit proposals for both single-authored books and edited volumes focused on particular qualitative designs situated within their historical, theoretical, and disciplinary/cross-disciplinary contexts. Pieces might include a tradition's or design's historical roots and key scholars, ways the approach has changed over time, as well as ethical and methodological considerations in the use of that particular research approach. They may also provide an introduction to contemporary designs created at the intersection of multiple, theoretical, and often assumed incommensurable historical paths. In addition, we encourage authors to submit proposals for books focused on the pedagogy of qualitative research methodologies that interrogate how we prepare researchers new to qualitative research methodologies with the theoretical, methodological, and ethical understandings and skills for their work.

Those interested in being considered for inclusion in the series should send a prospectus (https://zfrmz.com/rmlvGq7xgL2RTgPkByk9), CV, and cover letter to: Kathleen deMarrais (kathleen@uga.edu).

Books in the Series:

Focus Groups: Culturally Responsive Approaches for Qualitative Inquiry and Program Evaluation
by Jori N. Hall (2020)

Exploring the Archives: A Beginner's Guide for Qualitative Researchers
by Kathryn Roulston and Kathleen deMarrais (2021)

Transformative Autoethnography for Practitioners: Change Processes and Practices for Individuals and Groups
by Kathy-Ann C. Hernandez, Wendy Bilgen, and Heewon Chang (2022)

Quests for Questioners: Inventive Approaches to Qualitative Interviews
edited by Kathryn Roulston (2023)

The Action Research Dissertation: Learning from Leading Change
by Karen E. Watkins, Erica Gilbertson, and Aliki Nicolaides (2023)

Qualitative Research Design and Methods: An Introduction
by Kathleen deMarrais, Kathryn Roulston, and Janie Copple (2024)

QUALITATIVE RESEARCH DESIGN AND METHODS

 An Introduction

BY KATHLEEN DEMARRAIS,

KATHRYN ROULSTON,

AND JANIE COPPLE

Myers
Education
Press

Gorham, Maine

Copyright © 2024 | Myers Education Press, LLC
Published by Myers Education Press, LLC
P.O. Box 424
Gorham, ME 04038

Myers Education Press is an academic publisher specializing in books, e-books and digital content in the field of education. All of our books are subjected to a rigorous peer review process and produced in compliance with the standards of the Council on Library and Information Resources.

Library of Congress Cataloging-in-Publication Data available from Library of Congress.

13-digit ISBN 978-1-9755-0566-0 (paperback)
13-digit ISBN 978-1-9755-0567-7 (library networkable e-edition)
13-digit ISBN 978-1-9755-0568-4 (consumer e-edition)

Printed in the United States of America.

All first editions printed on acid-free paper that meets the American National Standards Institute Z39-48 standard.

Books published by Myers Education Press may be purchased at special quantity discount rates for groups, workshops, training organizations and classroom usage. Please call our customer service department at 1-800-232-0223 for details.

Cover design by Teresa Lagrange Design Service from Portland, ME.

Visit us on the web at **www.myersedpress.com** to browse our complete list of titles.

Contents

List of Figures, Tables and Text Boxes

Acknowledgments

W E THANK CHRIS MYERS, STEPHANIE Gabaree, and the whole team at Myers Education Press for their fine support through the writing and production of this book.

Gratitude to former students at the University of Georgia from whom we have learned much, and who graciously gave permission to share details of their doctoral dissertations for the Appendix of this volume: Lisbeth Berbary, Roshaunda Breeden, Sean Halpin, Kate Hobgood (also published as Guthrie), Brigette Herron, Seon-Joo Kim, Edward Muhammad, Amber Neal, Oksana Parylo, and Joseph Pate. Thank you to Parker Forest and Michael Stilson at Georgia State University for granting permission to share your research memos on transcription in narrative inquiry and participant observation.

Thanks to our colleagues Melissa Freeman and Jori Hall for providing feedback on earlier drafts of this manuscript, and to Maureen Flint for giving permission to share details of her dissertation study.

Thank you to Caprial Farrington for assistance with editing and indexing.

Thanks to SAGE College and SAGE Publications Inc. Journals for permission to reproduce tables first published in *Naturalistic Inquiry* by Y. S. Lincoln and E. G. Guba (1985) and "Qualitative quality: Eight 'Big-Tent' criteria for excellent qualitative research", by S. J. Tracy (2010).

And thanks to our spouses who have continued to help us in countless ways and graciously put up with late nights, early mornings, and midnight meanders: Jamie Lewis, Mike Healy, and Josh Goodman. We appreciate you!

Preface

Kathleen deMarrais, Kathryn Roulston, and Janie Copple

THERE ARE NUMEROUS WAYS TO generate knowledge about the world. Stereotypical images of researchers in popular media frequently show them as "mad" scientists in white coats, conducting experiments without regard to ethics in laboratories. Although there are many thousands of laboratories in which scientists work on biomedical advances, new technologies, and any number of topics, many researchers choose to conduct research using qualitative methods. Rather than testing their hypotheses in a series of experiments, these researchers examine research questions through talking to people, visiting social settings to understand what is going on, and examining virtual and archival documents. The main methods of qualitative researchers are those of inquiring, examining, and observing, rather than experimentation. How qualitative researchers design their studies varies widely, as do the analytic and representational methods they use. Although newcomers to research might be tempted to look for recipes to follow when designing a qualitative study, we do not recommend this as an approach to research. Yet, given the proliferation of theories and methods used by qualitative researchers, in combination with the democratization of research in which citizens engage with research as co-researchers, participants, and audience-makers, how can novice researchers proceed?

In this book, we introduce newcomers to qualitative research to the design process in qualitative research. After introducing key characteristics of qualitative research, we begin by centering ethics as crucial to the research process. Conducting research with human subjects involves thinking through the implications of methodological decisions involved in sampling and recruitment, generating and collecting data, and writing up and reporting findings. In our view, every aspect of research involves ethical decision-making. We then discuss the role of theory in qualitative design, providing brief introductions to a range of theoretical approaches, and outlining key decisions in the design process. The chapters that follow focus on how to design studies using interviews, narrative inquiry, ethnographic and autoethnographic methods, documents and archives, and arts-based approaches. In these chapters we provide examples of studies that employ different theoretical approaches. This book is not intended to be an all-encompassing guide to either the theories or methodologies used by qualitative researchers. We know that research designs we discuss represent a fraction of the approaches employed. By examining the basic methods used in interview, ethnographic, and archival research (i.e., those of inquiring, examining, observing), we provide novice qualitative researchers keys of sorts to unlock other creative paths to designing quality qualitative studies. This book should be seen as an entrée to the exciting world of qualitative inquiry.

We conclude the book by discussing issues to consider to do with the assessment of quality. And for those researchers who are planning to conduct research studies for graduate degrees, we include examples of actual studies conducted by graduate students in an appendix. Our aim in providing these examples is to showcase a variety of theoretical perspectives and research designs used by researchers who have completed graduate degrees.

Our hope is to provide newcomers to qualitative inquiry an accessible guide to beginning their studies. We recognize that any introductory textbook is just that—and we encourage readers to explore the references cited to explore primary sources related to the theories and methods discussed. We want qualitative researchers to be inspired to conduct studies on topics they are passionate about, contributing to the generation of knowledge about the human condition and how we might live differently. Most of all, we want readers to enjoy the pleasures of learning about the world through talking to people, observing what is going on, and examining documents and artifacts. We hope you enjoy your journeys into qualitative research just as much as we have. If you'd like to read about our journeys to qualitative inquiry, read on . . .

About the Authors

Kathleen's Story

I began my teaching career in classrooms referred to as "personalized instruction" and aimed at educating young children with learning difficulties. This was prior to the passing of P.L. 94-142 in 1975, the *Education for All Handicapped Children Act* that guaranteed special education services for children in the least restrictive environment. When graduate programs designed to address special needs children opened up, I returned to school for a master's degree in special education to enhance my knowledge and skills. Much of what I learned was informed by a behaviorist framework of rewards and reinforcement, a perspective that didn't always work for me with the children in my classrooms. One of my professors at the time, Dr. Sally Pruden, encouraged me to pursue my education at the doctoral level, which I did just a couple years later. Almost on a whim, at the urging of a fellow teacher, I applied to a doctoral program at the University of Cincinnati (UC) in Social Foundations of Education. At the time, I had no idea what Social Foundations of Education was, but at the interview it became clear I was in the right place. The professors talked with each of us, one at a time, about what they taught in the program and their research interests. Dr. Jeff Shultz mentioned he taught courses in ethnography and ethnographic field methods. My reaction was immediate—I wanted to learn about that! The Social Foundations of Education doctoral program turned out to be my entrée into the world of qualitative research, although during the late 1970s and early 1980s, the term "qualitative research" was not used. The Social Foundations program at UC was an interdisciplinary program that brought together faculty from different disciplines around the study of school—sociologists, anthropologists, historians, philosophers, and comparative educators. It married my interest in the social sciences with my love of teaching and the field of education. The primary organization for programs such as this, The American Educational Studies Program, was established in 1968, as was the American Anthropology Association's Council for Anthropology and Education. Membership in both these organizations were critical to my development as a scholar.

At the beginning of the UC program, I took a three-course sequence called *Ethnographic Field Methods* as well as numerous independent studies with Dr. Jeff Shultz and was introduced to and influenced by the newly developing field of anthropology and education. Jeff was a student of Frederick Erickson. The course content was influenced by both school ethnography as practiced by educational anthropologists, particularly George Spindler (1982), and illustrated in his edited volume, *Doing the Ethnography of Schooling: Educational Anthropology in Action*. It was also influenced by the work of micro ethnographers and sociolinguists who used video ethnography to focus on interactions within classrooms. Central to my studies was work by Courtney B. Cazden,

Vera P. John, and Dell Hymes later published in Cazden and colleagues' (1972) *Functions of Language in the Classroom* as well as the micro video ethnography of ethnomethodologist Hugh Mehan (1979). At that time, the methodological focus was on what was commonly termed, "fly-on-the-wall ethnography." This approach acknowledged the presence of observers as participants in the setting, but the goal was for researchers to primarily observe rather than participate to minimize any bias or influence. Through involvement with the American Anthropology Association's Council of Anthropology and Education, I was heavily influenced by school and classroom ethnographies of the late 1970s and early 1980s.

A second key aspect of the Social Foundations Program, the Pro-Seminar required during my first year, was the context for my journey into sociology of education and social theory. Berger and Luckmann's (1966) *The Social Construction of Reality: A Treatise in the Sociology of Knowledge* was a text that spoke to me in ways much different from the behaviorist notions I had learned in special education. It gave me a language consistent with my view of reality as constructed within our everyday interactions. Through a sociology of education course, I encountered the "new sociology of education" in Michael F. D. Young's (1971) *Knowledge and Control: New Directions for the Sociology of Education* and began to look at the critical ethnographic work coming out of the United Kingdom at the time. I was particularly drawn to Nell Keddie's (1971) ethnographic work that examined teachers' perceptions of students' identities and documented differential academic outcomes based on social class and their teachers' perceptions of them. These theories embedded in the new sociology of education led me to Henry Giroux's (1983) *Theory and Resistance in Education: A Pedagogy for the Opposition*, a foundation for critical social theory in the United States and the works of scholars in the Frankfurt School of critical theory.

Excited by my readings in critical theory, I developed a research proposal informed by these theories that enabled me to ask critical questions of social class and differential achievement within an ethnography based in an urban Appalachian classroom (Bennett, 1986, 1991). My research topic was informed by my experiences as a special educator working with both rural and urban Appalachian children. As an educational specialist, I was responsible for the evaluation and placement of children into special education programs. I found that the school system simply did not meet the needs of Appalachian children, and consequently, to access services it was necessary to label children rather than change the structures and practices of schooling.

While I was quite comfortable marrying critical social theory and ethnography into what was soon to become labeled a "critical ethnography," not all the professors on my committee were convinced. Some viewed this work as ideological—so informed by the theory as to "bias" my findings. I realized it jarred with the notion of the fly on the wall ethnography I had been trained in. Despite these critiques, after rewriting the prospectus with attention to how I would ensure quality in the ethnography, I gained approval to begin and, over the next year, produced a critical ethnography that carefully documented teachers' and students' interactions in a first-grade classroom. Specifically, I explored how the talk and instructional activities for three distinct reading groups led to differential achievement based on those group assignments. The study demonstrated how the school district's policies and required practice set the context for this differential achievement despite the resistance practices of the teachers. Critical theory not only provided a theoretical framework for my questions regarding equity but informed how I approached ethnography and other qualitative research methodologies.

Following the completion of my doctoral studies, I worked at the University of Alaska, Fairbanks' program called X-CED, a teacher education program informed by educational anthropology with the aim of certifying Native Alaskan paraprofessionals as certified teachers for their communities. While I found this work engaging, in 1985 I was invited to apply for a position in social foundations, including teaching courses in qualitative research. At that time, Richard Wisniewski, dean of the University of Tennessee's college of education and trained as an educational anthropologist, had begun a series of seminars for faculty in what had become known then as qualitative research methods. His goal was to create space in the college for this emerging field of research methods. This position changed the course of my career, and over the next decade I developed courses in qualitative research for students at the University of Tennessee. At that time, the Qualitative Interest Group (QUIG) Conference, the first conference in the United States focused on qualitative research, was held annually at the University of Georgia (UGA), so it was a wonderful opportunity to take students there to engage with other qualitative research scholars and methodologists. I was fortunate in 1999 to be hired at UGA to work with Judith Preissle and others in developing a qualitative research program.

Over the past two decades, my teaching and scholarly work has focused on qualitative research methodologies, theories that inform qualitative work, and qualitative pedagogy. Critical theories continued to inform the research I did, particularly my work in examining the ways conservative philanthropists have impacted educational policy and practice through systematic, highly funded efforts to support a 50-year agenda of change (cf. deMarrais, 2006).

Kathy's Story

I came to qualitative methodology via a scenic path. After high school I worked in a bank before earning a degree in music education and becoming an elementary music specialist. Early in my teaching career, a mentor introduced me to the Kodály method of instruction developed by the Hungarian composer Zoltán Kodály (1882–1967). The state department for which I worked in Australia had adopted this approach to music education in elementary schools. I quickly found that weekend and summer Kodály workshops weren't sufficient to equip me with what I needed to know to teach effectively, and turned to the work of Lois Choksy (1981, 1988), a music educator in Canada. I applied to study with her and completed my master's degree in music education at the University of Calgary. Every week, Professor Choksy would take her graduate students to a local school and model how to teach with a 5th grade class, while her graduate students circulated through the school, planning and delivering lessons, and observing one another. Although I had read and used her books on teaching, through observing Professor Choksy's teaching, I came to a deeper understanding of the value of adjusting one's teaching strategies to whatever emerged. Professor Choksy's teaching was no rote application of what she had written, and there were no recipes to follow in the pedagogical strategies she demonstrated. Instead, she was always revising her practice and orienting lessons specifically to the students with whom she worked. This lesson has stayed with me and also applies to research—I've learned the importance of being flexible in dealing with whatever emerges in teaching or research.

My master's degree involved completing a research thesis, and this is where I first learned about qualitative research from a graduate of the Ontario Institute of Studies in Education, Dr. Carol Harris. She introduced me to participant observation (Schatzman & Strauss, 1973), a primary method used in ethnography (Woods, 1986). Although I had already observed classrooms as a student teacher, a practicing teacher, and in my graduate studies, I now had a name for this method of generating qualitative data. I read about how to design and conduct interviews and case studies (Merriam, 1988; Stake, 1978) and discovered that the problems I had encountered as a teacher were well-studied by music education researchers. As a thesis topic I settled on a problem of practice: how do teachers help inaccurate singers to learn to sing? I studied the work of music education researchers and talked to prominent music educators who were attending an international symposium for the Kodály society in Calgary. I interviewed music advisors in several school districts who recommended teachers who had demonstrated excellence in working with children's voices that I could talk to and observe. The findings of this first qualitative study changed my teaching irreversibly and ignited an interest in learning more about qualitative research methods.

Returning to the music classroom after completing my degree, I implemented findings from published research together with what I had learned from observing and interviewing expert teachers. I also learned that some ideas did not transfer well into the context in which I worked. I came to understand that when it comes to teaching, research cannot, and will never be able to, produce the "sacred seven steps" to effective teaching (Eisner, 1991, p. 205). As Eisner (1991) commented, research provides "considerations to be shared and discussed, reflected upon, and debated" (p. 205). Implementing findings from research in practice taught me that research is incremental, findings are not always transferable, and researchers continually update what is known about any topic.

On my return to Australia in the early 1990s, I shared the findings from my study in articles directed to practitioner audiences. I also brought an inquiry lens to my forays in the classroom. I found that qualitative research methods provide tools to reflect on practice, problem solve, and share findings with others. Due to the administration of instructional and planning time for classroom teachers across the state in which I worked, the time budgeted for music education in the school in which I taught was reduced. Whereas I had felt comfortable working with 700 students each week, I was allocated one day per week at an additional school of 150 students an hour's drive away. Facing an increased workload with decreasing support from classroom teachers to which I had become accustomed, I applied to graduate school to examine the topic of itinerant teaching. How did specialist teachers working in multiple schools manage their work? I sought out an advisor in the school of education with expertise in qualitative methods to mentor me through a PhD program. As it turned out, as well as learning about how itinerant music teachers managed their work and how they had adapted to the changes in their work structure, I also learned a lot about qualitative theory and methods. My advisor Dr. Carolyn Baker had expertise in ethnomethodology, and my doctoral research took on a methodological focus.

Ethnomethodology (EM) is an approach to research that was developed by sociologist Harold Garfinkel (1917–2011). EM studies examine the methods that people or "members" use to make sense of one another's utterances and actions—that is, how people accomplish social order. Although there are multiple approaches to EM studies, one tool is that of conversation analysis (CA), an approach to the analysis of talk-in-interaction developed by sociologist Harvey Sacks (1935–1975). As I learned more about EM and CA, I re-analyzed a puzzling excerpt from an interview I had conducted during my master's research (Roulston, 2001). This helped me understand the performative work that interviewers and interviewees engage in to produce interview data and how researchers can cut and categorize interview transcripts in ways that distort the talk. If not applied with great care, coding-based approaches to data analysis can hide how researchers contribute to the generation of interview accounts. To use feminist scholar Dorothy Smith's (1974) term, this results in "theorizing as ideology." One day, as I met with Dr. Baker, she pointed out that interviewees I talked to complained a lot. Her comment took me by surprise, and I initially felt insulted. After all, I was interviewing people in a group to which I belonged! But when I looked at the phenomenon of complaints in my transcripts, I learned that as an interviewer I had co-participated in the generation of those complaints. This was the topic of my first methodological article (Roulston, 2000). Examining interview transcripts led to a deeper interest in interviewing, which has since branched into research and writing on qualitative interviewing, teaching interviewing, and analysis of interaction in research interviews. I found that methodological interests in qualitative research begin with observations concerning the process of conducting research. While my methodological interests have focused on interview methods, there are innumerable topics yet to be examined.

After I completed my doctoral degree, I continued to teach and research, working in a school and in a community-based research center. This center brought university researchers and community members together to address practical problems to do with education and health. This experience taught me about how researchers can work with collaborators to address problems in communities and added to my knowledge of qualitative methods. I learned that together with theoretical and methodological topics of interest, qualitative research is suited to examining practical problems in communities.

My interests in teaching and qualitative research intersected when I took a postdoctoral position at the University of Georgia that involved teaching qualitative research. This position led to a permanent position that I've been in ever since. And because I teach qualitative methods, I've continued to explore topics to do with teaching by examining the preparation of qualitative researchers.

Janie's Story

I stumbled into qualitative methodology by accident, sparked mostly by my interest in stories and storytelling. Early in my undergraduate studies, I knew I wanted to major in history—not because I was particularly interested in memorizing facts and dates, but because I was interested in stories. Even as a young reader, historical fiction and nonfiction were my favorite genres. When I was 8 years old, my prized possession was a paperback collection of Laura Ingalls Wilder's *Little House on the Prairie* books, which told stories of Wilder and her family's experiences in the American Midwest in the late 1800s. I not only loved reading history, I loved listening to it as well. My paternal grandmother was born at the turn of the 20th century, and she had great stories! My personal favorite was a story she told about her sister, her father, and a pot-bellied wood stove she and her sister used to cook meals for their family in rural North Carolina. I remember visiting my grandmother's house, just a few miles from where she'd grown up. I loved wiggling my way next to her on the sofa, asking "Can you tell me a story from when you were a little?"

Fast forward to 1999 when I graduated with a bachelor's degree in history from Gardner-Webb University where I focused my major in post-Civil War, U.S. history. Following my bachelor's degree, I taught for 1 year in a private school before returning to graduate school to pursue a master's in history at the University of North Carolina at Greensboro (UNCG). In the year prior to beginning my master's studies, I read Howard Zinn's (1980) *A people's history of the United States, 1492-present.* Up to that point, my formal study of history had focused on renowned, powerful, predominantly white, male actors. As I read Zinn's history of the United States, written largely from the perspectives of people omitted from traditional history textbooks (e.g., women, people of color, poor people, immigrants, children), I wondered about the countless stories waiting to be written, stories of people like my grandmother. In Fall 2000, I was admitted to the history program at UNCG as a full-time master's student where I focused on 20th century U.S. women's history. Although I did not have explicit training in qualitative research methodology during my master's program, my master's thesis project was my first foray into qualitative research.

In my first semester of graduate studies, I took a course entitled *Histories of Gender, Illness and the Body.* The assigned readings for this course included Margaret Charles Smith and Linda Janet Holmes' (1996) *Listen to Me Good: The Life Story of an Alabama Midwife.* I was intrigued to read stories of Margaret Charles Smith's experience as a Black midwife and community caregiver in Eutaw, Alabama and was struck by the way historian Linda Janet Holmes situated Smith's experiences within the broader historical context of midwifery. During my master's program, I worked as a part-time instructor teaching GED classes at a local community college. In an offhand conversation with a former student in the GED program, I learned that the former student's grandmother, a woman named Sarah, had been a midwife for more than 40 years in rural North Carolina. I asked the former student if perhaps her grandmother might be willing to talk with me about her experiences. Sarah invited me to her house, and I went not knowing what to expect or how long we'd talk. We talked for 5 hours! Following my conversation with Sarah, I couldn't wait to talk to my advisor, Dr. Tom Jackson, to ask if I could do an oral history project for my master's thesis. He pointed me towards examples of history written by scholars such as Charles M. Payne (1995), whose work incorporated interviews and archival methods, and oral history examples from Judith Porter Adams (1990), Brett Harvey (1994), and Studs Terkel (1970, 1992). My master's program did not provide explicit coursework in research methods, and most of my student colleagues were using archival sources for their thesis projects. There was no coursework or training in using archival methods, much less training on interview methods or transcription. All I knew going into my oral history thesis project was that I needed a tape recorder, a way to take notes, and the ability to listen. Everything else felt like guesswork, and

I had a lot of questions along the way. Questions such as: *How do I ask good interview questions? When and how much do I need to interact in conversations? How do I ask follow-up questions? How do I write dialogue and verbatim language in ways that honor participants' voices? How do I corroborate conflicting accounts or blurry details of an event? How do I address my identity as a white, female graduate student doing an oral history project in a rural, Black community?* I didn't realize it at the time, but I was asking questions about qualitative methods and qualitative methodology.

After completing my master's program, I re-entered the ranks of K–12 education and enjoyed a 15-year career as a public educator working as a classroom teacher, site-level curriculum facilitator, and district-level curriculum coordinator. I began my public school teaching career in 2002, just as the U.S. Department of Education ushered in a new phase of accountability in public education through high stakes assessment under the No Child Left Behind Act. I came of age as an educator in an environment where phrases like "data-driven instruction" and "teaching to the test" were gaining ground. I was struck by the disconnection between what districts and departments of education called data (score reports on district benchmarks or end-of-grade tests) and the data I generated with students in class. I wondered why samples of student work and observations of student success counted less than standardized measures. I remember end-of-year evaluation meetings with administrators where I brought portfolios of student classwork, examples of student projects, and stories situated in everyday conversations with students about their learning and their lives. This was data, too! And yet, this was not the data that counted. During my years as public educator, my family and I moved four times to four different states. Regardless of geography or my role in the school district, conversations about data and educational research in public school districts looked and sounded the same.

In 2015, my spouse accepted a job in Georgia and our family relocated once more. I accepted a teaching position in an Atlanta-area school district as an English/language arts and reading teacher. As a reading teacher, I regularly collected individual data on reading performance using a structured questionnaire created by the reading intervention program my school had adopted. As I listened to students read aloud and asked questions about their comprehension, I was struck by how much these conversations felt like interviews and how the data I was collecting was both systematic and observational.

Over my years in public education, I reflected on my oral history project with Sarah. I often found myself wishing I could go back to school, learn about interviewing and oral history, and do my thesis project all over again. As luck would have it, there was a PhD program just an hour and a half down the road at the University of Georgia (UGA) specializing in qualitative research methodology. I began reading about the program and the courses offered. It felt like qualitative methodology was the thread tying together experiences from my master's program and my teaching career.

In 2018, I enrolled in UGA's Qualitative Research and Evaluation Methodologies Program. I entered the program not exactly knowing what topic I wanted to study, but open to developing my skills as a methodologist. At the suggestion of my advisor, Dr. Kathleen deMarrais, I took a course in autoethnographic approaches to qualitative inquiry with Dr. Kathy Roulston in my first semester. In this course, I realized I could use my interest in stories and narrative writing to represent research focused on personal experience. My final paper for this course, an autoethnographic reflection on motherhood and parenting, informed my dissertation research topic on mothers' experiences of preparing menstruating children for puberty and led to my first solo authored publication (Copple, 2021). As I inquired into my experiences as a mother preparing a child for puberty, I wondered what stories other mothers might share on this topic. Following this question, I designed a qualitative interview study examining mothers' experiences preparing menstruating children for puberty. Courses in qualitative research design and analysis helped me think about issues to do with quality, ethics, and subjectivity in my study. As I took courses in theory, philosophies of social science, and qualitative methodology, I became interested in feminist critical materialist theories and considered how concepts such as Karen Barad's (2007) notion of entanglement troubled understandings of fixed, stable narratives. Although Barad, a physicist by training, wrote about entanglement to explain the behavior of quantum particles, her explanation of the way humans and the world engage together to make and remake reality resonated with the way I thought about stories and storytellers. I thought about the stories mothers shared during our interviews together and how my own stories entangled with theirs in my research. Given my interest in narrative and arts-based methods, my dissertation took the form of a multi-genre project incorporating constructed narratives and poetry from mothers' accounts as well as autoethnographic pieces narrating my journey as a mother-researcher-storyteller.

I graduated in 2022 with a PhD from UGA in Qualitative Research and Evaluation Methodologies and now hold a position as Assistant Professor of Research, Measurement and Statistics in the Department of Educational Policy Studies at Georgia State University. I teach introductory graduate courses in qualitative research methods as well as special topics courses to help students design theoretically informed qualitative educational research and mentor future qualitative methodologists. My research focuses on feminist critical materialist and posthuman approaches to narrative, autoethnographic, and arts-based methodologies and explores how motherhood narratives show up in formal and informal educational contexts with a specific focus on puberty education.

References

Barad, K. (2007). *Meeting the universe halfway: The entanglement of matter and meaning.* Duke University Press.

Bennett, K. P. (1986). *A study of reading ability grouping and its consequences for urban Appalachian first grade students* (Publication No. 8722050) [Doctoral dissertation, University of Cincinnati]. ProQuest Dissertations Publishing.

Bennett, K. (1991). Doing school in an urban Appalachian first grade. In C. Sleeter (Ed.), *Empowerment through multicultural education* (pp. 27–48). SUNY.

Berger, P. L., & Luckmann, T. (1966). *The social construction of reality: A treatise in the sociology of knowledge.* Anchor.

Cazden, C. B., John, V. P., & Hymes, D. (1972). *Functions of language in the classroom.* Columbia University Press.

Choksy, L. (1981). *The Kodály context: Creating an environment for musical learning.* Prentice-Hall.

Choksy, L. (1988). *The Kodály method: Comprehensive music education from infant to adult* (2nd ed.). Prentice-Hall.

Copple, J. (2021). Earnin' your raising: How mother-daughter stories and memories inform-reflections on parenting. *Qualitative Inquiry, 27*(3/4), 346–325. https://doi.org/10.1177/1077 800420917425

deMarrais, K. (2006). "The haves and the have mores:" Fueling a conservative ideological war on public education. *Educational Studies, 39*(3), 204–242.

Eisner, E. W. (1991). *The enlightened eye: Qualitative inquiry and the enhancement of educational practice.* Macmillan.

Giroux, H. A. (1983). *Theory and resistance in education: A pedagogy for the opposition.* Bergin & Garvey.

Harvey, B. (1994). *The fifties: A women's oral history.* Harper Collins.

Keddie, N. (1971). The organization of classroom knowledge. *English in Education, 5*(63), 63–68. https://doi.org/10.1111/j.1754-8845.1971.tb00172.x

Mehan, H. (1979). *Learning lessons: Social organization in the classroom.* Harvard University Press.

Merriam, S. (1988). *Case study research in education: A qualitative approach.* Jossey-Bass.

Payne, C. M. (1995). *I've got the light of freedom: The organizing tradition and the Mississippi freedom struggle.* University of California Press.

Porter Adams, J. (1990). *Peacework: Oral histories of women peace activists.* Cengage Gale.

Roulston, K. (2000). The management of 'safe' and 'unsafe' complaint sequences in research interviews. *Text, 20*(3), 1–39.

Roulston, K. (2001). Data analysis and 'theorizing as ideology.' *Qualitative Research, 1*(3), 279–302. https://doi.org/10.1177/146879410100100302

Schatzman, L., & Strauss, A. (1973). *Field research: Strategies for a natural sociology.* Prentice-Hall.

Smith, D. (1974). Theorizing as ideology. In R. Turner (Ed.), *Ethnomethodology* (pp. 41–44). Penguin Education.

Smith, M. C., & Holmes, L. J. (1996). *Listen to me good: The story of an Alabama midwife.* Ohio State University Press.

Spindler, G. (1982). *Doing the ethnography of schooling: Educational anthropology in action.* Holt, Rinehart and Winston.

Stake, R. (1978). The case study method in social inquiry. *Educational Researcher, 7,* 5–8.

Terkel, S. (1970). *Hard times: An oral history of the Great Depression.* Pantheon.

Terkel, S. (1992). *Race: How blacks and whites think and feel about the American obsession.* New Press.

Woods, P. (1986). *Inside schools: Ethnography in educational research.* Routledge & Kegan Paul.

Young, M. F. D. (1971). *Knowledge and control: New directions for the sociology of education.* Collier-Macmillan.

Zinn, H. (1995). *A people's history of the United States, 1492–present.* Harper Collins.

PART I

◌ GETTING STARTED WITH THEORY AND DESIGN

P ART 1 OF THIS BOOK introduces you to the field of qualitative research. The content, examples, and activities included in each of these chapters provide the foundation for the remainder of the book, which focuses on how to design qualitative studies. Comprised of four chapters, we begin Part 1 with a general introduction to qualitative methods outlining the primary characteristics of these approaches. At the end of Chapter 1, we outline five current challenges we see in today's contexts that influence all aspects of this work. These challenges include (a) technology, (b) globalization, (c) social justice, (d) global problems that span the natural/human world, and (e) accountability and control. While these are not the only challenges, they do shape how we see and do research.

Chapter 2, *Ethics and qualitative research*, was deliberately placed at the beginning of the book so you will understand the historical events that have led to institutional requirements for the ethical conduct of research. We also want you to understand what we mean by research integrity as you begin to design your own studies, whatever approach you choose. We review principles of practice that guide researchers in the ethical conduct of research as well as the role of institutional review boards (IRBs) in overseeing all kinds of research. The next portion of the chapter is focused on ways to build ethical practice into each aspect of qualitative research from data management through the publication of the study. We offer insights into particular issues related to the conduct of qualitative research, including cross-cultural research, online settings, working with specific groups of participants, using different methodologies and topics, how research is represented, and finally, thinking about the safety of the researcher. We offer resources for guiding decision-making and a protocol for applying ethical analysis with potential dilemmas.

Chapter 3 focuses on *The role of theory in designing qualitative research*. The placement of this chapter at the beginning of the book reflects our belief in the importance of considering theory and how it influences all aspects of the research design from your research purpose and questions to your choice of approaches, to the way you engage with participants, generate data, and analyze and represent your work. Theory conveys to readers the scholarly context in which you situate your research. We recognize that novice researchers may be unsure of the appropriate theoretical frameworks to employ, so this chapter begins with basic definitional elements, types, and categories of theory. We outline strategies for identifying the theoretical home that will inform your work. We also understand that researchers bring a range of backgrounds to reading theory, and offer strategies to engage with theory so you can become more familiar with theory and apply theoretical concepts in your work.

Chapter 4, *Designing qualitative research*, bridges theory with research design. As with previous chapters, we start with definitions and what we mean by design, then move to a discussion of the term conceptual framework, or that which pulls together the theoretical framework for your work with the existing scholarly literature informing your particular study. We provide examples of studies that use a range of theorical frameworks to show how theory informs research questions and research design. Since new researchers have different experiences with literature reviews, we guide you through this process and offer tips for locating and managing relevant published studies. We address issues of research significance and offer guidance for developing an argument for how your research will make a significant contribution to current literature. We address the political nature of research to encourage your thinking on any potential consequences or risks for you as researcher. Turning from the external context of the research to you as a researcher, we engage you in a discussion of the role of subjectivities and positionalities as a way to think about who you are and what you bring to your study, with strategies on how to do this. A key component of all research design is the articulation of the research purpose and research questions, so to conclude the chapter we engage you with questions aimed at this aspect of design with practical questions regarding resources of time, access to participants, and ensuring ethical practice in explaining your study to these participants.

Introducing Qualitative Research

QUALITATIVE RESEARCH AS A FIELD of inquiry is a relative newcomer to academic areas of inquiry. Brinkmann et al. (2014) noted that the term "qualitative" was originally used at the beginning of the 20th century in the natural sciences and is first found in reports from studies in chemistry. Yet the methods that qualitative researchers use—including talking to people, examining documents and artifacts, and observing what is going on—have been used for hundreds, if not thousands of years by people studying the world around them (Erickson, 2018). In this chapter we review multiple disciplinary influences and significant scholars who contributed to the development of what is now a "big tent" of qualitative inquiry (Denzin, 2010). We review key characteristics of qualitative inquiry, consider some of the issues impacting how researchers conduct qualitative studies in the 21st century, and outline questions to think about when designing studies.

The development of qualitative inquiry as a field of interest blossomed in the latter part of the 20th century as citizens across the world gained increasing access to higher education. Yet the methods that are now seen as commonplace—ethnography and autoethnography, interview studies, oral and life histories, archival research, narrative inquiries and so forth—have been practiced across disciplines for a variety of purposes for a much longer period.

The discipline of anthropology has roots in the colonization of other countries by Western nations. As explorers fanned out across the globe to claim new territories to support imperialist agendas, monarchs sent natural scientists on expeditions to study the potential for settlements in other countries, collect specimens of native flora and fauna, and to gather information concerning Indigenous peoples. Anthropology as a discipline was founded on understanding other cultures—and the method of "being there"—which is now typically referred to as "participant observation" or "witnessing" (Tracy, 2020) is frequently identified with the field of anthropology, even though other disciplines such as sociology and social work also used this approach to understanding social life. For example, sociologist W. E. B. Du Bois (1868–1963) undertook fieldwork to report on Black life in the city of Philadelphia in the late 19th century (Du Bois, 1996 [1899]), while some years later, anthropologist Zora Neale Hurston (1891–1960) conducted fieldwork to collect life stories and folklore of African American people during the 1920s and 1930s (Hurston, 1927).

Meanwhile, ethnomusicologists and folklorists spread out across the world to make recordings of folk songs and musical traditions (May, 1980). For example, Hungarian composers Zoltán Kodály (1882–1967) and Béla Bartók (1881–1945) collected folksongs that inspired their compositions, while in the United States, John Avery Lomax (1867–1948) and his children Alan, John Jr., and Bess all became noted folklorists who documented musical traditions from different parts of the United States and other countries. Although these early collectors did not identify themselves as "qualitative researchers," they were in fact doing similar sorts of fieldwork as is practiced today by researchers all over the world. They traveled extensively to meet, observe and talk to people, and record local knowledge, and presented their findings to others through writings, recordings, and images. Similarly, in conjunction with observing and interviewing, anthropologists such as Margaret Mead (1901–1978) and Gregory Bateson (1904–1980) used various technologies and recording devices to record photos and create films—all methods that continue to this day.

Interviewing both elites and ordinary citizens had already grown in popularity within the field of journalism during the mid-1800s and was later used by fieldworkers in social work and sociology. Whereas early interviews resembled what we now see as social surveys (e.g., the work of social reformer

Charles Booth [1840–1916] in London), sociologists involved in the Chicago School (Musolf, 2003) began to develop approaches to the study of urban life that involved recording life histories through written narratives, talking to people and observing everyday life. The roots of qualitative research may be traced to both the developing disciplines of anthropology and sociology in the late 19th and early 20th centuries, as well as other disciplines such as journalism and social work.

Methodological writing on how researchers approached their inquiries followed. For example, a section on research methods was initiated in the journal *Human Organization*, published by the Society for Applied Anthropology, beginning in 1949. In the Winter edition, the editors noted "we believe that an increasing awareness of field methods and techniques and a pooling and refining of existing ideas on these matters will produce better investigations and more dependable results" (Editors, 1949, p. 26). Through review of this section, we learn how sociologist Howard Becker approached interviewing (e.g., Becker, 1954), along with tips on how to map a new field setting upon entry (Editors, 1949) as well as other practices used by researchers. Figure 1.1 shows some of the sources for contemporary qualitative methods.

Early methodological texts show how methods were disseminated via autobiographical accounts, such as anthropologist Hortense Powdermaker's (1900–1970) account of her work (1966), and treatises forwarding grounded theory (Glaser & Strauss, 1967) and ethnographic fieldwork (Schatzman & Strauss, 1973; Spradley, 1979, 1980). Later, scholars contributed methodological texts to specific fields, such as education (Lincoln & Guba, 1985; Merriam, 1988; Preissle & LeCompte, 1984), and feminist scholars contributed texts that proved influential across disciplines (Bell & Roberts, 1984; Reinharz, 1992). By the early 1990s Norman Denzin and Yvonna Lincoln published the first edition of their influential *Handbook of Qualitative Research* (1994), which gathered scholars from multiple disciplines to discuss qualitative research methods, contributing to a steady and growing stream of publications on qualitative research methods on narrative methods, case study, interviewing, and ethnography (e.g., Clandinin & Connelly, 2000; Mishler, 1986; Stake, 1995; Wolcott, 1990, 1994, 1995, 1999). Thus far, we have talked about some of the roots of qualitative inquiry. Next we discuss key characteristics of qualitative research.

Origins of qualitative research

Qualitative research methods involve observing what goes on, listening to people's stories and examining documents and artifacts. This figure highlights key moments in the development of qualitative research as a field of inquiry.

1800s and early 1900s

European colonization, exploration and expansion, accompanied by anthropological fieldwork to understand "other" cultures; use of interviews in the field of journalism.

1920s and 1930s

Chicago School field studies of urban life.

1940s-1960s

Field studies and ethnographies using qualitative methods in the social sciences; increasing interest in promoting understanding of research methods.

1970s

An increase in the publication of articles and books focused on qualitative methods in sociology; realist fly-on-the wall ethnographies.

1980s and 1990s

The proliferation of approaches to research, including emancipatory, critical, feminist, and postmodern approaches to research, including arts-based inquiry, narrative methods, and autoethnography, among others. Methodological writing on qualitative methods developing across disciplines.

2000s

Attendance to the material and non-human aspects of inquiry, and decentering of the human, using critical, new materialist, and posthuman philosophies. Mixing of methods.

Key Early Methodological Publications

Powdermaker, H. (1966). *Stranger and friend: The way of an anthropologist.* Norton.

Glaser, B. G., & Strauss, A. L. (1967). *The discovery of grounded theory: Strategies for qualitative research.* Aldine Publishing.

Lofland, J. (1971). *Analyzing social settings: A guide to qualitative observation and analysis.* Wadsworth.

Schatzman, L., & Strauss, A. (1973). *Field research: Strategies for a natural sociology.* Prentice-Hall.

Spradley, J. P. (1979). *The ethnographic interview.* Wadsworth.

Spradley, J. P. (1980). *Participant observation.* Holt, Rinehart & Winston.

Preissle, J., & LeCompte, M. D. (1984). *Ethnography and qualitative design in educational research.* Academic Press.

Lincoln, Y. S., & Guba, E. G. (1985). *Naturalistic inquiry.* Sage.

Reinharz, S. (1992). *Feminist methods in social research.* Oxford University Press.

Denzin, N. K., & Lincoln, Y. S. (Eds.). (1994). *The handbook of qualitative research.* Sage.

Figure 1.1. Origins of Qualitative Research.

What is "Qualitative" Research?

Qualitative inquiry involves generating data using the senses—it includes what we can see (e.g., via observation, or using still and moving images), what we can hear (e.g., using audio and/or video recording of naturally occurring interaction or researcher-generated events such as interviews), what we can touch and feel (e.g., objects and artifacts), or smell and taste. Researchers use these data to develop narrative accounts of what is going on in the world. More recently, researchers have attended to not only phenomena related to humans, but to the "more-than-human," including spaces, places, objects and technologies, plant and animal life, and affect (Roulston, 2022).

Qualitative researchers examine the particular, ordinary details of human experience, looking for the multiple patterns in the ways people understand and engage with their worlds. To help conceptualize qualitative research, think of an impressionist painting. If you stand very close to the painting you will see many separate splotches of color on the canvas but cannot clearly make out the whole picture. As you get more distance from the painting, the separate bits of color merge into shapes and patterns so that you can clearly see the whole. The patterns may change as the light in the room changes, thus allowing for various perspectives on the painting. Much like such a painting, qualitative researchers generate data from participants in the form of interview talk, ethnographic fieldnotes, documents, and artifacts. While looking at these discrete bits of data, we may not see patterns, but as we analyze the data, we begin to discern patterns within that database and make meaning from these observations.

Since qualitative research is an interactive process, it entails getting closely involved with other people, sharing in their lives, and trying to make sense of it all. Qualitative research necessitates embracing ambiguity—it can be a messy process and is certainly not predictable. There is no one best way or one set of tools and methods to do qualitative research, but researchers make decisions about how to design and engage in research based on the theories they are using, the work done by previous scholars on the topic, and their specific research questions. Furthermore, it requires a healthy balance of improvisation and organization, involvement and distance. Curiosity, a sense of playfulness, and an enjoyment of the creative process enhance one's ability to do good qualitative research. And finally, because so much of the qualitative process involves writing, good writing skills are crucial.

Characteristics of Qualitative Research

Qualitative research design is concerned with human behavior and human interpretations. Researchers ask research questions to get at the what, how, and why of phenomena. Often research questions focus on interpretations of meaning people place on their experiences and rely on in-depth data derived from methods that require longer periods of time spent with participants and/or in the contexts in which participants live and work. Table 1.1 summarizes key characteristics of qualitative research.

Table 1.1. Characteristics of Qualitative Research

Characteristic	Description
Interpretive	Relies on the notion that people continually make or construct and modify meanings in their lives through social interactions with others. Qualitative researchers attempt to understand the meanings, constructs, and categories that people use to make sense of their worlds from their perspectives.
Preference for the emic perspective	Many qualitative researchers prefer to understand human experience from the point of view of an insider, although this is not the only way to conduct a qualitative study.
Descriptive	Uses documentary evidence, including people's written and spoken words, written descriptions of people's behaviors, and visual images of human experiences.
Empirical	Generates data from people's descriptions of their perspectives and experiences, researchers' observations in the research site, and the artifacts and documents people use and produce.
Naturalistic settings	Involves researchers going to participants' settings.
Holistic perspective	Understands the context in which qualitative research is conducted as critical to exploring the experiences of people within that setting.
Idiographic	Interpretations and meaning are constructed from the particular data of the case and are context specific rather than nomothetical, which aims for generalizations, explanations, and predictions across cases and contexts.
Abductive and inductive reasoning	Inductive reasoning begins with the particularistic, concrete data with analyses and interpretations grounded in this data. Qualitative researchers also make use of abductive reasoning by making creative leaps during the analytic process that explain something more clearly than pre-existing theory.
Researcher as instrument	Researchers collect, analyze, and interpret data, serving as the filtering lenses through which the research data move.
Emergent design	Maintaining openness to what occurs in a setting—the researcher does not always know exactly what the design of the research will be, but develops and changes the design over the course of the study.

Characteristic	Description
Variety of approaches and strategies	Uses multiple approaches—there is no one "right" method in qualitative research. Researchers use a variety of methods to construct the fullest understanding of the phenomena under study in response to their research purposes and questions.
Generates theory	Qualitative researchers attempt to explain human behavior—generating theory from their data.

Qualitative Research Is Interpretivist

Different philosophical positions, with their accompanying assumptions, provide the basis for qualitative and quantitative research methodologies. Quantitative research, with its origins in the work of positivist philosophers such as August Comte (1798–1857) and Emile Durkheim (1858–1917), assumes that there are "social facts with an objective reality apart from the beliefs of individuals" (Firestone, 1987, p. 16). Durkheim (1938) defined a social fact as "every way of acting, fixed or not, capable of exercising on the individual an external constraint; or again, every way of acting which is general throughout a given society, while at the same time existing in its own right independent of its individual manifestations" (p. 13). He further explained the "first and most fundamental rule is: Consider social facts as things" (p. 14). Keat and Urry (1975) explained: "Positivism is concerned only with observable phenomena and consists of the establishment of law-like relations between them through the careful accumulation of factual knowledge. This occurs by means of observation, experimentation, comparison, and prediction" (p. 72). Researchers steeped in positivist traditions are concerned with the discovery of universal laws, of "truth." They aim to make true statements about the world (Eisner, 1991) and examine "the factors that influence social behaviors as if they were concrete objects and external to the individual" (Best, 2003, p. 17). Through quantitative analyses, researchers working in this paradigm attempt to explain causes of change in these social facts and to make predictions.

Interpretive paradigms are based on assumptions that knowledge is socially constructed, and it is possible to understand the social world from the actor's point of view. This interpretive worldview leads qualitative researchers to explore and understand the meaning people place on their daily experiences.

Qualitative researchers are interested in trying to understand the meanings, constructs, and categories that people use to make sense of their world from their perspectives. In other words, we seek to discover the meaning people make of their experiences rather than impose researcher constructs on them. As explained by Clifford Geertz (1973a):

> Believing, with Max Weber, that man [sic] is an animal suspended in webs of significance he himself has spun, I take culture to be those webs and the analysis of it to be therefore not an experimental science in search of law but an interpretive one in search of meaning. (p. 5)

You might think of examples from your own experiences of ways you and another person have differed in your perceptions, in the meanings you have given to a particular situation or relationship. For example, you may have had a relationship that you considered "just" a good friendship, whereas your friend believed the relationship to be a romantic one that would lead to a more permanent partnership. Despite mutual participation in conversations and activities together, you interpreted them quite differently based on your unique perspectives. If you happened to discover this difference in perceptions, you may have acted to modify your perceptions or worked with your friend to alter the relationship to come to closer agreement as to what the relationship would be. The different meanings you and your friend placed on the relationship were equally "real" to both of you.

Interpretive paradigms include a wide range of differing theoretical positions including phenomenology, symbolic interactionism, ethnomethodology, social constructivism, and critical and feminist frames. Each of these theories lead researchers to ask different research questions and position themselves differently as researchers within the project. Phenomenologists seek to describe the nature of human experiences of the life world, with a specific focus on prereflective experiences. Symbolic interactionists examine how people interpret and make meaning of lived experience through interaction and symbols. Feminist qualitative researchers ask questions where women's experiences are central to the project. They often view projects as collaborative ventures where researcher and participants work together throughout all phases of the research. Critical theorists ask questions related to power and powerlessness, usually related to questions of social class differences. They focus on determining whose interests are served in a given situation or set of experiences. Critical race theorists examine race and power as core constructs of their work. Each of these theoretical frameworks —and there are many more—is a lens through which we can explore aspects of the ways human experience is constructed in social interactions.

Qualitative Researchers' Preference for Understanding Emic Perspectives

Although not all qualitative researchers emphasize understanding phenomena from participants' points of view, many do; and there is much debate about whether this is possible. Pelto and Pelto (1978) attribute the origins of the "emic" approach to anthropologist Franz Boas (1858–1942), who emphasized careful, verbatim collection of data to maintain the meaning of our participants. Boas argued, "If it is our serious purpose to understand the thoughts of a people the whole analysis of experience must be based on *their concepts, not ours*" (Boas, 1943, p. 314; italics our emphasis).

Anthropologists have been debating the meaning of the words etic and emic since they were coined by linguist Kenneth Pike (1967). Pike used portions of the words phonetic and phonemic as the source of these constructed terms. His operational definitions of etic and emic are as follows: "Two units are different etically when instrumental measurements can show them to be so. Units are different emically only when they elicit different responses from people acting within the system" (Pike, 1967, p. 38). When an outsider can hear differences, words are etically different. When only an insider understands differences, they are emically different. Emicists rely heavily on in-depth interviews in the participants' language to understand the meaning systems of these participants.

Anthropologist Marvin Harris (1976), an outspoken critic of the emic viewpoint (Pelto & Pelto, 1978), did not claim to understand what goes on in people's heads, but rather, wanted to study human behaviors with the intent of interpreting observable patterns of behavior. This approach requires intensive, systematic observations, sometimes using videotaping to produce a database for analysis. The etic approach as presented by Harris examines what people do, but neglects to account for the meaning people attribute to their actions. Similarly, scholars using ethnomethodology, an approach to research developed in sociology, are not interested in examining people's viewpoints or what they profess to believe, preferring to examine the mundane methods that people use to construct social actions that are recognizable to one another in naturalistic contexts (e.g., classrooms, workplaces).

Nevertheless, many anthropologists still concentrate on understanding emic perspectives in order to construct analyses that are consistent with the meanings of the cultural group they are studying. Ward Goodenough's (1970) explanation of emics as "the method of finding where something makes a difference for one's informants" (p. 21) is helpful in understanding the term. In *Argonauts of the Western Pacific*, Bronislaw Malinowski (1961, first published in 1922 [and consequently full of dated language]) eloquently explained that the goal of ethnography, the anthropological study of cultures, is "to grasp the native's point of view, his [or her] relation to life, to realise his [or her] vision of his [or her] world" (2014 [1922] p. 24). Anthropologists have vigorously debated the dilemma posed by gaining emic perspectives. James Lett (1987) in an essay problematizing the anthropological debate around the etic/emic distinctions, defines etic and emic as:

> Emic constructs are descriptions and analyses conducted in terms of the conceptual schemes and categories considered meaningful by the participants in the event or situation being described and analysed. Etic constructs are descriptions and analyses conducted in terms of the conceptual schemes and categories considered meaningful by the community of scientific observers. (p. 62)

He argued that one cannot have etic and emic "things," because events, situations, or relationships in themselves are neither. Our analyses, descriptions, or explanations can be etic or emic. He further argued regardless of how the data are collected—whether by observation or by participant interviews — our descriptions and analyses "must be measured against other standards— namely, the judgment of natives (for emics) and the evaluation of scientists (for etics)" (p. 63). In other words, emic accounts are those validated by a consensus of participants in the study and etic accounts are those that measure up to a scientific standard where the accounts (a) satisfy the scientific ideals of precision, reliability, and accuracy; (b) can be validated by independent observers; (c) satisfy the canons of scientific knowledge and evidence in that they cannot be contradicted by other available evidence; and (d) are applicable cross culturally.

The ongoing etic–emic debate is one facet of an argument about whether researchers can actually gain understanding of the viewpoint of the participants.

At its extreme, this debate suggests two different research approaches based on the different theories and goals inherent in the two viewpoints. Eticists rely heavily on observational data gained from the outside looking in to understand cultural behaviors, while emicists rely heavily on interview data gained from people to get at participants' meanings embedded in cultural forms of behavior and interactions. Most qualitative researchers recognize the value of both positions and move back and forth between emic and etic interpretations in their own work.

Qualitative Research Is Descriptive

We often hear the phrase "thick description" used in relation to qualitative research, particularly ethnography. In his essay *Thick Description: Toward an Interpretive Theory of Culture*, Clifford Geertz (1973b) borrowed Gilbert Ryle's phrase *thick description* to describe ethnography, the anthropological method used to study cultures. Through a lengthy and humorous depiction of the difference between a twitch and a wink, Ryle illustrated the difference between thick and thin description. In brief, the actual physical description of what the actor is doing, "rapidly contracting his right eyelids," is thin description (p. 7). Explanation of the varied and multiple meanings implied by actors within their cultural contexts is thick description. For example, the wink may be a physical reaction to an itch, serve as a sexual invitation, or as a conspiratorial signal that something stated as true is actually false. In other words, a thick description provides us with the complexity of meaning underlying the physical behavior of the wink. As we saw in our discussion of emic and etic perspectives, qualitative researchers are concerned with these underlying meanings participants give to their worlds. The ways researchers are able to describe these human meanings through "thick description" is uniquely qualitative. The strengths of qualitative research lie in its depiction of concrete detail and the portrayal of process in those studied (Firestone, 1987).

Qualitative Research Is Empirical

In order to capture participants' meanings and convey these meanings through thick description, qualitative researchers gather firsthand, sensory accounts of phenomena as they occur in natural settings of their participants.

LeCompte and Preissle (1993) argued the term empirical is often used errone-ously to describe quantitative or experimental approaches to research. They defined empirical as phenomena that are:

> capable of being found in the real world and assessed by means of the senses. Since both qualitative and ethnographic research are preeminently concerned with observation and recording of real-world phenomena, they clearly *are* empirical. In fact, all social science research, especially ethnography, is empirical. (LeCompte & Preissle, 1993, p. 31, italics in original)

These sensory accounts of people's behaviors and perceptions provide the database for our analyses of human behavior and furnish the evidence from which our categories, themes, narrative presentations, and theories are con-structed in the qualitative research process.

Qualitative Research Is Conducted in Natural Settings

Traditionally, qualitative researchers conducted their work by observing and talking to people in their natural settings with as little disruption to those set-tings as possible. "Natural" settings are those in which participants typically live, work, and interact with others, and contrasts with contexts in which re-searchers create settings and conditions for experimental studies. When re-searchers spend weeks and months in a research site, they become partici-pants in the setting and can share in the experiences of the participants. The longer they spend in the field, the more they become part of it. Lincoln and Guba (1985) used the term naturalistic inquiry to suggest that "inquiry be car-ried out in a 'natural' setting because phenomena of study, whatever they may be—physical, chemical, biological, social psychological—take their meaning as much from their contexts as they do from themselves" (p. 189). By taking their research to the natural setting of the participants, researchers attend to the complexities of the context, understanding the ways in which the context and participants interact.

Qualitative Research Is Holistic

Since qualitative research takes place in the natural setting where partici-pants live and work, researchers assume a holistic stance in order to construct a complex description of the cultural or social group they are studying (Fetterman, 1989). Lett (1987) suggested the discipline of anthropology is the only one among the social sciences that "has established holism and comparison as ideals to be pursued" (p. 61). This anthropological approach to human inquiry is holistic in that it attempts to examine the whole of human experience, looking beyond social, economic, political, historical, linguistic, and biological factors to see the connections between them (Lett, 1987).

Qualitative researchers who are able to study human beliefs and behaviors within particular contexts and over time can capture some of the complexity of the participants' experiences. They must describe in as much detail as possible the context surrounding the particular phenomena under study. For example, if we were to conduct research within a classroom, in order to provide a holistic picture of the setting, we would need to consider not only what happens within that particular classroom, but how that classroom is embedded within the school, neighborhood, and larger community context. We would want to explore the sociopolitical context of that community, learn about district policies and practices that influenced the pedagogical practices of the teacher, and develop understandings about the teacher and the children in the classroom. We would also want to convey to the readers of the study the way in which the researcher gained access into the site and situated themself there. What role or roles did they play in relation to the teacher and students in the classroom? How did they interact with others in the school? The researcher attempts to understand and explain the multiple and interrelated contexts surrounding the participants holistically to adequately describe and understand the phenomena under study.

Qualitative Research Is Ideographic Rather Than Nomothetic

Qualitative research aims to make meaning from systematically generated data constructed within particular settings and contexts. Lincoln and Guba (1985) argued that ideographic interpretations are a characteristic of qualitative research where researchers:

> draw conclusions ideographically (in terms of the particulars of the case) rather than nomothetically (in terms of lawlike generalizations) because different interpretations are likely to be meaningful for different realities; and because

interpretations depend so heavily for their validity on local particulars, including the particular investigator-respondent (or object) interactions, the contextual factors involved, the local mutually shaping factors influencing one another, and the local (as well as investigator) values. (p. 42)

Qualitative researchers are concerned with studying particular contexts and the participants in those settings for generating meanings and interpretations. As O'Reilly and Kiyimba (2015) asserted, qualitative research is idiographic in that it "focuses on understanding the individual as unique and complex" (p. 4). Qualitative researchers recognize the aim of their approach is not to generalize or predict, but to offer interpretations based in context-specific data. Further, qualitative researchers account for their relationships to both the research topic and the participants of a study.

Qualitative Research Involves Both Inductive and Abductive Reasoning

Qualitative research is like detective work in that it is an inductive process of working out the puzzle, looking for patterns, trying out different interpretations, and reconstructing the whole picture. Rather than beginning with a hypothesis, qualitative researchers begin with an open-ended problem, research purpose, and research questions. They go about the tasks of understanding this problem by selecting the research methods that will enable them to get at the particular details of human behaviors, experiences, and perceptions. As researchers generate data, they begin to make sense of it inductively, moving back and forth between data collection and analysis. After the completion of the data generation phase of the project, researchers continue to handle the data inductively looking for categories and patterns of behavior within the data. We can illustrate this process with an example of a garden. Think of a small English cottage garden in which flowers, herbs, and vegetables are planted together in a small yard. The garden is alive with colors, textures, and smells. It crawls with caterpillars, butterflies, ladybugs, and other living creatures, both helpful and harmful to the gardener. It changes with the weeks and months during the growing season and even through the colder winter months. In summer, the overall look of the garden is fantastic, with a variety of brilliant yellows, reds, blues, purples and with many shades of green as a backdrop. We might know little about gardens and gardeners but can appreciate the beauty and complexity of the garden as a whole.

If we wanted to understand the garden in depth, we would need to systematically study it. Since a garden has clear borders in the form of stones, fences, garden timbers, or simply the edge of a lawn, we could focus or "bound" our study of the garden to whatever is inside these borders. Our study is also bounded by the particular time frame in which we study it. It is not the same garden it was in previous seasons and will be different in subsequent seasons and will change over the years. We might study the garden by examining each individual plant or animal that contributes to the whole picture. We could categorize these plants in a variety of ways. For example, we might group them by type (herb, flower, vegetable, grasses, annual or perennial, etc.), color, texture, smell, size, or by the time in which they produce blossoms or fruit. We could keep detailed fieldnotes on the way in which the plants grow and develop, and the way in which the insects live with the plants. As we build an extensive database of information about the garden, we will be able to see patterns of texture, light, smell, and color that contribute to the overall appearance and experience of the garden. If we wanted to understand the garden more fully, we could interview the gardener about their experience in building and maintaining the garden. We might talk to them regularly over weeks and months. Through analysis of this interview data we would see patterns in the way the gardener interacts with the garden. We would gain an emic understanding of the gardener's perspective on the garden and their relationship to it. This whole process of exploring the garden from whole to parts and back to whole again is an inductive process. We can never fully capture the complexity of the garden, but we can better understand it and the meaning it has for its gardener through this inductive process of data collection and analysis. A qualitative researcher develops the ability to use this inductive process to make sense of qualitative data.

Qualitative researchers also make use of abductive reasoning processes. Reichertz (2014) explains that abduction "attempts as far as possible to being its observations without presuppositions and, above all, without theories" (p. 126). Yet, through the research process, researchers create new ideas. Reichertz (2014) describes the steps in abductive reasoning as follows: (a) observing scenes to look *"for a rule to explain"*; (b) recognizing a case in which the rule may be applied (pp. 132–133, italics in original). In this way, "[a]bduction 'proceeds', therefore, from a known quantity (= result) to two unknowns (= rule and case)" (p. 127).

In the example of the garden above, an observer could note that plants in a particularly damp and shady spot characterized by acid soil do not flourish. When transplanted to a sunnier and drier spot with less acidic soil, the same plants grow prolifically. Through experimenting where these plants are placed with respect to light, water source, and soil, we might come to a rule and case in which we can expect a particular plant to grow and mature under optimum conditions.

The Qualitative Researcher as "Human Instrument"

In the first few sentences of her book, *Stranger and Friend: The Way of an Anthropologist*, Hortense Powdermaker (1966) explained the reasons why it is important for researchers to identify their own interests in a project. She wrote:

> . . . it is an illusion for him [or her] to think he [or she] can remove his [or her] personality from his [or her] work and become a faceless robot or a machinelike recorder of human events. It is important to accept that this human instrument is as much a project of biological, psychological, and social conditioning as are the people he [or she] studies. Often we catch glimpses of an anthropologist or sociologist and have hunches about what he [or she] is like and of his biases as we read his [or her] books. (p. 19)

In many qualitative research texts since Powdermaker, scholars have taken up the task of recognizing researchers' roles in their projects as "research instruments." This notion was recognized by early anthropologists and field sociologists who understood that the researcher produces the written database for interpretation through careful, systematic recording of observations and interviews.

Lincoln and Guba (1985) explained unlike other types of instruments, humans-as-instruments have, among others, the following characteristics: (a) the ability to be responsive to personal and environmental cues in order to make explicit sense of the situation; (b) the ability to be adaptable to collecting information about multiple factors and levels simultaneously; (c) the ability to look holistically at phenomena within its context; and (d) the capability to summarize data immediately in order to get clarification and correction from a participant (pp. 193–194). These characteristics help us to understand the unique and central role qualitative researchers play in the process.

Although the term "instrument" harkens to the influence of the positivist paradigm, none of the aforementioned scholars use the phrase in a positivistic way—the notion of an instrument as something mechanical, able to be "objective," with perhaps more abilities than are humanly possible. There is no doubt that the qualitative researcher plays the central role in the entire research process from design through interpretation and dissemination of findings. Consequently, there are serious implications for the way researchers go about their work and the theoretical lenses they use to interpret data. We may think of researchers as having complex sets of filters or lenses in the form of personal attributes, experiences, and beliefs that influence and shape the research questions they ask and the way in which they engage in their practice, and the interpretations they make of their data.

A researcher's identity characteristics such as gender, race, ethnicity, social class, ability, and so forth have an impact on the research. Therefore, part of the research process is to interrogate what you, as the researcher, bring to your process. This reflective process applies to all researchers—not just those who engage in qualitative research. Reflection should be ongoing throughout the research process. Once in the research setting, the researcher decides what to observe and what not to observe, what questions to ask and what questions to omit, what fieldnotes to take, and what fieldnotes to omit. Many of these decisions are conscious, but some resulting from what the researcher brings to the project may not be evident to even the most thoughtful researcher. Because of the central role the researcher plays, it is helpful to engage others in the process to help make the implicit more explicit.

Qualitative Research Has an Emergent Design

In qualitative research, we cannot always know ahead of time what will best lead us to understanding the phenomena we are studying. We may begin with a question that makes sense to us but has little to do with the way the participants in our study view their worlds and consequently does not make sense within their contexts. Further work within that context will require a revision in the initial research purpose. As we engage in our research we are always learning, and consequently, ready to change our questions if necessary, change our strategies, and develop different approaches to our study. Qualitative researchers are open to reformulating their questions, changing the focus of the study, and using whatever methods it takes to understand the problem they have selected to investigate.

Qualitative Researchers Use a Variety of Data Collection Methods

Qualitative researchers begin with a problem of interest, generally consistent with their worldviews and theoretical frameworks, which leads to selection of the research approach and subsequent choice of methods or research techniques. There are a range of qualitative methodologies, some more appropriate than others for particular research problems. Within these approaches there are three basic research techniques or tools qualitative researchers use: interviewing people, observing people, and examining documentary evidence. Table 1.2 illustrates methodological approaches to qualitative research under the categories of archival, narrative, and observational ways of knowing. This categorization is aimed to illustrate the primary data sources used for each of these methodological approaches, recognizing such categories can use the other data sources as well. While these basic tools are similar, researchers vary in the way they use these techniques depending on their theoretical framework and disciplinary training.

Table 1.2. Ways of Knowing in Qualitative Research

	Archival knowing: Artifacts*	Narrative knowing: Stories*	Observational knowing: Actions and behaviors*
Methodological Approaches	• Historical research • Biography	• Autobiography • Autoethnography • Self-study • Interview studies • Narrative inquiry • Oral history • Life history • Phenomenology • Arts-based research	• Ethnography • Participatory action research
Data Sources	• Journals • Diaries • Letters • Newspapers • Images and photographs • Films • Objects • Online data • Other archives and documents	• Interviews • Stories • Written Narratives	• Participant observation (fieldnotes) • Audio and videorecording of naturally occurring interaction

*We acknowledge material, affective, and embodied ways of knowing in qualitative research embedded across the categories shown here. Material knowing describes the relations between human and nonhuman agents. Embodied knowing describes sensory, bodily experiences. Affective knowing describes processes of intensity within and among human and nonhuman elements. Material, embodied, and affective ways of knowing are not limited to specific methodological approaches or data sources but may be used across the spectrum of methodological approaches used to design qualitative research studies.

We will explore a range of research designs and methods in this book. The approach you select for your study should lead to a holistic understanding of the research problem so that the complexity of human meaning and behavior can be carefully portrayed.

Qualitative Research Studies Generate Theory

Through a process that begins with a detailed exploration of phenomena, qualitative researchers use inductive analyses to construct findings. Sometimes these are represented as categories and themes that contribute to developing theory grounded in the data to explain the phenomena under study. There are other ways to analyze data and build theory, too. Although qualitative researchers are informed by theoretical frameworks and previous scholarly research through a literature review on the research topic, they focus on data to guide their analyses. This is where we move back and forth between emic and etic interpretations of data. Although the process of data analysis or interpretation is intertwined with data collection in qualitative studies, for clarity, we'll consider data analysis possibilities in later chapters. Next, we consider contemporary issues that may influence how you go about designing and conducting research.

Responding to Global Contexts of Qualitative Research

Throughout this chapter, we have noted the importance of context in examining people's experiences. Likewise, context shapes the kinds of questions researchers ask and the methods they use. In this section, we consider the ways global issues shape contemporary practices in qualitative research design. We provide a brief description of some global issues that have influenced how qualitative research is conducted along with key questions related to these issues. We acknowledge the issues listed here are selective rather than exhaustive, although you will see that we rely on illustrative examples in our descriptions. As you read our descriptions of these global issues, you may recall other examples (e.g., events, social movements, innovations) related to each topic. You may notice how particular events or social movements intersect across multiple categories. In short, there are many ways you could bound these topics and countless examples that you might include. We simply offer these issues and key questions to get you thinking about larger issues that might shape your research questions, design, and methods.

Technology

The 1980s through the early 2000s witnessed massive proliferation of technological innovation. Personal computers became smaller and cheaper to manufacture, making them more accessible for consumers. By the late 1990s, modem-based internet was being replaced with wireless internet, enabling mobile access to the World Wide Web. Further developments in smartphone and satellite technology provide people with instant access to information via the internet and immediate communication with one another via voice, video, or text message. Social media platforms provide yet another venue for people to connect with one another and create and share user-generated content. Such technological innovation has led to the growth of "big data" and tracking of people's activities in real and virtual life via digital tracking and surveillance tools. Further innovation in robotics and artificial intelligence has enabled the elimination of workers (e.g., self-checkout lines, automated teller machines, robots on assembly lines) and portends drastic changes among workers dealing with language and communication. In short, technology intersects with almost every aspect of life.

These innovations have implications for not only the types of questions qualitative researchers might ask about people's interactions with one another and with the world around them, but the ways qualitative researchers generate and analyze data. Digital tools such as videoconferencing software, increasing digitization of materials (e.g., archival documents), and the move to archiving "born-digital" documents (e.g., texts, emails) have opened possibilities for online interviewing and secondary data analysis of archived data. In recent years, voice-to-text transcription services powered by artificial intelligence have become more prevalent and affordable for qualitative researchers to transcribe interviews.

The perils of technological innovation have implications for qualitative research as well. For instance, ease of access to online information and user-generated content has led to disinformation and the proliferation of predatory or fake online journals. Another challenge is that as researchers adopt new technologies, ethical guidelines for research are always outpaced by new methods. Related challenges for researchers may involve increasing regulation from Institutional Review Boards regarding the conduct of research in online settings and ethical issues to do with storage and secondary analysis of research data. In Box 1.1 below, we include questions qualitative researchers might consider regarding the role of technology in conducting qualitative research studies.

Box 1.1. Key Questions for Qualitative Researchers: Technology.

- How might you integrate online research methods in your study? What are the benefits and limitations of doing so?
- What are the implications of using online data?
- If conducting research using data generated through social media, how will you consider respect for persons in relation to company user agreements, privacy protocols, and so forth?
- What are the implications of archiving your research data in an online repository?
- What are the implications of storing data on your computer? On cloud-based storage?

Globalization

The term globalization is often used to describe the interdependence of economies and cultures around the world (International Monetary Fund, 2002). As communities across the world become more diverse, this has led to cross-cultural, multi-disciplinary and interdisciplinary research teams involving researchers across countries. Diversity of experiences and approaches to research fuels cross-fertilization of concepts, theories, and methodologies. At the same time, the perils of globalization raise ethical issues for qualitative researchers conducting research in other countries. Despite promises that multinational corporate growth would improve living standards, economic inequity disproportionately affects people living in the Global South (López, 2007). This has led to both global mass migration and to the outsourcing of jobs from Western countries to maximize corporate profits through hiring poorly compensated workers in other countries. Worries over the negative impacts of globalization have raised concerns over economic policies that reinscribe a form of modern-day Western imperialism (López, 2007). Additionally, in Western countries like the United States the impacts of globalization and outsourcing has disproportionately impacted marginalized communities resulting in an ever-widening income gap between the poorest and richest Americans.

Researchers engaged in multicultural or international research must be sensitive to the negative impacts of globalization and employ culturally sensitive and decolonizing methodologies to resist colonizing research practices. For instance, ethical review board protocols typically require written informed consent. Researchers may have to seek ways to avoid documenting informed consent with vulnerable populations (e.g., nondocumented people), and translate research protocols and findings for people who speak other languages. If you choose to conduct research in another country, it will be important to familiarize yourself with the ethical protocols for conducting research in that country and consider the local customs when working with communities. In Box 1.2 below, we pose questions for qualitative researchers to consider regarding the role of globalization in conducting qualitative research studies.

Box 1.2. Key Questions for Qualitative Researchers: Globalization.

- If you are going to be conducting research in another country, what are the ethical guidelines for doing so in the country where you will be working?
- What are the implications of storing and sharing data with research team members across international borders?
- How might protocols such as informed consent and assent vary across cultural contexts?
- What are the ethical implications of using images of minoritized communities?
- How will you address interpretation, translation, and transcription when interviewing community members?
- How will your research be enriched or limited by the data you incorporate into your study (e.g., archival documents, artifacts, interviews, observation)?
- How will you conduct culturally responsive research?

- How will you resist recolonizing practices in your research?
- How will you address your researcher positionality and subjectivities?

Social Justice

In the past 10 years, there has been increased public attention to issues of injustice perpetrated on women and communities of color. In 2017, reporting of sexual abuse by prominent women led to powerful men losing their jobs and being charged with criminal offenses. In 2020, the murders of George Floyd, Breonna Taylor, and Ahmaud Arbery sparked nationwide protests in the United States and drew increased attention to demands for social justice and equity. There has been public recognition of longstanding abuse of Indigenous people (e.g., Stolen Children in Australia, child abuse and murder in institutions in Canada and the United States, and calls for repatriation of stolen artifacts now housed in art galleries and museums in the Global North). And yet, while these issues have become amplified in mainstream news and social media, they are not "new." For centuries, Western political, religious, and social institutions controlled mostly by White men have perpetrated acts of violence on women and Black, Indigenous, and People of Color (BIPOC) and their communities.

For over a century, critical scholars have researched and written about these atrocities (e.g., W.E.B. Du Bois, Zora Neale Hurston, Ida B. Wells). Heightened awareness of social injustice both inside and outside the academy affords space for qualitative researchers adopting intersectional approaches to explore the interconnections of race, gender, ethnicity, and ability to dismantle systems of oppression. An emphasis on democratization of research focuses on including voices that have been traditionally omitted from research. Application of critical theories (e.g., BlackCrit, LatCrit, AsianCrit, IndigenousCrit, DisCrit) center the epistemologies and experiences of BIPOC individuals and disability communities.[1] Even as critical researchers work to dismantle unjust systems of power and privilege, their work is met with opposition from traditional forms of authority subject to political critique. Such critiques favor maintenance of the status quo and reinscribe White supremacy. In doing so, many traditional forms of authority reproduce White-washed, hegemonic narratives of the past and the present. Qualitative researchers who engage in justice-oriented research will likely navigate such resistance to their work. In Box 1.3 below, we include key questions regarding justice-oriented approaches to qualitative research.

Box 1.3. Key Questions for Qualitative Researchers: Social Justice.

- How will your research be enriched or limited by the data you incorporate into your study (e.g., archival documents, artifacts, interviews, observation)?
- How will you conduct culturally responsive research?
- How will you resist recolonizing practices in your application of qualitative research methods and your analysis and representation of findings?
- How will you address your researcher positionality and subjectivities?
- What might be potential benefits or drawbacks for community members participating in your study?
- Who is the audience for your research?
- How will you disseminate your research?
- How might your study and future publications impact policy and/or practice?
- If conducting research with community partners, how will you negotiate authorship for future publications?

Global Problems That Span the Natural/Human World

As with issues surrounding social justice, we acknowledge that research on topics like climate change and global health is not "new." For example, since the 1960s, scientists have pointed to the long-term effects of environmental pollution and greenhouse gas emissions on planet ecosystems (see for example Rachel Carson's 1962 book *Silent Spring*, or reports from Charles Keeling's research with the Scripps Institution of Oceanography on carbon dioxide emissions, 1958–2005). Regarding global health crises, there are numerous historical accounts chronicling the flu pandemic of 1918 (see for example John M. Barry's *The Great Influenza: The Epic Story of the Deadliest Plague in History*) and the Ebola virus (see for example Paul Farmer's *Fevers, Feuds and Diamonds: Ebola and the Ravages of History*). In recent years, the intensity and frequency of climate-related natural disasters and the COVID-19 global pandemic have drawn increasing attention to environmental and health issues affecting our planet.

In the field of qualitative research, we have seen an increase in studies drawing on new materialist and posthuman concepts to examine the entanglements between humans and the environment. Qualitative research studies in fields such as public health, geography, and ecology are growing. Qualitative studies investigating people's experiences during the global COVID-19 pandemic have been published across a range of disciplines (e.g., health, education, family studies, organizational studies, counseling, psychology). Research studies investigating the social inequities amplified by the pandemic include topics such as equitable access to healthcare, risks to frontline workers, and access to technology and internet for online learning. Qualitative researchers conducting research during the pandemic relied almost exclusively on online modes of communication, and this has led to greater acceptance of online research methods. Challenges for researchers conducting research on COVID-19 include the ability to keep up with the latest findings and publish relevant, timely studies.

While the worst of the COVID-19 pandemic appears to be in the past, each year people all over the world deal with both natural disasters and those created by humans (e.g., oil spills, gun violence). When conducting research to do with global issues such as climate change or health crises, researchers may well encounter mistrust from the public in the research process, especially when topics have been politicized in popular media. As we noted earlier in this chapter, research is emergent. As researchers learn more, they ask different questions of the data. Misunderstanding of the research process may pose difficulties communicating your research to public audiences. In Box 1.4 below, we offer some key questions for you to consider on research related to global problems spanning the natural and human world.

Box 1.4. Key Questions for Qualitative Researchers: Social Problems Spanning the More-Than-Human.

- What "more-than-human" phenomena manifest in the research topics you want to examine (e.g., technologies, geography, climate, nonhuman animals, matter)?
- How might you bring knowledge from other disciplines to the study of your topic of interest?
- What are the challenges of engaging in interdisciplinary and transdisciplinary research?

- How is interdisciplinary research valued among the community of scholars to whom you want to address your work?
- What are the implications for how you construct your researcher identity?
- How might you communicate complex theoretical ideas to the public?

Accountability and Control of Education

In the early 2000s, legislation outlined in the No Child Left Behind Act ushered in an era of high stakes standardized testing for U.S. K–12 public schools. As a result, think tanks funded by wealthy philanthropists sponsored educational research for ideological ends (deMarrais, 2006; deMarrais et al., 2019, 2020). The Scientific Research in Education (SRE) report (Shavelson & Towne, 2002) endorsed quasi-experimental and causal studies as the "gold standard" for educational research. The SRE report sparked vigorous debate among scholars as to its usefulness. Qualitative scholars challenged the report's exclusion of critical and postmodern theories in educational research and argued excluding such theoretical perspectives produced White-washed, hegemonic histories (Freeman et al., 2007).

More recently, there has been a concerted effort on the part of conservative activists in the United States to censor and exclude conversations about certain topics (e.g., Critical Race Theory, LGBTQIA topics, diversity, equity, and inclusion) in K–12 and higher education contexts. This activity has led to legislation aimed at curtailing scholars' academic freedom to pursue particular research agendas since they may be viewed as openly ideological. At the same time, increased accountability and control in higher education has led to more pressure on faculty to produce publications and direct their research to particular topics that are fundable. Early career scholars are faced with the dual pressures of conducting research considered to be "objective" by reviewers and the public, who may not be sympathetic to researchers' aims, while meeting the demands of a "publish or perish" culture in higher education.

While early-career qualitative scholars have multiple reputable outlets to publish their work, the influx of online, predatory journals introduces new challenges as scholars decide where to submit studies for publication. The rush to publish to meet annual review or tenure and promotion guidelines can lead to poor quality publications. As peer-refereed journals move increasingly online this expedites the publishing process and places increased pressure on reviewers to review articles quickly. We note here a few possibilities and challenges for qualitative researchers arising from increased accountability and control of education. As you look to Box 1.5 below, consider some key questions qualitative researchers might ask concerning this topic.

Box 1.5. Key Questions for Qualitative Researchers: Accountability and Control of Education.

- What forms of research design are valued in your discipline?
- What are the significant issues and important problems discussed in your field of study?
- How might you shape your research agenda in a way that is significant to academic peers?
- What, if any, are the public conversations surrounding the theoretical frameworks that you intend to use in your study?
- How might you craft the findings of your research for nonscholarly audiences?
- What standards of quality will be used by members of your advisory committee to judge your research?
- How will reviewers judge your work for publication?
- What are the peer-reviewed journals in your field that publish qualitative research?
- How might you add to existing conversations in your field of inquiry?

Conclusions

In this chapter we introduced readers to qualitative research within its historic contexts and illustrated how what we now know as qualitative research began in disciplines like anthropology, sociology, social work, and journalism starting in the late 19th century. We offered a brief overview of the history of qualitative research and examples of early methodological texts, followed by a discussion of the primary characteristics of qualitative research. We concluded the chapter by discussing some of the key questions that qualitative researchers need to consider as they conduct their research in a global context in which people are intricately connected via technology, where sustained inequities among people have led to social movements and calls for social justice, and where the conduct of research is both increasingly interdisciplinary, and subject to the demands of surveillance for accountability purposes. In the next chapters, we focus first on research ethics, followed by the role of theory as used in qualitative research, then move to engaging readers in research design before focusing on a variety of methodological approaches to qualitative research. These include interview studies, narrative inquiry, ethnography and autoethnography, documents and archives, and arts-based approaches to research. We conclude by discussing how qualitative researchers attend to quality in the design of their studies. The appendix provides examples of a range of approaches to dissertation research, demonstrating the numerous possibilities for designing studies that represent diverse theoretical perspectives and approaches to representing research.

Activities

1. What research courses and experiences have you had? Compare those to the characteristics of qualitative research described in this chapter.
2. Considering the characteristics of qualitative research, make a list of the abilities and/or skills a qualitative researcher might possess to do this type of research.
3. Given the current climate for qualitative researchers, make a list of potential research topics related to significant global, national, or local events. What interests you about these topics? What is your relationship to these topics? What opportunities and/or challenges might arise when investigating these topics?

Further Reading

Denzin, N. K., Lincoln, Y. S., Giardina, M. D., & Cannella, G. S. (Eds.). (2024). *The SAGE handbook of qualitative research* (6th ed.). SAGE.

Hammersley, M. (2023). The history of qualitative research in education. In R. J. Tierney, F. Rizvi, & K. Erkican (Eds.), *International Encyclopedia of Education* (4th ed., pp. 14–23). Elsevier. https://doi.org/https://doi.org/10.1016/B978-0-12-818630-5.11002-4

Note

1. Here we choose to use identity-first, rather than person-first language, realizing there is much debate among communities on naming practices. See Dunn and Andrews (2015) and Andrews et al. (2019).

References

Andrews, E. E., Forber-Pratt, A. J., Mona, L. R., Lund, E. M., Pilarski, C. R., & Balter, R. (2019). #SaytheWord: A disability culture commentary on the erasure of "disability." *Rehabilitation Psychology, 64*(2), 111–118. https://doi.org/10.1037/rep0000258

Barry, J. M. (2004). *The great influenza: The epic story of the greatest plague in history*. Viking.

Becker, H. S. (1954). A note on interviewing tactics. *Human Organization, 12*(4), 31–32. https://doi.org/10.17730/humo.12.4.n2416271h4242904

Bell, C., & Roberts, H. (Eds.). (1984). *Social researching: Politics, problems, practice*. Routledge & Kegan Paul.

Best, S. (2003). *A beginner's guide to social theory*. SAGE.

Boas, F. (1943). Recent anthropology. *Science, 98*(2545), 311–314. http://www.jstor.org/stable/1669676

Brinkmann, S., Jacobsen, M. H., & Kristiansen, S. (2014). Historical overview of qualitative research in the social sciences. In P. Leavy (Ed.), *The Oxford handbook of qualitative research* (pp. 17–42). Oxford University Press.

Carson, R. (1962). *Silent spring*. Fawcett Crest.

Clandinin, D. J., & Connelly, F. M. (2000). *Narrative inquiry: Experience and story in qualitative research*. Jossey-Bass.

deMarrais, K. (2006). "The haves and the have mores:" Fueling a conservative ideological war on public education. *Educational Studies, 39*(3), 204–242. https://doi.org/10.1207/s15326993es3903_3

deMarrais, K., Brewer, T. J., Atkinson, J.C., Herron, B., & Lewis, J. B. (2019). *Primer for concerned educators: Philanthropy, hidden strategy, and collective resistance*. Myers Education Press.

deMarrais, K., Herron, B., & Copple, J. (Eds.). (2020). *Conservative philanthropies and organizations shaping US educational policy and practice*. Myers Education Press.

Denzin, N. K. (2010). *The qualitative manifesto: A call to arms*. Left Coast Press.

Denzin, N. K., & Lincoln, Y. S. (Eds.). (1994). *The handbook of qualitative research*. SAGE.

Du Bois, W. E. B. (1996 [1899]). *The Philadelphia negro: A social study*. University of Pennsylvania.

Dunn, D. S., & Andrews, E. E. (2015). Person-first and identity-first language: Developing psychologists' cultural competence using disability language. *The American Psychologist, 70*(3), 255–264. https://doi.org/10.1037/a0038636

Durkheim, E. (1938). *The rules of sociological method*. University of Chicago Press.

Editors. (1949). Field methods and techniques. *Human Organization, 8*(1), 26–27. http://www.jstor.org/stable/44123925

Eisner, E. W. (1991). *The enlightened eye: Qualitative inquiry and the enhancement of educational practice*. Macmillan.

Erickson, F. (2018). A history of qualitative inquiry in social and educational research. In N. K. Denzin & Y. S. Lincolns (Eds.), *The SAGE handbook of qualitative research* (pp. 36–65). SAGE.

Farmer, P. (2020). *Fevers, feuds and diamonds: Ebola and the ravages of history*. Macmillan.

Fetterman, D. M. (1989). *Ethnography: Step by step*. SAGE.

Firestone, W.A. (1987). Meaning in method: The rhetoric of quantitative and qualitative research. *Educational Researcher, 16*(7), 16–21. https://doi.org/10.2307/1174685

Freeman, M., deMarrais, K., Preissle, J., Roulston, K., & St. Pierre, E. A. (2007). Standards of evidence in qualitative research: An incitement to discourse. *Educational Researcher, 36*(1), 25–32. https://doi.org/10.3102/0013189x06298009

Geertz, C. (1973a). *The interpretation of cultures*. Basic Books.

Geertz, C. (1973b). Thick description: Toward an interpretive theory of culture. In Y. Lincoln & N. Denzin (Eds.), *Turning points in qualitative research: Tying knots in a handkerchief* (pp. 143–168). Altamira Press.

Glaser, B. G., & Strauss, A. L. (1967). *The discovery of grounded theory: Strategies for qualitative research*. Aldine Publishing.

Goodenough, W. (1970). *Description and comparison in cultural anthropology*. Aldine.

Harris, M. (1976). History and significance of the emic/etic distinction. *Annual Review of Anthropology, 5*, 329–350. http://www.jstor.org/stable/2949316

Hurston, Z. N. (1927). Cudjo's own story of the last African slaver. *The Journal of Negro History, 12*(4), 648–663. https://doi.org/10.2307/2714041

International Monetary Fund. (2002). *Globalization: A framework for IMF Involvement*. Retrieved June 15, 2023. https://www.imf.org/external/np/exr/ib/2002/031502.htm

Keat, R., & Urry, J. (1975). *Social theory as science*. Routledge & Paul.

LeCompte, M. D., & Preissle, J. (1993). *Ethnography and qualitative design in educational research* (2nd ed.). Academic Press.

Lett, J. (1987). *The human enterprise: A critical introduction to anthropological theory*. Westview.

Lincoln, Y. S., & Guba, E. G. (1985). *Naturalistic inquiry*. SAGE.

López, A. J. (2007). Introduction: The (Post) Global South. *The Global South, 1*(1), 1–11. http://www.jstor.org/stable/40339224

Malinowski, B. (2014 [1922]). *Argonauts of the western Pacific: An account of native enterprise and adventure in the archipelagoes of Melanesian New Guinea*. Routledge.

May, E. (Ed.). (1980). *Musics of many cultures: An introduction*. University of California Press.

Merriam, S. (1988). *Case study research in education: A qualitative approach*. Jossey-Bass.

Mishler, E. G. (1986). *Research interviewing: Context and narrative*. Harvard University Press.

Musolf, G. R. (2003). The Chicago School. In L. T. Reynolds & N. J. Herman-Kinney (Eds.), *Handbook of symbolic interactionism* (pp. 91–118). AltaMira Press.

O'Reilly, M. & Kiyimba, N. (2015). *Advanced qualitative research: A guide to using theory*. SAGE.

Pelto, P. J., & Pelto, G. H. (1978). *Anthropological research: The structure of inquiry* (2nd ed.). Cambridge University Press.

Pike, K. (1967). *Language in relation to a unified theory of human behavior.* Mouton.

Powdermaker, H. (1966). *Stranger and friend: The way of an anthropologist.* Norton.

Preissle, J., & LeCompte, M. D. (1984). *Ethnography and qualitative design in educational research.* Academic Press.

Reichertz, J. (2014). Induction, deduction, abduction. In U. Flick (Ed.), *The SAGE handbook of qualitative data analysis.* (pp. 123–135). SAGE.

Reinharz, S. (1992). *Feminist methods in social research.* Oxford University Press.

Roulston, K. (2022). Bursting forth: Attending to the more-than-human in qualitative research. In N. K. Denzin & M. D. Giardina (Eds.), *Transformative visions for qualitative inquiry* (pp. 65–84). Routledge.

Schatzman, L., & Strauss, A. (1973). *Field research: Strategies for a natural sociology.* Prentice-Hall.

Scripps Institution of Oceanography. (n.d.). Scripps CO2 Program, Charles David Keeling, Technical Reports. https://scrippsco2.ucsd.edu/publications/technical_reports.html

Shavelson, R. J., & Towne, L. (Eds.). (2002). *Scientific research in education.* National Academy Press.

Spradley, J. P. (1979). *The ethnographic interview.* Wadsworth.

Spradley, J. P. (1980). *Participant observation.* Holt, Rinehart & Winston.

Stake, R. E. (1995). *The art of case study research.* SAGE.

Tracy, S. J. (2020). *Qualitative research methods: Collecting evidence, crafting analysis, communicating impact* (2nd ed.). Wiley-Blackwell.

Wolcott, H. F. (1990). *Writing up qualitative research* (Vol. 20). SAGE.

Wolcott, H. F. (1994). *Transforming qualitative data: Description, analysis, and interpretation.* SAGE.

Wolcott, H. F. (1995). *The art of fieldwork.* Altamira Press.

Wolcott, H. F. (1999). *Ethnography: A way of seeing.* AltaMira Press.

Ethics and Qualitative Research

THIS CHAPTER DISCUSSES ETHICS IN designing and conducting qualitative research studies. Conducting social sciences research involves not only abiding by institutional policies, but interacting with people and organizations in respectful and ethical ways. Designing, conducting, and representing findings involves ethical decision-making throughout the process. Unfortunately, researchers do not always act ethically and conduct research of integrity. Unethical practices lead to mistrust of research by the public and create lingering problems for participants and other researchers. Complicating matters, what researchers have viewed as acceptable in the past may now be regarded as problematic if not unethical due to changing norms of behavior across time and cultural context.

Federal funding agencies in the United States now require universities to provide training on research integrity known as Responsible Conduct of Research (RCR). In this chapter we begin by discussing components of RCR pertaining to all researchers. We review problematic research that led to the institutionalization of ethical review of research protocols around the world and resources that researchers can use to inform ethical courses of action. Finally, we discuss potential ethical issues in qualitative research via several cases. Let's start with ethics: what does it mean to be ethical?

Ethics

Ethics refers to what we consider to be right and wrong and our moral responsibilities in how we conduct ourselves in relation to others and the world around us. Although in society we generally can agree on certain norms of behavior—that it is wrong to lie, steal, cheat, or commit murder—how people decide what is the right thing to do draws on upbringing, religious beliefs, cultural norms and values, and professional guidelines. The philosopher Kwame Anthony Appiah (2008) reminds us that the goals of ethics are not only to "study the good life, but to sustain what's good in our lives" (p. 204). This good underlies how researchers pursue individual research agendas, work with others, and contribute to understanding the natural and social world in which we live.

Research ethics involves treating participants, collaborators, and the larger scientific community with respect and communicating findings with scholarly, practitioner, and public audiences in ways that satisfy accepted professional standards of conduct. Ethical researchers aim to develop trusting and honest relationships with others and contribute to the good of society. When faced with ethical dilemmas, researchers must develop compelling moral arguments to support thoughtful actions. Over time the scientific community has developed codes of conduct to guide how researchers conduct research of integrity, as we discuss next.

Fostering Research Integrity

The National Research Council (2002) defined research integrity in individual and institutional terms:

> For the individual scientist, integrity embodies above all a commitment to intellectual honesty and personal responsibility for one's actions and to a range of practices that characterize responsible research conduct. These practices include:
>
> - intellectual honesty in proposing, performing, and reporting research;
> - accuracy in representing contributions to research proposals and reports;
> - fairness in peer review;
> - collegiality in scientific interactions, including communications and sharing of resources;

- transparency in conflicts of interest or potential conflicts of interest;
- protection of human subjects[1] in the conduct of research;
- humane care of animals in the conduct of research; and
- adherence to the mutual responsibilities between investigators and their research teams. (pp. 34–35)

Universities and institutions such as hospitals or schools support integrity in research by putting in place policies and processes that monitor what researchers do to ensure best practices are followed. The National Academies of Sciences (2017) recommended that accomplishing research integrity requires that researchers, institutions, journals, and professional organizations work collaboratively to ensure that best practices are followed in all aspects of the research process. As already mentioned, in the United States, RCR training has been implemented in an effort to ensure that researchers understand how to conduct research of integrity.

Responsible Conduct of Research

Professional development for researchers in RCR who gain federal funding in the United States (e.g., National Science Foundation and National Institutes of Health) is mandatory. Because RCR training is not required for unfunded research or research funded by nonfederal sources and not all qualitative researchers see themselves as scientists, they can overlook RCR. We think that RCR offers useful things to think about in relation to research integrity for *all* researchers—regardless of methods used.

Research Misconduct

Researchers are human and make mistakes. But when researchers engage in intentionally dishonest acts, their actions can constitute researcher misconduct. From an institutional viewpoint, researcher misconduct is defined as involving cheating, lying, or stealing—that is, (1) falsification of data; (2) fabrication of data; or (3) plagiarism. Learning about appropriate professional codes of conduct early in a research career can help researchers avoid research misconduct. Irrespective of discipline or approach to research all researchers are subject to institutional guidelines concerning research misconduct. Yet, because researchers explore research problems using many theoretical and methodological approaches, it can sometimes be challenging to differentiate "misunderstood" actions from "transgressions" (Macrina, 2014, pp. 6–7).

RCR deals with much more than ethical treatment of human subjects, which is a well-rehearsed topic in methodological literature on qualitative research. The four areas covered include (1) subject protection; (2) research integrity; (3) environmental and safety issues; and (4) fiscal accountability (Macrina, 2014, p. 18) (See Table 2.1). This chapter focuses primarily on subject protection and research integrity and briefly addresses safety issues and fiscal accountability.

Table 2.1. Topics Covered in Responsible Conduct of Research

Subject protection	Research integrity	Environmental and safety issues	Fiscal accountability
• Human subjects • Nonhuman animal species	• Data management: – Collection – Management – Storage – Sharing – Ownership • Collaborative research • Mentoring • Authorship and publication • Peer review	• Hazardous substances • Scientific research subject to regulation	• Conflicts of interest • Responsible use of research funds

Let's begin by exploring subject protection.

Scientific Research and Protection of Human Subjects

The history of science reveals numerous experimental studies conducted for medical research that resulted in harm to, and even death of, participants.[2] For example, during World War II Nazi doctors conducted experiments on prisoners leading to death and disfigurement. Yet, during the Nuremburg Trials when doctors were being tried for experimenting on prisoners, defense lawyers argued that the very same thing was being done in the United States (Reverby, 2009, p. 66). Nuremberg Trial defense lawyers were referring to experimental studies conducted by pharmaceutical researchers with prisoner populations that were considered acceptable at the time (Hornblum, 1999).[2]

Beecher (2001 [1966]) also documented published studies that reported experimental treatments on patients by medical doctors that resulted in harm to participants. And more recently, Human Rights Watch and the Physicians for Human Rights accused psychologists James Mitchell and Bruce Jessen of breaching codes of ethical conduct for medical research as part of the Central Intelligence Agency's (CIA) post-9/11 experiments on detainees to develop enhanced methods of torture. A lawsuit filed by the American Civil Liberties Union (ACLU) against Mitchell and Jessen was settled out of court (Fink, 2017, August 17).

Let's look at one infamous study. The Public Health Service's (PHS) study of untreated syphilis in Alabama from 1932 to 1972 achieved notoriety because of its unethical treatment of human subjects. African American sharecroppers in Alabama were recruited to participate in a study of the effects of untreated syphilis over time. Even when effective treatment for syphilis was developed in the 1940s, and despite complaints made to the Public Health Service, investigators continued to collect data from participants, who were not referred to treatment. Physician Irwin Schatz, among others, on reading a 1964 article about the study published in *Archives of Internal Medicine*, wrote a letter of protest to the PHS that went unanswered. The study ended only when Peter Buxtun, who had worked for the PHS, gave information about the study to a reporter that became public. The resulting scandal led to the appointment of a special committee to examine the study, congressional hearings, a lawsuit that sought reparation for the participants and their families, and an official apology that President Bill Clinton delivered to participants and their descendants in 1997 (Reverby, 2009). The immense harm caused by this study has lingered long after the study was shut down, and contributed significantly to mistrust of researchers among African-American people (for another example, see Skloot, 2010).

Debates about ethics and research have led to a series of agreements concerning how human subjects should be treated. These include the Nuremburg Code, the Declaration of Helsinki, and the Belmont Report. After the trials of those involved in war crimes in Nazi Germany during World War II, 10 principles pertaining to scientific research with human subjects were enshrined in the Nuremberg Code in 1947. These principles were developed to prevent the atrocities that occurred during experiments on prisoners that occurred during the war:

1. The voluntary consent of the human subject is absolutely essential.
2. Experiments must only be conducted for the good of society if not possible by other means, and must not be random or unnecessary.
3. Experiments involving humans should be based on previous animal experimentation.
4. Experiments should avoid all unnecessary physical and mental suffering and injury to participants.
5. No experiment should be conducted if it is believed to cause death or disability (except perhaps if experimental researchers are also subjects).
6. The risks of research should never exceed the benefits for addressing humanitarian problems.
7. Appropriate preparation and adequate facilities should be used to protect human subjects.
8. Experiments should only be conducted by qualified scientists.
9. Subjects should be able to end their participation at any time.
10. Scientists must terminate experiments when injury, disability, or death is likely to occur. (https://history.nih.gov/display/history/Nuremberg+Code)

The Declaration of Helsinki, which outlined ethical principles for medical research involving human subjects, centers around the welfare of patients. This was adopted in 1964 by the World Medical Association, but has been updated several times to attend to advances in medical technologies and research, most recently in 2013. (See https://www.wma.net/policies-post/wma-declaration-of-helsinki-ethical-principles-for-medical-research-involving-human-subjects/) For instance, genetic research provokes complex ethical questions concerning what is acceptable research. In one notable example, a Chinese researcher, He Jiankui, was dismissed from his university and later received a prison sentence after he announced in 2018 that his team had engaged in gene editing of unborn babies. Consider that cloning animals is now considered acceptable, while cloning of human beings is not. Juan Enriquez (2020) argued that new technologies constantly transform our understanding of right and wrong. This means that perceptions of ethical practice in research are subject to change. In the future, people will likely have different views on what counts as ethical research.

In the United States, the National Commission for the Protection of Human Subjects of Biomedical and Behavioral Research was established in 1974. The

Commission developed principles for ethical research that could be applied to medical and behavioral research. These are described in the Belmont Report (https://history.nih.gov/display/history/Belmont+Report). The three principles, those of respect for persons, beneficence, and justice, underlie the ethical approach to research with human subjects taken in the United States.

Respect for persons encapsulates two ideas: "first, that individuals should be treated as autonomous agents, and second, that persons with diminished autonomy are entitled to protection" (National Commission for the Protection of Human Subjects of Biomedical and Behavioral Research, 1979). Researchers are responsible for attending to the needs of vulnerable participants (e.g., children, the ill, disability communities.). This might involve ensuring that participants are fully aware of what participation involves via offering continuous consent throughout a project, or using inclusive approaches to generating data and involving participants in a project (e.g., as co-researchers). *Beneficence* means that researchers should do no harm, but rather maximize the benefits of research and minimize potential harms for participants and larger society. *Justice* entails that researchers ensure that the burden of participating in research studies and the subsequent benefits of research are fairly distributed among the population. Poor and vulnerable populations should not assume a greater proportion of participation in research studies than other members of society (National Commission for the Protection of Human Subjects of Biomedical and Behavioral Research, 1979).

The Nuremburg Code, the Declaration of Helsinki, and the Belmont Report have been crucial to how institutional oversight of biomedical and behavioral research has been implemented in universities through Institutional Review Boards (IRBs) and ethical review boards in other organizations such as schools and hospitals. Requirements for ethical review extend to forms of social research that use qualitative methods.[3]

IRBs and Ethical Review

IRBs and ethical review boards have oversight of research protocols that involve human subjects, while Institutional Animal Care and Use Committees (IACUCs) review protocols for animal research. Although research on nonhuman animals has been crucial to scientific research historically, animal rights groups have made steady inroads into raising awareness of the suffering and death inflicted on animals for research purposes. Associations such as the Physicians Committee for Responsible Medicine argue for alternatives to use of animals in medical research, and it is plausible that in future research using animals will become less common.

Within qualitative methodological literature much has been written on the ethical oversight of research and how IRB regulations based on biomedical research do not fit qualitative research (e.g., Bosk & de Vries, 2004; Johnson, 2008). These critiques have been relevant for action and participatory forms of research, ethnography, autoethnography, and self-studies, especially when members of IRB boards know little about qualitative research. Qualitative scholars have critiqued IRBs' "mission creep" (Gunsalus et al., 2007) and argued that IRBs interfere with the academic freedom of researchers to design and conduct qualitative studies (Katz, 2007). Researchers' use of new technologies can also outpace existing regulations, leading to delays in gaining permission to conduct studies. How federal regulations are implemented across institutions varies depending on who serves on IRBs. This has meant that research protocols approved in one institution have been denied by another. Rather than be overly concerned about gaining an IRB's approval for a study, we have found that researchers can work with IRB staff members to provide sufficient information about their protocols to ensure timely approval for their studies (Roulston & Preissle, 2018). With the implementation of the Revised Common Rule in 2018, oversight of unfunded research of a noninvasive nature decreased (see https://www.hhs.gov/ohrp/education-and-outreach/revised-common-rule/index.html).

Conducting Qualitative Research With Integrity

As indicated in Table 2.1, conducting research with integrity involves all aspects of research, including working with participants, managing data (collecting, storing, managing, owning and sharing), and publishing findings (writing and reviewing). Let's first look at data management.

Data Management

When conducting a qualitative study, researchers typically draw on a range of data sources: transcripts of interviews and focus groups, fieldnotes of observations, documents, texts and artifacts from field settings, and visual data (e.g., photos and videos). Researchers usually ensure that participants' identities are protected throughout the process of research (e.g., using pseudonyms in transcripts and field texts), or blurring or omitting details in images using photo-editing software. In some instances, participants provide their consent to use their names and images in publications. Naming participants in publications can be respectful in some communities (e.g., Fournillier, 2016). Researchers must take precautions to protect digital files stored in cloud storage and/or hard drives through using strong passwords to prevent others accessing files. Corti et al. (2020) outlined protocols for managing, storing, and sharing research data. In keeping with good practice, we recommend routinely backing up digital files on external drives.

Researchers should be aware that when working on team projects, the institution owns the data collected. Principal investigators (PIs) and team members need to collaboratively agree on the projects pursued by individual members and who is responsible for different parts of a project. In lab-based research, research notebooks belong to the institution and must not be removed when team members move to other institutions. All team members must take responsibility for accurately maintaining files and research records while working at an institution and ensuring that the PIs have access to these should they leave an institution. Further use of research records must always be negotiated with a project's PIs. Some funders require submission of a data management plan that outlines what happens to research data at the conclusion of a project, how and where it will be stored, and whether it will be archived for sharing with other researchers. Ownership of data becomes particularly important when financial compensation for investigators and institutions is involved (e.g., through commercial products), or when legal protection of ideas or research products is sought.

Mays and Macrina (2014) identified four forms of intellectual property: patents, copyrights, trademarks, and trade secrets. Governments extend patents to grantees for a specific period of time to exclude others from "making, using, selling, offering to sell, or importing. . . . the claimed invention" (p. 305). Copyright protects "the *expression or presentation* of an idea" (p. 298, emphasis in original). This entails that researchers accurately acknowledge the work of others in their writing, teaching and presentations, and pay for re-use of others' words and images in publications (e.g., textbooks or monographs).

Copyright law currently safeguards "fair use" of copyrighted material for research and teaching purposes under certain conditions (Mays & Macrina, 2014, p. 301). Because fair use requirements are integral to teaching and research, be sure to check the fair use requirements at your institution.

The U.S. Trademarks and Patent Office defines a trademark as "a word, phrase, symbol, and/or design that identifies and distinguishes the source of the goods of one party from those of others" (https://www.uspto.gov/). Trademarks identify the brand for products and services. For example, Apple™ lists dozens of trademarks for different products. Finally, trade secrets include information that is not publicly known that conveys economic worth to the owner. For example, the formula for Coca Cola™ remains a closely guarded trade secret.

Authorship and Peer Review

When writing up reports from studies, ethical issues extend to author credit for a manuscript submitted for publication, protocols for submission of manuscripts, and the process of peer review.

Authorship Credit. "Ghost authorship," in which someone writes an article yet another person is given author credit; "gift authorship," in which noncontributors are given credit for authorship; and "coercive authorship," in which people in authority assume authorship of supervisees' work without contributing, are all unethical practices, and should be avoided (National Academies of Sciences & Medicine, 2017). How authors are listed on a publication varies depending on discipline. We know one discipline in which the leader of a lab-based team is listed as the final author with the primary author listed first. Sometimes a large team of authors lists authors in alphabetical order without regard to primary authorship. In our field of education, the primary author is typically listed as first author. In some departments, advisors of doctoral dissertations are credited as co-authors in ensuing publications. The different practices that exist across disciplines and departments means that researchers should always discuss credit for co-authorship early in a project to avoid hurt feelings when authors believe that they were not given sufficient credit for their work, or others were given undue credit.

Manuscript Submission. Prior to submission of a manuscript for publication, the submitting author should seek permission from all authors and provide each with a copy of the manuscript for approval. Ethical practices in publishing require scholars to submit a manuscript to one journal at a time.

Peer Review. When reviewing others' manuscripts for journal editors, reviewers should (a) only review manuscripts within their purview of expertise;[4] (b) not take advantage of others by borrowing ideas from unpublished manuscripts during the review process; and (c) not share unpublished manuscripts without editors' and authors' permission. We believe that fairly reviewing others' manuscripts involves ethical decision-making: that is, reviewers should never reject manuscripts without providing a reasoned argument and evidence (e.g., competition with a reviewer's own work is not a legitimate reason to reject a manuscript!); and take time to write informed and pedagogical reviews that assist authors to improve their work.

Dual Use Research of Concern

One issue that has become relevant in scientific publishing since the beginning of the new millennium is that of "Dual Use Research of Concern" (DURC). This refers to research developed for one purpose that can be used by bad actors for detrimental purposes. Qualitative researchers are unlikely to conduct research developed for one purpose that can be used for the purposes of bioterrorism, which is the focus of DURC. While qualitative researchers typically do not need to concern themselves with DURC, it is important to recognize that audiences can apply the findings of any study in ways unintended by author/s. While in some circumstances this may be something to applaud, researchers may have qualms about others. Kathy, for example, was approached by a military contractor who wanted to use her writing on teaching interviewing to teach soldiers in war zones how to interview local community members to collect intelligence.

Publishing

Early career scholars should be aware that in the age of fake news, academic journals can also be faked or hijacked. Fake websites have emulated legitimate journals in order to accept manuscripts published for a fee. This activity is part of what is known as "predatory publishing." For those unfamiliar with predatory journals, a group of 35 scholars published a definition:

Predatory journals and publishers are entities that prioritize self-interest at the expense of scholarship and are characterized by false or misleading information, deviation from best editorial and publication practices, a lack of transparency, and/or the use of aggressive and indiscriminate solicitation practices. (Grudniewicz, 2019, p. 211)[5]

The Committee on Publication Ethics' (2019) statement on predatory publishing provides more detail on the forms that predatory publishing can take:

Predatory publishing generally refers to the systematic for-profit publication of purportedly scholarly content (in journals and articles, monographs, books, or conference proceedings) in a deceptive or fraudulent way and without any regard for quality assurance. Here, '*for-profit*' refers to profit generation per se. Whereas predatory publishers are profit-generating businesses, some may conceivably pose as non-profit entities such as academic societies or research institutions. This is not to suggest that '*for profit*' is, in itself, problematic but that these journals exist solely for profit without any commitment to publication ethics or integrity of any kind. Predatory publishers may cheat authors (and their funders and institutions) through charging publishing-related fees without providing the expected or industry standard services. Predatory publishers may also deceive academics into serving as editorial board members or peer reviewers. In short, fake scholarly publications lack the usual features of editorial oversight and transparent policies and operating procedures that are expected from legitimate peer-reviewed publications. (p. 3)

New and early career scholars should be aware that conducting research of integrity involves publishing in the best journals in a field of inquiry. If you are not sure what these are, check where experts in your discipline publish. Because any field of research is immense and always growing, learning the hidden curriculum of academic work can appear insurmountable. This is why mentorship is integral to the responsible conduct of research.

Mentorship

Macrina (2014) wrote that the term mentor "has come to mean a loyal and trusted friend, enlightened advisor, and teacher" (p. 53). Faculty advisers serve as mentors to graduate students, providing advice concerning research topics and methodology and the requirements of academic careers. Effective mentorship involves a trusting relationship between an adviser and advisee. No single person can attend to all aspects of a novice researcher's development. Kathleen has used the idea of "an invisible college" to encourage new students to develop mentoring relationships with a range of people, both inside and outside their institutions, who can support them in completing graduate research projects and preparing for academic careers. Developing an effective mentoring relationship requires that mentees show themselves to be mentorable. This entails attending to mentors' advice, assuming responsibility for managing one's program of study and career development, and understanding what is required by the program, department, and institution. Fortunately, there is much work to guide novice researchers on how to complete a graduate degree and pursue a scholarly career (Calarco, 2020; Kelsky, 2015; Tanggaard & Wegener, 2017).

Collaborative Research

Societies face complex, ill-structured problems that rely on teams of researchers. Whereas in some disciplines such as humanities and history individual scholarship is highly valued, in others (e.g., public health, ecology), team-based research brings together experts with different areas of expertise. Much funded research relies on teams working across departments and institutions. In cases where collaboration extends beyond the bounds of one institution, collaborative agreements are needed to outline the roles and responsibilities of each team member. Macrina (2014) recommended that these agreements outline how team members will communicate and what processes will be used to manage conflict (p. 253). While most readers of this book are scholars designing a first qualitative research project, involving oneself in a team-based research study or writing project will assist in preparing for collaborative research.

Environmental and Safety Issues

Qualitative researchers usually do not engage in research involving hazardous procedures and toxic substances. Although qualitative researchers do not usually conduct research that involves procedures that cause physical harm to participants, research can be harmful in other ways. For example, research involving undocumented immigrants or people committing crimes (e.g., illicit drug use) could harm participants should members of the justice system subpoena research records to identify people for deportation or arrest. Employees who provide accounts that will be read critically by employers could be penalized or fired if they can be identified via research reports. In the case of research on sensitive topics (e.g., intimate partner violence, human trafficking, or suicide), the process of participating in data generation (e.g., interviews) could result in re-traumatization of survivors or family members. In these sorts of studies, IRBs require that researchers outline what safety protocols they have in place should participants encounter emotional difficulties during the study. Ensuring the safety of participants in a qualitative study involves a number of questions, including:

- Can participants and research contexts be identified using the descriptive detail included?
- What are the potential harms for participants of being identified by readers from descriptions (including other participants in the research setting)?
- What are potential outcomes if the researcher's data sources (fieldnotes, interview transcripts etc.) are subpoenaed by a court of law?
- What psychological harms could potentially ensue for participants during data generation?
- What needs to be put in place to support participants who suffer psychological harm for participating in a research study?

In some cases, researchers may witness harm to people during fieldwork (e.g., Alice Goffman's [2014] *On the Run*). For some participant groups (e.g., children and adolescents), institutions require that researchers report instances of child abuse or suicidal ideation they have observed, and this potential is stated in consent agreements. Because every qualitative study is different, we do not have prescriptions for what to do. Rather, each researcher must consider particular research contexts and relevant factors. Ethical decision-making is necessarily contingent.

Fiscal Accountability

Institutions require researchers to keep accurate records of expenditure of research funds, maintain research equipment (e.g., digital recorders, computers) and submit appropriate reports when due. Again, since a large proportion of master's and doctoral students engage in unfunded research, this aspect of RCR may be less relevant for early career scholars.

Novice researchers should be aware that researchers must avoid both actual and apparent conflicts of interest (COI). Bradley (2014) defined conflicts of interests as a broad range of situations that involve the "possibility of receiving something of financial or personal value that, in turn, may introduce bias or corrupt the judgment of the scientist" (p. 209). Financial conflicts of interest occur when "an individual exploits, or appears to exploit, his or her position for personal gain or the profit of a member of his or her immediate family or household" (Bradley, 2014, p. 217). This is why journals require authors to identify funding sources for research when submitting manuscripts for publication. In the United States, scholars have been dismissed because they did not identify COIs in their work for foreign institutions suspected of stealing research.

Other conflicts of interest include those of "effort" and "conscience" (Bradley, 2014). A conflict of effort occurs when a researcher spends too much time on compensated activities with an external entity that prevents them from completing assigned responsibilities for their primary employer. For example, a researcher might engage in consulting at other institutions on their topic of expertise. While this is a valued part of a scholarly career, institutions limit the amount of time that faculty members can spend consulting to ensure that faculty expend sufficient time on their assigned duties (i.e., administration, research, teaching, and service). A conflict of conscience occurs when a researcher's own values and beliefs about an issue prevent them from making fair decisions. For example, a researcher whose religious beliefs prohibit in vitro fertilization (IVF) treatments to assist couples in conception could potentially encounter a conflict of conscience in reviewing a research proposal or manuscript examining couples' experiences with fertility treatments. Similarly, researchers with deeply-held beliefs and values that forbid abortion or euthanasia may need to recuse themselves with respect to decision-making concerning research related to these topics.

Ethical Issues in Qualitative Research

Ethical decision-making occurs throughout the life of a research project (see Figure 2.1). Points at which ethical issues related to planning for and conducting a project might emerge include:

1. conducting research in specific contexts and/or sites (e.g., cross-cultural research; online settings);
2. working with particular groups and participants (e.g. undocumented people, Indigenous people, vulnerable groups, disabled communities; children etc.) and ensuring continuing informed consent throughout the life of a project;
3. using specific methodologies (e.g., Participatory Action Research (PAR), Community Based Participatory Research (CBPR), oral history, narrative, autoethnography) and methods (observations, interviews, photovoice, images, secondary data analysis);
4. examining sensitive and/or taboo topics (e.g., intimate partner violence);
5. representing findings to a variety of audiences (e.g., maintaining confidentiality, avoiding harmful stereotypes); and
6. ensuring safety for the researcher/s.

Next, we discuss examples of ethical issues that researchers have discussed in relation to these decision points. To assist with ethical decision-making, scholars talk about navigating institutional regulations, using a range of scholarly theorizations and philosophical approaches to ethical decision-making. Let's look at these ethical issues in turn.

Conducting Research in Specific Contexts

Researchers must consider what ethical issues pertain to the specific contexts that they will be working in. All contexts have unique features—here we discuss an example of ethical issues arising in a cross-cultural research study and problems that can arise in online spaces.

Cross-cultural Research. Susan Kiragu and Molly Warrington (2013) discussed the ethical and methodological challenges they faced in a study involving young girls in Kenya. These included positionality and power, the tensions between maintaining confidentiality and protecting girls from harm, and the researchers' involvement and advocacy in relation to project participants. Kiragu and Warrington reported that the status differentials between themselves and participants impacted recruitment for the study and the negotiation of the informed consent process. Differences in status (such as adult researchers working with adolescents) may result in people feeling compelled to participate in a study. When this occurs, consent becomes less than voluntary. These researchers came to a deeper understanding of the stark differentials in wealth that separated them from participants. For example, they discussed their own access to bottled water while in the presence of participants who had suffered during drought-stricken conditions. They also learned of potentially

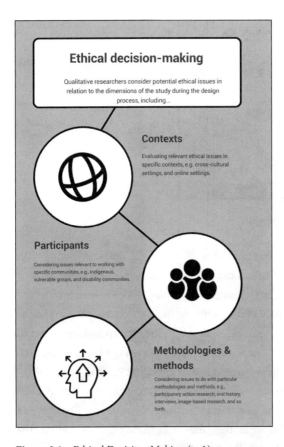

Figure 2.1a. Ethical Decision-Making (p. 1).

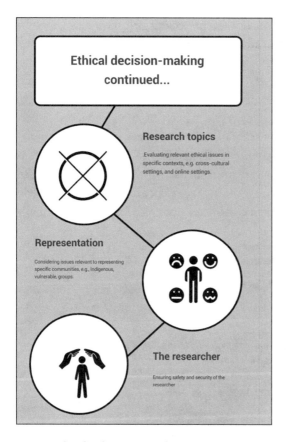

Figure 2.1b. Ethical Decision-Making (p. 2).

harmful situations faced by the girls they interviewed, and contended with the ethical dilemma of how to handle this information in instances where they believed the safety of participants was threatened. In response to the challenging circumstances revealed by some of the participants, the research-ers chose to involve themselves in advocacy activities that provided material support. This study entailed ethical dilemmas specific to the Kenyan context. Yet, from this study researchers can learn that engaging in cross-cultural re-search entails being open to recognizing challenges relating to differences in cultural norms and traditions and particular local conditions. Researchers should also keep in mind that when they share a cultural heritage and/or eth-nicity with participants, they may still be viewed as outsiders by participants.

Online Settings. Conducting research in online settings such as virtual communities, or using asynchronous or synchronous tools to generate data, involves a range of ethical issues. Peter Newman et al. (2021) discussed ethical considerations for qualitative researchers who turned to online methods during the COVID-19 pandemic that profoundly affected how researchers proceeded with their research during lockdowns. These included the increased potential for interruptions to occur when participants are engaging in research from their homes, the possibility for online meeting spaces to encourage oversharing, the ease with which online tools (e.g., Voice Over Internet Protocols such as Zoom™ or Facetime™) can generate visual data that is not needed to examine a study's research questions, the inability of researchers to ensure that participants can ensure confidentiality when group meetings occur online (e.g., participants could potentially record and disseminate meetings), and the potential exclusion from research of marginalized people who lack access to technology.

Researchers examining questions related to online communities must also consider how they identify whether spaces are public or private, and whose consent is needed to engage in research. Use of data sources identified as public does not excuse researchers from seeking permission from participants to conduct research, nor does it necessarily give researchers permission to take covert roles. When researchers use data from publicly available online sources such as social media sites, blogs, or websites, researchers must think about consent. For example, this is discussed in relation to online mourning in Myles et al. (2019). Other issues include those of copyright, confidentiality, anonymization, identification of minors, and potential risks of online recruitment to researchers (Burles & Bally, 2018; Gerrard, 2021; Kurtz et al., 2017; Roberts, 2015). Assistance for researchers conducting online research is found in the ethical guidelines developed by the Association of Internet Researchers, updated in 2019 (https://aoir.org/reports/ethics3.pdf).

Working with Specific Groups and Participants

Ethical issues can arise with almost any particular group. Increasing attention has been paid in the literature to conducting research with minors and vulnerable groups, such as undocumented migrants. "Vulnerability," however, can also relate to "sensitive" or "taboo" topics. And when researchers work with any participants, they may face challenges in coming to mutual understanding. This can be based on differences in subject positions (identities related to occupations, education, ability, race, ethnicity, language, and so forth), as well as our biases, prior assumptions, and preconceptions about topics.

As one case, Ariana Mangual Figueroa (2016) discussed the risks for the mixed-status families (i.e., some were undocumented) involved in participating in her research study, and the "brokering activities" in which she engaged (p. 73). The parents in one of the focal families requested that she formally adopt two of their children so they would gain American citizenship. Mangual Figueroa discussed an approach that treats beneficence "as an emergent set of practices and possibilities" that must be reconsidered throughout a study (p. 81). To that end, she advocated that researchers engage participants in the research process (e.g., by encouraging participants to articulate their own goals), and continually reflect on ethical codes of conduct in order to shape these in ways that help community members (pp. 82–83).

As another example, Nadia Bashir (2018) highlighted experiences of interviewing people in vulnerable health and financial circumstances in their homes. The participants' emotional states, sometimes combined with unsanitary conditions and unexpected life circumstances, produced potentially unsafe contexts for the researcher, and in some cases increased the vulnerability of participants. Bashir discussed strategies that research teams might use to support the researcher's safety and wellbeing, as well as the kinds of questions that researchers might think about when conducting research that involves physical and emotional risks, especially in the context of conducting longitudinal research.

Using Specific Methodologies and Methods

Specific methodologies and methods might also implicate ethical concerns. For example, use of still or moving images in qualitative studies needs to be carefully thought through, since the confidentiality of participants might be compromised if images are shared with audiences (e.g., Creighton et al., 2018). Research involving participatory approaches entails a range of ethical issues (Salazar, 2022), including covert to overt research (e.g., observations) and issues related to research pertaining to sensitive and/or taboo topics (e.g., intimate partner violence).

Research Topics

Sensitive and/or taboo topics can present problems for researchers, including recruiting participants and managing data collections. For example, how might conversations be initiated about sensitive or painful topics? Paxton (2018), for example, employed an interactive approach to interviewing about the topic of bereavement, recommending that researchers need personal experience with the topic, and either have, or be willing to develop, strong ties with participants (p. 154).

Representation

Ethical decision-making is also required when representing others' stories. Questions to consider here relate to whether participants will have the opportunity to provide feedback on preliminary drafts of findings, or have right of reply to the researcher's interpretations. Researchers must also think about how to represent participants fairly and respectfully, even when they might not agree with their perspectives.

The Researcher

Finally, we remind readers to be aware of their own safety. Researchers have been harmed while conducting fieldwork or subject to sexual harassment in field settings (e.g., Hanson & Richards, 2019). When conducting fieldwork or arranging interviews with unknown participants, researchers must attend to what is going on and make wise decisions if they need to withdraw from potentially dangerous situations.

Ethical Quandaries For Qualitative Researchers

As mentioned earlier, research using any method entails ethical decision-making. This is complicated when working with human subjects. Special considerations might relate to the type of data one works with (e.g., online, archival, visual data); the needs of special populations that one works with (e.g., refugees, children, the ill, the elderly, disability communities); or research concerning sensitive, illegal, or taboo topics. Once one has identified ethical issues that could occur, potential action/s can be planned. For example, in the case of working with a vulnerable population such as people with expressive language disabilities, the research design could involve methods that cater to the special characteristics of participants, such as inclusion of a family member in dyadic interviews (e.g., Verseghy et al., 2020). Because qualitative inquiry involves researchers in relationship with participants, it is plausible that any study—involving both "sensitive" and topics that appear as nonsensitive—will entail both researchers and participants encountering moments of vulnerability. Let's look at some ideas for how qualitative researchers can plan for how they respond to ethical dilemmas.

Identifying Presuppositions

First, before a study has even begun, researchers can identify their presuppositions about right and wrong with respect to research. You may be surprised when talking to peers just how varied others' perspectives are concerning ethical conduct. Part of identifying presuppositions involves reflecting on the sources used for deciding what is right and wrong. People use moral philosophies, cultural values, professional guidelines, and religious authorities to guide decision-making. Identifying presuppositions involves not only reflecting on your beliefs about right and wrong, but examining the warrants upon which your views are based and considering how your beliefs and values shape what you do as a researcher. For example, researchers following the Christian principle that people should not lie would likely not choose to engage in deceptive research. Researchers following a utilitarianist perspective of moral philosophy in which the pursuit of the "greater good" of society can lead to overlooking the needs of the vulnerable could argue that the benefits of learning about a taboo topic for society outweigh the risks to a small number of participants.

Identifying and Avoiding Moral Quagmires

Second, some researchers have deceived participants in the process of collecting data (Milgram, 2009 [1974]), engaged in sexual relationships with participants (Goode, 2002), and over-identified with participants (Goffman, 2014), leading to unexpected outcomes for both participants and themselves. It is helpful to remember that ethical challenges are not static, but change shape throughout a study. This is because relationships between participants and researchers vary over time. For example, when beginning any study, researchers occupy varying positions on the spectrum from insider to outsider in relation to the groups that they study, and the power relationships between researchers and participants likewise vary. Because institutional guidelines ensure that participants can voluntarily cease their involvement in a study at any point prior to publication, participants have a good deal of say in what happens in a study. Nevertheless, researchers must be vigilant about what they do and say, how this is communicated to participants, and monitor potential ethical issues that emerge in order to avoid stepping into a quagmire.

Resources To Guide Decision-Making

We have mentioned important documents that have been developed in the course of ethical oversight. These are supplemented by professional codes of ethics. Professional associations typically have a code of ethics, and guidelines have been developed for specific methods (e.g., oral history, online research, visual methods). Be sure to identify the professional code of ethics that guide research in your discipline. Moral philosophies (Birsch, 2023; Rachels & Rachels, 2015; Wolff, 2021) also provide guidelines for thinking through courses of action with respect to ethical dilemmas. Gert (2020) wrote that:

the term "morality" can be used either

1. descriptively to refer to certain codes of conduct put forward by a society or a group (such as a religion), or accepted by an individual for her own behavior, or
2. normatively to refer to a code of conduct that, given specified conditions, would be put forward by all rational people. (para 2)

Let's look further at the resources offered by the field of moral philosophy.

Applying Ethical Analysis

Let's look at a protocol for dealing with moral dilemmas and ethical problems that arise in research. Rachels and Rachels (2015) concluded that we should maximize the interests of all sentient beings by living according to our best plan; asserting that "the single moral standard is not human welfare, but all welfare" (p. 183). The following questions can be used to identify the core issues, stakeholders, and potential courses of action. It is important to recognize that in the face of any ethical dilemma there is not one right approach to be taken. Bebeau et al. (1995) proposed working through the following questions when faced with an ethical dilemma[6]:

- What are the ethical issues at stake?
- Who are the parties involved? What are their expectations? What is the legitimacy of their expectations?
- What are the issues and points of ethical conflict in this situation?
- What courses of action are open to the researcher?
- What are the consequences for actions? For whom?
- What are the duties and obligations for persons concerned?
- What are the professional norms and values that give rise to these obligations?

Let's look at a fictional case. Using the questions above, develop a potential course of action for the dilemma posed in Box 2.1 below.

Box 2.1. Jennifer's Ethical Dilemma.

Jennifer is a doctoral researcher conducting an interview study about eating disorders among young women from 18 to 25 years of age. Jennifer is following participants over the course of a year as they engage in treatment for eating disorders. The study also involves interviewing parents about their experiences supporting a daughter with an eating disorder. One of her participants, Kim, texts to say that she has dropped out of college and is no longer participating in therapy since she no longer needs it. The friend with whom she is now living has provided her with an herbal therapy. Kim reports that she is happier than she has been for a long time and lets Jennifer know that she would like to participate in further interviews as she wants to help with Jennifer's research. Kim asks Jennifer to keep details of what she is doing confidential, as she has not told family members about her decision. The next day, Jennifer receives a phone call from Kim's mother. Kim's mother has tried to get in touch with Kim at college, but has not been able to do so. She is very concerned about Kim's welfare, and asks Jennifer if she knows Kim's whereabouts. What should Jennifer do?

Conclusions

This chapter has examined the institutionalization of ethical review boards, what is entailed in Responsible Conduct of Research, and discussed ethical issues in qualitative research. The chapter concludes with a brief review of resources that researchers can use to develop moral arguments to attend to ethical dilemmas and make ethical decisions.

Activities

1. Choose a book or film from Table 2.2 that reports or depicts ethically problematic research. For the book or film, analyze the ethical problems that occurred in the research studies described. What could researchers have done differently?

Table 2.2. Books and Films Related to Research Ethics

Books	Films based on the books (several of these films take some poetic license)
Milgram, S. (2009 [1974]). *Obedience to authority: An experimental view* (Reprint ed.). Harper Perennial Modern Thought..	*Experimenter* (2015)
Skloot, R. (2010). *The immortal life of Henrietta Lacks*. Crown Publishers.	*The immortal life of Henrietta Lacks* (2017)
Zimbardo, P. G. (2007). *The Lucifer effect: Understanding how good people turn evil*. Random House.	*The Stanford prison experiment* (2015)
Reverby, S. (2009). *Examining Tuskegee: The infamous syphilis study and its legacy*. University of North Carolina Press.	*Miss Evers' boys* (1997)

2. Complete training in Responsible Conduct of Research and research ethics required by your university prior to applying to conduct human subjects research.

Further Reading

National Center for Professional and Research Ethics. https://ethicscenter.csl.illinois.edu/

Responsible Conduct of Research cases at Columbia University. https://ccnmtl.columbia.edu/projects/rcr/

Shamoo, A. E., & Resnik, D. B. (2022). *Responsible conduct of research* (3rd ed.). Oxford University Press.

Notes

1. As qualitative researchers, we typically use the term research participants and do so throughout the book, but here we are using the term human subjects to be consistent with RCR and IRB language and protocols.

2. This is no longer the case, and prisoners are now regarded as "vulnerable populations."

3. Because some approaches to research do not meet the federal guidelines of "research," in the United States IRB review might not be required (e.g., evaluation studies, oral history studies, and autoethnography). We advise all researchers to check with their local ethical review board prior to conducting a study to see if permission is required for a research study.

4. We recognize that expertise is developed over time. This is why mentors should ensure that they provide opportunities for mentees to develop the skills to review manuscripts during graduate programs.

5. We recognize that use of the term "predatory publishing" has been debated and some scholars have called for abandoning use of this term in favor of focusing on the problems of deception and low quality in publishing.

6. For another reasoning protocol, RICE (Reflect, Investigate, Contemplate, Evaluate) see Whiteford, L. M., & Trotter, R. T. (2008). *Ethics for anthropological research and practice.* Long Grove, Ill.

References

Appiah, K. A. (2008). *Experiments in ethics.* Harvard University Press.

Bashir, N. (2018). Doing research in peoples' homes: fieldwork, ethics and safety – on the practical challenges of researching and representing life on the margins. *Qualitative Research, 18*(6), 638–653. https://doi.org/10.1177/1468794117731808

Bebeau, M. J., Pimple, K. D., Muskavitch, K. M. T., Borden, S. L., & Smith, D. H. (1995). *Moral reasoning in scientific research: Cases for teaching and assessment.* Indiana University.

Beecher, H. K. (2001 [1966]). Ethics and clinical research. *Bulletin Of The World Health Organization, 79*(4), 367–372. (Reprinted from *The New England Journal of Medicine, 274* (24).)

Birsch, D. (2023). *Introduction to ethical theories* (2nd ed.). Waveland Press, Inc.

Bosk, C. L., & de Vries, R. G. (2004). Bureaucracies of mass deception: Institutional Review Boards and the ethics of ethnographic research. *The Annals of the American Academy of Political and Social Science, 595,* 249–263. https://www.jstor.org/stable/4127623

Bradley, S. G. (2014). Competing interests in research. In F. L. Macrina (Ed.), *Scientific integrity: Text and cases in responsible conduct of research* (4th ed., pp. 209–241). ASM Press.

Burles, M. C., & Bally, J. M. G. (2018). Ethical, practical, and methodological considerations for unobtrusive qualitative research about personal narratives shared on the internet. *International Journal of Qualitative Methods, 17*(1). https://doi.org/10.1177/1609406918788203

Calarco, J. M. (2020). *A field guide to grade school: Uncovering the hidden curriculum.* Princeton University Press

Corti, L., Van den Eynden, V., Bishop, L., & Woollard, M. (2020). *Managing and sharing research data: A guide to good practice* (2nd ed.). SAGE.

Creighton, G., Oliffe, J. L., Ferlatte, O., Bottorff, J., Broom, A., & Jenkins, E. K. (2018). Photovoice ethics: Critical reflections From men's mental health research. *Qualitative Health Research, 28*(3), 446–455. https://doi.org/10.1177/1049732317729137

Enriquez, J. (2020). *Right/wrong: How technology transforms our ethics.* The MIT Press.

Fink, S. (2017, August 17). Settlement reached in C. I. A. torture case. *The New York Times.*

Fournillier, J. B. (2016). An act of remembering: Making the 'collective memories' my own and confronting ethical issues. In I. F. Goodson (Ed.), *The Routledge International handbook on narrative and life history* (pp. 493–504). Routledge.

Gerrard, Y. (2021). What's in a (pseudo)name? Ethical conundrums for the principles of anonymisation in social media research. *Qualitative Research, 21*(5), 686–702. https://doi.org/10.1177/1468794120922070

Gert, B. (2020). *The definition of morality.* Stanford University https://plato.stanford.edu/entries/morality-definition/

Goffman, A. (2014). *On the run: Fugitive life in an American city.* Chicago University Press.

Goode, E. (2002, Winter). Sexual involvement and social research in a fat civil rights organization. *Qualitative Sociology, 25*(4), 501–534.

Grudniewicz, A., Moher, D., Cobey, K. D., Bryson, G. L., Cukier, S., Allen, K. Ardern, C., Balcom, T. B., Berger, M., Ciro, J. B., Cugusi, L., Donaldson, M. R., Egger, M., Graham, I. D., Hodgkinson, M., Khan, K. M., Mabizela, M. Manca, A., Milzow, K., ...Lalu, M. M. (2019). Predatory journals: No definition, no defence. *Nature, 56,* 210–212. https://www.nature.com/articles/d41586-019-03759-y

Gunsalus, C. K., Bruner, E. M., Burbules, N. C., Dash, L., Finkin, M., Goldberg, J. P., Greenough, W. T., Miller, G. A., Pratt, M. G., Iriye, M., & Aronson, D. (2007). The Illinois White Paper: Improving the system for protecting human subjects: Counteracting IRB "mission creep." *Qualitative Inquiry, 13*(5), 617–649. https://doi.org/10.1177/1077800407300785

Hanson, R., & Richards, P. (Eds.). (2019). *Harassed: Gender, bodies, and ethnographic research.* University of California Press.

Hornblum, A. M. (1999). *Acres of skin: human experiments at Holmesburg prison. A true story of abuse and exploitation in the name of medical science.* Routledge.

Johnson, T. S. (2008). Qualitative research in question: A narrative of disciplinary power with/in the IRB. *Qualitative Inquiry, 14*(2), 212–232. https://doi.org/10.1177/1077800407308821

Katz, J. (2007). Toward a natural history of ethical censorship. *Law & Society Review, 41*(4), 797–810. https://doi.org/10.1111/j.1540-5893.2007.00325.x

Kelsky, K. (2015). *The professor is in: The essential guide to turning your Ph.D. into a job* (1st ed.). Three Rivers Press.

Kiragu, S., & Warrington, M. (2013). How we used moral imagination to address ethical and methodological complexities while conducting research with girls in school against the odds in Kenya. *Qualitative Research, 13*(2), 173–189. https://doi.org/10.1177/1468794112451011

Kurtz, L. C., Trainer, S., Beresford, M., Wutich, A., & Brewis, A. (2017). Blogs as elusive ethnographic texts. *International Journal of Qualitative Methods, 16*(1). https://doi.org/10.1177/1609406917705796

Macrina, F. L. (Ed.). (2014). *Scientific integrity: Text and cases in responsible conduct of research* (4th ed.). ASM Press.

Mangual Figueroa, A. (2016). Citizenship, beneficence, and informed consent: the ethics of working in mixed-status families. *International Journal of Qualitative Studies in Education, 29*(1), 66–85. https://doi.org/10.1080/09518398.2014.974722

Mays, T. D., & Macrina, F. L. (2014). Research data and intellectual property. In F. L. Macrina (Ed.), *Scientific integrity: Text and cases in responsible conduct of research* (4th ed., pp. 287–328). ASM Press.

Milgram, S. (2009 [1974]). *Obedience to authority: An experimental view* (Reprint ed.). Harper Perennial Modern Classics.

Myles, D., Cherba, M., & Millerand, F. (2019). Situating ethics in online mourning research: A scoping review of empirical studies. *Qualitative Inquiry, 25*(3), 289–299. https://doi.org/10.1177/1077800418806599

National Academies of Sciences, Engineering and Medicine. (2017). *Fostering integrity in research*. The National Academies Press. https://doi.org/https://doi.org/10.17226/21896

The National Commission for the Protection of Human Subjects of Biomedical and Behavioral Research. (1979). *The Belmont Report: Ethical principles and guidelines for the protection of human subjects of research*. Retrieved June 15, 2023, from https://www.hhs.gov/ohrp/regulations-and-policy/belmont-report/read-the-belmont-report/index.html

National Research Council. (2002). *Integrity in scientific research: Creating an environment that promotes responsible conduct*. The National Academies Press. https://doi.org/10.17226/10430

Newman, P. A., Guta, A., & Black, T. (2021). Ethical considerations for qualitative research methods during the COVID-19 pandemic and other emergency situations: Navigating the virtual field. *International Journal of Qualitative Methods, 20*, 1–12. https://doi.org/10.1177/16094069211047823

Paxton, B. (2018). *At home with grief: Continued bonds with the deceased*. Routledge.

Rachels, J., & Rachels, S. (2015). *The elements of moral philosophy* (8th ed.). McGraw Hill.

Reverby, S. (2009). *Examining Tuskegee: The infamous syphilis study and its legacy*. Chapel Hill.

Roberts, L. D. (2015). Ethical issues in conducting qualitative research in online communities. *Qualitative Research in Psychology, 12*(3), 314–325. https://doi.org/10.1080/14780887.2015.1008909

Roulston, K., & Preissle, J. (2018). Debating ethical research with human subjects. *Acta Paedagogica Vilnensia, 40*, 11–24. https://doi.org/DOI: https://doi.org/10.15388/ActPaed.2018.0.11885

Salazar, C. (2022). Participatory action research with and for undocumented college students: Ethical challenges and methodological opportunities. *Qualitative Research, 22*(3), 369–386. https://doi.org/10.1177/1468794120985689

Skloot, R. (2010). *The immortal life of Henrietta Lacks*. Crown Publishers.

Tanggaard, L., & Wegener, C. (2017). *A survival kit for doctoral students and their supervisors: Traveling the landscape of research*. SAGE.

Verseghy, J., Atack, L., & Maher, J. (2020). Key considerations when interviewing individuals with expressive language difficulties. *Qualitative Research, 20*(6), 960–970. https://doi.org/10.1177/1468794120909038

Whiteford, L. M., & Trotter, R. T. (2008). *Ethics for anthropological research and practice*. Long Grove, Ill.

Wolff, J. (2021). *An introduction to moral philosophy* (2nd ed.). W. W. Norton & Company.

THREE

 # The Role of Theory in Designing Qualitative Research

LEARNING OBJECTIVES

After reading this chapter you should be able to:

- Define key concepts including axiology, ontology, epistemology, theory, theoretical framework, and paradigm.
- Explain the role of theory in qualitative research design.
- Identify theory(ies) useful to your own research.
- Articulate strategies for reading theoretical texts.

WHAT IS THEORY? WHAT IS a concept? What are different levels of theory? How might different types or levels of theory be used in qualitative studies? What is a theoretical perspective or framework? What do we mean by the philosophical terms axiology, ontology, and epistemology? What is the relationship between these terms and theoretical frameworks? How do all these terms relate to research design? Students new to qualitative research are often confused by these abstract ideas and may approach theory with varying levels of trepidation or anxiety when asked to identify the theoretical framework they are using to inform their studies. In this chapter, we first examine these philosophical terms and how various scholars have used them in relationship to qualitative research. We then move to a discussion of how scholars have categorized and labeled the types and levels of theory as well as how these theories are used in designing and implementing qualitative studies. We discuss strategies you might use to begin your journey into theory and how you might theorize topics related to your research. We suggest ways to manage the confusion and anxiety you may experience in reading dense texts and identify theoretical frameworks that resonate with your experiences and perspectives.

Defining Terms

As humans, we are constantly identifying, comparing, grouping, categorizing, and theorizing as necessary means to know, understand, and simplify our worlds. We engage in all of these activities in our daily lives. For example, when you set out to drive from point A to point B and find yourself stuck in a traffic jam, you might imagine potential causes: a car accident has occurred, a water main has broken, or you may have forgotten that a marathon was scheduled to block your route. You are engaging in theorizing as an everyday activity to explain what is going on in your world.

Our understanding of the world begins with who we are in relation to families, local communities, as well as state and national citizenship. We learn early what is valued and what is not, how people are grouped within a community, and how we fit into that community. We learn through observations and interactions with others how we are viewed and how to view others. Historical and cultural events inform and shape our worldviews. Coming of age during particular eras influences how we view reality and understand the world. For example, the Vietnam War, Civil Rights, and Feminist movements of the 1960s and 1970s, and the 2008 recession and housing crash are all pivotal moments occurring in the last 60 years that have shaped views of people who grew up during those times. Even as children, we are theorizing our understanding of reality, how the world around us works, and how we come to know that reality. How we know the world and how we see reality depends on our standpoints in the world, and as a result, the theories and research topics we are drawn to. For example, if you grew up in a family or community with strict gender roles, racial biases, or unequal treatment, you may see reality in terms of power, privilege, and inequities and may be drawn to critical theories. The more abstract or scholarly terms for (1) what we value and what we believe is ethical, (2) how we understand reality, and (3) how we understand where our knowledge about this reality comes from are *axiology*, *ontology*, and *epistemology*. These concepts are the assumptions that inform theory, theoretical perspectives, and overall research design.

Let's look at these terms in more detail. *Axiology* refers to "the study of what things are good and how good they are, or more simply, the philosophical study of value or value theory" (Schwandt, 2015, p. 15). Axiology is concerned with values, ethics, and ethical behavior. As researchers we want to be aware of what we value, how we conduct ourselves ethically and make decisions within our research studies. Schroeder (2021), in *The Stanford Encyclopedia of Philosophy* explained:

> Traditional axiology seeks to investigate what things are good, how good they are, and how their goodness is related to one another. Whatever we take the "primary bearers" of value to be, one of the central questions of traditional axiology is that of what stuffs are good: what is of value. (https://plato.stanford.edu/entries/value-theory/)

What you believe to be valuable guides your ethical decisions as a researcher. For example, if you value social justice, you may believe reciprocity with participants within research to be an important feature of the design.

Another philosophical concept central to research is the notion of *ontology*, which refers to the nature of reality. Webster's dictionary defines ontology as "a particular theory about the nature of being or the kinds of things that have existence" (https://www.merriam-webster.com/dictionary/ontology). When we talk about ontology in relationship to research design, we are concerned with the nature of reality or of being. What is reality? What does it mean to be in the world? Do you see reality in the sense that there is a common, fixed reality to be studied or conversely, is reality constructed, fluid and open to multiple understandings and interpretations? Or perhaps you view reality as somewhere along a continuum from fixed to fluid reality to a bit of both? Killam (2013) explained "a person's ontological beliefs will dictate how objective the relationship between the researcher and what can be known is" (p. 11). Identifying our ontological assumptions about the world helps us think about what kinds of evidence we need to understand the world. Is reality something people construct in their daily lives with one another at the microlevel of interactions? Is the world an inequitable place based on race, class, gender, and other categories? How you view the nature of reality will shape the research you undertake, how you design that research, and the role you take as a researcher in that study.

A third concept central to consider here is the notion of *epistemology*, the branch of philosophy that examines the nature of knowledge or how we get to know that reality. How do we know what we know? What is our theory of knowledge? How is knowledge acquired? How do you think we generate knowledge through research? Schwandt (2015) described one view of epistemology within social inquiry that is useful in relation to how many qualitative researchers view the concept:

> that knowledge is by definition uncertain and that the best we can do is make a stand on the basis of (admittedly fallible) human judgement that requires the use of both reason and evidence. This response abandons epistemology with a capital "E"—the search for the foundations or essences of knowledge—but retains the idea of epistemology with a lowercase "e"—reflection of various kinds about what it means to know. (p. 90)

Later theorists have critiqued this separation of concepts and emphasized the interconnectedness of the concepts ontology and epistemology. For example, Barad (2007) introduced the term ontoepistemology, arguing, "We don't obtain knowledge by standing outside the world; we know because we are in the world" (p. 185). This change in language and how we understand concepts is a good example of how concepts and theories change over time as some ideas are found inadequate and new language is introduced. From a new materialist standpoint, then, the notion of being/reality and epistemology cannot be seen as discrete concepts. In short, while ontology traditionally answers the question, *What is reality?* and epistemology answers the question, *How do we know reality?* you might recognize how these concepts work together in research and how they influence how you think about theoretical frameworks, your research questions, and research design.

Philosophical ideas are deeply embedded into the theories we use in research design. While they may not be immediately evident, by asking how theorists see the nature of reality, how knowledge is obtained and created, and how the notion of values and ethics is expressed in the theory, you will begin to understand these relationships and the relationship to research. For example, critical qualitative researchers from various theoretical standpoints (e.g., critical theory, critical race theory, critical feminist theory) emphasize issues of equity and social justice at the center of their work. They see research participants within their sociocultural, political contexts and examine how those contexts have shaped the experiences of the participants. Researchers from this standpoint value the experiences and stories of participants and see their roles as researchers as working with participants to transform unjust/inequitable structures toward more inclusive knowledge and understandings.

Now that we've briefly introduced these philosophical terms, let's begin our journey into theory with the notion of *concepts* as key elements of theory and theorizing. Concepts are simply abstract ideas or as Bernard (1994) suggests, "mental creations" (p. 24). Concepts are based in historical and sociocultural contexts and may differ from the ways others outside that context understand or make sense of the same concept. Examples of typical demographic concepts used in research are social class, race, gender, ethnicity, and age. These are constructed terms used to categorize and classify people. While we may share understandings of these concepts within a particular culture, they can vary from others based on who we are within our specific cultural contexts. Other examples of common human concepts, not linked to demographics, might include ideas to describe emotions and patterns of behavior. In scholarly work, concepts are typically developed through research and are then used to build increasingly abstract theoretical perspectives.

A *theory* is a statement about how we understand and explain the world and how things are connected. As LeCompte and Preissle (1993) explained, theories are "statements about how things are connected. Their purpose is to explain why things happen as they do. Theories vary in size, density, abstractness, completeness, and quality" (p. 118). Similarly, Bennett deMarrais and LeCompte (1999) wrote, "In very simplistic terms, a *theory* is a world view, a way we organize and explain the world we live in. Theories are not necessarily impractical or complex. In fact, all human beings use theoretical thought every day" (p. 3, italics in original). In his glossary of qualitative terms, Thomas Schwandt (2015) explained,

> A formal understanding common in the natural and social sciences is that theory is a unified, systematic causal explanation of a diverse range of social phenomena. Theory of this kind is evaluated in terms of the familiar criteria of parsimony, completeness, predictive power, and scope. Examples from different social science disciplines include exchange theory, kinship theory, cognitive dissonance theory, and Keynesian economic theory. (p. 301)

Across disciplines, however, there are various levels of "theory" that are used for different purposes within a research project. Schwandt (2015) is worth quoting at length to explain how scholars use the term theory and theoretical concepts in less formal ways as:

theory may be said to come in many shapes and sizes depending on levels of sophistication, organization, and comprehensiveness. At the simplest level there are theoretical ideas or, more simply, concepts that function as analytical tools. Concepts point the inquirer in a general direction but do not give a very specific set of instructions for what to see. A step up the ladder of sophistication, one finds theoretical orientations or perspectives (e.g., functionalism, symbolic interactionism, behaviorism, phenomenology, hermeneutics, feminism, social constructionism, poststructuralism). These, more or less, are social theories that explain the distinguishing features of social and cultural life, and thus, they serve as approaches to identifying, framing, and solving problems, as well as understanding and explaining social reality. Substantive theories, however, are different from these theoretical frameworks because they are about some specific social or behavioral phenomena—for example, a social constructionist theory of living with a particular cancer, a feminist theory of nursing work, or a behavioral theory of children's play. Substantive theories can develop into formal theories; the difference is one of the comprehensiveness or scope of their explanation. The former, more or less, hover low over the data, as Clifford Geertz once noted; the latter are more removed from the case at hand. (pp. 301–302)

As you can see, Schwandt (2015) used the terms theoretical perspectives, orientations, or frameworks interchangeably and lists different perspectives that have been influential broadly across disciplines in social science research. Like Schwandt, LeCompte and Preissle (1993) defined *theoretical perspectives* as larger social science models or theories that include interrelated concepts that explain a view of the world. Goetz and LeCompte (1984) used the terms *theoretical models* and *perspectives* synonymously defining them as "loosely interrelated sets of assumptions, concepts, and propositions that constitute a view of the world" (p. 37).

Despite variations in definitions, what is important here is that theories, theoretical perspectives, and theoretical models are all human constructions social science researchers use to inform their work within particular contexts. By articulating the theoretical perspectives underlying our research, we are communicating to a larger scholarly audience how our research is both informed and contributes to the ongoing work in the field. Theories and theoretical perspectives are living human constructions that change over time as other scholars engage in research, develop new perspectives, critique what has gone before, and revise and innovate conceptualizations based on research.

As the historic and sociocultural contexts change, so do the theories we develop and use in social science research. Theories are our attempts to try to understand and explain to others how we make meaning in the world based on personal experiences, worldviews, empirical research, and the interplay of those. Throughout this book, we will use the terms theoretical perspectives, theoretical frameworks, and theoretical paradigms interchangeably.

Let's turn to two examples of heuristics or scaffolds scholars have used to show the interrelationships among the concepts we've discussed. In a conceptualization of the relationship of theoretical perspectives within research, Crotty (1998) used a leveled explanation to describe how we might think about theoretical perspectives within a research study. He described epistemology as informing one's theoretical perspective which in turn informs the research methodology or research design as well as the specific methods or tools used within that design. He posed the four following key questions for researchers to consider: "1) What *methods* do we propose to use? 2) What *methodology* governs our choice and use of methods? 3) What *theoretical perspective* lies behind the methodology in question? 4) What *epistemology (and ontology)* informs this theoretical perspective?" (Crotty, 1998, p. 2, italics in original). We could easily reorder these questions and start from epistemologies and theoretical framework, then move to methodology and methods, one informing the other. These questions encourage researchers to articulate how they see the connections between and among these concepts. In the next chapter, we discuss the process of research design in more depth, but for now we encourage you to consider these questions as you think about your research interests.

As another approach, Lather (2006) organized a table of research paradigms for use in teaching qualitative research according to the aims or purposes of the theoretical perspective or paradigms: (1) to predict, (2) to understand, (3) to emancipate, and (4) to deconstruct. Those with an aim to *predict* include experimental and (some) mixed methods research. Those that seek to *understand* human behavior include interpretive, naturalist, constructivist, phenomenological, ethnographic, symbolic interactionist, and interpretive mixed methods. *Emancipatory and critical work* includes neo-Marxist, feminist, critical race theory, praxis-oriented, and Freirian participatory action research; gay and lesbian theories; and critical ethnography (although Lather noted these perspectives can work across various aims). Finally, those included in *deconstruction* paradigms or perspectives are poststructural, postmodern, queer theory, discourse analysis, postcolonial, post-Fordism, posthumanist, postcritical, postparadigmatic diaspora. Lather then illustrated how our notions of reality and truth map onto these theoretical perspectives. For example, reality for the positivist is objective; for the interpretivist, reality is subjective and constructed; for the critical theorist, "reality is subjective and constructed on the basis of issues of power" (Lather, 2006, p. 38); and for the deconstructivist, "reality is ultimately unknowable; attempts to understand it subvert themselves" (Lather, 2006, p. 38).

These two examples above show how by understanding and articulating your values and views of reality, you can begin to examine theoretical perspectives that may be useful as you begin to construct your own research design.

Categorizing Theories

Let's look more closely at theories and theorizing. The purpose of theories is to help us sort out our world and make sense of it. Theories come in different sizes, shapes, and levels of abstraction. Theories are made up of *concepts* that are basic elements of theory. In describing relationships among and between concepts, we begin to build theories. Considering levels of theory may be useful as you begin to theorize your way into a research design. As we mentioned above, we categorize things to better understand how they are similar and different and how one category relates to another. Different scholars have named and grouped theories differently based on their levels of abstraction from substantive theories, those generated from individual research studies, to broad social science theoretical frameworks such as phenomenology, feminist theory, critical theory, poststructural theory, or new materialist theories.

LeCompte and Preissle (1993) identified four levels of theory, including: (1) formal theory, (2) substantive theory, (3) middle range theory, and (4) grand theories—the latter are those that seek to explain general aspects of the world and fall outside the scope of qualitative research and our discussion here. Before we explain these further, let's first look at how they illustrate the constructed nature of theorizing:

> Theories are created by developing a set of propositions, postulates, or generalizations which establish relationships between things in some systematic

way. Theories are *human* constructions; they are derived from information which people collect by seeing, hearing, touching, sensing, smelling, and feeling. This information is put together into formal or informal theories by means of cognitive processes or thinking. We call this type of thinking, or set of cognitive processes, "theorizing." (LeCompte & Preissle, 1993, p. 120, emphasis in original)

By *formal theory*, LeCompte and Preissle referred to theoretical perspectives or models developed within disciplines and used across disciplines that are "little more than conceptual frameworks or typologies. Their significance derives primarily from their influence on the way social scientists perceive and interpret the empirical world" (LeCompte & Preissle, 1993, p. 126). They provided an extensive table of eight major theoretical perspectives in the social sciences, many of which continue to inform researchers today: functionalism, conflict theory, symbolic interactionism and ethnomethodology, critical theory, ethnoscience or cognitive anthropology, exchange theory, psychodynamic theory, and behaviorism (pp. 128–133). You may find this table useful in that for each perspective they list the focus, assumptions, major concepts, and major questions and topics for investigation. In a similar table, Bennett deMarrais and LeCompte (1999) examined major sociological theoretical frameworks including functionalism, conflict theory, interpretive theory, and critical theory along with their foci, assumption, major concept, levels of analysis, major questions and topics of investigation, critiques, and contributors. As you begin to explore these more abstract levels of theorizing, you may find tables like those mentioned in this chapter useful in helping you identify your own assumptions, beliefs, and research interests.

At a much less abstract level of theorizing, we find substantive theories; those theories based on specific research studies and focused on specific phenomenon in specific populations at particular times and within particular contexts. Glaser and Strauss (1967) viewed substantive theory as "that developed for a substantive, or empirical, area of sociological inquiry such as patient care, race relations, professional education, delinquency, or research organizations" (p. 32). Similarly, LeCompte and Preissle (1993) defined substantive theories as "the simplest form of scientific theory [that] are interrelated propositions or concepts which create explanations for the existence of phenomena lodge in particular aspects of populations, settings, or times" (p. 134). Schwandt's (2015) notion of substantive theories is that they hover close to data and are then developed by other researchers. For example, a commonplace notion in the field of teacher education today is one of "wait time" or the belief that teachers need to provide enough time for students to consider their questions before answering. This concept was originally developed by educational anthropologists Mohatt and Erickson (1981) in a study of White and Indigenous teachers' questions of students in a First Nations school in Canada. Subsequently, researchers and practitioners found the idea of wait time applicable across many school settings to inform ways teachers interacted with students from various socioeconomic, racial, and ethnic backgrounds.

Another example of substantive theory is that of "emotional work" or "emotional labor." The concept was developed by sociologist Hochschild (1983) to describe the invisible emotional work of flight attendants and bailiffs. According to Hochschild (1983), jobs requiring emotional labor have three common characteristics:

> First, they require face-to-face or voice-to-voice contact with the public. Second, they require the worker to produce an emotional state in another person—gratitude or fear for example. Third, they allow the employer, through training and supervision to exercise a degree of control over the emotional activities of employees. (p. 147)

This concept was then viewed as applicable to other fields and applied in research across other disciplines and professional fields.

At the next level, those theories that are more abstract than substantive theories, but not as abstract as theoretical models, perspectives, or paradigms, have been referred to as middle range theories (Preissle & LeCompte, 1993). Previously, Glaser and Strauss (1967) described middle range theories as those theories that "fall between 'minor working hypotheses' of everyday life and 'all-inclusive' grand theories" include those that deal with larger topics of research in sociology, such as stigma, deviant behavior, and social mobility (pp. 32–33). Those broader theories developed from numerous substantive studies, where scholars have applied concepts from research studies that have wider applicability for the discipline. These theories are used to inform subsequent research and professional practice. Building on earlier work by Glaser and Strauss (1967), Strauss and Corbin (1990) described how substantive theory can be used more broadly:

If theory is faithful to the everyday reality of the substantive area and carefully induced from diverse data, then it should fit that substantive area. Because it represents that reality, it should also be comprehensible and make sense both to the persons who were studied and to those practicing in that area. If the data upon which it is based are comprehensive and the interpretations conceptual and broad, then the theory should be abstract enough and include sufficient variation to make it applicable to a variety of contexts related to that phenomenon. (p. 23)

This description of theory building illustrates the link between substantive and middle-range theories. As in the examples of Mohatt and Erickson (1981) and Hochschild (1983) above, the concepts of "wait time" and "emotional work" constructed within specific studies were then able to be used by other researchers across a range of contexts and thus, developed into broader, middle-range theories used within and across disciplines.

Creating Your Research Path

How does all this theory talk relate to you and your research? It is useful to think about how theory is used by scholars in your discipline. While the larger social science theoretical frameworks and their embedded values, beliefs, and assumptions inform our thinking, you may find that researchers in your specific discipline rely primarily on theories at the substantive and middle-range level. We encourage you to contribute to that work, but to be aware of how those theories are informed by theory at all levels. In considering your own research interests, what concepts intrigue you? Who are the scholars and researchers who have done work in those concepts? What did they find? At the next level of mid-range theory, what are the common concepts across research studies that disciplinary scholars are using to understand and explain a particular phenomenon or aspect of professional practice? At the level of theoretical orientations, you might ask: What are the larger social science theoretical frameworks that help you think through your research design and focus your study? For instance, if you use a critical theoretical framework, you will examine issues of power and ask questions around equity and social class. Critical race theory will point you toward questions of power and race.

Feminist questions work across theoretical perspectives and can ask questions of understanding, emancipation, deconstruction, or questions arising from new materialisms. For instance, emancipatory feminist theories might engage ways gender, power, and privilege operate in women's experiences to create safer and more equitable spaces for women and girls. Feminist deconstructionist approaches combine deconstructive readings of textual documents with feminist critical theory to inquire how gendered subjects are produced, surveilled, and disciplined in texts. Feminist critical materialist and feminist posthuman perspectives engage both feminist critical and new materialist or posthuman theories to examine how human and nonhuman bodies produce gendered subjectivities. Some students begin at the level of larger social science theories and read widely in those before coming to a specific research project. Others begin with a question or problem more specific to their personal and professional experiences and eventually come to find a more macro theoretical perspective useful. There is no one right way to approach the design of your study. The key, though, is to start somewhere as you read more and think through how others have conceptualized the question or problem that interests you.

In this section, we examine how you might approach identifying what we like to call your "theoretical home" (deMarrais et al., 2018) to think about those theories that reflect your beliefs, assumptions, and explanations of how the world works. Duster (cited in Torres, 1998) often argued in his lectures, "If you scratch a theory, you'll find a biography." Who you are and how you view the world will shape your ontological and epistemological understandings, how you approach theory, and which theories speak to you and reflect your worldviews. What experiences have led you to thinking about yourself, theoretically, in one way rather than another? How do I find a theoretical home? When we think about a theoretical home, we think about how you might come to the language of theory that resonates with you. What is it in your experience that resonates in the world of theory and scholarship? Do some theories make more sense to you than others? Are there theoretical perspectives that provide a language to explain your worldview and how you approach your research topic? What concepts are you interested in? What are the current problems in your field? What questions are being asked in your field? What theories are other researchers who are doing that work interested in? How do they reflect beliefs about the way the world works? As you consider these questions, keep a journal of your readings and begin to think and write about the concepts that describe the work that interests you. Reading and reflection are critical to situating yourself theoretically and methodologically.

Emotional Work and Strategies For Reading Theory

Throughout our reading of others' texts, sometimes we fail to apprehend what the author is communicating. When we are learning about a new topic, these challenges to understanding occur because we as readers have insufficient knowledge to understand what the author is trying to communicate. St. Pierre (2011) pointed out that "we hesitate to read outside our comfort areas and too casually reject texts that seem too hard to read" (p. 614). St. Pierre advised her students to:

> take seriously Lacan's (as cited in Ulmer, 1985) advice, "to read does not obligate one to understand. First it is necessary to read . . . avoid understanding too quickly" (p. 196). I have little sympathy with excuses not to read difficult texts, and I advise students to read harder when the text seems too hard to read, to just keep reading, letting the new language wash over them until it becomes familiar. (p. 614)

Similarly, in our experience, students new to qualitative research have had a variety of experiences with reading and understanding theoretical texts. Students with little background in theory develop a level of anxiety when faced with difficult theoretical reading. They struggle with the complex language of theoretical texts. While we as authors appreciate that clear and concise writing can help to understand new topics, we also recognize that explaining complicated ideas may require the use of more complex language. As instructors, we think about how to support students with navigating difficult texts. The following are a few strategies we've found useful:

- Read secondary sources that focus on key concepts of theories in more accessible language in getting the lay of the theoretical landscape. As you read more, you may resonate with some theories more than others. From here you may want to read the original scholars within those perspectives.

- Read slowly. Often the reading load in doctoral programs is quite heavy, but it is important to read slowly to think with these more complicated concepts.
- Keep a journal to assist you in thinking further about your readings.
- Use an organizational system to take notes on specific concepts within theories and how they are related. You may find notecards, visuals, or spreadsheets useful for thinking with theory. If you're a visual learner, try drawing the various aspects of a theory you are working with.
- Through your reading, you'll find numerous scholars writing within a theoretical perspective. Which of these resonates with the way you see the world? Then focus on that scholar. For example, many scholars are currently working within a new materialist framework or a feminist framework, or perhaps a feminist new materialist framework. It is nearly impossible to read deeply in each of those scholars' works. Which scholar do you find more likely to inform your thinking about a research project? What concepts within that framework are useful to your topic?
- Consult a dictionary as you read and develop your own glossary for new terms to keep track of how different scholars define these.
- Be willing to take sidetracks by locating and reading an article cited in the text that you are reading. This sometimes helps to explain a point that the author is making by providing context. By locating references in the bibliography, you will locate resources to help you understand the topics an author is discussing. This helps to develop a deeper and broader understanding of a new topic, including debates about ideas presented.
- Develop a network of colleagues who are working with these theories and develop a reading group with these theories as a focus. Be sure to set up regular meetings and expectations within the group.

Conclusion

In this chapter we began with unpacking key terms related to theory including ontology, axiology, epistemology, theory, concepts, theoretical perspectives, and paradigms. We examined the relationship of these terms with one another and explored how epistemologies inform theoretical perspectives, research methodologies, or design as well as the tools or specific methods of research. We then addressed strategies for reading and understanding theoretical texts. In the next chapter we build on this chapter as we work through the component parts of a theoretically informed research design.

Activities

1. Draw a timeline of major or figural events during your lifetime to date. You might consider experiences close to home or major national/international events and cultural shifts. How did you react to and understand those events? How did they influence your understanding of the world around you?

2. Think of a typical family dinner at your home growing up. Who made and served the dinner? What food was prepared? Where did you eat dinner? With whom? If you ate around a table, who set it? Who cleaned up after dinner? How were family members seated? What kind of conversations were had? What topics were discussed? Did some family members speak more than others? How might those family dinner experiences have shaped your early conception about gendered roles, hierarchy within families, appropriate language usage, how the family was situated in relation to others in the community, and issues of power and privilege? How might these experiences inform your values, beliefs, understandings?

3. Draw a picture of your theoretical home. What concepts are included? How do those concepts relate to one another?

Further Reading

Collins, C. S., & Stockton, C. M. (2018). The central role of theory in qualitative research. *International Journal of Qualitative Methods, 17*(1), https://doi.org/10.1177/1609406918797475

Jackson, A. Y., & Mazzei, L. A. (2022). *Thinking with theory in qualitative research* (2nd ed.). Routledge.

Lather, P. (2006). Paradigm proliferation as a good thing to think with: Teaching research in education as a wild profusion. *International Journal of Qualitative Studies in Education (QSE), 19*(1), 35–57. https://doi.org/10.1080/0951839050045014

Prasad, P. (2018). *Crafting qualitative research: Beyond positivist traditions* (2nd ed.). Routledge.

Ravitch, S. M., & Riggan, M. (2012). *Reason and rigor: How conceptual frameworks guide research*. SAGE.

References

Barad, K. (2007). *Meeting the universe halfway: Quantum physics and the entanglement of matter and meaning.* Duke University Press.

Bennett deMarrais, K., & LeCompte, D. (1999). *The way schools work: A sociological analysis* (3rd ed.). Longman.

Bernard, H. R. (1994). *Research method in anthropology: Qualitative and quantitative approaches.* SAGE.

Crotty, M. (1998). *The foundations of social research.* SAGE.

deMarrais K., Moret, L., & Pope, E. M. (2018). I found a fit: Doctoral student narratives of coming to a theoretical home in a qualitative research class. *International Research in Higher Education 3*(2), 83–98. https://doi.org/10.5430/irhe.v3n2p83

Glaser, B. G., & Strauss, A. L. (1967). *The discovery of grounded theory: Strategies for qualitative research.* Aldine Publishing.

Goetz, J. P., & LeCompte, M. D. (1984). *Ethnography and qualitative design in educational research.* Academic Press.

Hochschild, A. R. (1983). *The managed heart: Commercialization of human feeling.* University of California Press.

Killam, L. A. (2013). *Research terminology simplified: Paradigms, axiology, ontology, epistemology and methodology.* Author.

Lather, P. (2006). Paradigm proliferation as a good thing to think with: Teaching research in education as a wild profusion. *International Journal of Qualitative Studies in Education, 19*(1), 35–57. https://doi.org/10.1080/09518390500450144

LeCompte, M. D. & Preissle, J. (1993). *Ethnography and qualitative design in educational research* (2nd ed.). Academic Press.

Mohatt, G., & Erickson, F. (1981). Cultural differences in teaching styles in an Odawa classroom: A sociolinguistic approach. In H. Trueba, H. Guthrie, & K. Au (Eds.), *Culture and the bilingual classroom* (pp. 105–119). Newbury House.

Schwandt, T. A. (2015). *The SAGE dictionary of qualitative inquiry* (4th ed.). SAGE.

Schroeder, M. (2021). Value Theory. In E. N. Zalta (Ed.), *The Stanford Encyclopedia of Philosophy.* https://plato.stanford.edu/archives/fall2021/entries/value-theory/

St. Pierre, E. A. (2011). Post qualitative research: The critique and the coming after. In N. K. Denzin & Y. S. Lincoln (Eds.), *The SAGE handbook of qualitative research* (4th ed., pp. 611–625). SAGE.

Strauss, A., & Corbin, J. (1990). *Basics of qualitative research.* SAGE.

Torres, C. A. (Ed.). (1998). *Education, power, and personal biography: Dialogues with critical educators.* Routledge.

Ulmer, G. L. (1985). *Applied grammatology: Post(e)-pedagogy from Jacques Derrida to Joseph Beuys.* Johns Hopkins University Press.

FOUR

Designing Qualitative Research

LEARNING OBJECTIVES

After reading this chapter you should be able to:

- Articulate the components of a conceptual framework.
- Identify a research problem through a review of relevant literature.
- Articulate the significance of the research problem.
- Develop a research purpose and research questions.
- Engage in a thorough, critical literature review.
- Articulate your subjectivities and positionalities in relation to the study.
- Consider each component part in developing a theoretically informed research design.
- Develop a written explanation to present the study to participants.

IN PREVIOUS CHAPTERS WE DISCUSSED qualitative research generally, and ethics in relation to research. We then turned to the language of theory and the relationship with theory and theoretical concepts in qualitative research. In this chapter we move to a closer focus on research design, the core components within this design, and how theory is integrated throughout the study. Learning to conduct qualitative research can involve struggle with the design aspects. By persevering, we learn how to think about an issue or research problem and how to develop that problem into a quality research plan. We begin with the notion of a *conceptual framework*. We think of the conceptual framework as the guiding framework for the study to include both the theoretical framework or key concepts as well as the literature base for the study. Both of these aspects are crucial to informing other scholars of your thinking process and where your study is situated both theoretically and in relationship to current scholarship in the field. In the last chapter, we offered strategies for identifying the various levels of theories you are interested in. In this chapter we transition to strategies for constructing a critical review of relevant literature focused on your topic, thus creating an argument for the need or significance of your study within current scholarship. Both the theoretical framework and relevant literature will inform your entire research design including the research purpose, research questions, participant sampling and selection, and specific methodological approaches you will use to implement your qualitative study. This chapter is intended to actively engage you in all aspects of qualitative research design. In short, we emphasize the importance of a theoretically informed design, well-grounded in scholarly literature, and one that results in a significant contribution to that literature. In subsequent chapters we delve more deeply into a variety of commonly used qualitative research designs and typical methods of data generation and analysis for those designs.

Defining Terms

In the previous chapter we focused on the idea of a theoretical framework to inform your research. In this chapter we introduce the idea of a *conceptual framework* to frame your specific study. While some scholars use the terms theoretical framework and conceptual framework synonymously, we see value in using these ideas differently. As discussed, theoretical frameworks are the larger social science theories shared and used widely by scholars across disciplines as well as disciplinary theories based on empirical work in the field. For our purposes here, we use the term conceptual framework as the framework unique to you and your research design. Your conceptual framework includes your theoretical framework, a critical examination of the disciplinary and substantive literature that informs your topic, as well as the argument grounded in these to inform your research purpose, research questions, and research design. Ideas included in the conceptual framework ask the following questions:

1. What theoretical concepts and or frameworks inform this study?
2. What research has been done in the field around this topic to date?
3. What are the key findings of that research?
4. In the conclusions of their articles, what further research do the authors suggest? What further research needs to be done on this topic?
5. How will this study contribute to the knowledge in the field? What is the significance of the study?

As you can see from these questions, the conceptual framework situates your work within relevant theoretical frameworks and scholarly literature and provides an argument for why this study is needed. It points to the significance of the study within the community of scholars who have done research on the topic. Table 4.1 illustrates how theoretical perspectives make possible different research approaches and research questions through qualitative studies that explore the topic of bullying. You might look for examples of studies on your topic of interest that use different theoretical perspectives and research designs.

Table 4.1. How Theoretical Perspectives Make Possible Different Research Questions

Research topic: Bullying

Theoretical perspective & focus of research	Methodological approach	Research questions posed by researchers
The interpretive traditions: Research for understanding		
Symbolic Interactionism focuses on understanding situations, contexts, and interactions from participants' perspectives (Blumer, 1969).	Grounded theory and ethnographic fieldwork	• How might school bullying be understood as a social process? • What are the main concerns and perspectives of children with respect to bullying? (Thornberg, 2018)
Ethnomethodology focuses on understanding how members of society produce and make sense of everyday actions and interactions (Garfinkel, 1967).	Ethnographic fieldwork with conversation analysis and membership categorization analysis of children's language practices	• What are the micropolitics of an extended gossip dispute among children? • How might this be understood in relation to a school's bullying intervention practices? (Evaldsson & Svahn, 2012)
Phenomenology focuses on constructing a detailed or thick description of an experienced phenomenon (Van Manen, 2014).	Interview study	• How does it feel to be bullied? (Corney, 2008)
Critical traditions: Research for social justice		
Critical Theory focuses on examining and critiquing the institutional structures and practices that reproduce social inequalities and oppressive ideologies. Through both critique and/or participatory forms of inquiry, researchers aim to change oppressive structures and practices (Kincheloe et al., 2018). *Intersectionality* focuses on the intersections of race, class, gender, ability, sexuality, age, and so forth.	Semi-structured interviews	The purpose of the study was to "apply a critical, intersectional analysis of student, parent and teacher perspectives of bullying and cyberbullying to better understand these phenomena" (Mishna et al., 2020, p. 2).

Theoretical perspective & focus of research	Methodological approach	Research questions posed by researchers
Critical traditions: Research for social justice		
Critical Race Theory and LatCrit LatCrit is a branch of Critical Race Theory that examines the experiences of Latinas/os in relation to the intersections of race, power, and privilege with the aim to promote (Donnor & Ladson-Billings, 2018; Solórzano & Yosso, 2002). ***Disability Critical Race Studies (DisCrit)*** Critical examination of the social norms surrounding the conceptualization of race and ability/disability with the aim to alter these norms and the practices surrounding them (Annamma et al., 2017).	Participant observation, interviewing, and grounded theory	• "How do Latina/o students experience special education?" • "How do Latina/o students respond to their special education experiences?" (Dávila, 2015, p. 444)
Feminist Theory focuses on the problems of women in patriarchal society via a sociology for women (Smith, 1987) with the aim of promoting equality for women.	Semi-structured interviews	• What is the impact of cyberbullying on women's livelihoods? (Jane, 2018)
Black Feminist Thought (BFT) focuses on critically examining Black women's experiences and identities and the production of experiential counter-narratives as a means to transform persistent oppressive structures and practices (Collins, 2009).	Autoethnography	• How was I unable to affirm my identity as a doctoral student within the program when faculty viewed me with a deficit, minoritized lens? • How can gaslighting and BFT as frameworks validate my experiences in my previous doctoral program? (Grant, 2021, p. 943).
Post-traditions: Research for deconstructing and troubling understandings		
Poststructural Feminism deconstructs the ways language, discourse, power, and knowledge construct gendered subjectivities within and across disciplines and institutions (St. Pierre, 2000).	Focus groups	• How is gendered violence constructed in school? (Rawlings, 2019)
Queer Theory focuses on disrupting heteronormative assumptions related to gender identities and the politics of sexuality (Butler, 1990, 1993).	Focus groups	• What are students' perceptions of bullying situations? • How are intelligible masculinities and femininities performed through violence? (Carrera-Fernández et al., 2018, p. 343)

Theoretical perspective & focus of research	Methodological approach	Research questions posed by researchers
Post qualitative inquiry: Research that experiments with knowing and being		
New Materialisms and Critical Posthumanism		
Agential Realism examines how the human and nonhuman bodies intra-act and produce particular subjectivities and entangled performances of matter and meaning (Barad, 2007).	Group interviews	• How do human and nonhuman intra-actions shape bullying events? (Ringrose & Rawlings, 2015)
Critical Posthumanism focuses on accounting for the interdependence of humans and the nonhuman world, with a view to creating new ways of thinking and becoming (Braidotti, 2019).	Document analysis Interviews	• How can critical posthumanism inform work with lesbian, gay, bisexual and transgender (LGBT) diversities in school education? (Ferfolja & Ullman, 2017)

What is Design?

First, let's consider the term *design*. Selections from Merriam-Webster (n.d.) are useful here:

1. To create, fashion, execute, or construct according to plan
2. To conceive or execute a plan
3. To have as a purpose
4. To devise for a specific function or end
5. To make a drawing, pattern, or sketch of
6. To draw the plans for
7. To draw, lay out, or prepare a design (https://www.merriam-webster.com/dictionary/design)

If we think of the word *design* outside the context of designing qualitative research, we find many different uses for the word as both a verb and a noun. We may design vegetable gardens through the process of thinking about what we want to plant and when based on our growing seasons. After looking through seed catalogs, researching the qualities of specific varieties, talking with other gardeners, and deciding which plants we want to grow, we might create a drawing or plan for where we'll plant these crops in relationship to one another within the garden. In other disciplines, for example, architects *design* new homes and other buildings, engineers *design* bridges and roads, software engineers *design* the applications we use in our daily lives, and artists *design* the beautiful sculptures, paintings, and other *objets d'art* we enjoy. While a design may result in a plan or object, much of the work of a design is head work—deep thinking and reflection. It is also a process with many starts, stops, and changes. Not all designs work, so we change course or make modifications. We try out different ways to enact the plan. The process of designing qualitative studies is no different. This aim of this chapter is to get you excited about all the possibilities for researching a topic that interests you.

Getting Started in Research Design

As with most designs, we simply start with something we find intriguing. You might think about what interests you in life. What are the themes in your own life that keep calling to you? What are you truly curious about? You might have an idea for research that stems from your own personal experiences. For example, you might have experienced a major illness and want to learn more about others' experiences with that illness. You may come to a research topic through a particular problem you've faced in your professional life. For example, teachers, healthcare workers, and practitioners in many other applied fields may have faced problems of practice that have stymied them and engage in research to better understand how to address those problems. There is no right way to come to a research topic. We always ask our students *why* they want to explore a particular topic. Invariably, they reply they had a similar experience in their own lives and want to better understand the experience. The topics we want to explore are often those closest to our own experiences, and therefore, to our hearts, and are topics that will sustain our interest over time.

While experiences lead to research projects, so do theories. You may have read particular theories or theorists whose explanations interest you or reflect how you view the world. You might wonder how those concepts may play out in researching a topic you are interested in. For Kathleen, as a doctoral student in the 1980s, her interests in urban Appalachian communities, coupled with a focus on critical theory, led her to asking critical questions focused on social class and power differences in a first-grade classroom in this community. By way of a more recent example, Janie started with an interest in how mothers prepare their daughters for puberty. When she became interested in new materialist theorists, she read theorist Karen Barad (2007) and wondered how she might use specific concepts developed by Barad in examining mothers' stories of their experiences with their daughters around menstruation. In this example, Janie was fascinated by a particular topic—mothers and menstruation—but also by the work of a particular new materialist theorist. In Table 4.2 you will see Janie's conceptual framework for her dissertation study. As you can see, she has clearly articulated the major elements of her research design including the theoretical concepts that informed all aspects of the work, the research purpose and questions, her methodological approaches, how she recruited participants for the study, strategies for generating and analyzing data, how she represented the data in text and visual form, and how she considered ethics throughout the study. As you think of your own work, creating a table such as this will guide your planning and design.

Table 4.2. Conceptualizing a Dissertation Study

Research purpose: To understand experiences of mothers preparing children for menarche	
Research questions: What are the experiences of mothers preparing children for menarche? How do narratives materialize among human and nonhuman actors in mothers' experiences preparing children for menarche?	
Theoretical framework: Karen Barad's (2007) theory of agential realism	
Research methodologies: Object-interviewing, narrative inquiry	
Elements of design	**Guiding concepts**
Theoretical approach	*Entanglement*: Describes relationship among human and nonhuman entities. Refuses notion of pre-existing boundaries between humans–nonhumans, self–other, nature–culture. Rather, humans and the world exist in relation making and remaking one another.
	Intra-action: Describes how entangled entities enact agency with one another. Unlike interaction, intra-action reconceptualizes agency as produced as humans and nonhumans enact boundaries together rather than upon one another.
	Apparatuses: Describes the relationship between boundary-making practices and conceptualizing phenomena. Apparatuses make certain phenomena visible and obscure others; apparatuses are inseparable from the phenomena they produce. Apparatuses are not fixed, rather they are dynamic, ongoing reconfigurations.
Recruitment/sampling	Entanglement describes the web of researcher-participant, participant-participant, and participant-child relations produced through *purposive network sampling*.
	The researcher's experience, extant literature, research questions, and criteria comprise (in part) the recruitment apparatus of the research study. Recruitment makes visible mothers' experiences as they navigate menarche with their children.

Elements of design	Guiding concepts
Data generation	*Object-interviews* (Nordstrom, 2013) engage the entanglement of humans (mothers) and nonhumans (objects) in lived experience.
	Mothers, objects, interview questions, technology (e.g., recording devices, online meeting platforms) comprise the interview apparatus. They simultaneously inform and are inseparable from stories mothers share.
Analysis	Concept mapping, collaging with paper transcripts, watercolor, and multimodal memos are intra-active processes to think with data.
Representation	Entanglement troubles linear storytelling. Dissertation zigzags across mother and researcher stories to illustrate the connection and tensions across experiences.
	Stories and poems show intra-action among mothers and objects.
	Narratives and poems are apparatuses comprised of actors, objects, spaces, times, genres, and storytellers (to name a few). These entangled entities produce particular phenomena and obscure others.
Ethics	Ethical considerations regarding entangled researcher subjectivities (e.g., researcher as friend, researcher as mother, researcher as storyteller). How does negotiating these entangled subjectivities matter across the research process?
	Ethics of enacting boundaries with data—Why this participant's story and not another? Why these stories/poems in this section? What might these intra-actions produce for readers?
	Researcher as storyteller/poet is always part of the telling. Why this genre and not another? Does this representation honor the experiences of mothers and their children? How might research practices such as member-checking address this concern?

Identifying a research topic is the first critical step in the research process, but good research design requires developing a deep understanding of current theories and research literature to inform the topic you've selected (see Box 4.1). We turn now to the role of the literature review, how that contributes to your conceptual framework, and points you toward the need for the study in the field, and thus, the significance of the study.

Box 4.1. Identifying a Research Topic.

1. Is there an aspect of your personal or professional life you want to explore? Are you interested in extending the work of other researchers on a particular topic?
2. What specifically is the phenomenon you want to study?
3. Are there theories or theoretical concepts that fascinate you? How might you use these theoretical concepts to examine your topic of interest?

4. Is there a community, person, or group of people you are interested in learning more about? This can be virtual.
5. Is there a particular time period you find fascinating? What aspect of that period might you focus on?

Thinking through the questions in Box 4.1 will focus and refine your thinking, leading you to a general topic to explore further in the scholarly literature.

Learning From the Scholarly Literature

As mentioned above, a key component of the conceptual framework is the literature review. In this section we examine the purpose of the literature review and ways in which to go about the task. A literature review is a process in which you find out more about your topic. It is also a noun, in the form of an essay you write that carefully articulates for your reader what research has already been completed related to your topic and how it forms the context for the work you will do. You might think of the literature review as linking your interest in a topic to current *scholarly conversations* into which your research project will be a contribution. While you might think of the audience for your literature review as your professors, it is useful to consider a larger audience—that of other scholars who are working in the same or similar research area. The literature review is a critical component of the research process and perhaps the least favorite part for many beginning students. However, it is not a one-time project. You will examine research related to your study as you begin to think about constructing your research project, but will want to revisit and update that literature throughout each phase of your work. Once you have engaged in data generation and analysis, you may find that the literature you used to inform your study is peripheral to what you actually found in your study. If so, returning to the scholarly literature related to your findings will connect your work to relevant ideas and will inform your conclusions and recommendations for further research. But let's not get ahead of ourselves here.

In the early stages of research design, coming to a clear understanding of what scholars have written about your topic, how they have designed studies around that topic, and the relevant findings all help to deepen your understanding of the scholarly context in which you're working. As you enter this work, consider:

- Where do you begin reading?
- How do you bound the literature?
- How do you synthesize the literature?
- How do you know when you have read enough?
- How do you know when to stop reading the literature?

Rather than feeling overwhelmed, we encourage you to imagine the literature review as an engaging space for learning more about your topic of interest. You've identified a research topic, but how do you move that topic into a "doable" research study?

As with theoretical perspectives, most research studies begin with an autobiography. As we noted above, you may be drawn to research topics that hold a personal interest. But this is not enough. You will want to figure out how your interest in a research topic fits with what other researchers have discovered on this topic. Where does your personal interest align with the work of an academic community of scholars? The literature review helps you do this. As Machi and McEvoy (2016) explained, a literature review is a written document that presents a logically argued case founded on a comprehensive understanding of the current state of knowledge about a topic of study. Similarly, Hart (2018) defined a literature review as:

> The selection of available documents (both published and unpublished) on the topic, which contain information, ideas, data and evidence written from a particular standpoint to fulfil certain aims or express certain views on the nature of the topic and how it is to be investigated, and the effective evaluation of these documents in relation to the research being proposed. (p. 13)

In other words, a literature review lays out the background, context, and current empirical base to argue the need for one's study. Why does one need a literature review? Literature reviews help you become more knowledgeable about the background and current state of your research topic and provide a space to demonstrate a need for further research on a topic. They help you become more familiar with the community of scholars working within an area of research. You might think about this as your *informal or "invisible" college*, those colleagues whose work you will build on and who will cite your findings as you move them into publication. These will also be the scholars who may serve as mentors, review your submitted articles, serve as external reviewers for promotion and tenure, and other aspects of academic life.

Where to Start to Explore the Relevant Literature

Google Scholar™ is a good start, but it is not your only tool for searching the literature. You'll want to rely on library searches for work across a variety of publications including journal articles, books, dissertation abstracts, handbooks, and academic encyclopedias. Handbooks and academic encyclopedias are a great way to introduce you to a particular community of scholars. These publications typically invite authors who are well known for their research in a particular area to contribute chapters or entries on that topic. Think of the literature review as detective work with yourself as the detective trying to solve a puzzle or mystery. How can you discover what has been done on the topic in your academic field as well as related fields? Try not to narrow your search too quickly. Sometimes new researchers rush to the conclusion that no research has been done on their topic of interest. However, in looking at other academic disciplines and searching more broadly, it may be that your topic has been well-researched in another field and can provide useful literature to research within your field of study.

One of your first stops in conducting a review of the literature should be the reference librarian. Make friends with the reference librarians in your institution. Although we may know quite a bit about using library resources, reference librarians are professional experts in tracking down resources and are especially skilled in helping researchers come up with useful key words to guide their literature searches. What might we identify as key words to guide our search? First, look to the key words used by your academic community. You might examine key words appearing in articles on your research topic, conference program indices, and academic handbooks and encyclopedias. As you delve further into the literature review, you may find yourself narrowing your topic, and thus refining your search terms.

Organizing the Literature Review

A plan for how you will organize your literature is critical to a successful process. Again, reference librarians are wonderful resources for helping you organize and manage this work. You may decide to use programs such as RefWorks®, Endnote™, Zotero™, and Mendeley™ to organize the literature. We encourage students to consider an online management tool to store and organize literature in ways that don't take up precious space on your own computer hard drive. You might consider using data analysis software to manage literature reviews. Scholars often use software systems to store, code and categorize relevant literature. Like the process of analyzing qualitative data, a literature review is an inductive analysis of the literature in which you are looking for key findings. These key findings will enable you to organize and write a critical review of the literature based on themes rather than a chronology of studies. What are the common findings across research studies? The key to a good organizational system or tool is to select and use one that fits with your work style and technological abilities.

What types of scholarly articles make up the literature base? Most literature falls across four main categories: (a) theoretical, (b) methodological, (c) empirical studies, and (d) practice-based. Theoretical articles focus on theory and theoretical constructs and may or may not be connected to an area of research but are essential as you engage with the theoretical framework for your study. Methodological articles are focused on research methodology and are typically useful for the methods section of a research article or dissertation study. They describe how researchers have employed particular approaches and methods. Empirical studies are articles reporting research studies using qualitative, quantitative, mixed, and historical methods where a researcher has gone into a field and subsequently reported findings through journal publications and books. Literature reviews focus primarily on these empirical studies to situate research within relevant scholarship. Practice-based articles, typically written in lay language, are those that share research findings with a professional community with the aim of improving practice and are typically follow-up articles from research studies. While these articles are useful for practitioners, they are less useful for researchers since they probably don't describe the theories, previous literature, methodologies, and findings in the detail you need in a literature review.

As you are engaging in this process, you'll want to read these articles carefully and critically. Using a spreadsheet or bibliographic tool that helps track references and manage your reading, start with the abstract and key words, note the research problem, purpose, and research questions. Next, look at the methods used and population studied. What are the key findings? In the conclusion, it is typical for authors to provide recommendations for further research. These recommendations will assist you in building the need for the study, the argument necessary for the study to be a significant contribution to the field. Be sure to look at the article's reference list for citations relevant to your work; follow those resources as well. Creating a tracking system for your literature review (e.g., a table, spreadsheet, analysis software) will help you stay organized. See suggestions in Box 4.2 below for the items you might track.

Box 4.2. Possible Headings or Tags for Your Literature Review Management.

- Full citation
- Key words
- Theoretical framework
- Research purpose and research questions
- Overall research design
- Specific research methods
- Sampling/selection of participants
- Comments on anything you want to note about the article
- Selected key quotes for use in your written literature review

How much literature should you review? What if the research around your topic is huge? What if you can't find relevant research? Beginning researchers sometimes ask these questions. We like to use the analogy of a bird's nest to think about the size of the literature around your topic—with the nest as the literature base for your study and the eggs as various studies situated in that nest. Not all nests are the same; neither are all eggs the same. For example, the hummingbird's nest is an exquisite, tightly woven construction of about three-quarters of an inch in diameter and half an inch deep that rests in the saddle of a tree branch. Its symmetrical cup is lined with a soft down of plant fibers. On the other end of the spectrum, birds such as ospreys and eagles build large, shallow nests high up in tall trees—rough structures—with course sticks and grasses (Comstock, 1986, first published in 1911). Depending on how much literature is already available about your particular study, you might find a cozy, tight little body of literature, like the hummingbird's nest, in which to rest your egg. However, you may find few studies related to your research topic—not enough to construct a nest. If you don't find literature directly tied to your particular topic in your own field you might expand your search to related fields or disciplines. If you are still not finding relevant literature, this may signal a lack of scholarly interest in the topic or researchers do not see this as a problem worthy of study. If so, it will be difficult to construct an argument for the study. If there is no literature base, it will be difficult not only to establish a need for the study but to argue the study will be a significant contribution to the literature in the field. That said, some researchers conduct studies that are not viewed as significant and may actually be ahead of their time, with recognition coming much later.

At the other end of the continuum, the literature base for your study might be substantially larger and looser, like the osprey's nest, perhaps not so snug, but still a good foundation for your study. If there is so much literature that is it unwieldy, you might ask yourself if what you are interested in is too broad. How might you focus your research so it is more specific? For instance, are the key words you are using close enough to your research topic? How might you think about temporally bounding the literature (e.g. studies published within the past 5 years)? However, be sure to include those classic studies scholars have relied on for years to inform their work. Perhaps you have defined your research problem and research purpose in such a way that your literature search will yield a good literature base without overwhelming you.

As noted above, you'll return to the literature throughout the research process, but for graduate students who need to complete the milestones of a research proposal or prospectus to be approved for doing the research, a written literature review is required and serves to articulate the conceptual framework you have constructed for your research. Many students stall in the literature review process waiting for new studies to emerge on their topic, or chase topics related to their research. It is important to know when to stop. After spending considerable time in the literature, you might notice you are coming back to the same authors and same articles. At this point, you should also have a good idea of how those scholars have described the research that still needs to be done on the topic. If you find the same scholars cited over and over again—congratulations! You have found your academic community and are ready to write up the literature review and move forward to argue the need for this study with colleagues and professors who can provide critical feedback on your work and who can assess the quality of the argument you have made.

In sum, the steps to completing a literature review are to first identify a research topic and make a list of key words for searching the academic literature related to your topic. Be sure to spend some time with a reference librarian to help you refine key words and organize your literature findings. Librarians are often available for face-to-face and virtual help sessions. Many institutions provide an online chat resource for students and faculty to encourage communication with librarians for assistance with library resources. Make a plan ahead of time for surveying, organizing, and analyzing the literature. As you survey the literature, note key thematic findings and develop an argument about how the literature addresses your topic. Look for gaps in the academic literature and consider how your research can fill a gap around your topic. Be sure to write as you read and revise your review as needed. You may likely find you need to revisit your research questions as you survey the literature. Lastly, be sure to ask a peer to edit your review. You may consider publishing this critical literature review as a contribution to the field. Before doing so, you'll want to explore journals in your field dedicated to publishing critical literature reviews. For example, the *Review of Research in Education* is a journal dedicated to critical literature reviews of education research. As you begin your literature review, look for resources on writing literature reviews. Machi and McEvoy's (2016) *The Literature Review: Six Steps to Success* and Galvan and Galvan's (2017) *Writing Literature Reviews: A Guide for Students of the Social and Behavior Sciences* are wonderful resources to guide students through the steps to writing a successful literature review. See our recommendations for further reading around this topic.

Arguing for the Significance of the Study

What makes a study significant and how do you convince your major professor, committee, and other scholars in the field that the study is needed and will make a solid contribution to the field? Establishing this level of significance demands rhetorical skill to argue the need for the study. As you saw with articles in your literature review, most offered an argument for the study that included the following questions:

1. What is the research problem or dilemma you want to address?
2. What have scholars in the field already done in relation to this research problem?
3. Based on your review of the literature, what have they found or what knowledge has already been contributed to our understanding of the problem?
4. What is missing from the literature—what is the gap in the literature?
5. Why it is critical that this gap in the literature be addressed by the research study that you are planning?
6. How do you propose to fill this gap and thus make a significant contribution to the literature?

Kelsky (2015) offered an extensive discussion and template for writing grant proposals that lead to this type of rhetorical argument for a research study. You may find this helpful in creating your argument for your research study, thesis, or dissertation proposal. One of the ways you might think of the gap in the literature is that previous scholars may have done studies using a particular theoretical framework, but not the framework you are using. If this is the case, how will a different theoretical framework inform the work or focus the study differently to further understanding, knowledge, or critique? It is good practice to get to the know the journals and scholars in your field to see what work is getting published. What are the current theories and discussions in the field as evidenced in journal articles and significant scholarly texts? Situating your work within these scholarly conversations enables you to establish the significance of your work, get your articles published, and become recognized in the field. In short, the decisions you make about your research in graduate school impact the way you situate yourself in the field for future positions and success in those positions.

Politics and Research

Research decisions are *political*, so identifying the field around your topic and how you will contribute to this work is critical. This decision has ramifications for your academic career. How research has been taken up in your field and what counts as significant research is a question you'll want to ask yourself. The research you undertake shapes your scholarly identity and development of that invisible college we mentioned earlier. It influences your ability to have your work published and secure funding as you move toward getting an academic position in your field, and gain tenure and promotion. That said, innovative research may not be recognized by other scholars at the time it is done, but that recognition in some cases has come years and perhaps decades later. For instance, there is a long history of ignoring the contributions of Black and Indigenous women scholars in the anthropological literature (Esposito & Evans-Winters, 2022; McClaurin, 2001). One of the most notable examples can be seen in the work of Zora Neale Hurston (Hurston et al., 2018), whose work *Barracoon: The Story of the Last "Black Cargo,"* an oral history of the last Black survivor of the Atlantic slave trade, was published decades after her death in 1960.[1]

Subjectivities, Positionalities, and Researchers' Emotions

Our focus so far in this chapter has been outward toward situating your work within the work of other scholars—those theorists and researchers who have informed your work. Now, we turn that focus inward to you as the researcher and primary instrument of the research. An important part of the research design is to look inward—to examine yourself as researcher in relation to the study. We encourage you to think deeply about who you are as a researcher and what you bring to the study. What experiences have you had that informs your thinking about the topic? What beliefs do you hold about this topic? Would you consider yourself an insider or outsider to the community(ies) you intend to work with? What implications might this insider/outsider status have on your work with participants? Who are you in terms of your demographics—gender, race/ethnicity, social class, abilities, age, physical attributes, and other social identity characteristics. How might these impact your work? In other words, what is your position in relation to the study? The concepts of *subjectivity* and *positionality* are the concepts we use to think about ourselves as researchers in relation to the study. Peshkin (1988) described subjectivity as that quality that "affects the results of all, not just observational, investigation. It is an amalgam of the persuasions that stem from the circumstances of one's class, statuses, and values interacting with the particulars of one's object of investigation" (p. 17). He further argued:

> that researchers, notwithstanding their use of quantitative or qualitative methods, their research problem, or their reputation for personal integrity, should systematically identify their subjectivity throughout the course of their research. When researchers observe themselves in the focused way that I propose, they learn about the particular subset of personal qualities that contact with their research phenomenon has released. These qualities have the capacity to filter, skew, shape, block, transform, construe, and misconstrue what transpires from the outset of a research project to its culmination in a written statement. (p. 17)

As we see from Peshkin's examination of subjectivities, they include one's values, beliefs, attitudes, and one's position in the world in regard to social identity categories. More recently, the term positionality has been used with an emphasis on these demographic categories. When researchers are explicit about what they personally bring to their studies, including descriptions of "biography, background assumptions, and beliefs—and how these have shaped the research process and its products," they are engaging in one form of "reflexivity" (Hammersley, 2023, p. 108). In his review of the concept of reflexivity, Hammersley (2023) pointed out that reflexivity has been used to refer not only to properties of persons or practices, but also to features of objects. He proposed three forms of researcher reflexivity: those of "existential reflexivity" (i.e., the researcher is part of the world that they study); "practical reflexivity" (i.e., the researcher's acknowledgement of potential threats to the validity of their study); and "reporting reflexivity" (i.e., providing sufficient information for readers to understand the research process) (p. 109).

To help you consider how your biography intersects with your study, you might think of your positionalities in relation to your research study across all phases of the process. The terms subjectivity and positionality call for us as researchers to thoroughly examine our identity categories, values, experiences, and beliefs and how they may impact our work—in other words, to exhibit researcher reflexivity. For those less familiar with qualitative research the term subjectivities may call up a binary of objective–subjective with one valued over the other. While this is not the case, to avoid this binary, you may want to use the term positionality. Hammersley (2023) asserted that being reflexive is not in conflict with objectivity, since by examining how we engage in our research and the implications for the generation of research findings we can aim to maximize the accuracy of the answers to the research questions examined (for more on this, see p. 110). The key is to communicate to your readers how you are using concepts such as subjectivity, positionality, and reflexivity and to consider what is important in relation to your study. Table 4.3 may assist you to think through these aspects related to your biography that will influence your research.

Table 4.3. Thinking Through Your Subjectivities/Positionalities

Identity characteristics (age, gender, race, ethnicity, ability, social class, education, profession, language, etc.)	Personal experiences	Beliefs and values related to the research topic

As you think about the relationship between your subjectivities/positionalities and your research topic, it is important to remember that these are multiple. Research incorporating an intersectionality perspective, which pays attention to how people's *multiple* identities are entwined, also has a long history (Collins, 1989; Cooper, 2017; Crenshaw, 1991). In the decades since Crenshaw first coined the term intersectionality to refer to intersections of race and gender in the late 1980s, scholars have expounded on this idea to include LGBTQIA+ identities and disabled identities, among others (Esposito & Evans-Winters, 2022). Researchers using an intersectional framework attend to the ways power functions in the experiences of people who sit at the intersection of specific identities (see Table 4.1). We draw your attention to intersectionality here to emphasize the complexities of reflecting on your subjectivities/positionalities as researcher. As you consider your multiple identities in relation to your research phenomenon, this might evoke issues of power, privilege, and agency.

One strategy for examining your subjectivities/positionalities is to include a statement in your work that explains how you relate to your research study both at the beginning and throughout the study. You may find yourself rewriting and refining this statement as the work progresses to account for new understandings. For example, Peshkin (1988) explained how he knew his subjectivities were at play when he felt his emotions aroused at points in his research. At these times, he wrote notes about his reactions and what he was reacting to in the work. *Researchers' emotions* can be valuable signals for how you are reacting and relating to your research. You'll want to be sure to write about these emotions in your research notes/journal, and in your subjectivity/positionality statements. Emotions are a critical part of the research process. They enable us to build rapport (or not), empathize with participants, and for ourselves as researchers, signal how we are reacting and relating to that work.

Using a Research Journal

A research journal is an effective tool for documenting your entire process and you'll want to start your research journal prior to gaining entry. The journal is the place for you to work through the study design as well as a place to brainstorm your ideas for the study, refine your purposes and research questions, and think about your criteria for participant selection. As you gain entry into the field, document your progress. Develop how you will present your research explanation and keep notes on who you talk to, what your experience was in that interaction, and what stood out for you in the process.

Kathleen remembers in the process of gaining entry to her dissertation research site, the principal introduced her to Ms. Jones, a teacher he thought was the "best" first grade teacher in the school. When Kathleen talked with her about the study, Ms. Jones seemed uneasy, quickly referring her to another first grade teacher who was "exceptional" and "much more experienced" than she. Kathleen was puzzled by the teacher's discomfort but chalked it up to lack of interest or willingness to participate in the research project but was able to gain the consent of the second teacher and conducted the study in her classroom. While she included a summary of these discussions with the two teachers in her research journal, it was quickly forgotten once involved in the study. At the end of the school year, Kathleen was invited to the final teachers' meeting of the school year. At that meeting, the principal announced that he and Ms. Jones had been secretly married all year (despite district policy prohibiting spouses working in the same school) and that Ms. Jones would be moving to another school for the following year. Kathleen read her initial journal entries and understood why Ms. Jones was so fearful of participating in the ethnographic study—she couldn't afford to have any-one suspect the marriage. As Kathleen did, you may find by journaling your experiences from early on throughout the study, you are reminded of these earlier experiences. Your initial reactions may provide clues or explanations for people's actions and/or comments during the data collection period of the research project. Continuing to write in your journal through all phases of the research—gaining entry, data generation, data analysis, and writing up—provides a place for you to mull over ideas, document your progress, jot down questions you need to find answers to, and to regularly reflect on what you are doing in the study. We turn now to the specifics of the research design.

Designing the Study

In the previous sections, we examined how your conceptual framework—including both the theories and literature that guide and provides an argu-ment for your study—informs the research problem, research purpose, and research questions. We explored the role of subjectivities, positionalities, and researchers' emotions in relation to the research. We turn now to the primary components of a qualitative research design—the problem statement, re-search purpose, research questions, and methods. What do we mean by these terms? These terms can be confusing, particularly for students engaged in the process of writing a research proposal or dissertation prospectus. Erlandson et al. (1993) clearly and succinctly explained the difference between the re-search problem and research purpose:

> The problem statement in naturalistic research is not a question or even an objective, but rather, as we have noted, an expression of a dilemma or situation that needs to be addressed for the purposes of understanding and direction. The purpose of a research inquiry is to seek to resolve the problem by accumulating pertinent knowledge and information and, in collaboration with the various stakeholders in the social context being studied, construct meaning directed toward that end. (p. 49)

In looking for research problems, as noted above, we usually "find" or iden-tify problems from our own personal experiences, from our work with col-leagues who are already involved in research projects, or through explorations of the literature on topics of interest to us. Sometimes, we even identify re-search problems as a result of potential funding sources; however, we want to be sure if we use this route to get to a research problem, that the work is something for which we have clear and sustained interest. LeCompte and Preissle (1993) provided another way of understanding the research purpose:

> Statements of *purpose* or *goals* delineate what is to be the overall, ultimate product of the research. These statements describe what is yet unknown which a study will reveal and how it will fill gaps in the existing knowledge base, expand the knowledge base, initiate investigation in a neglected line of inquiry, or facilitate integration of an emerging conceptual field. (p. 37, italics in original)

It is essential to spend the necessary time to think about, read about, and write about your research problem and purpose. It can be a time-consuming process to get the research purpose articulated as a clear, simple statement. Wolcott (1994) warned that "a researcher lacking a clear sense of purpose—the ability to set a problem—cannot narrow the research focus sufficiently to achieve any purpose at all" (p. 402).

Once you have identified your topic, have explored what you already know about the topic from existing literature, and have some ideas for a research project, you may find it especially helpful at this stage of the research process to explain to your friends or colleagues what it is you want to explore. Get to-gether with a research group to refine your research purpose. Explaining your ideas for others will help you further clarify your thinking. Journaling about your process may also help. Keep notes from your library work as well as your reflections about the topic. Wolcott (1992) highlighted the importance of refining the research purpose:

> . . . I take as its single most critical feature the "purpose" guiding the research. Research purpose is the only basis on which decisions about process can be made; the clearer the purpose, the clearer the ways to achieve it. The greatest service anyone can provide to another researcher is to help with the formation of, and then with constantly reviewing and refining, that basic key question. Stripped of eloquence that can be added later, this key feature of qualitative (and any other) research begins with the phrase, "The purpose of this study is . . ." The fewer the words needed, the better; wordiness is a dead giveaway to an ill-formed, or at least not-yet-framed, idea. (p. 7)

When you have established your research purpose you can then begin to generate more specific research questions. These come directly from the purpose. In other words, the research questions point to the specific ways the research purpose will be carried out. Since qualitative research is an iterative process, research questions are usually more concretely stated than the purpose, and may be altered as needed in the process of doing the study. As the researcher gains better understandings through the process of the study, it becomes clear that initial research questions may need to be refined or refocused. In summary, the research questions point specifically to how you will go about the research process. Who will be your research participants? What data will you need to gather? How will you generate and analyze data? In thinking about how to design your research purpose statement, start with the following phrase:

- The purpose of my research is to . . . . . .

The more concise you can make this statement, the clearer the intention and focus of your research will be. Perhaps you will be able to explain your research purpose in an elevator by the time you get from the first to the third floor. Ask yourself:

- Is the study too broad or too narrow?
- Is it "do-able"?
- What specific research methodologies or approaches will you use?
- Why?

The research purpose should lead to specific methodological approaches. The purpose statement will point to the participants you will be working with in the study. As we saw in Table 4.2, Janie's research purpose was *to understand experiences of mothers preparing children for menarche.* Her statement is simple and clear. With the words "understand experiences" she signals she will be using interviews as a primary research approach. With the focus on mothers, we know that her participants are at the point of preparing children for menarche. So, in searching for participants, she wanted to talk with mothers of preteens and early teenagers. Hers was a singular focus on the experiences of these mothers.

You may find yourself wanting to *compare* one thing to another through qualitative research methods. In our introductory qualitative research classes, many students lean toward research questions that compare one group to another. Their interest in such comparisons usually comes from familiarity with quantitative studies where comparison is frequently used. Although it is possible to conduct comparative qualitative studies (e.g., Parvez [2017] conducted a comparative case study concerning the politicization of Islam in France and India), qualitative research approaches lend themselves to understanding the depth of human experience. You will want to assess your ability to get the richness and depth you need for good qualitative work. A way of focusing a study is to explore an issue in one context. As qualitative researchers, we can better spend our limited energies attempting to get to the heart of the matter, as Wolcott (1994) suggests below.

> I became "anticomparativist", resolved never to engage in the potentially mindless activity of simply cataloging similarities and differences. That may explain my lingering bias against comparative approaches in the social sciences such as the much touted "constant comparative method" suggested by Glaser and Strauss . . . (p. 181)

Wolcott (1994) went on to note:

> I was heartened during a recent rereading of Geertz's (1983) *Local Knowledge* to find him quoting Santayana's "famous dictum" that "one compares only when one is unable to get to the heart of the matter" (p. 233). Perhaps we should restate that idea as our own aphorism: Get to the heart of the matter if possible; if not, compare. (p. 183)[2]

If you opt to do a comparative study, that, of course, will take more resources, particularly in regard to the time it will take. As part of the research design, you will want to consider your resources as a researcher. Let's discuss what we mean by those resources next.

Consideration of Time and Resources

Throughout our process of constructing the research design, you need to keep in mind the practical issues involved in carrying out the study. Do you have the time and resources to spend on the study? If you have a family, a full-time job, and limited financial resources, it is unlikely that you will be undertaking a year-long ethnographic study in another country. The study must be able to fit into your life given other responsibilities and resources. Your topic should sustain your interest over a sufficient period of time, since it may take longer to complete your study than you expect. In addition you need to consider whether you are able to undertake the study emotionally. The project you select may be much too close to home for comfort. While qualitative research evokes difficult emotions on the part of the researcher, you will want to assess the extent you are able to emotionally take on a topic of interest. For example, topics related to personal trauma, illness, or loss may require time and distance from personal events before you are ready to conduct research on the topic. Silverio and colleagues (2022) explored the challenges of conducting qualitative research on difficult topics such as childhood sexual abuse, severe mental illness, and professional trauma and traumatic stress, among others. They offered suggestions for practicing self-care in research that might be helpful when conducting research on difficult topics. Some suggestions included forming peer support networks, avoiding overscheduling data collection (e.g., multiple interviews or focus group sessions in a single day), reflective journaling, and debriefing with colleagues following difficult data collection events (pp. 7–9).

The point is to construct a study that you are able to do within a reasonable amount of time considering your resources—both material and emotional. If you are undertaking a master's thesis or doctoral dissertation, you might remind yourself, this is not your life's work, as a colleague of ours continually reminds students, but a *beginning* to your scholarly process. It is important to construct a study you are able to complete successfully, to gain skills as a qualitative researcher, and to make a solid contribution to the body of knowledge in your field. It may not be a major theoretical contribution, but can contribute to an increased understanding of one aspect of human experiences.

Gaining Access

Once conceptual framework, research purpose, research question, and overall design are clear to you and you have selected possible participants, it is time to plan for how you will approach potential participants. Although research designs may differ, the general way in which to approach people to explain research is quite similar. In this section we examine the construction of a research explanation to be used to gain access in qualitative research studies, including various questions you need to answer prior to approaching potential participants. Before you arrange to meet with a potential participant, it is helpful to compose a written explanation of your study and to practice this explanation with someone who can give you honest feedback on your explanation. A research group is helpful for rehearsing these research explanations.

Depending on your study, you may need to talk with several people to gain access to a site or to a group of people. If you intend to do an ethnographic study in a particular site, you will not only need to talk with the owner or manager of the site, you will need to talk to participants at the site. Consider both the official channels as well as informal channels accessible through personal networks as ways to make connections with possible participants. Networking can be accomplished through friends, classmates, acquaintances, or other relationships you have developed.

Despite the approach you use, your explanations need to be appropriate for the various people to whom you will be talking. If you intend to talk with a school superintendent or school district research officer to attempt to get consent to conduct your study within a school system, your presentation of self may be a bit different from a situation that is less formal. Box 4.3 offers a list of questions to assist you in thinking through your research explanation. As you can see, these questions harken back to our discussion in Chapter 2 of the IRB requirements, so your IRB application should inform how you explain your research to potential participants.

Box 4.3. Constructing a Research Explanation for Participants.

1. What is the purpose of your research in clear language?
2. Why is the study important?
3. Why have you selected these participants to participate in the study?
4. What will the participants be required to do as part of the study?
5. What will you be doing in the study related to the participants?
6. How long will it take? How much time will the study require from the participants?
7. How much control do the participants have over their own stories?

8. How will you share the research results with the participants at the end of the study?
9. What will you do with the results of the study?

Glesne (2016) referred to this as your "lay summary" or the "summary of the research purpose and procedures presented (written or oral) to participants" (p. 59). Fetterman (1989) suggested using a "go-between," someone who has credibility with the group and who can provide you with an introduction to the setting. You will need to be careful that the person you select will not later limit your choices of participants within the setting. For example, you may select a go-between who is related to one faction within the community. Those who represent another faction or group may be hesitant to work with you if you are viewed as aligned with the "other" group. This is quite a bit easier in dealing with individuals for interview studies. You may be able to find one person who fits all the criteria you have established for participant selection. They then may refer you to someone they know who fits your criteria and may talk with that person on your behalf. This process is referred to as "network selection" (LeCompte & Preissle, 1993).

In constructing your research explanation, you will want to begin with an introduction of yourself—who you are and where you are from. You will also need to attend to the questions listed in Box 4.3 above. Your research purpose should be clear to you and to your participants. What is the purpose of the study and why do you want to do it? If your explanation of the purpose of the study is unclear, too lengthy, or full of academic jargon, you will have difficulty conveying to participants what you are doing. Describe to your potential participants why you want them, rather than someone else, to participate in your study. Explain what exactly you will be doing to gather data for the study and what you expect participants to do as part of the study. If you are planning an ethnography, you will become a player in the participants' daily lives over a long period of time and they will need to know this in order to make an informed decision if they want to permit you into the setting. If you are engaged in an interview study, the time and energy commitment from your participants is significantly less. Your participants will want to know what is required of them for your study.

In keeping with ethical practices, ensuring the confidentiality of the participants is required in most qualitative studies and accomplished through the use of pseudonyms. You might give your participants the option to select their own pseudonyms. Several of our students have had the experience of asking participants to select a pseudonym and the name selected was meant to be fun and did reflect how they were seeing themselves, but looked silly in research reports (e.g., "Tinkerbell"). You may want to explain to your participants that the name they select will be used in written publications to avoid unnecessary complications.

IRB guidelines require an explanation of how the study will benefit those involved in it. This may be in the form of monetary rewards or in the benefits of having someone listen to their stories. Some researchers offer compensation to participants for their time in the form of money, gift cards, and other small tokens. In some studies, the researchers may consider it fair to pay participants for their involvement in data generation. Be sure to check with your IRB and individual department about protocols for offering incentives to participants. If your research is connected to grant funding, review grant guidelines or provisions regarding participant incentives.

Finally, you might talk about how much control the participants will have over the final product. Questions to consider are:

- Will you share your fieldnotes and interview transcripts with them?
- Will they be able to take out what they don't want reported?
- Will you share a draft of the research report for their consideration?
- Will you change it if they want it changed?
- What if you report something that is not what the participants want to hear?
- Will you and your participants write the research report together? If so, how will you negotiate authorship for potential publications?
- What will happen to the final product of the research?

All these are considerations to think about prior to talking with potential participants. By considering these aspects of the research process prior to conducting the study, you might avoid surprises, discomfort, and hard feelings later in the process.

Once you have planned your research explanation, you are ready to begin. Think about the context of your setting to decide if you need official sanction first before you talk with others in the setting. Decide who to contact first. Decide whether you want to phone for an appointment, write a letter or email, or simply stop by in person. This will depend on your study. Although it is usually better to explain your study in person, it may be difficult to do so without first calling for an appointment or sending a written request. You need to weigh your options and make the best decision for your study.

Conclusions

In this chapter, we examined all aspects of a theoretically informed research design and provided examples. In the remaining chapters we turn to methodological approaches qualitative researchers use in their work. We focus on six different research designs including interview studies, narrative inquiry, ethnography and autoethnography, archival research and document analysis, and arts-based inquiry. We situate these designs within their disciplinary histories and theoretical frameworks and discuss data generation, data analysis, and representation within those traditions. While we present the approaches in separate chapters, we encourage flexibility in their use. Based on your conceptual framework, you may use these approaches in combination with one another. As we saw with Janie's design in Table 4.2, she used a variety of methodological approaches that were woven carefully within the theoretical framework and research questions of her study. As you read through the following chapters, consider each in light of your research. How will you construct a rigorous, theoretically informed design?

Activities

1. Jot down your ideas for research topics, then write about why you want to study these topics. What experiences have you had related to the topics?
2. Using Table 4.1 as a model, build your own table by selecting one topic in your field and follow it through different theoretical frameworks, research purposes, research questions, and methods.
3. Talk with a reference librarian about your study and the key words you are using prior to engaging in your literature review. Plan and use a system for organizing your review.

4. Using Table 4.3, think through all aspects of your positionality and write a positionality statement.
5. Using Box 4.3, write a research explanation you will use to present your study to potential participants.

Further Reading

Boote, D. N., & Beile, P. (2005). Scholars before researchers: On the centrality of the dissertation literature review in research preparation. *Educational Researcher, 34*(6), 3–15. https://doi. org/ 10.3102/0013189X034006003

Cooper, H. (1998). *Synthesizing research: A guide for literature reviews* (3rd ed.). SAGE.

Fink, A. (2019). *Conducting research literature reviews: From paper to the internet* (5th ed.). SAGE.

Pan, M. L. (2017). *Preparing literature reviews: Qualitative and quantitative approaches* (5th ed). Routledge.

Pillow, W. S. (2015). Reflexivity as interpretation and genealogy in research. *Cultural Studies* ↔ *Critical Methodologies, 15*(6), 419–434. https://doi.org/10.1177/1532708615615605

Poulson, L., & Wallace, M. (Eds.). (2004). *Learning to read critically in teaching and learning.* SAGE.

Wallace, M. (2021). *Critical reading and writing for postgraduates* (4th ed.). SAGE.

Notes

1. The manuscript for the book was submitted for publication in 1931 but rejected because Hurston refused to revise the use of dialect. More recent historical work has found that Kossula, the narrator featured in Hurston's book, was outlived by another survivor, Sally "Redoshi" Smith (Durkin, 2019).

2. However, Wolcott may have misinterpreted Geertz's (1983) comment in *Local Knowledge: Fact and Law in Comparative Perspective.* Geertz quotes Santayana then argues the opposite as follows: "Santayana's famous dictum that one compares only when one is unable to get to the heart of the matter seems to me, here at least, the precise reverse of the truth: it is through comparison, and of incomparable, the whatever heart we can actually get to is to be reached" (p. 233).

References

Annamma, S. A., Jackson, D. D., & Morrison, D. (2017). Conceptualizing color-evasiveness: Using dis/ability critical race theory to expand a color-blind racial ideology in education and society. *Race Ethnicity and Education, 20*(2), 147–162. https://doi.org/10.1080/13613324.20 16.1248837

Barad, K. (2007). *Meeting the universe halfway: Quantum physics and the entanglement of matter and meaning.* Duke University Press.

Blumer, H. (1969). *Symbolic interactionism: Perspective and method.* Prentice Hall.

Braidotti, R. (2019). *Posthuman knowledge.* Polity Press.

Butler, J. (1990). *Gender trouble: Feminism and the subversion of identity.* Routledge.

Butler, J. (1993). *Bodies that matter: On the discursive limits of 'sex.'* Routledge.

Carrera-Fernández, M. V., Lameiras-Fernández, M., & Rodríguez-Castro, Y. (2018). Performing intelligible genders through violence: Bullying as gender practice and heteronormative control. *Gender & Education, 30*(3), 341–359. https://doi.org/10.1080/09540253.2016.1203884

Collins, P. H. (1998). It's all in the family: Intersections of gender, race, and nation. *Hypatia, 13*(3), 62–82. https://www.jstor.org/stable/3810699

Collins, P. H. (2009). *Black feminist thought: Knowledge, consciousness, and the politics of empowerment* (2nd ed.). Routledge.

Comstock, A. B. (1986). *Handbook of nature study.* Comstock Publishing Associates.

Cooper, B. C. (2017). *Beyond respectability: The intellectual thought of race women.* University of Illinois Press.

Corney, B. (2008). Aggression in the workplace. *Journal of Health Organization and Management, 22*(2), 164–177. https://doi.org/10.1108/14777260810876321

Crenshaw, K. (1991). Mapping the margins: Intersectionality, identity politics, and violence against women of color. *Stanford Law Review, 43*, 1241–1299. https://doi.org/10.2307/1229039

Dávila, B. (2015). Critical race theory, disability microaggressions and Latina/o student experiences in special education. *Race Ethnicity and Education, 18*(4), 443–468. https://doi.org/10.1080/13613324.2014.885422

Donnor, J. K., & Ladson-Billings, G. (2018). Critical race theory and the postracial imaginary. In N. K. Denzin & Y. S. Lincolns (Eds.), *The SAGE Handbook of Qualitative Research.* SAGE.

Durkin, H. (2019). Finding last middle passage survivor Sally 'Redoshi' Smith on the page and screen. *Slavery & Abolition, 40*(4), 631–658. https://doi.org/10.1080/0144039X.2019.1596397

Erlandson, D. A., Harris, E. L., Skipper, B. L., & Allen, S. D. (1993). *Doing naturalistic inquiry: A guide to methods.* SAGE.

Esposito, J., & Evans-Winters, V. (2022). *Introduction to intersectional qualitative research.* Routledge.

Evaldsson, A.-C., & Svahn, J. (2012). School bullying and the micro-politics of girls' gossip disputes. In S. Danby & M. Theobald (Eds.), *Disputes in everyday life: Social and moral orders of children and young people* (Vol. 15, pp. 297–323). Emerald Group Publishing Limited. https://doi.org/10.1108/S1537-4661(2012)0000015016

Ferfolja, T., & Ullman, J. (2017). Exploring 'thing-power' and the 'spectre of fear' on schooling subjectivities: A critical posthuman analysis of LGBT silencing. In K. Malone, S. Truong, & T. Gray (Eds.), *Reimagining sustainability in precarious times* (pp. 187–198). Springer Singapore. https://doi.org/10.1007/978-981-10-2550-1_13

Fetterman, D. M. (1989). *Ethnography: Step by step.* SAGE.

Foote, M. Q., & Bartell, T. G.(2011). Pathways to equity in mathematics education: How life experiences impact researcher positionality. *Educational Studies in Mathematics, 78*, 45–68. https://www.jstor.org/stable/41485940

Galvan, J., & Galvan, M. (2017). *Writing literature reviews: A guide for students of the social and behavior sciences*. (7th edition). Routledge.

Garfinkel, H. (1967). *Studies in ethnomethodology*. Prentice-Hall.

Geertz, C. (1983). *Local knowledge*. Basic Books

Glesne, C. (2016). *Becoming qualitative researchers: An introduction* (5th edition). Pearson.

Grant, J. (2021). No, I'm not crazy: A Black feminist perspective of gaslighting within doctoral socialization. *International Journal of Qualitative Studies in Education, 34*(10), 939–947. https://doi.org/10.1080/09518398.2021.1930258

Hammersley, M. (2023). *Methodological concepts: A critical guide*. Routledge.

Hart, C. (2018). *Doing a literature review: Releasing the social science research imagination* (2nd ed). SAGE.

Hurston, Z. N., Plant, D.G., & Walker, A. (2018). *Barracoon: The story of the last "Black cargo."* Amistad, an imprint of Harper Collins.

Jane, E. A. (2018). Gendered cyberhate as workplace harassment and economic vandalism. *Feminist Media Studies, 18*(4), 575–591. https://doi.org/10.1080/14680777.2018.1447344

Kelsky, K. (2015). *The professor is in: The essential guide to turning your PhD into a job*. Three Rivers Press.

Kincheloe, J. L., McLaren, P., Steinberg, S. R., & Monzo, L. D. (2018). Critical pedagogy and qualitative research: Advancing the bricolage. In N. K. Denzin & Y. S. Lincoln (Eds.), *The SAGE handbook of qualitative research* (pp. 235–260). SAGE.

LeCompte, M. D. & Preissle, J. (1993). *Ethnography and qualitative design in educational research* (2nd ed.). Academic Press.

Machi, L. A., & McEvoy, B. (2016). *The literature review: Six steps to success*. (3rd edition). Corwin.

McClaurin, I. (Ed.). (2001). *Black feminist anthropology: Theory, politics, praxis and poetics*. Rutgers University Press.

Merriam-Webster. (n.d.). Design definition & meaning. Merriam-Webster. http://www.merriam-webster.com/dictionary/design

Mishna, F., Sanders, J. E., McNeil, S., Fearing, G., & Kalenteridis, K. (2020). "If somebody is different": A critical analysis of parent, teacher and student perspectives on bullying and cyberbullying. *Children and Youth Services Review, 118*, 105366. https://doi.org/https://doi.org/10.1016/j.childyouth.2020.105366

Parvez, Z. F. (2017). *Politicizing Islam: The Islamic revival in France and India*. Oxford University Press.

Peshkin, A. (1988). In search of subjectivity: One's own. *Educational Researcher, 17*(7), 17–22. https://www.jstor.org/stable/1174381

Rawlings, V. (2019). 'It's not bullying', 'It's just a joke': Teacher and student discursive manoeuvres around gendered violence. *British Educational Research Journal, 45*(4), 698–716. https://doi.org/10.1002/berj.3521

Ringrose, J., & Rawlings, J. (2015). Posthuman performativity gender and 'school bullying': Exploring the material-discursive intra-actions of skirts, hair, sluts, and poofs. *Confero:*

Essays on Education, Philosophy and Politics, 3(2), 80–119. https://doaj.org/article/8260705f
d42c4f72a7a5178c0be5d16f

Rowe, W. E. (2014). Positionality. In D. Coghlan & M. Brydon-Miller (Eds.), *The SAGE encyclopedia of action research*. SAGE. https://doi.org/10.4135/9781446294406

Savin-Baden, M., & Major, C.H. (2013). *Qualitative research: The essential guide to theory and practice*. Routledge.

Silverio, S. A., Sheen, K. S., Bramante, A., Knighting, K., Koops, T. U., Montgomery, E., November, L., Soulsby, L. K., Stevenson, J. H., Watkins, M., Easter, A., & Sandall, J. (2022). Sensitive, challenging, and difficult topics: Experiences and practical considerations for qualitative researchers. *International Journal of Qualitative Methods, 21*, 1–16. https://doi.org/10.1177/16094069221124739

Smith, D. E. (1987). *The everyday world as problematic: A feminist sociology*. Northeastern University Press.

Solórzano, D. G., & Yosso, T. J. (2002). Critical race methodology: Counter-storytelling as an analytical framework for education research. *Qualitative Inquiry, 8*(1), 23–44. https://doi.org/10.1177/107780040200800103

St. Pierre, E. A. (2000). Poststructural feminism in education: An overview. *International Journal of Qualitative Studies in Education, 13*(5), 477–515. https://doi.org/10.1080/09518390050156422

Thornberg, R. (2018). School bullying and fitting into the peer landscape: A grounded theory field study. *British Journal of Sociology of Education, 39*(1), 144–158. https://doi.org/10.1080/01425692.2017.1330680

Van Manen, M. (2014). *Phenomenology of practice: Meaning-giving methods in phenomenological research and writing*. Routledge.

Wolcott, H. F. (1992, April). *What qualitative research has revealed about education's researchers*. Paper presented at American Educational Research Symposium, San Francisco.

Wolcott, H. F. (1994). *Transforming qualitative data: Description, analysis, and interpretation*. SAGE.

PART II

℘ GENERATING DATA BY TALKING, OBSERVING, AND EXAMINING

THE PURPOSE OF PART 2 is to introduce you to the three primary methods typically used in qualitative research design: (a) interviewing, (b) participant observation, and (c) documents and material culture. As with all chapters in the book, we situate these methods within the disciplinary contexts in which they were originally used. With all three of the methods, we offer detailed descriptions of the method itself, guidelines for how it is used, and specific suggestions on planning for and conducting research. Since we believe your theoretical frameworks should inform your work, we've provided examples of different theoretically informed practice in each of the chapters.

Chapter 5, *Designing studies that use interviews*, begins with a discussion of the types and formats for interview research design and is followed by various roles researchers might play based on the theoretical orientations of the study. We walk you through key aspects of designing interview studies: (a) formulating a purpose and research questions, (b) considering the potential participants of your study, and (c) thinking through the process of selecting those participants. In this section, we review different approaches to sampling. The next portion of the chapter is focused on the practical considerations of planning an interview study, beginning with developing and posing interview questions. Here we consider the various types of questions you might use as well as the actual conduct of the interviews, with attention given to building rapport and recording the interview. We turn to the post-interview phase with a discussion of the transcription of interview data, along with practical examples. Since there are many ways to analyze qualitative research data based on the type of design as well as the theory(ies) used to inform the work, the process of data analysis is integrated throughout this book. Reading across all chapters you will be introduced to many approaches to analysis, but it is up to you, your theoretical frameworks, and research aims as to which data analysis approach you'll select. These are your choices, but you'll want to read about that approach in more depth than what we can offer in this introductory text. In Chapter 5, we introduce two approaches: the constant comparative and thematic analysis methods within the history and context in which they were developed.

Chapter 6, *Participant observation, ethnography, and ethnographic designs*, focuses your attention to the next primary method of data generation—that involving observation. We begin with ethnography and the culture concept. Historically, anthropology is the discipline in which ethnography and ethnographic practices were developed. We follow with critiques of the field and those scholars and traditions where the critiques are situated. Next, we move to the actual conduct of participant observation studies with discussions on site selection, researchers' roles, planning the work and entering the field, establishing rapport, and engaging researchers' emotions. We then turn to the actual work of participant observation—taking fieldnotes and engaging in ethnographic interviews. We share a description of different kinds of fieldnotes and strategies for taking them, approaches to ethnographic interviews, and how to think about the kinds of documents that might be available to you in this work. Our discussion of analysis in this chapter focuses on ethnographic data analysis including taxonomic analysis as well as a variety of descriptive writing activities that can be used in representing ethnographic and participant observation studies.

Chapter 7, *Designing studies that use documents and archives*, is the final primary method in qualitative research. The examination of documents and archives is the focus here. We first examine documents including both institutional records and personal records, then move to a description of archives, what we mean by archives, and how archival collections are created. We provide you with many examples of archives and offer practical suggestions for accessing archival collections, handling materials in those collections, and asking critical questions of the archives. Qualitative studies based in archival work can be quite different from interview or participant observation studies. Due to the limitations of archival collections, qualitative studies typically begin through an examination of what is available and accessible, rather than by developing research questions and generating data. With archival studies, you will be surveying what is available on a particular topic of interest and developing leads and questions for research using those materials. The final portion of the chapter describes numerous examples of studies using archival data and the many ways used to represent findings.

Designing Studies That Use Interviews

THIS CHAPTER DISCUSSES INTERVIEWS—CONVERSATIONS THAT researchers facilitate with participants that are directed towards generating information to inform research questions. Researchers use participants' verbal descriptions to develop narratives that respond to research questions about peoples' lives, experiences, beliefs, meaning-making, and perspectives. Just as interviews take many forms in society (e.g., police interviews, clinical interviews, journalistic interviews, etc.), formats for research interviews vary. Survey researchers use highly structured standardized interview guides to generate data that are subject to *deductive analysis* using preformulated coding schemes. In contrast, qualitative researchers use semi-structured or open-ended interviews to generate data and analyze data inductively. Among a range of approaches to *inductive analysis* is qualitative coding, in which researchers develop coding schemes through reading and re-reading data sources. In practice, qualitative researchers use a combination of deductive, inductive, and abductive reasoning (in which cognitive leaps occur to better explain what is going on) when analyzing qualitative data (Reichertz, 2014).

Interviews can also be subject to numerous forms of analysis, including narrative, phenomenological, and discursive analysis among others. In this chapter we focus on qualitative approaches to semi-structured and open-ended interviews.

What Makes an Interview "Qualitative"?

Whereas *standardized interviews* involve asking questions using the same wording in identical order for every participant, qualitative interviewers are flexible in guiding conversations, and can use conversational approaches (San Pedro, 2021) as well as *semi-structured interview* guides in research. Although interviewers have topics in mind, they strive to provide opportunities for participants to answer questions in their own words and follow the interviewee's leads in what to discuss. Interviewers generate storytelling by asking *open* rather than *closed questions* and following up on participants' accounts with open-ended prompts. For example, rather than the closed question "Did you enjoy that experience?" that could be answered with a yes/no response, open prompts such as "Tell me more about that," or "Tell me what that experience was like for you" can elicit storytelling.

There are many variations in the ways that interviews can be conducted. Three well-used forms used for interviewing individuals are phenomenological interviews (Van Manen, 2014), oral history interviews (Janesick, 2010; Ritchie, 2015), and ethnographic interview (Heyl, 2001; Spradley, 2016). Researchers use interviews to generate descriptive accounts of lived experiences, and histories of people, events, and cultural phenomena. The theoretical frameworks that researchers use also informs how they conduct interviews (e.g., feminist approaches to interviewing). Interviews can be conducted in pairs (known as joint interviews or dyads) (Polak & Green, 2016) and incorporate a variety of sensory modes of knowing (Alam et al., 2018; Harris & Guillemin, 2012). For example, interviewers have invited interviewees to (a) talk about objects and visual stimuli (e.g., photos) that they bring to the interview encounter (Copple, 2023; Jaumot-Pascual et al., 2023; Nordstrom, 2023) and vignettes (Sampson & Johannessen, 2020); (b) discuss space and place using mobile methods (e.g., by traveling with participants in cars, buses, or trains, or walking through a neighborhood) (Kusenbach, 2018; Roulston & Flint, 2023); and (c) generate maps, diagrams, or drawings that they talk about in interviews (Bravington, 2023; Bravington & King, 2019).

Researchers also make use of groups formats to conduct interviews. The "focused interview" (Merton et al., 1956/1990), which was developed during World War II to understand peoples' responses to experiences such as viewing a film, has since transformed into the discussion format known as focus groups. Researchers and evaluators use focus groups to generate dialogue on a range of perspectives, opinions, and beliefs concerning research topics (Barbour, 2018; Hall, 2020).

The Interviewer's Role

Interviewers take a range of roles depending on the theoretical approach and research design used in a study. On the one hand, interviewers can assume a nondirective and neutral role in which they ask nonleading questions and contribute minimally to the conversation. This form of interview draws on the model of talk used in psychotherapy developed by the psychoanalyst Carl Rogers (1902–1987) (Lee, 2011). In contrast, interviewers can take on a more active role in interviewing in which they challenge interviewees to provide rationales for their accounts, and may even contribute their own viewpoints to the conversations (Brinkmann, 2007; Dinkins, 2005; Johnston, 2016; Way et al., 2015). Between these two extremes, researchers can take on a collaborative role in which they invite questions from interviewees and readily answer questions posed. This more "active interview" (Holstein & Gubrium, 1995) is illustrated by feminist approaches to interviewing (Herron, 2022). Regardless of format, what all qualitative research interviews have in common is that researchers ask research participants questions in order to generate descriptions to learn about topics of interest.

Qualitative interviews have historically entailed face-to-face interaction between an interviewer and interviewee/s. With the digital revolution beginning in the late 20th century researchers have also made use of online formats to conduct interviews. Whether conducting interviews via telephone, online, or in person, researchers need to be aware of their assumptions about a topic, and what they bring to an interview context in relation to both the topic of research and the participants of a research study. This entails identifying subjectivities and positionalities and engaging in reflexive practices that examine the implications of these for the study and related stakeholders as discussed in the previous chapter.

Designing a Study That Uses Interviews

Researchers begin the design process by first considering interviews as a form of evidence. When researchers want to learn about people's perceptions, opinions, beliefs, experiences, rationales, values, or meaning-making, interviews serve as a useful method to generate descriptions for analysis. Interview descriptions are also analyzable as discourse, and are suited to research questions that focus on the circulation of discourses, or methodological questions that examine the interactional and performative features of interview talk (Roulston, 2019, 2024). In the latter case, analysis of interview talk is typically undertaken as a complementary form of analysis that examines interview talk methodologically.

Unless accompanied by participant observations in which researchers spend lengthy periods of time in a field setting gaining knowledge of what is going on, interview descriptions are less valuable for learning about what people actually do. This does not mean that researchers cannot ask questions concerning what people do. Researchers need to remember, however, that people do not always do what they say they do and might even intentionally lie or misrepresent their experiences. People can misremember and represent themselves differently to various audiences. Think, for example, how you might describe a first date in a conversation with a minister of religion as opposed to a peer.

Once you have decided that interviews will be helpful to explore a topic of interest, you will need to develop a research purpose statement and research questions. A generic purpose statement worded in an interpretivist format might look like this:

- The purpose of this study is to examine [*Y population's*] experiences and perspectives of [*X phenomenon*].

As one example, a purpose statement from a study Kathy conducted was formulated as:

- The purpose of this study is to examine adults' perspectives and experiences of learning music. (Roulston et al., 2015)

The openness and flexibility of qualitative research designs means that there are many decisions in the process of designing a study to examine a topic of interest. Let's begin by looking at selection and sampling. How will you identify a potential population to study, by what criteria will participants be sampled, and how will you recruit them?

Selection and Sampling in Qualitative Studies

Selection is the process by which you identify a potential site and population for your study. Researchers first define the unit of analysis they intend to examine. This could be individuals, groups, lived experiences, or other phenomena such as events, social settings, institutions, or contexts. Patton (2002) advised that "[t]he key issue in selecting and making decisions about the appropriate unit of analysis is to decide what it is you want to be able to say something about at the end of the study" (p. 229, bolding in original). Mason (2018) suggested that researchers ask themselves the question: "What is the nature of the phenomena, or entities, or social world, that I wish to investigate?" (p. 4). If the phenomenon that you wish to study can be explored using people's accounts and reports, then interviews can be a useful source of evidence. In the example from Kathy's study above, the research team first selected a broader population—adult music learners, from which they identified people willing to participate in an interview study.

Sampling is the process by which researchers choose data sources from a population of data sources available. Qualitative researchers typically use criterion-based sampling, which is a purposeful, rather than random, approach to sampling. For example, in the aforementioned study, the criterion for selecting participants was that they were adult music learners who were currently engaged in learning to sing or play a musical instrument. One member of the research team was a music educator who recruited participants by asking for recommendations from instructors who taught in studio settings as well as instructors involved in a community music program as part of the local branch of the Osher Lifelong Learning Institute. In this study, Kathy and the research team wanted to recruit participants learning a variety of instruments in a range of contexts (*typical-case sampling*). Researchers use other forms of sampling to select participants, including unique-case, reputational-case, and deviant case sampling (LeCompte & Preissle, 1993).

Unique-case sampling refers to the use of criteria for sampling that are rare in comparison to typical cases (e.g., blind music learners). In *reputational-case sampling*, researchers identify the characteristics of a population for which they seek expert recommendations (e.g., prize-winning adult instrumental students). *Deviant case sampling* involves outlining sampling criteria that would deviate from the typical case. For example, in the study discussed we found that many of the adult learners had returned to learning an instrument that they had engaged with as children. Had we wanted to pursue this further, we could have sought to sample for deviant cases by specifically recruiting adults who had no prior experience learning an instrument.

Network sampling refers to the process by which participants are located. After a person has been recruited for a study, researchers seek recommendations for other parties willing to participate from those already interviewed (e.g., a final interview question could be: "Do you know anyone who might be interested in being interviewed for this study?"). This approach is sometimes referred to as "snowball sampling."[1]

Convenience sampling is an approach in which researchers sample data sources from what is immediately available to them. Although convenience sampling may be useful in the early stages of a project (e.g., when piloting interviews), it is considered to be a weak form of sampling, since researchers are relying on a limited circle without regard to the wider population available. Findings from a study using convenience sampling may be flawed because the researcher has not taken the opportunity to gain wider perspectives and (perhaps) divergent views concerning the topic of interest. For certain kinds of study designs (e.g., autoethnography), convenience sampling would be appropriate.

Theoretical sampling refers to a late-stage sampling strategy associated with grounded theory methods. Once researchers have identified a phenomenon of interest from analysis of data they recruit participants or select data that speaks to this phenomenon. Kathy Charmaz (2014) explained that theoretical sampling involves "seeking and collecting pertinent data to elaborate and refine categories in your emerging theory" (p. 192). She continued: "You conduct theoretical sampling by sampling to develop the properties of your categories until no new properties emerge. Thus, you *saturate* your categories with data and subsequently *sort* and/or diagram them to integrate your emerging theory" (pp. 192–193, italics in original). Charmaz (2006) illustrated the process using Jane Hood's study of dual-career families. Hood began her study with an examination of married women's self-concepts and friendships, but identified an emergent issue related to how women negotiated household chores and childcare when they returned to work (Charmaz, 2006, p. 97). After analyzing interviews with women, Hood realized that she needed to learn more about how husbands conceptualized their wives' work, so she recruited more participants to this end. Charmaz (2006) reminded researchers that theoretical sampling is different from sampling that (a) addresses the initial research questions; (b) reflects population distributions; (c) searches for negative cases; and (d) locates additional data until no new concepts are found (p. 100).

Practical Considerations

How many interviews? How many participants? How long should an interview be? These are all questions to ask in the design process, although there are no precise answers that will work for all studies. Deciding what to do entails deliberately planning your study and providing clear rationales for your decisions. For example, how many people to recruit will be impacted by the contexts in which you conduct your study, your personal context (e.g., time constraints and financial considerations), any special considerations involving the participant group (e.g., working with Indigenous peoples, elites, children, the ill, elderly, or people with disabilities), or whether a study involves sensitive topics, cross-cultural engagement, or multiple languages (e.g., interpreters or translators). Since methodological literature on qualitative interviews describes a range of interview forms (e.g., unstructured and semi-structured interviews, conversational interviews, phenomenological interviews and ethnographic interviews) and theorizations of interviews that range from feminist, epistemic, postmodern, decolonizing, and Indigenous and new materialist approaches (Roulston, 2022), the approach that you take needs to align with the theoretical assumptions that you bring to your study. Let's look at the planning, conducting, and post-interview stages in more detail.

The Planning Phase

When interviews are used as a primary method it is important to identify people who can provide in-depth descriptions about the research topic and are willing to take the time to talk to a researcher. Thinking about the potential relationships with interviewees will assist researchers to make informed decisions about what interview format will be most effective in eliciting detailed descriptions. Since any interviewer and interviewee each bring a multitude of positionalities to the interview context, interviewers can begin by considering which interview format will work best for a particular study. For example, researchers who have worked with children and adolescents have found that participatory approaches are helpful in generating talk about topics (e.g., play-based methods or photo-elicitation).

Developing an Interview Guide

Developing interview guides goes hand-in-hand with reflecting on what you hope to learn. For any research study, you might start with two or three research questions, and develop topical areas and interview questions that will elicit information that responds to each research question. We begin by outlining how to develop a semi-structured interview guide in which an interviewer asks open questions of multiple participants in ways that facilitate spaces for participants to generate descriptions in their own words. Interviews are semi-structured when the same topics are discussed with multiple interviewees, but the ways in which interviews unfold differ because the interviewer formulates follow-up questions based on what each participant has said.

Let's look at a worked-out example. To generate questions to do with a research topic, begin by brainstorming a list of potential topics (see column 1, Table 5.1) and then formulating interview questions that relate to each topic (column 3). Table 5.1 shows interview questions generated for the previously mentioned study on adults' experiences learning music (Roulston et al., 2015). As a planning step, it is useful to write down what you hope to learn from each interview question (column 2) as this needs to relate to the research questions posed. Once you've formulated interview questions, double check that each interview question relates to a research question, and that background information is gained about each participant as appropriate.

Table 5.1. Brainstorming Potential Interview Topics and Questions

Potential topics	What I want to learn	Potential interview questions
Pathways to learning music in adulthood	How do adults come to adult music learning?	Tell me how you came to be involved in learning music/taking music lessons. • Why did you become involved in learning music/taking music lessons? • Tell me about your childhood experiences in learning music/taking music lessons.

Potential topics	What I want to learn	Potential interview questions
Adults' experiences of learning and making music	How do adults describe their experiences in learning and making music?	What stands out for you in your experiences of learning music? • What were your expectations when you began [as an adult]? • Have your expectations been met? If not, why? • Are there any aspects of learning music/taking music lessons that surprised you? If so, what? Why? • What aspects of learning music do you find most rewarding? • What aspects of learning music do you find most challenging? What stands out for you in your experiences of making music? • Performing for others? • What aspects of performing do you find most rewarding? • What aspects of performing do you find most challenging? Describe a typical music lesson. Describe a typical music-making event. • Rehearsals • Performances
Role of the music teacher	What are adult music learners' perspectives of the teacher's role?	Tell me what you see as the role of your teacher. Possible probe: • How does your teacher impact your learning? What helps you as a music learner? What else do you think would be helpful? Tell me about your plans to engage in music further.

If you have a specific interview format in mind (e.g., a phenomenological or ethnographic interview), your research questions should be formulated accordingly. For example, if you are using a phenomenological interview to examine the "experience of loss of a parent," a single question to prompt storytelling could suffice. For example,

• Think back to when you experienced the loss of your mother, and tell me about that.

Ensuing questions would be formulated from what the participant has already said, for example:

- You mentioned _____, tell me more about that.
- What happened then?
- Can you describe what that felt like?
- Is there anything else you would like to share about losing your mother?

In the same way, if you were taking an ethnographic approach to interviewing, your interview questions would depend on what you have observed and experienced in ongoing fieldwork related to your study's purpose. The development of interview questions in an ethnographic study is embedded within extended fieldwork in which the researcher develops an ethnographic record through observation and participation in the setting, before going on to conduct informal and formal interviews (see Chapter 6 for more information on interviewing in ethnographic research). Spradley (2016) suggested a sequence for doing this kind of work through asking descriptive questions, and then later structural and contrast questions. Some of Spradley's suggestions for asking descriptive questions (e.g. "grand tour" or "mini-tour") have provided question types that are commonly used in interviews that are not ethnographic, for example:

- Walk me through a typical day.
- Tell me how you would typically go about doing *x*.

We conclude this section by offering tips for formulating interview guides. When developing interview questions:

- Pose open, rather than closed questions (e.g., "Tell me about *x* . . ." rather than "Were you _____ when that happened?")
- Avoid the inclusion of possible responses in questions (e.g., "Tell me what you thought of *x*" rather than "Did you enjoy *x*?"). Completely avoiding assumptions about what might be learned is not possible in most studies, since by pursuing a topic, researchers come to any study with assumptions about what can be potentially learned and what a participant is thought to know concerning a topic.

- Avoid formulating multi-part questions (e.g., "Describe the challenges you've encountered learning *x*" rather than "Describe the challenges and benefits of learning *x*").
- Sequence interview questions from broad to narrow.

Finally, we offer some cautions as you develop your interview guide.

Cautions in Developing Interview Guides

Distinguishing Research Questions from Interview Questions. This means that thought should be given to the topics that participants can talk about that relate specifically to each research question. Phenomenological research questions most closely resemble an interview question that might be asked. For example, in one of Kathleen deMarrais's studies (Liljestrom et al., 2007) the research question was: "What are women teachers' experiences of anger in school settings?" The initial interview question was: "Think of a time when you experienced anger in a school setting, and tell me about that." There is much more to the conduct of a phenomenological study than asking open-ended questions, however. We advise new researchers to delve deeply in methodological literature on the topic (Freeman, 2021).

Collecting Demographic Data. Questions to do with attributes of a population (e.g., age, race and ethnicity, income, professional qualifications, no. of years of work experience) might be better examined using a cover sheet that each participant completes *after* an interview has been conducted, as these sorts of questions do not typically generate conversation.

Deciding Whether to Use Standardized Surveys or Qualitative Interviews. If you want to seek factual information, you may be better served by using a standardized survey. As mentioned earlier, qualitative interviews are useful for eliciting people's descriptions of perceptions, events, experiences, opinions, beliefs, understandings, and so forth. This is best done by asking questions in a way that elicits stories (e.g., use "Tell me about. . . ." openings).

Pursuing Research Questions That Examine the "Factors That Impact *x*." Interview questions that aim to elicit accounts to examine these sorts of questions can be included in a semi-structured interview. Think about the evidence generated by interview accounts. Interviewees' answers provide *perception/s* of "factors that impact *x*"—that is, what people *attribute* to be the reason for *x*. It has long been known that people do not necessarily know everything about themselves, or perhaps believe things that are not actually true. If you want to examine research questions about "what are the factors that [actually] impact x," consider what additional forms of evidence would contribute understanding of those.

Posing Knowledge Questions. Interviewees sometimes respond to knowledge questions as threatening, since people can (mis-)perceive that they are being examined or evaluated. If you want to learn about a participant's knowledge state, you can introduce this topic using these sorts of questions:

- Tell me what you have noticed about x.
- What stands out to you with respect to y?

Formulating Open-ended Questions. When formulating open-ended questions, be sure that sufficient information is included for participants to respond. If open-ended questions are too broad, participants might need further guidance from the interviewer concerning what they need to talk about. It is useful to experiment with different wordings prior to an interview. For example, "Tell me about your education" could be too broad for a participant to answer. Consider what you want to learn and ask an open-ended question that is sufficiently focused for participants to understand the information you are seeking. For example, if you want to learn about a person's educational history you could start with: "Tell me about your high school years," or "Walk me through your educational history before you came to study at x university."

Drafting Fewer Interview Questions. If you have a long list of questions, consider drafting fewer questions that can be followed by prompts that elicit more detail. When asking follow-up questions, the easiest and most effective way to do this is by using the participant's words, e.g.,

- You mentioned x, describe an example of how that works.
- You talked about y, what usually happens then?

Using Interview Guides Flexibly. If people have already answered a question, you might not need to ask the next question on the interview guide. That is something you will have to judge on a case-by-case basis in the interview. You cannot draft follow-up questions in advance, since you do not know what people will say. The sentence starters included above will be helpful. These formulations focus on *what the participants have said* (e.g., "You mentioned *x*, tell me more about that") rather than the *interviewers' interpretations of what participants have said* (e.g., "What I hear you saying is *y*"). This does not mean that interviewers should not clarify their understanding of participants' talk by asking clarification questions. Clarification can and should be used judiciously, however, since whatever interviewers say contributes to the co-construction of interview talk.

Conducting Interviews Phase

Once you are ready to conduct an interview, you will need to decide where it will be conducted, how, and by what means talk will be recorded. Historically, interviews have been conducted in person. This entails locating a space that is comfortable and quiet for both interviewer and interviewee. Researchers need to ensure that they make arrangements where both parties will feel secure since researchers have reported experiences of sexist remarks in interview research (Gailey & Prohaska, 2011) and sexual harassment in ethnographic research (Hanson & Richards, 2019). Researchers need to ensure that they conduct research safely. When interviewing participants in different cultural contexts, thought should be given to what is appropriate for the context. For example, in some cultures it might not be appropriate for a researcher to interview a participant of another gender alone, or to conduct interviews with people in the absence of other family members.

With social distancing guidelines and travel restrictions worldwide during the COVID-19 pandemic, many researchers needed to conduct interviews online. This continued a long tradition of using multiple technologies to conduct interviews. Researchers have conducted interview by telephone (Trier-Bieniek, 2012), email (James, 2016), Voice over Internet Protocol (VoIP) technologies such as Skype™ or Zoom™ (Lobe & Morgan, 2021), or podcasting apps such as Zencastr™ and text-based applications such as WhatsApp™ (Chen & Neo, 2019). Research on these different forms of communication modalities suggests that they can be used successfully to generate in-depth descriptions. Challenges have been reported, however. Effective use of these technologies relies on participants who have sufficient knowledge and expertise to use the applications selected, and interviewers' and interviewees' access to up-to-date equipment and stable internet connections to facilitate and sustain communication. Researchers must take care that any data generated in online formats is stored securely so that participants' confidentiality will not be breached.

Researchers have typically recorded what is said in interviews via note-taking (as in ethnographic and journalistic interviews), or audio or video recording. In contemporary practice, researchers use a variety of technologies to record interviews. These include cell phones, laptops, tablets, and digital audio and video recording devices. Whatever device you choose to use to record your interview, be sure that the file is downloadable and in a format that can be easily transcribed. Use of an external microphone can improve the quality of audio recordings for in-person interviews. Irrespective of what recording device is used, we have found it useful to make a secondary recording of interviews in case one fails. Researchers should take precautions to ensure that all equipment is fully charged or that there will be access to an external power supply, and that there is sufficient storage space on devices to ensure that interviews are fully recorded. After interviews, audio files should be backed up on secure external drives to ensure that they are not lost or accidentally deleted. In cases when interviews are being recorded within an application (e.g., VoIP), the files should be downloaded, backed up, and deleted from cloud storage systems. When backed up on local devices, be sure to password protect folders containing audio and video files and associated transcriptions.

Conducting interviews effectively entails a process in which researchers develop sufficient rapport with participants that they willingly answer questions in detail. Researchers typically explain the consent process and what they plan to do with the interview data either in correspondence prior to the interview or at the beginning of the interview. Interviewers should be well-prepared for interviews. This means knowing what topics to explore and completing sufficient background research on the topic and/or participants where applicable. In the actual interview, however, interviewers must judge on a moment-by-moment basis how to best facilitate talk. Our best advice here is to be respectful, listen intently, and follow the interviewee's leads. If an interviewee gets off topic, argues, or avoids answering questions, the interviewer will need to improvise. Once an interview is completed, thank the participant for their time, let them know if you will be in touch, and if more is expected of them (e.g., if you will send the interviewee a copy of the transcript or preliminary findings to comment on).

Post-Interview Phase

Once an interview has been conducted we recommend that researchers transcribe it as soon as possible. There are many transcription applications available that provide support. These allow researchers to upload an audio file and modify the speed of playback in order to transcribe talk incrementally. The services traditionally provided by professional transcribers have rapidly been replaced by automated voice-to-text transcription services that are fee-based (e.g., Otter.ai; Sonix™). Although these applications are powered by artificial intelligence, be sure to allow time to listen to the audio recordings and edit transcripts carefully. Whatever approach we have taken to transcription, and these have included paying professional transcribers, using transcription software, and using voice-to-text applications, we have found that transcriptions *always* need editing due to a variety of factors (i.e., people's accents, specific terminology that is not identifiable in an application or by a transcriber, the speed at which people talk, overlapping talk, and background noise). Listening to the audio files is part of the analytic process and will allow you to gain deep familiarity with the interview data.

Also think about the transcription conventions you will use. These vary considerably based on your approach to analysis (i.e., various forms of discourse analysis use different conventions to those used for thematic analysis). There is some key information that you should include on all transcriptions, irrespective of the transcription conventions used (see Box 5.1).

Box 5.1. Information to Include on an Interview Transcription.

Interviewer:	Sally Smith (ST)
Participant:	Jane Brown (JB) (Use a pseudonym.)
Date:	19 August 2022
Place of interview:	(e.g., Participant's home/office/synchronous online interview)
Beginning/Ending time:	2:30-4:00 pm
File name and duration:	XXXX.mp3
Transcriber:	Sally Smith

We recommend beginning a transcription by writing down all words spoken, including descriptions of other phenomena (e.g., laughter, crying), and anonymizing the transcription to preserve the confidentiality of the participant. As mentioned in the previous chapter, this entails using pseudonyms for the participant, and replacing real names of people and places mentioned that could lead to identification of a participant. Anonymization of transcriptions entails ethical decision-making, since omitting details can also entail loss of meaning of the interview accounts.

Analyzing Interview Data

In qualitative research, *inductive analysis* is commonly used to develop findings from repeated examination of data in the form of interview transcripts, documentary and archival data, and fieldnotes of observations. In contrast to *deductive analysis*, inductive analysts do not begin their research with preconceived analytic constructs into which they fit findings. Rather, analysts show how concepts generated from the data relate to and interconnect with one another. Thus, via inductive analysis the researcher builds interpretations from qualitative data, while deductive analysis tests hypotheses using data. In this section, we discuss inductive approaches to analysis that involve coding and categorization (Freeman, 2017), although we recognize that there are many forms of inductive analysis that do not involve coding (e.g., hermeneutic analysis, narrative analysis, conversation analysis, discursive psychology, phenomenological reduction). Coding practices are used widely by qualitative researchers across disciplines for different purposes (e.g., to develop grounded theory, to develop themes). There are many ways to move from codes (in which data have been reduced to core ideas), to themes (in which concepts are put back together again and interpreted). Here, we discuss *constant comparative analysis* and approaches to *thematic analysis* as two widely used forms of inductive analysis.

Constant Comparison Method

The constant comparison method was first described by the grounded theory researcher Barney Glaser (1965) and reprinted in the first book on grounded theory that he published with Anselm Strauss (1967). As the name suggests, this method "constantly compares" pieces of data. Groves (1988) described the purpose as "generating explicit categories which can help to provide an understanding of the data" (p. 277). The basic method was first described as encompassing four phases:

1. Comparing incidents applicable to each category.
2. Integrating categories and their properties.
3. Delimiting the theory.
4. Writing the theory (Glaser & Strauss, 1967, pp. 105–113).

Groves (1988) explained how Lincoln and Guba (1985) extended Glaser and Strauss's model by adding the concepts of "unitizing" to Stage 1 (pp. 344–345). By this, Lincoln and Guba were referring how to go about assigning "incidents" or "units" to broader categories. They suggested James Spradley's semantic domains as one approach (e.g., "x is a kind of y"; for more detail see Spradley [1979]). Lincoln and Guba (1985, p. 342) asserted that *memo writing* provides a way to help researchers during this stage. The process of "categorizing" in Stage 2 is explained by Lincoln and Guba as "a shift from comparing incidents to the primitive versions of the rules (properties) describing the category" (p. 342). During this process, researchers make explicit the properties (i.e., qualities or characteristics) of the categories (or larger groupings) by which preliminary codes are groups. During Stage 3, the researcher's task is to refine the developing theory until there is no need to add further examples (p. 344). Finally, Lincoln and Guba (1985) outlined a process for using member checks with both participants of the study and external auditors for further assessment of the interpretations.

How might you begin using this method? The first phase of the process involves coding the data set and comparing these codes or labels within and across interview transcripts. Charmaz (2000) suggested some points of comparison that analysts might consider:

- comparisons of different people (such as their views, situations, actions, accounts, and experiences);
- comparisons of data from the same individuals with themselves at different points in time;
- comparisons of incident with incident;

- comparisons of data with category; and
- comparisons of a category with other categories. (p. 515)

Glaser and Strauss split theoretically when Strauss and Juliet Corbin began developing their distinctive approach to grounded theory. In earlier versions of their book, *Basics of Qualitative Research*, Strauss and Corbin (1990) described the development of codes and the process of connecting these codes to one another as *axial coding*. In later versions of this book Corbin de-emphasized axial coding. Explanations of axial coding typically discuss identifying the "properties" and "dimensions" (i.e., a measurable property, such as speed or direction) of a code in relation to one another (Charmaz, 2014; Dey, 1999). To do this, researchers must constantly compare data and codes with one another.

Kathy Charmaz's (2014) approach to qualitative data analysis is known as "constructivist grounded theory." Charmaz's approach differed from those of Glaser and Strauss and Corbin in substantial ways. First, Charmaz rejected the idea of generating a "central or core category" (Strauss & Corbin, 1990) and did not explicitly use the family of codes developed by Glaser (1978) ("The Six Cs: Causes, Context, Contingencies, Consequences, Covariances and Conditions" [Charmaz, 2014]). In her work on identity and chronic illness, Charmaz developed *themes* to describe social-psychological processes. Second, Charmaz used a process of open and focused coding with memo writing throughout to develop her analyses. She did not emphasize the idea of elaborating on the properties and dimensions of each code in her methodological writing—although examples of her practice suggest that this may be implicit. She favored the use of gerunds (the noun form of a verb) in order to code her data (e.g., "reflecting on teaching" rather than "reflections"; "leading" rather than "leaders"). She argued that the use of gerunds "helps to define the implicit meanings and actions, gives researchers directions to explore, spurs making comparisons between data, and suggests emergent links between processes in the data to pursue and check" (Charmaz, 2014, p. 121).

Thematic Analysis

In a much-cited article, Braun and Clarke (2006) argued that "thematic analysis" (TA) should be accorded separate status as an analytic approach to qualitative data (e.g., along with narrative analysis or grounded theory). They have since refined their approach, which they now call "reflexive thematic analysis" (Braun & Clarke, 2020), arguing that a researcher's subjectivity is an "analytic *resource*" (p. 3). Braun and Clarke asserted that reflexive thematic analysis emphasizes a researcher's "reflexive engagement with theory, data and interpretation" (p. 3). Their 2020 article reiterated their guidelines for doing thematic analysis as involving six steps, those of: "1) data familiarization and writing familiarization notes; 2) systematic data coding; 3) generating initial themes from coded and collated data; 4) developing and reviewing themes; 5) refining, defining and naming themes; and 6) writing the report" (p. 4). In an effort to highlight how their initial paper (Braun & Clarke, 2006) has been widely misconstrued, Braun and Clarke (2020) have described 10 problems in the way that their approach to TA has been poorly applied, along with questions to ask in evaluating the quality of TA.

A core strategy associated with qualitative data analysis is writing memos. Through memo writing you will begin to make meaning and interpret your data, and generate more questions to ask of your data set. This is a very important step—so be sure to continue memo writing begun in the research process as you read your transcripts and begin coding. Rather than aiming to code your data *correctly*, we urge you to consider generating a plausible analysis that you can support with robust evidence from your data set. Working with others in small data analysis groups will assist this work, as you will find that others do not always interpret data similarly. When faced with disagreement to our analyses, we try to consider what we've missed and revise the coding to take account of others' viewpoints. And when we disagree with others' interpretations of our analyses, we work to build a stronger case using evidence for our interpretations.

Conclusions

In this chapter, we have discussed the steps entailed in planning for and conducting research interviews (i.e., How will participants be selected and recruited? What interview format will be used? What interview questions will be asked? Where should interviews be conducted? What technologies, if any, will be used to conduct interviews? How are interviews transcribed and analyzed?). Although the planning, conducting, and post-interview phases may seem overwhelming at first, remember that any large project proceeds one step at a time. In our own research, we have found that each phase of the research process brings its own rewards and helps us to keep going to completion. For examples of purpose statements and research questions for studies using interviews that were designed using a variety of theoretical perspectives, see the Appendix for studies by Oksana Parylo, Brigette Herron, Joseph Pate, Seon-Joo Kim, Kate Guthrie, and Janie Copple. These studies illustrate how interview research can be informed by different theoretical perspectives.

Activities

1. Review examples of others' interviews (peers, research interviews, media interviews) and analyze how questions are asked. Did interviewees answer the questions posed? Was information gained from the answers?

2. Select a theoretical perspective of interviewing (e.g., phenomenological, feminist, postmodern, decolonizing, new materialist) and locate as many articles as possible that discuss this approach. How might you apply this approach in your research?

3. Select an interview that augments talk with other sensory modes (e.g., photo elicitation, photovoice, object elicitation, graphic elicitation) and locate as many articles as possible that discuss this approach. How might you apply this approach in your research?

4. Select an approach to interviewing other than in-person individual interviews (e.g., telephone interview, synchronous or asynchronous online interviews, text-based interviews) and locate as many articles as possible that discuss this approach. How might you apply this approach in your research?

5. Develop an open-ended interview guide that will generate information relating to your research questions.

6. Consider the potential interviewees for your research study. In what ways does this group have special characteristics? Locate methodological literature that speaks to conducting interviews with participants who share these characteristics? (e.g., race, gender, language, age, status).

7. Plan and conduct three different types of interview to generate information concerning a research topic (e.g., in-depth individual interview, photo-elicitation interview, focus group).

Further Reading

Resources for Designing and Conducting Interview Studies

Gubrium, J. F., Holstein, J. A., Marvasti, A. B., & McKinney, K. D. (Eds.). (2012). *The SAGE handbook of interview research: The complexity of the craft* (2nd ed.). SAGE.

Roulston, K. (2022). *Interviewing: A guide to theory and practice.* SAGE.

Roulston, K. (Ed.) (2023). *Questions for questioners: Inventive approaches to qualitative interviews.* Myers Education Press.

Epistemic Interviews

Brinkmann, S. (2007). Could interviews be epistemic? An alternative to qualitative opinion polling. *Qualitative Inquiry, 13*(8), 1116–1138. https://doi.org/10.1177/1077800407308222

Postmodern Interviews

Denzin, N. K. (2001). The reflexive interview and a performative social science. *Qualitative Research, 1*(1), 23–46. https://doi.org/10.1177/146879410100100102

Decolonizing Interviews and Indigenous Methodologies

Chilisa, B. (2020). *Indigenous research methodologies* (2nd ed.). SAGE.

New Materialisms and Interviewing

Kuntz, A. M., & Presnall, M. M. (2012). Wandering the tactical: From interview to intraview *Qualitative Inquiry, 18*(9), 732–744. https://doi.org/10.1177/1077800412453016

Interviewing Elites

Lancaster, K. (2017). Confidentiality, anonymity and power relations in elite interviewing: Conducting qualitative policy research in a politicised domain. *International Journal of Social Research Methodology, 20*(1), 93–103. https://doi.org/10.1080/13645579.2015.1123555

Nir, E. (2018). Approaching the bench: accessing elites on the judiciary for qualitative interviews. *International Journal of Social Research Methodology, 21*(1), 77–89. https://doi.org/10.1080/13645579.2017.1324669

Interviewing Children and Adolescents

Clark, A. (2005). Ways of seeing: Using the Mosaic approach to listen to young children's perspectives. In A. Clark, A. T. Kjørholt, & P. Moss (Eds.), *Beyond listening: Children's perspectives on early childhood services* (pp. 29–49). The Policy Press.

Koller, D., & San Juan, V. (2015). Play-based interview methods for exploring young children's perspectives on inclusion. *International Journal of Qualitative Studies in Education, 28*(5), 610–631. https://doi.org/10.1080/09518398.2014.916434

Interviewing People with Disabilities

Benford, P., & Standen, P. J. (2011). The use of email-facilitated interviewing with higher functioning autistic people participating in a grounded theory study. *International Journal of Social Research Methodology, 14*(5), 353–368. https://doi.org10.1080/13645579.2010.534654

Hollomotz, A. (2018). Successful interviews with people with intellectual disability. *Qualitative Research, 18*(2), 153–170. https://doi.org/10.1177/1468794117713810

Interviewing the Deaf Community

Anderson, M. L., Riker, T., Gagne, K., Hakulin, S., Higgins, T., Meehan, J., . . . Wolf Craig, K. S. (2018). Deaf qualitative health research: Leveraging technology to conduct linguistically and sociopolitically appropriate methods of inquiry. *Qualitative Health Research, 28*(11), 1813–1824. https://doi.org/10.1177/1049732318779050

Interviewing Older People

Pleschberger, S., Seymour, J. E., Payne, S., Deschepper, R., Onwuteaka-Philipsen, B. D., & Rurup, M. L. (2011). Interviews on end-of-life care with older people: Reflections on six European studies. *Qualitative Health Research, 21*(11), 1588–1600. https://doi.org/10.1177/1049732311415286

Cross-cultural Interviewing

Griffin, G. (Ed.). (2016). *Cross-cultural interviewing: Feminist experiences and reflections.* Routledge.

Griffin, G. (2018). "It's not just a matter of speaking...": The vicissitudes of cross-cultural interviewing. *Qualitative Research Journal, 18*(2), 105–114. http://www.emeraldinsight.com/doi/10.1108/QRJ-D-17-00050

Translation and Interpretation

Clark, L., Birkhead, A. S., Fernandez, C., & Egger, M. J. (2017). A transcription and translation protocol for sensitive cross-cultural team research. *Qualitative Health Research, 27*(12), 1751–1764. https://doi.org/10.1177/1049732317726761

Santos, H. P. O., Black, A. M., & Sandelowski, M. (2015). Timing of translation in cross-language qualitative research. *Qualitative Health Research, 25*(1), 134–144. https://doi.org/10.1177/1049732314549603

Note

1. We do not use the term snowball sampling since this derives from research in which participants were first randomly sampled from a target population and then interviewed. Additional participants were recruited by asking interviewees for referrals to others with specific kinds of relationships with those interviewed (e.g., friend, parent). Snowball sampling was initially conceptualized as a way for researchers to make statistical estimations about the relationships among participants. See Goodman, L. A. (2011). Comment: on respondent-driven sampling and snowball sampling in hard-to-reach populations and snowball sampling not in hard-to-reach populations. *Sociological methodology, 41*(1), 347–353.

References

Alam, A., McGregor, A., & Houston, D. (2018). Photo-response: Approaching participatory photography as a more-than-human research method. *Area, 50*(2), 256–265. https://doi.org/10.1111/area.12368

Barbour, R. (2018). *Doing focus groups*. SAGE.

Braun, V., & Clarke, V. (2006). Using thematic analysis in psychology. *Qualitative Research in Psychology, 3*(2), 77–101. https://doi.org/10.1191/1478088706qp063oa

Braun, V., & Clarke, V. (2020). One size fits all? What counts as quality practice in (reflexive) thematic analysis? *Qualitative Research in Psychology*, 1–25. https://doi.org/10.1080/14780887.2020.1769238

Bravington, A. (2023). Experience in the abstract: Exploring the potential of graphic elicitation. In K. Roulston (Ed.), *Questions for questioners: Inventive approaches to qualitative interviews* (pp. 169–193). Myers Education Press.

Bravington, A., & King, N. (2019). Putting graphic elicitation into practice: tools and typologies for the use of participant-led diagrams in qualitative research interviews. *Qualitative Research, 19*(5), 506–523. https://doi.org/10.1177/1468794118781718

Brinkmann, S. (2007). Could interviews be epistemic? An alternative to qualitative opinion polling. *Qualitative Inquiry, 13*(8), 1116–1138.

Charmaz, K. (2000). Grounded theory: Objectivist and constructivist methods. In N. Denzin & Y. S. Lincoln (Eds.), *Handbook of qualitative research* (2nd ed., pp. 509–535). SAGE.

Charmaz, K. (2006). *Constructing grounded theory: A practical guide through qualitative analysis*. SAGE.

Charmaz, K. (2014). *Constructing grounded theory* (2nd ed.). SAGE.

Chen, J., & Neo, P. (2019). Texting the waters: An assessment of focus groups conducted via the WhatsApp smartphone messaging application. *Methdological Innovations, 12*(3). https://doi.org/https://doi.org/10.1177%2F2059799119884276

Copple, J. (2023). Object lessons: Considering object-interviews and narrative representation in qualitative research. In K. Roulston (Ed.), *Quests for questioners: Inventive approaches to qualitative interviews* (pp. 147–167). Myers Education Press.

Dey, I. (1999). *Grounding grounded theory: Guidelines for qualitative inquiry*. Academic Press.

Dinkins, C. S. (2005). Shared inquiry: Socratic-hermeneutic interpre-viewing. In P. M. Ironside (Ed.), *Beyond method: Philosophical conversations in healthcare research and scholarship* (pp. 111–147). University of Wisconsin Press.

Freeman, M. (2017). *Modes of thinking for qualitative data analysis*. Routledge.

Freeman, M. (2021). Five threats to phenomenology's distinctiveness. *Qualitative Inquiry, 27*(2), 276–282. https://doi.org/10.1177/1077800420912799

Gailey, J. A., & Prohaska, A. (2011). Power and gender negotiations during interviews with men about sex and sexually degrading practices. *Qualitative Research, 11*(4), 365–380. https://doi.org/10.1177/1468794111404315

Glaser, B. G. (1965). The constant comparative method of qualitative analysis. *Social Problems, 12*(4), 436–445.

Glaser, B. G. (1978). *Theoretical sensitivity: Advances in the methodology of grounded theory*. The Sociology Press.

Glaser, B. G., & Strauss, A. (1967). *The discovery of grounded theory: Strategies for qualitative research*. Aldine de Gruyter.

Goodman, L. A. (2011). Comment: on respondent-driven sampling and snowball sampling in hard-to-reach populations and snowball sampling not in hard-to-reach populations. *Sociological methodology, 41*(1), 347–353.

Groves, R. W. (1988). An analysis of the constant comparative method. *International Journal of Qualitative Studies in Education, 1*(3), 273–279.

Hall, J. N. (2020). *Focus groups: Cultural responsive approaches for qualitative inquiry and program evaluation*. Myers Education Press.

Hanson, R., & Richards, P. (Eds.). (2019). *Harassed: Gender, bodies, and ethnographic research*. University of California Press.

Harris, A., & Guillemin, M. (2012). Developing sensory awareness in qualitative interviewing: A portal into the otherwise unexplored. *Qualitative Health Research, 22*(5), 689–699. https://doi.org/10.1177/1049732311431899

Herron, B. A. (2022). 40 Years of qualitative feminist interviewing: Conceptual moments and cultivating ecosystems of care. *Qualitative Inquiry, 29*(6), 659–668. https://doi.org/10.1177/10778004221139611

Heyl, B. S. (2001). Ethnographic interviewing. In P. Atkinson, A. Coffey, S. Delamont, J. Lofland, & L. Lofland (Eds.), *Handbook of ethnography* (pp. 369–383). SAGE.

Holstein, J. A., & Gubrium, J. F. (1995). *The active interview* (Vol. 37). SAGE.

James, N. (2016). Using email interviews in qualitative educational research: Creating space to think and time to talk. *International Journal of Qualitative Studies in Education, 29*(2), 150–163. https://doi.org/10.1080/09518398.2015.1017848

Janesick, V. J. (2010). *Oral history for the qualitative researcher: Choreographing the story*. The Guilford Press.

Jaumot-Pascual, N., Smith, T., Ong, M., & DeerInWater, K. (2023). Photo elicitation with Native STEM students and professionals. In K. Roulston (Ed.), *Questions for questioners: Inventive approaches to qualitative interviews* (pp. 215–236). Myers Education Press.

Johnston, M. S. (2016). Men can change: Transformation, agency, ethics and closure during critical dialogue in interviews. *Qualitative Research, 16*(2), 131–150. https://doi.org/10.1177/1468794115569561

Kusenbach, M. (2018). Go-Alongs. In U. Flick (Ed.), *The SAGE handbook of qualitative data collection* (pp. 344–361). SAGE.

LeCompte, M. D., & Preissle, J. (1993). *Ethnography and qualitative design in educational research* (2nd ed.). Academic Press.

Lee, R. (2011). "The most important technique . . .": Carl Rogers, Hawthorne, and the rise and fall of nondirective interviewing in sociology. *Journal of the History of the Behavioral Sciences, 47*(2), 123–146. https://doi.org/10.1002/jhbs.20492

Liljestrom, A., Roulston, K., & deMarrais, K. (2007). "There's no place for feeling like this in the workplace": Women teachers' anger in school settings. In P. Schutz & R. Pekrum (Eds.), *Emotion in education* (pp. 267–284). Academic Press.

Lincoln, Y. S., & Guba, E. G. (1985). *Naturalistic inquiry.* SAGE.

Lobe, B., & Morgan, D. L. (2021). Assessing the effectiveness of video-based interviewing: A systematic comparison of video-conferencing based dyadic interviews and focus groups. *International Journal of Social Research Methodology, 24*(3), 301–312. https://doi.org/10.108 0/13645579.2020.1785763

Mason, J. (2018). *Qualitative researching* (3rd ed.). SAGE.

Merton, R. K., Fiske, M., & Kendall, P. L. (1956/1990). *The focused interview: A manual of problems and procedures* (2nd ed.). The Free Press.

Nordstrom, S. N. (2023). Past, present, futures of assembling object-interviews. In K. Roulston (Ed.), *Questions for questioners: Inventive approaches to qualitative interviews* (pp. 127–144). Myers Education Press.

Patton, M. Q. (2002). *Qualitative research and evaluation methods* (3rd ed.). SAGE.

Polak, L., & Green, J. (2016). Using joint interviews to add analytic value. *Qualitative Health Research, 26*(12), 1638–1648. https://doi.org/10.1177/1049732315580103

Reichertz, J. (2014). Induction, deduction, abduction. In U. Flick (Ed.), (pp. 123–135). The SAGE handbook of qualitative data analysis: SAGE.

Ritchie, D. A. (2015). *Doing oral history a practical guide* (3rd ed.). Oxford University Press.

Roulston, K. (Ed.). (2019). *Interactional studies of qualitative research interviews.* John Benjamins Publishing Company.

Roulston, K. (2022). *Interviewing: A guide to theory and practice.* SAGE.

Roulston, K. (2024). Examining the inside lives of interviews. In N. K. Denzin, Y. S. Lincoln, M. D. Giardina, & G. S. Cannella (Eds.), *The SAGE handbook of qualitative research* (6th ed., pp. 317–331). SAGE.

Roulston, K., & Flint, M. (2023). Mobile methods, go-alongs, and walking interviews. In K. Roulston (Ed.), *Questions for questioners: Inventive approaches to qualitative interviews* (pp. 195–214). Myers Education Press.

Roulston, K., Jutras, P. J., & Kim, S. J. (2015). Adults' perspectives of learning musical instruments. *International Journal of Music Education, 33*(3), 325–335. http://dx.doi.org/10.1177/ 0255761415584291

Sampson, H., & Johannessen, I. A. (2020). Turning on the tap: the benefits of using 'real-life' vignettes in qualitative research interviews. *Qualitative Research, 20*(1), 56–72. https://doi. org/10.1177/1468794118816618

San Pedro, T. (2021). *Protecting the promise: Indigenous education between mothers and their children.* Teachers College Press.

Spradley, J. P. (1979). *The ethnographic interview.* Wadsworth.

Spradley, J. P. (2016). *The ethnographic interview.* Waveland Press, Inc.

Strauss, A. L., & Corbin, J. (1990). *Basics of qualitative research: Grounded theory procedures and techniques.* SAGE.

Trier-Bieniek, A. (2012). Framing the telephone interview as a participant-centred tool for qualitative research: a methodological discussion. *Qualitative Research, 12*(6), 630–644. https://
doi.org/10.1177/1468794112439005

Van Manen, M. (2014). *Phenomenology of practice: Meaning-giving methods in phenomenological research and writing*. Routledge.

Way, A. K., Zwier, R. K., & Tracy, S. J. (2015). Dialogic interviewing and flickers of transformation: An examination and delineation of interactional strategies that promote participant self-
reflexivity. *Qualitative Inquiry, 21*(8), 720–731. https://doi.org/10.1177/1077800414566686

Participant Observation, Ethnography and Ethnographic Designs

---

LEARNING OBJECTIVES

After reading this chapter you should be able to:

- Understand the concept of culture as a theoretical framework for traditional ethnography.
- Articulate a definition of the term "culture."
- Consider critiques of traditional ethnography as well as various contemporary theoretical frameworks used to inform ethnographic practice.
- Identify and explain the planning of ethnographic work including site selection, writing a cover story, gaining entry, and establishing rapport with participants.
- Explain the role(s) you expect to assume in the field.
- Explain the different types of fieldnotes and create a strategy for taking fieldnotes in the site you have selected.
- Engage in data analysis/writing strategies for making sense of and representing ethnographic data.

Introduction

ETHNOGRAPHY IS A PRIMARY METHOD used by cultural anthropologists—the scientists whose goal it is to understand cultures and communicate this understanding to others (Spradley & McCurdy, 1990). The word *ethnography* is derived from two Greek words—*ethnos*, meaning a "nation, people, culture" and *graphos*, meaning "written" or "writing" (Brown, 1993, pp. 857, 1152). Not only is ethnography the written document about people in cultural groups, it is a method or approach to research—in that one *does* ethnography.

For decades, anthropologists have been studying cultural groups using a variety of research techniques associated with ethnography or fieldwork.

Spradley (1980), an anthropologist, described ethnography as the "work of describing a culture" (p. 3). Atkinson (2015), a sociologist, described ethnographic fieldwork as following the "dimensions of the everyday—spatial, temporal, interpersonal," with a view to tracing the "dimensions of culture—material, aesthetic, semiotic" (pp. 5–6). With a focus on what ethnographers actually do, Hammersley and Atkinson (2019) commented that:

> ethnography usually involves the researcher participating, overtly or covertly, in people's daily lives for an extended period of time, watching what happens, listening to what is said, and/or asking questions through informal and formal interviews, collecting documents and artefacts—in fact, gathering whatever data are available to throw light on the issues that are the emerging focus of inquiry. (p. 3)

Early 20th century anthropologists studied cultures considered "exotic" or "primitive" at the time. They lived among the "natives" for years, recorded and interpreted cultural behaviors, and reported back to the world of western academics.[1] The research was conducted on, not with, these communities. Researchers made their reports accessible to the public in Western countries through monographs and accounts in periodicals, excluding local community members as audience members. Training for such a huge undertaking was minimal. In the 21st century, both the role of the anthropologist and the approach to training ethnographic fieldworkers is considerably different. Those who intend to become involved in qualitative studies in fields like anthropology, sociology, education, and health often take courses in ethnographic research methods. Coursework on ethnography can help you develop expertise in participant observation, ethnographic interviewing, and report writing. By reading deeply in the literature, you can also reflect on documented and contemporary challenges of this method and how to avoid making unintentional mistakes and causing harm to participants and communities.

In this chapter, we examine the work of traditional ethnographers within the field of anthropology beginning with an exploration of the theoretical concepts of culture that inform this work. We present a discussion of the critiques of traditional ethnography that were developed by scholars from other fields before discussing the specific methods that ethnographers use from the beginning to the end of their fieldwork.

The Theoretical Underpinnings of Ethnography: The Culture Concept

Traditional ethnography was firmly based in a worldview focused on the goal of understanding the meanings people make of their experiences within their cultural contexts—insiders' or *emic* perspectives. Over time, scholars have debated what culture is and how it should be studied. Margaret Mead (1967 [1949]) described the work of early anthropologists:

> An anthropologist's materials of study are the behaviours of living peoples living together in ways that they have learned from their forebears, who shared common patterns of behaviour. The anthropologist's laboratories are primarily primitive societies, small, isolated groups of people who because of their geographical or historical isolation have remained outside the mainstream of history, and preserved special practices of their own that contrast vividly with behavior in large societies. (p. 23)

Assumptions embedded in this description were that the cultures studied by early anthropology were both "primitive" and "isolated." While anthropologists still travel and study widely around the world, the ubiquity of international travel and global communications ensure that there are few communities that remain "isolated" from Western countries. Further, recognition of the knowledge and wisdom among non-Western and Indigenous communities has led to understanding the racist origins of labels such as "primitive." Many anthropologists no longer seek out the "exotic," but work in their home communities exploring cultures of classrooms, schools, churches, public agencies, corporate settings, and other cultural sites.

The culture concept remains a central focus of anthropological work, but a precise definition is elusive. We include a few common definitions here to give you a sense of this variation based on different disciplinary perspectives. Garbarino (1977) explained that E. B. Tylor (1832–1917), known as the founder of cultural anthropology, defined culture as "that complex whole which includes knowledge, belief, art, morals, custom, and any other capabilities and habits acquired by man[2] as a member of society" (p. 31). This definition provided a unifying concept for American anthropologists in the 20th century. From a cognitive anthropological perspective, Spradley and McCurdy (1990) described culture as "the acquired knowledge that people use to generate behavior and interpret experience" (p. 16). With a focus on symbols and meaning, Geertz (1979) elaborated:

> The culture concept to which I adhere has neither multiple referents nor, so far as I can see, any unusual ambiguity; it denotes an historically transmitted pattern of meanings embodied in symbols, a system of inherited conceptions expressed in symbolic forms by means of which men communicate, perpetuate, and develop their knowledge about and attitudes toward life. (p. 89)

What is apparent in these definitions is the focus on culture as something both "exterior" and "interior" to people. Chang (2009) asserted that culture is a "product of interactions between self and others in a community of practice" (p. 23). Given the variation in how culture is defined, it is useful to remember that this concept is an invention of anthropology (Wagner, 1981). Nevertheless, the aim of anthropologists is to understand the culture of a group of people in particular contexts using ethnographic methods. At their best, anthropological accounts open doors through which we can read stories of others' lives and come to greater understandings of ourselves.

Critiques of Traditional Ethnography and Critical Theoretical Contributions

Ethnography has its roots in colonialism. Critics have pointed out the historical ties that anthropologists have had to Western expansion. While conducting research in colonial settings, researchers ignored how Western governments exploited local communities. Often funded by colonial governments, anthropologists chose to focus on topics such as kinship patterns and language while ignoring social injustices that shaped the very assumptions guiding their research. Since the 1960s anthropology and thus, ethnography, has been critiqued for this by Indigenous peoples, people of color, feminists, critical theorists, and other groups for not recognizing the assumptions embedded in the work as well as the fact that ethnography was often done *on* rather than *with* people. The slogan with roots in the disability rights movement "nothing about us without us" (Charlton, 2000, p. 1) is relevant here and reflects this critique. The "fly-on-the-wall," neutral observer stance adopted by early anthropologists has long been critiqued by scholars who argue that researchers are neither neutral nor dispassionate (Denzin, 1997).

Within the fields of anthropology and sociology, and applied fields such as education, nursing, and medicine, scholars have recognized these critiques but maintained a belief in the value of ethnography and ethnographic methods. By adopting theoretical stances informed by critical, feminist and Indigenous scholarship, researchers argued that they could create a critical ethnography, thereby rehabilitating the practices of ethnography and avoiding the exploitation of participants and communities. For example, in the late 1970s and 80s critical scholars in the field of education who were trained in traditional field methods began employing critical theory in what was labeled critical ethnography (cf. Anderson, 1989; Carspecken, 1996; Willis, 1977). During that same time period, feminists, Black feminists (Collins, 2009), and critical feminists used ethnographic methods to examine gendered spaces and address injustices (Madison, 2005). Later, critical race theorists, postcritical theorists (Noblit et al., 2004), and those using postcolonial (Brill de Ramírez, 2007) and critical Indigenous methodologies (Deyhle, 2009) critiqued colonial ethnographic practices (Dutta, 2020) and developed decolonizing approaches to inquiry (Smith, 1999). Some ethnographers have explicitly taken up participatory methods (e.g., Dazzo et al., 2023).

As scholars have continued to experiment with and develop new theoretical approaches to research, they applied these to well-established methods such as ethnography in efforts to attend to power relationships, the researcher's role, and the entanglements of the human with material and nonhuman entities. For example, you will now find methods texts that ponder the question of if and how new materialist theory could be used with ethnographic methods (e.g., Gullion, 2018). Like other qualitative methods, ethnographic methods are not static, but are continually subject to change and revision.

We offer examples of scholarship that has applied critical and poststructural theories to ethnography. Annette Markham (1998) used postmodern theories from the French sociologist Jean Baudrillard in her online ethnography. Lizbeth Berbary (Berbary & Johnson, 2012) used feminist poststructural theories to examine the experiences of sorority women at a land-grant university in the southern United States, while Begoña Aretxaga (1997) explored the gendered nature of political violence in Northern Ireland using poststructural theories. Philippe Bourgois and Jeff Schonberg (2009) drew on the work of Pierre Bourdieu, Karl Marx, and Michel Foucault to interpret data from their photo-ethnography of unhoused people in San Francisco. Khiara Bridges

(2011) drew on critical theories of race and legal theory in her ethnography of an obstetrics clinic that examined the racialized experiences of poor women. Nicole Gonzalez van Cleve (2016) took a critical approach to her ethnographic study of Crook County criminal court in Chicago.

As theories come under critique, new perspectives are created to address those critiques. While the methods of participant observation, ethnographic interviews, documents, and archives appear similar in different studies, the focus of the work and the ways methods are employed in a field differ depending on the particular theoretical framework used. This is especially apparent in regard to how researchers engage with participants in the field (e.g., relationships and collaboration), make ethical decisions, represent findings, and address audiences. For example, Henson (2020) reflected on the dilemmas of being a Black male ethnographer, using critical theory in his ethnography of hip-hop culture in Brazil. He concluded with a reimagined view of ethnography and the role of the critical ethnographer:

> Rather than conceiving of how Black people may become ethnographers, I want to instead conceive that the critical Black ethnographer illustrates how ethnography, and the idea of the ethnographer must change to foreground Black people as knowledge creators who interrogate the political stakes of cultural practices within larger social relations of power. In other words, rather than Blackness attempting to enter the category of the ethnographer, we would better serve to imagine how ethnography would have to be accommodated by Blackness to have a truly more radical and emancipatory critical ethnography. (p. 333)

As you can see from our brief review of traditional ethnography and recent critical contributions, ethnographers today use different theories to inform the questions they ask and the methods they use. As you design your ethnography, we provide questions to ask as you situate your work:

- What theories are informing your work?
- What scholars are you reading?
- What are the questions that can be asked using that theoretical framework?
- What might be the focus of your study?
- How will the theories you draw on inform:
  - the site(s) you select,

- your relationships with your participants,
- the ethics you employ as you do the work,
- the questions you ask of your data set as you analyze and interpret it, and
- the ways you represent the work in written and visual form?

We now turn to the methods of ethnography—what ethnographers actually do. In the next section, following a discussion of site selection, researchers' roles, entering the field, and emotions in the field, we examine the three primary methods used in ethnographic work: (a) participant observation, (b) ethnographic interviews, and (c) document and archival analysis.

Engaging in Ethnography

In ethnography the purpose is to understand what is happening in a particular site. As a social science researcher, your selection of a site will be informed by your theoretical framework and research purpose. Your personal and professional history may also inform your approach to human inquiry. You may be interested in understanding particular communities, organizations, schools, classrooms, or other configurations of human groups. Once you have selected the group you want to explore, your research questions are simple: What is happening here? What is the culture of this group of people? You may have other, more specific questions related to your particular frameworks, but these are stated in open-ended ways and are subject to change as we become immersed in the site. We do not always know at the beginning what the focus of an ethnography will be other than to explore aspects of the group you have selected. As you become more immersed in the field and learn about the community, you may hone in on particular aspects of the human experience within the group. Some researchers may lack the affordance of time required to conduct an ethnographic study, but may rely on ethnographic methods (e.g., participant observation, document analysis, informal and formal interviewing) in their research. Thus, we suggest strategies for engaging in ethnography that are useful for studies using ethnographic methods but are not ethnographies.

Site Selection

Prior to entering the field, you need to decide which "field" to enter—whether an in-person field or one found in the digital world. What site will you choose? You may know the purpose of your research, but still be without a site. You might find it helpful to brainstorm a list of all the possible sites that would suit your purpose, noting the possibilities and problems associated with each. Then you may want to visit those sites that seem most suitable. In selecting your site, consider places about which you do not already have intimate knowledge. The less knowledge and fewer assumptions you have about the site, the more you can bring fresh eyes to the setting. Your challenge is, to paraphrase Erickson's (1973) words, *to make the strange familiar and the familiar strange.* In studying something that is somewhat unfamiliar, you tend to have fewer assumptions about the phenomenon and consequently can be more open to it. For example, de Rond (2017) was invited to conduct an ethnography of a war-time field hospital in Afghanistan—as an embedded ethnographer and nonsurgeon, he witnessed and described the horrifying scenes involving medical teams working at the front lines.

One of the issues for some studies is that unless one has insider status and credibility, it will be difficult to enter a site. For example, Ho (2009) had worked at an investment bank before she began her ethnography of Wall Street. De Los Ríos (2020) had close ties to a Latinx bookstore in East Harlem, New York, where she conducted an ethnographic study of how the bookstore challenged, affirmed, and developed patrons' understanding of Latinx history and literature. There are numerous other examples of ethnographers studying within their home communities and with those familiar to them. Dennis et al.'s (2020) project *WomenWeLove* involved a research team comprised of an ethnically and racially diverse group of women ethnographers talking with women they love—including a friend, grandmother, mother, daughter-in-law—across generations with a focus on love, storytelling, and digitization. Informed by a feminist approach to ethnography and ethics in research, they argued for a loving relationship despite how familiar or strange the site may be:

> Contemporary ethnographers can, also, benefit from thinking relationally with their participants in the long term. Perhaps in specific situations ethnographers cannot start with those they love, but they can take up a loving attitude in relation to their participants. Such an orientation does not, by default, result in bias. Our

idea of beginning with love is to maximize good will and character throughout the process without assuming that such an orientation automatically produces biased work. Love is an aspect of knowing rather than an impediment to it. (p. 770)

In these familiar settings, the challenge is to continually reflect on your assumptions, insights, beliefs, relationships, and interpretations, and perhaps, like Dennis and her colleagues, begin with an orientation of love and good will.

Researchers' Roles

As you think about your site, consider the role you will take as a researcher. Spradley (1980) described five possible types of participation: nonparticipatory, passive, moderate, active, and complete. These align with the roles described by Hammersley and Atkinson (2019, citing Junker 1960), namely those of complete participant, participant as observer, observer as participant, and complete observer. The ethnographer functioning as a complete participant is totally immersed in the field. Those they work with are unaware of the research activities. This could be someone who is already a member of a group or organization or takes a job at a site in which they want to study. The covert nature of this role places strain on the researcher, may restrict the researcher's ability to move about freely within the site, and raises serious questions about the ethics of the work. On the opposite side of this continuum, we find the complete observer who has no contact with participants but uses distanced observation usually in public places or observes through one-way glass. The two roles in the middle of this continuum are those most frequently used by ethnographers: observer as participant and participant as observer. The observer as participant is in the setting with participants but tends to rely on the role of observer from an unobtrusive vantagepoint and may always be perceived as an outsider by participants. The participant as observer is a more fully functioning member of the cultural group. In this latter role, you are more likely to come to be viewed by participants as an insider.

As an ethnographer, you will want to reflect on possible roles prior to immersion in the site. If you choose, you can move from observer to participant within the context. The theoretical orientation you bring to the work will help you think about your role within that work. For example, Gross

(2023), a white woman in her early thirties from an upper middle-class background, conducted a 2-year ethnography with a group of Black teenage boys in a Philadelphia high school. She described herself as a full participant in the life of the school through ethnographic observations, interviews with students, teachers, administrators, and parents, and also used social media (Instagram™) with students' consent. Using a framework of Black masculinity and emotion management, Gross (2023) described how her roles and relationships with participants changed over time:

> Over time, students began to seek me out as a confidante, sharing thoughts they claimed they did not share with teachers or friends. In other work I have reflected on the complexities of the relationships that develop between youth participants and ethnographic researchers across identity differences, particularly in highly ordered school contexts (Gross 2022). Of course, my identity was also a limitation in that there are fundamental ways in which I can never fully access the depth of these boys' emotional lives and the risks that confront them. As Claudia Rankine (2020) vividly puts it, "there really is no mode of empathy that can replicate the daily strain of . . . being black." This surely played out both in the field and in my analysis. (p. 268)

The particular site you choose as well as your access within that site will shape your participation and will enable some relationships and constrain others. In the example above, if Gross had assumed the role of a teacher, she may have had more limited access to this group of teenagers.

Scholars taking a critical orientation to the work are faced with the possibility that community members might not agree with their theoretical orientations. That is why critical ethnographers address power and positionality in relation to their studies. For example, critical ethnographer Michelle Fine (2006) wrote that strong objectivity—a concept forwarded by Sandra Harding (1993)—is "achieved when researchers work aggressively through their own positionality, values and predispositions, gathering as much evidence as possible, from many distinct vantage points, all in an effort not to be guided, unwittingly, by predispositions and the pull of biography" (p. 89, italics in original). One example is provided by critical ethnographer De Los Ríos (2020), who noted her intent to serve as a "worthy witness" to the bookstore community, who stood in "solidarity to promote social change" (p. 429).

Beginning the Work

Once you have received participants' consent, begin your ethnography by go-ing to "the field." Remember that consent must be navigated throughout a project as you develop relationships with participants (Klykken, 2022). In or-der to avoid ethical breaches in long-term research contexts, some researchers choose to implement a "continuous consent" process in which they remind participants throughout a project that they are generating data for research purposes and that participation is voluntary. Navigating the informed con-sent process is challenging, however, since participants might misconstrue reminders of continuous consent as invitations to discontinue participation.

Like the early anthropologists, spend as much time as possible in your site. You may not be living among the cultural group, but you will participate in many activities of the group for a period of time. Let's use an example of class-room ethnography. If you have chosen this site, you have already "bounded" your study by the length of the academic year, the number of days in a week and the number of hours a day at school. Once that academic year is finished, the students move on to new teachers, so you will never be able to reconstruct the same cultural group, thus bringing a natural end to your fieldwork. Other field sites may not be quite so restricted by external structures and practices and therefore may not have such a natural stopping point. You will need to make decisions about when to observe in the site and how long to stay during each visit. You may want to start with several short visits until you become more experienced with and comfortable taking fieldnotes. While in the site, decide where to place yourself, what to observe, and what role you want to play in the research process. It is important to begin by being open to what is happening in the site rather than focusing in too quickly on one particular aspect of the site. In other words, you are a learner in that site, so you will want to be open to the understandings the group has to offer you. Sometimes, the ethnography produced may not be in keeping with the narrative that of-ficials from an organization wish to tell. For example, publication of de Rond's (2017) ethnography of a field hospital was delayed due to objections from the Ministry of Defense in the United Kingdom.

Establishing Rapport

You may find yourself feeling awkward or uncomfortable during your first visits to the site. You may not be sure what to do, what to watch, or how to act in the site. Perhaps the best advice is to find a comfortable spot where you are away from the center of attention while you *watch* and *listen* to what is going on. You may want to just hang around and get to know the site rather than trying to record field notes right away. Be sure you are introduced to everyone in the setting with an explanation of your research so there are no questions as to who you are and how you will fit into the setting. Still, they may be wary of you if you are a stranger in the site. In an ethnography based in a small Appalachia community, George Hicks (1976) recounted this initial uncertainty of his participants, who at various times reported him to be an "FBI man," "a psychiatrist," "a tourist," and "a schoolteacher." It took him a full 6 months before he came be accepted as someone who community members could trust with their stories, rather than an outsider, or as old-timers called him, a "furriner" (p. 1). Hicks reported that:

> The longer I stayed, however, the more willing were people to accept me as a person with whom they could indulge their pleasure in talking about themselves. My curiosity about the community people soon became just one aspect of my interest in local history and customs. Few people had any conception of what an anthropologist was, and I explained my study as an historical one. This seemed to satisfy everyone. (p. 1)

Although this study took place decades ago, like Hicks, you will need sufficient time to establish rapport with participants and become more comfortable with the roles you have selected for yourself while in the site. The time it takes for you to be accepted into the community depends on many factors. We have found in our own qualitative studies, the more genuinely interested you are, the more likely people are to construct relationships with you. In addition to feeling a more comfortable fit within the community, you begin to develop technical skills as an ethnographer and begin to feel more competent in your abilities.

Emotions in Fieldwork

Human inquiry is never free from emotions. Ethnography, perhaps more than any other type of qualitative research, provides opportunities for a wide range of emotional experience during the course of the work. Since ethnographers spend long time periods in the field, they often experience the same range of emotions they do in their daily lives outside research projects. As with other endeavors, researchers begin fieldwork with a sense of anticipation and excitement. They might feel frustration over their initial lack of skill in the process of recording fieldnotes when so much is going on around them. As the work continues, ethnographers experience loneliness, boredom, and might even question the point of their work. Ethnographers have more opportunities than other researchers to develop relationships with participants because of the length of time they spend in the field and the nature of ethnographic research. As researchers become more immersed in the lives of participants, they have more opportunities to experience anger, passion, love, apathy, pleasure, pride, confusion, dismay, embarrassment, empathy, and other human emotions. You can be sure that you will experience both pleasant and unpleasant emotions during the course of your ethnographic work. Margery Wolf (1999) described these emotions for the beginning ethnographer:

> The first field trip is a stunning roller coaster of self-doubt, boredom, excitement, disorientation, uncertainty, exhaustion, bullying, being bullied, cajoling, being cajoled—in the course of which we somehow accumulate "data," precious notebooks packed with disorganized thoughts, detailed observations of minutiae, descriptions of rituals, transcripts of conversations, diagrams, and detritus. (pp. 354–355)

It helps to record this bombardment of emotions in your research journal. It may also help to talk with supportive people and/or mentors outside the field site to help sort out difficult emotions. In a recent essay focused on competencies for ethnographers working with vulnerable populations, Winfield (2022) described her emotions in a 3-year study working with cadet candidates at the U.S. Military Academy Preparatory School at West Point. She explained:

> I knew relationships were integral to the research process and had no difficulty building rapport but was not adequately prepared to build healthy boundaries and avoid emotional enmeshment. Moreover, I was away from friends and

loved ones completely immersed in an all-encompassing field site. Although I had read articles on emotions in the field, I was taken aback by the impact of this isolation on my mental health and had no self-care techniques ready at my disposal. (p. 143)

Be aware of your emotions and take them seriously as you progress through your work. Emotional reactions may signal a need to consider your relationships with participants, to change your approaches in some way, to think about ethical issues in the fieldwork, or to simply process very appropriate reactions to human experiences. When ethnographers work in dangerous contexts researching stressful topics, there may be experiences that cause intense distress. Warden (2013), for example, discussed how her ethnographic research with the sex worker community in Guatemala involved a "daily bombardment of violence" (p. 156). Warden experienced not only guilt when comparing her privilege to those of participants, but the symptoms of posttraumatic stress disorder (PTSD) as a result of her fieldwork experiences when she returned home.

Recording Cultural Behaviors: Taking Fieldnotes

Fieldnotes—the detailed notes that you take as a participant observer in the research site—form the primary database for ethnographic studies. In fieldnotes, you describe the site, what people say and do there, and what you make of what you're seeing. Taylor and Bogdan reminded us that "if it is not written down, it never happened" (Taylor et al., 2016, p. 53). An artist friend of the first author, Kathleen, described using his "art eyes" to scope out possibilities for paintings. When he has his art eyes on, he is keenly aware of the light, color, textures, and shapes in the landscape. As a participant observer, you go into the site with this kind of acute attention—with your "ethnographer's eyes" in sharp focus.

Ethnographers construct different kinds of fieldnotes during the course of their work. Spradley (1980) described four types of fieldnotes:

(a) *Condensed fieldnotes* are those notes the researcher takes in the site in the midst of complex and ongoing social interactions. Since it is impossible to document everything that happens, the condensed fieldnotes are reconstructions of the multitude of activities and interactions that take place. You can never hope to catch everything. Condensed notes can be in any form including notebooks, index cards, and/or the variety of digital equipment (cell phones, electronic notebooks, etc.) you have available.

(b) *Expanded fieldnotes* are the expanded versions of the condensed notes. It is essential for you to expand your condensed fieldnotes in electronic form as soon as possible after leaving the site for easier analysis later. Your condensed notes serve as reminders to help you elaborate on your field observations. You may find you spend at least as much time and probably more expanding your notes as you did in the field. Spradley's (1980) "Concrete Principle" in both condensed and expanded fieldnotes is helpful in learning to take fieldnotes. This principle refers to attempts to record descriptions of actions in specific, concrete *low-inference* detail. For example, a high inference statement might be "an elderly man crossed the street" where a low inference description is "a white-haired, bearded man using a walking stick slowly navigated the crosswalk." Fieldnotes should include verbatim narratives of what people say and do. Remember to use all your senses—see, hear, taste, smell, and feel—in making these records.

(c) *The fieldwork journal* is another form of fieldnotes in which, with dated entries, you write about your process during the course of the research. It is helpful for you to describe your research decisions, emotional reactions, hunches, questions, problems, and other reactions to the research process.

(d) *Analysis and interpretation fieldnotes* are where you record your understandings, observed patterns, interpretations, insights, and analyses. These records can be incorporated into the fieldnote journal. These *high inference* notes are where you put your thinking and theorizing into text form. Glaser and Strauss (1967) refer to these types of notes as theoretical memos.

Clifford (1990) provided another way to think about the different types of fieldnotes. He described (a) *inscription* as the quick notes—mental or written—that are made during the course of the action in the field; (b) *transcription* as the notes made in the form of dictation from conversations with our participants; and (c) *description* as "the making of a more or less coherent representation of an observed cultural reality. While still piecemeal and rough, such field descriptions are designed to serve as a data base for later writing and interpretation aimed at the production of a finished account" (Clifford, 1990, pp. 51–52). Descriptions are the work we do in our private places away from the interaction and activities of the field.

When you first enter your site you may feel clumsy and unsure of your notetaking. You may find it frustrating trying to "capture" everything—an impossible task. Break the work up. Begin by looking around and describing the site in as much detail as possible. Draw a map or sketch a picture. Take a photo. On subsequent days, you can focus in on different aspects of field activities. Think of all the things you might observe in the setting—the space itself; objects and artifacts in the space; the people; what people say and do; how people move about in the setting; the sounds, smells and feelings in the setting. Although you may feel a bit self-conscious in writing in the site, if you have carefully explained your project and your fieldnote practice, your participants may accept you as a new participant in the site and care little about your notetaking.

In addition to all the possibilities for observation, the quick pace of activities and interactions in your site might surprise you. You might feel you cannot possibly write enough to adequately describe what you see. The following excerpt from an ethnographer's journal captures the challenges of beginning fieldwork.

> I noticed that I would often make eye contact with people in the room. This made me a bit anxious, as I was worried that I would somehow break my cover as an observer. I would try to time out when I would look in that direction again. This was to avoid making eye contact with them for a second time. I am curious to think if my concern about making a connection inhibited my ability to objectively observe the participants. I also noticed that I seemed to veer from the purpose of the study (non-verbal interactions between others) as there were not a lot of interactions. For a while my mind drifted into thinking about objects, observing their phones, headphones, and drinks (water bottles vs coffee). By shifting my focus on objects in the room, I might have missed some nonverbal interactions between students. (Included with permission from a former student in Janie's qualitative research design course.)

Despite your first impressions, with time and experience, you will become more familiar with the site and more skilled at taking fieldnotes. The work will become routine. This process of participant observation and writing fieldnotes is the primary work of the ethnographer. As Geertz (1973) reminded us, the "ethnographer 'inscribes' social discourse; he [or she] writes it down. In so doing, he [or she] turns it from a passing event, which exists only in its own moment of occurrence, into an account, which exists in its inscriptions and can be reconsulted" (p. 19).

Designing a system of fieldnote-taking that fits your style is useful to your process. It is helpful to have a consistent header to introduce your fieldnotes consistently each day you are in the field. The following header ensures you get the information you need later as you summarize and analyze your date:

- Date
- Name of Observer
- Place of Observation
- Time Began
- Time Ended

In addition to this header information, within the body of the fieldnotes, write relevant information about your participants. Take notes on the actions and behaviors people engaged in and their utterances. Attend to what people say using direct quotes as much as possible. Be sure to note who is speaking for each quote. You'll have time later in your ethnographic interviews to find out more about these participants, including how they identify in terms of gender, race, social class, ethnicity, abilities, and so forth, so you may want to avoid making assumptions without checking. If you can't get full quotes, jot down key words and phrases to enable you to reconstruct the conversation as much as possible later in your expanded fieldnotes. Note any nonverbal behaviors such as expressions, gestures, locations in the site, postures, eye contact, and touch. Take notes on the artifacts or things that are present and being used in the site. Which are not used?

Box 6.1 provides a series of questions for you to use in evaluating fieldnotes throughout your process. If you find you are neglecting some of these aspects, you can focus on those more the next time you are in the field. Think of this work as a process where you begin with a focus on the whole site, then as you describe that, begin to focus in on more specific happenings in the site in relation to your research focus and questions. Once the site description and mapping are done, move on to another aspect of the site. Each time you plan to go into the site, set a goal for what you want to focus on. As you gain experience in the field and get to know it more, you'll begin to theorize about what is happening, you may refine or change your research questions, and may encounter the unexpected—surprises you didn't anticipate—leading to more questions or changed research focus.

Box 6.1. Evaluating Your Fieldnotes.

---

1. Do fieldnotes have identifying information such as date, time, place of observation?
2. Is there a thorough, concrete description of:
   a. the setting?
   b. the participants?
   c. the artifacts or things in the setting?
3. Is there a map of the setting?
4. Are direct quotations from the participants provided? Does each quote have a speaker identified?
5. Is there evidence and a description of:
   a. a sequence of events that occurred during the observation period?
   b. laughter, tone of voice, and speed of speech?
   c. nonverbal behaviors such as gestures, eye contact, etc.?
6. Have you noted your own reactions, questions, and comments about the observation period?
7. Have you noted questions you want to address in the next observation period?

What you are attempting to do is construct "thick description" of a social site, which will yield careful interpretations of the meanings people make within a site. However, consider how such thick description could compromise participant confidentiality. In a review of the practice of using thick description in ethnography, Goldensher (2023) cautioned researchers in its use, depending on the context. She explained:

Thick description has long been the standard for both credibility and quality in ethnographic, community action, and participatory observation research across the disciplines, but I argue that researchers have an ethical obligation to consider when to decline to describe thickly (p. 139). . . . We must be aware of our capacity to harm communities we depict entirely unintentionally—in the course, in fact, of the ordinary work of thick description. How do we reconcile the scholarly imperative to shore up the legitimacy of our claims through thick description with our ethical imperatives not to endanger the subjects of our research? (p. 151)

As you engage in the process of generating fieldnotes, you will be making many decisions about what to focus on, what to write, and who to include and omit. These detailed fieldnotes will ultimately be used in the construction of a written report. Goldensher's advice to consider the ethics of how we engage in thick description and its possible consequences for participants is important. For example, although Stein (2010) promised anonymity to the participants of her study of a small town divided by a local ballot initiative against gay and lesbian civil rights, when her book *The Stranger Next Door* was published, readers were able to identify participants based on her detailed descriptions. This not only created controversy in the town but outed several of her participants.

The digital age has changed the way ethnographers do their work. Smartphones with their capabilities to easily record and take notes and photos, as well as electronic notebooks, and a variety of digital means to store and manage data are convenient and provide new opportunities for the way we document and represent ethnographic work and may be less conspicuous. As Dennis et al. (2020) argued, "Digitization is not just a means to an end, not only a tool in the technical sense. Digitization is a dialogic mode of engaging where images, sound, text, and arrangement on the page reflect and resource our ongoing interpretations" (p. 766). Your technological interests, skills, and willingness to learn new tools will determine the extent to which you'll employ technology in your data generation, analysis, and representation.

Understanding Cultural Knowledge: Ethnographic Interviewing

In addition to the participant observation components to the research process, you will need to talk with participants in the field site. Since we have explored interview studies in detail in an earlier chapter, we touch briefly on the role of interviews in ethnography. Interviews in ethnographies are an additional way to understand the meaning people make within particular sites. You can make careful and systematic observations based on people's actions, but without talking to people in the site, you will be unable to gain an emic or insider perspective. You might think of ethnographic interviews as conversations with people on a continuum from brief, informal chats that take place during the course of regular social interactions to more formal, recorded interviews such as those we described previously. You will want to use ethnographic interviews throughout the study to gather information, get people's perspectives on what is happening in the culture, and confirm your own interpretations of what you have already observed.

We typically begin an ethnography with more emphasis on participant observations to give context from which to generate interview questions. You can learn much about a context by watching, listening, and participating in activities without jumping in too quickly with researcher questions. Time early in the field is better spent getting to know participants in the community, observing daily activities, and trying to figure out community relationships. Patience, relationship building, and getting into the natural flow of community activities can lead to rich understandings. For example, Matthew Desmond (2016), in his ethnographic study of eviction in a U.S. city, described his initial decision to move into a particular trailer park "after reading in the newspaper that its residents could face mass eviction" (p. 317). Although the expected mass eviction did not happen, Desmond wrote, "I decided to stay anyway because the park proved a fine place to meet people getting the pink [eviction] papers" (p. 317). He went on to note that his decision to remain in the trailer park afforded opportunities to make connections with two key informants in his study.

Selecting Key Actors

Traditionally, anthropologists talked about "key informants" and how to select these informants. These are the individuals who are insiders to the culture and serve as "culture brokers" by providing historical information about the context, explaining cultural behaviors, and answering the ethnographer's questions. Since the term informant carries negative connotations, we refer to these individuals as "key actors" as does Fetterman (1989). As you begin your study, you may find that a participant in the site may approach you with an interest in your study or with helping you to understand the culture. This person may become a key actor in your study and an invaluable source of information. You will probably develop a close relationship to this person while you are engaged in fieldwork. Often relationships with key actors continue long after projects are completed. Sometimes a key actor occupies a marginal status in the site and may have had experiences outside the culture that enable comparisons across cultural contexts and consequently, explain cultural understandings to you. Remember that any key actor is providing a situated perspective of the setting, which is why it is useful to work to gain multiple perspectives throughout the life of a study. Try to talk with a wide variety of people, exploring various interpretations of what you are observing and experiencing in the site to avoid generating one-dimensional interpretations. Keeping an inventory is helpful to document who you talked with, when you had the conversations, how long they lasted, and perhaps other details of these informal interviews. Through this inventory you can assess whether or not you have talked with people who provide the depth of knowledge you need to most adequately understand the multiple interpretations that are evident in any field study.

Exploring Archival and Documentary Evidence

While we learn about cultures through peoples' behaviors and their words, their artifacts and documents are important aspects of the setting. Artifacts come in a variety of forms. In ethnography, the site provides the context for the types of documentary evidence that might be available. People in some sites are more reliant on written documents than others. These might be in the form of official documents such as court or school records or they may be informal written documents such as notes or shopping lists. In addition to written documents, you may find drawings, paintings, photographs, or films, which portray aspects of the culture in visual form. All the documents available to you in the site become part of the ethnographic record and can contribute to your analysis and reconstruction of the cultural narrative. Written documents in both paper and digital forms may include memos, notes, diaries, journals, letters, autobiographies, newspaper accounts, court records, school records, books, curriculum guides, shopping lists, report cards, planning books, meeting agendas and minutes, datebooks, account ledgers, signs, instructions, emails, texts, and so on. Visual documents might include drawings, paintings, photographs, posters, videos, films, postcards, graffiti, and flyers. In the midst of your study, you might find it helpful to brainstorm a list of possible artifacts and documentary evidence you could examine.

We have discussed primary forms of evidence in ethnographic fieldwork: participant observation, interviews, and documents and material culture as evidence that enable you to gain understandings of a setting. Often called *triangulation* by qualitative researchers, the use of multiple sources can help you check one source against another. You can confirm some understandings and find contradictory evidence in others. Pitman and Maxwell (1992) noted that "this layering of data across time, informants, events, documents, and so on is an essential validation technique for conclusions and recommendations" (p. 763). You'll want to plan for specific ways you intend to use multiple data sources into your ethnographic research design before you enter the site and at different points in your ethnography, take stock of where you are and where you're going. Assessing exactly what you have done and what still needs to be done is useful in chronicling your process.

Fieldnotes
1. Number of observations completed, and total time spent in the field
2. Number of pages of condensed fieldnotes
3. Number of pages of expanded fieldnotes
4. List of various times/contexts sampled in field

Ethnographic Interviews
1. List of people talked to in informal conversations
2. List of people interviewed more formally
3. List of people to be interviewed and why

Artifacts and Documents
1. List of documents and material objects included in fieldnotes and descriptions
2. List of documents and other material objects still to review

We turn next to a discussion of how researchers conclude their ethnography.

Leaving the Field

You may never feel like you are finished with an ethnography. There is always more data to gather, more activities to observe, more people to interview, and more documents to study. At some point, however, you need to stop the participant observation portion of the study and leave the field. It may be a bit easier if there is a natural stopping point, such as the end of a school year. You may have come to the end of your time or resources. With enough time in the field what you are seeing becomes repetitive, which might suggest an end to fieldwork. In Kathleen's ethnography, she could anticipate what would happen next in the classroom—the activities stayed much the same from day to day until the end of the school year, a natural stopping point.

It is often difficult to leave the field. Spending days, weeks, and months with people in your field site, even a digital one, you become friends with many. Your participants have given you the privilege of entering and sharing their lives during this time. Finding ways to gradually leave the field is useful so that your participants don't feel abruptly abandoned as you transition to the writing stage of the work. Arranging to return to the field to share and get feedback on your findings can help with this transition.

Some participants will be eager to know about your interpretations, while others are less enthusiastic or even uninterested. As ethnographers, the study becomes central to our lives—we become totally immersed in our work. The study is not often the central feature of the lives of our participants, although it is useful to remember that participants can read reports and identify events and participants that you describe. Since participants have families, jobs, and a host of activities that consume them, it should not be surprising if they are just casually interested in the outcomes. That is not to say that the participants are not interested in what researchers do as people. Often these personal ties are lasting, and participants may not want you to leave. For example, Smith (2019) showed how children towards the end of her fieldwork in a classroom worked to prolong their interactions with her because they were upset that she was leaving. As the study draws to a close, consider how best to leave the field, how to explain your leaving to the community, and how to keep your relationships open to new possibilities.

Ethnographic Data Analysis

Data analysis in ethnography is ongoing from the beginning to the end of the process and can involve a wide variety of strategies including categorizing, synthesizing, interpreting, writing, and constructing data displays. In this section we describe a number of activities and approaches to assist you in making sense of your ethnographic study. There is no one correct way to systematize or analyze ethnographic data. You might think of this as the "head work" of the study. How do you make meaning of what you are seeing and hearing in the field site? Spradley, a cognitive anthropologist, focused on the language participants use to understand and categorize their worlds. Spradley (1980) provided guidelines for this work with a focus on domain and taxonomic analyses where a researcher focuses on participants' use of language to reflect the underlying culture. A domain might be all the ways participants refer to people and subsets of people in a site. For example, in a school setting, participants may use labels to describe kinds of teachers, administrators, or students by type or level. Their language may illustrate how they see the relationships among these people or may give clues as to the implicit and explicit culture of the site. Researchers may use taxonomies focused on all aspects of the site—places and spaces, actions, activities, events, objects, goals, and feelings—to categorize their observations in the site. A taxonomy is simply a way to categorize data. In the above example of domains, a taxonomy of a teacher might categorize all the different activities they engage in throughout the day or all the different objects and spaces within the classroom as used within these activities. Taxonomies show relationships as means to make sense of a cultural site. Building taxonomies is one analytic approach ethnographers use, but there are many other ways to make sense of one's data. For example, while thematic analysis is a common analytic approach, researchers also use narrative and discourse analysis and apply poststructural theories to analyze ethnographic data. In the next section, we explore writing activities that will assist you to better understand what is happening in the site.

Writing Up Ethnography

Writing *is* analysis. By writing we express what we are observing and understanding. We write throughout the ethnographic process to make sense of things. An early writing activity is a *site description*. Using fieldnotes as well as a map of the site, create a detailed description of the site. What does it look like? What does it feel like? What does it smell like? What are the sounds you hear in the site? What are the different parts or sections of the site? How do people use those? Ask yourself these and other questions as you write the site into being. If someone outside the site read your site description, they should have little difficulty imagining what it looks like. Similar to the site description, you'll want to write *participant descriptions* of the various people or types of people in the site. Through these descriptions you are introducing your readers to your site. The use of direct quotes may enhance readers' understanding of the participants. Another form of ethnographic writing is the *typical day vignette* where you articulate the flow of the day with the various activities involved. How does the day begin and end? What are the various changes within the day? How does one activity change to the next? In each of these writing activities, you discover what you know and where there are gaps in your knowledge of the site, and consequently, what information you need to find out during your next visit to the site. This is an iterative process in which the writing points to aspects you need to further explore. In addition to these suggested activities, you will want to write analytic memos based on your ongoing data analysis.

Traditionally, many ethnographies were written as *case studies*. Since the work focused on one community, the research was bounded by that community, and thus a case format was used to represent the work, often in monographs. In a recent example, Kurie's (2018) *In Chocolate We Trust: The Hershey Company Town Unwrapped* is an ethnography of Hershey, Pennsylvania with a focus on the Hershey Trust and its influence on the life of the community. Kurie presented the case study in five different chapters: the scandal, the man and the town, the company, the school, and the gift. Each of these chapters described an aspect of the case and contributes to a fuller understanding of the impact the Hershey Trust has had on this community. While scholars such as Merriam (1988, 1991, 1998), Stake (1995), Yin (2017), and Simons (2009, 2020) have all presented case studies as a type of research design, we chose not to single it out as its own design in this book, but as a way to represent the study. If you choose to use a case study format, you'll want to engage your reader in the context of the study, your research purpose, and questions and incorporate the writing activities suggested above (participant descriptions, typical day vignettes) in addition to your findings and conclusions. Researchers have great flexibility in how they want to structure and represent ethnographic studies in case study form.

As Wolcott (1994) reminded us, "qualitative researchers need to be storytellers" (p. 17) and encouraged writing activities such as critical or key events, use of plot and characters in play format to tell the story, or even the use of the mystery genre to organize the ethnography. More recently, ethnographers (e.g., Blackledge & Creese, 2019; Pachirat, 2018; Waterston, 2014) have used literary elements such as fictionized accounts, dramatic performance, poetry, or simply the use of constructed dialogue within a narrative description. Contemporary scholars treat ethnographies as a written genre, deconstructing their textual elements the way one would with other literary genres to better understand traditional ethnographic forms of writing with regard to its characterization, plot, point of view, and tone as presented to the reader. They call for explorations into alternative forms of ethnographic writing where the varied voices of researcher and researched are reflected in the texts and where a variety of literary forms are used to tell these stories (e.g., Clifford & Marcus, 1986; Coffey, 2018; Goodall, 2000).

Conclusions

In this chapter we introduced ethnography, beginning with a discussion of the culture concept as the basis of traditional ethnographic work. We explored the critiques of anthropology's, and thus, ethnography's, colonial history and offered theoretically informed examples of contemporary ethnography based in a variety of critical traditions and the ways those theories impact how scholars ask questions of the work, engage with participants, and represent their ethnographies. We then described the various phases of ethnography from the planning stage through to the finished product with sections on site and participant selection, gaining rapport, considering various researcher roles, and writing fieldnotes. We explored the emotional aspects of ethnographic research and introduced a variety of analytic writing activities used to represent this research design. The Appendix includes examples of ethnographic studies by Sean Halpin and Lisbeth Berbary.

Activities

1. Write a "thick description" of your field site with as much concrete, low inference description as possible. Share with a colleague for discussion and critique.
2. When you have been in your field site long enough to know the structures and patterns of the days' activities, write a *Typical Day Vignette*.

This *data analysis* activity helps you to write what you know about your site and points to things that you still need to know by further observations. Share your vignette with colleagues for their response and critique.

3. Select a 5–10 minute segment of a film where the social interactions are not too complicated. First, play the segment of the film without audio and take fieldnotes. Repeat the segment with audio, taking fieldnotes again. Share your fieldnotes with colleagues for discussion and critique.

4. Select a potato, orange, or other object. Describe in as much detail as possible using clear, low inference descriptions. Share your descriptions with colleagues for reflection and critique.

5. Design a system for taking fieldnotes in your site.

6. After you have been in your field site several times, write a site description statement including a detailed map of the site. Be as clear and thorough as possible in this statement. Read your statement to colleagues for response and critique. They should be able to visualize the site from your description.

7. Write a typical day vignette or participant description to illustrate your research site.

8. Select an approach to ethnography that reflects your theoretical orientation and review published studies using this approach. How did the authors' theories inform their ethnographic work in the questions asked, methods used, and ways of representation?

9. Examine your own use of technology. What is your comfortability level with different technologies? What digital tools will you use in your study? Why? How will you use digital and visual tools to represent your work?

Further Reading

Resources for Doing Ethnographic Research

Atkinson, P. (2017). *Thinking ethnographically.* SAGE.

Coffey, A. (2018). *Doing ethnography.* SAGE.

Emerson, R. M., Fretz, R. I., & Shaw, L. L. (2011). *Writing ethnographic fieldnotes* (2nd ed.). University of Chicago Press.

Pink, S. (2021). *Doing visual ethnography* (4th ed.). SAGE.

Examples of Ethnographic Texts

Behar, R. (1993). *Translated woman: Crossing the border with Esperanza's story.* Beacon Press.

Blackledge, A. & Creese, A. (2019). *Voices of a city market: An ethnography.* Multilingual Matters.

Desmond, M. (2016). *Evicted: Poverty and profit in the American city.* Crown.

Kurie, P. (2018). *In chocolate we trust: The Hershey Company town unwrapped.* University of Pennsylvania Press.

Waterston, A. (2014). *My father's wars: Migration, memory, and the violence of a century.* Taylor & Francis.

Notes

1. We intentionally use quotation marks here to signal language used by early 20th century anthropologists in descriptions of their work and recognize how such descriptions of people and culture exemplify imperialist and colonizing practices embedded in early anthropological research (Esposito & Evans-Winters, 2022).

2. Throughout we recognize the gender-exclusive language in classic references but choose to quote as stated in the publications. Although numerous women anthropologists such as Ruth Benedict (1887–1948), Zora Neale Hurston (1891–1960), Hortense Powdermaker (1900–1970), and Margaret Mead (1901–1978) have contributed to the field, we notice the androcentric nature of early methods texts on ethnography.

References

Anderson, G. L. (1989). Critical ethnography in education: Origins, current status, and new directions. *Review of Educational Research, 59*(3), 249–270.

Aretxaga, B. (1997). *Shattering silence: Women, nationalism, and political subjectivity in Northern Ireland.* Princeton University Press.

Atkinson, P. (2015). *For ethnography.* SAGE.

Berbary, L. A., & Johnson, C. W. (2012). The American sorority girl recast: An ethnographic screenplay of leisure in context. *Leisure/Loisir, 36*(3–4), 243–268. https://doi.org/10.1080/14 927713.2012.746072

Blackledge, A. & Creese, A. (2019). *Voices of a city market: An ethnography.* Multilingual Matters.

Bourgois, P., & Schonberg, J. (2009). *Righteous dopefiend.* University of California Press.

Bridges, K. M. (2011). *Reproducing race: An ethnography of pregnancy as a site of racialization.* University of California Press.

Brill de Ramírez, S. B. (2007). *Native American life-history narratives: Colonial and postcolonial Navajo ethnography.* University of New Mexico Press.

Brown, L. (Ed.). (1993). *The New Shorter Oxford English dictionary* (Vol. 1). Clarendon Press.

Carspecken, P. F. (1995). *Critical ethnography in educational research: A theoretical and practical guide.* New York.

Chang, H. (2008). *Autoethnography as method.* Left Coast Press.

Charlton, J. I. (2000). *Nothing about us without us: Disability oppression and empowerment.* University of California Press.

Clifford, J. (1990). Notes on (field)notes. In R. Sanjek (Ed.), *Fieldnotes: The makings of anthropology* (pp 47–70). Cornell University Press.

Clifford, J., & Marcus, G. (Eds.). (1986). *Writing culture: The poetics and politics of ethnography.* University of California Press.

Coffey, A. (2018). *Doing ethnography.* SAGE.

Collins, P. H. (2009). *Black feminist thought: Knowledge, consciousness, and the politics of empowerment.* Routledge.

Dazzo, G. P., Cúmez, C., Henderson, E., & Peccerelli, F. (2023). Restorative validity and healing through inquiry: A visual ethnographic case study in Guatemala. *Conflict Resolution Quarterly, 40,* 383–404. https://doi.org/10.1002/crq.21376

De Los Ríos, C. V. (2020). "Got libros?": Exploring patrons' experiences with Latinx history and literature at La Casa Azul Bookstore. *Anthropology & Education Quarterly, 51*(4), 422–439. https://doi.org/10.1111/aeq.12351

Dennis, B., Carspecken, L., Zhao, P., Silberstein, S., Saxena, P., Bose, S., Palmer, D., Washington, S., & Elfreich, A. (2020). Digital migrating and storyworlding with Women We Love: A feminist ethnography. *Journal of Contemporary Ethnography, 49*(6), 745–776. https://doi.org/10.1177/0891241620937758

Denzin, N. K. (1997). *Interpretive ethnography: Ethnographic practices for the 21st century.* SAGE.

de Rond, M. (2017). *Doctors at war: Life and death in a field hospital.* Cornell University Press.

Desmond, M. (2016). *Evicted: Poverty and profit in the American city.* Crown Publishers.

Deyhle, D. (2009). *Reflections in place: Connected lives of Navajo women.* The University of Arizona Press.

Dutta, U. (2020). The politics and poetics of "fieldnotes": Decolonizing ethnographic knowing. *Qualitative Inquiry, 27*(5), 598–607. https://doi.org/10.1177/1077800420935919

Erickson, F. (1973). What makes school ethnography "ethnographic?" *Council on Anthropology and Education Newsletter, 4*(2), 10–19. http://www.jstor.org/stable/3219522

Esposito, J., & Evans-Winters, V. (2022). *Introduction to intersectional qualitative research.* SAGE.

Fetterman, D. M. (1989). *Ethnography: Step by step.* SAGE.

Fine, M. (2006). Bearing witness: Methods for researching oppression and resistance—A textbook for critical research. *Social Justice Research, 19*(1), 83–108. https://doi.org/10.1007/s11211-006-0001-0

Garbarino, M. S. (1977). *Sociocultural theory in anthropology: A short history.* Waveland Press.

Geertz, C. (1973). *The interpretation of cultures: Selected essays.* Basic Books.

Geertz, C. (1979). *Meaning and order in Moroccan society: Three essays in cultural analysis.* Cambridge University Press.

Glaser, B. G., & Strauss, A. (1967). *The discovery of grounded theory: Strategies for qualitative research.* Aldine de Gruyter.

Goldensher, L. O. (2023). "Mimicked winks": Criminalized conduct and the ethics of thick description. *Journal of Contemporary Ethnography, 52*(2), 139–162. https://doi.org/10.1177/08912416221094653

Gonzalez van Cleve, N. (2016). *Crook county: Racism and injustice in America's largest criminal court*. Stanford University Press.

Goodall, H. L. (2000). *Writing the new ethnography*. Altamira Press.

Gross, N. (2022). A 'friend' or an 'experiment'?: The paradox of ethnographic relationships with youth. In V. Vasudevan, N. Gross, P. Nagarajan & K. Clonan-Roy (Eds.), *Care-based methodologies: Reimagining qualitatitve research with youth in US schools* (pp. 133–145). Bloomsbury Academic.

Gross, N. (2023). #LongLiveDaGuys: Online grief, solidarity, and emotional freedom for Black teenage boys after the gun deaths of friends. *Journal of Contemporary Ethnography, 52*(2), 261–289. https://doi.org/10.1177/08912416221105869

Gullion, J. S. (2018). *Diffractive ethnography: Social sciences and the ontological turn*. Routledge.

Hammersley, M., & Atkinson, P. (2019). *Ethnography: Principles in practice* (4th ed.). Routledge.

Harding, S. (1993). Rethinking standpoint epistemology: What is "strong objectivity?" In L. Alcoff & E. Potter (Eds.), *Feminist epistemologies* (pp. 49–82). Routledge.

Henson, B. (2020). "Look! A Black ethnographer!": Fanon, performance, and critical ethnography. *Cultural Studies ↔ Critical Methodologies, 20*(4), 322–335. https://doi.org/10.1177/1532708619838582

Hicks, G. L. (1976). *Appalachian Valley*. Waveland Press.

Ho, K. (2009). *Liquidated: An ethnography of Wall Street*. Duke University Press.

Junker, B. (1960). *Field work*. University of Chicago Press.

Klykken, F. H. (2022). Implementing continuous consent in qualitative research. *Qualitative Research, 22*(5), 795–810. https://doi.org/10.1177/14687941211014366

Kurie, P. (2018). *In chocolate we trust: The Hershey Company town unwrapped*. University of Pennsylvania Press.

Madison, D. S. (2005). *Critical ethnography: Method, ethics, and performance*. SAGE.

Markham, A. N. (1998). *Life online: Researching real experience in virtual space*. Altamira Press.

Mead, M. (1967 [1949]). *Male and female: A study of the sexes in a changing world*. Morrow Quill Paperbacks.

Merriam, S. B. (1988). *Case study research in education: A qualitative approach*. Jossey-Bass.

Merriam, S. B. (1991). *Case study research in education: A qualitative approach* (2nd ed.). Jossey-Bass.

Merriam, S. B. (1998). *Qualitative research and case study applications in education: Revised and expanded from case study research in education*. Jossey-Bass.

Noblit, G. W., Flores, S. Y., & Murillo, E. G. (Eds.). (2004). *Postcritical ethnography: Reinscribing critique*. Hampton Press.

Pachirat, T. (2017). *Among wolves: Ethnography and the immersive study of power*. Routledge.

Pitman, M. A., & Maxwell, J. A. (1992). Qualitative approaches to evaluation. In M. D. Le Compte, W. L. Millroy, & J. Preissle (Eds.). *The handbook of qualitative research in education* (pp. 729–770). Academic Press.

Rankine, C. (2020). "The condition of Black life is one of mourning." In *Grief and Grievance: New York Times*, June 22, 2015. https://www.nytimes.com/2015/06/22/magazine/the-condition-of-black-life-is-one-of-mourning.html.

Simons, H. (2009). *Case study research in practice.* SAGE.

Simons, H. (2020). Case study research: In-depth understanding in context. In Leavy, P. (Ed.). *The Oxford handbook of qualitative research* (2nd ed., pp. 676–703). Oxford Academic.

Smith, L. T. (1999). *Decolonizing methodologies: Research and indigenous peoples.* Zed Books Limited.

Smith, R. A. (2019). "What does it mean?" Methodological strategies for interviewing children. In K. Roulston (Ed.), *Interactional studies of qualitative research interviews* (pp. 103–124). John Benjamins Publishing Company.

Spradley, J. P. (1980). *Participant observation.* Holt, Rinehart & Winston.

Spradley, J. P. & McCurdy, D. W. (1990). *Culture and conflict: Readings in social anthropology.* HarperCollins.

Stake, R. E. (1995). *The art of case study research.* SAGE.

Stein, A. (2010). Sex, truth, and audiotape: Anonymity and the ethics of exposure in public ethnography. *Journal of Contemporary Ethnography, 39*(5), 554–568. https://doi.org/10.1177/0891241610375955

Taylor, S. J., Bogdan, R., & DeVault, M.L. (2016). *Introduction to qualitative research methods: A guidebook and resource* (4th ed.). Wiley.

Wagner, R. (1981). The invention of culture (rev. and exp. ed.). University of Chicago Press.

Warden, T. (2013). Feet of clay: confronting emotional challenges in ethnographic experience. *Journal of Organizational Ethnography, 2*(2), 150–172. https://doi.org/10.1108/joe-09-2012-0037

Waterston, A. (2014). *My father's wars: Migration, memory, and the violence of a century.* Routledge.

Willis, P. (1977). *Learning to labour: How working class kids get working class jobs.* Saxon House.

Winfield, T. P. (2022). Vulnerable research: Competencies for trauma and justice-informed ethnography. *Journal of Contemporary Ethnography, 51*(2), 135–170. http://dx.doi.org/10.1177/08912416211017254

Wolcott, H. F. (1994). *Transforming qualitative data: Description, analysis, and interpretation.* SAGE.

Wolf, M. (1999). Writing ethnography: The poetics and politics of culture. In R. T. McCutcheon (Ed.) *The insider/outsider problem in the study of religion: A reader* (pp. 354–361). A& C Black.

Yin, R. K. (2017). *Case study research and applications: Design and methods.* SAGE.

SEVEN

Designing Studies That Use Documents and Archives

DOCUMENTS AND ARCHIVAL DATA CAN be used as a primary method to explore research questions, or as one of multiple methods in a research design. There are numerous sources of documents and archival records that researchers can examine. This chapter discusses how to identify documents and archives to explore and what to do with this information once located.

Using Documents

The word "document" is both a noun and verb and refers to both the process for *locating* information that records actions and the *evidence* for actions that people have taken. Documents created as part of everyday life provide evidence to support assertions to do with what people do and say and how they represent their actions. This does not mean that documents should be equated with "truth." People *do* things with documents and records (e.g., record birth, deaths, and marriages) and also convey to others self-representations of identity, experiences, and viewpoints (e.g., a text or social media post) that may not be reflective of the "authentic" or "actual." As we know, sometimes these representations can be purposefully distorted or faked. Imagine, for example, if one were to take images of people that had been photoshopped as indicative of what actually happened. Kathy, for example, has a photo of a family gathering taken at a celebration for her parents' 60th wedding anniversary in which a professional photographer added images of several individuals who could not attend the celebration. While the image created provided a complete depiction of all of the family members, it should not be taken to indicate who actually attended the event. Whatever one's research topic, there are numerous material and digital documents to explore, including websites, newspapers, and the records used in everyday life. Let's begin by looking at institutional documents.

Institutional Records

Government agencies, nongovernment organizations, institutions, associations, and businesses all create records to plan for and implement organizational missions. For example, a study conducted in a school could include policy documents to do with teacher supervision and professional development, employment and financial records, school curricula, teachers' planning documents and assessment tasks, and students' work samples. School administrators record daily decision-making and activities through newsletters to parents, school websites, minutes of meetings, memos to teachers, and public correspondence. Documents also include photographs and videos and both material and born-digital records such as emails and texts.

What occurs in school contexts is reported in local newspapers and television programming. Searches could also be conducted for documents collected as part of homecomings, special events, and anniversaries and so forth. What to select from the range of documents and images available will depend on the research questions you want to examine and what materials you can readily access. Some materials may be protected. For example, in the United States, some student records are protected by the Federal Educational Rights and Privacy Act (FERPA).

Personal Records

Only a minute fraction of the documents that people generate in daily life are retained. Those that are, such as diaries and journals, personal correspondence, scrapbooks, and photo albums, all provide information about people's lives and activities. By examining these materials, you can locate further leads, such as relatives and people with whom a person associated and corresponded, places where a participant lived and worked, and activities that people engaged in. When working with family photos, Chalfen (1998) recommended asking the following questions:

1. Planning events: What information about formal or informal decisions around the production of the image is available?
2. On camera shooting: What action(s) structure the person(s) or thing(s) that happen in front of the camera? Who's included? What is not included? What kinds of "poses" get recorded?
3. Behind camera shooting: Is there a recognized routine of using the camera? Who uses the camera? Are there specific times and places that require snapshots? What is the relationship between the photo taker and the photographed? Are there directions for the photo taking activity? Are there props?
4. Editing events: What action(s) transform, accumulate, arrange, or rearrange images?
5. Exhibition events: What action(s) occur after shooting in the exhibiting of the photos? (pp. 218–222).

With the advent of social media in the 21st century, you can examine people's use of social media platforms and how they represent themselves online through text, images, and video. Whether searching for documents on- or offline, ask:

- What documents and artifacts do people produce as part of daily activities in the social setting for this study?
- What documents and artifacts are accessible?
- For what purposes did people create these documents and artifacts?
- Who were the intended audiences?

- What permissions will you need from the creator/s and owners to use documents and artifacts for research purposes? For example, in archives, authors of letters rightfully own the copyright of their letters, even if these are located in other people's manuscripts. To publish letters, you will need to seek permission from the authors. Where authors are deceased, you will also need to check if any provisions were added to the use of a collection by the donor or original owner of the collection. Similarly, you will need permission to reproduce visual images from the creators if you wish to include these in your reports and publications.

The vast majority of institutional and personal documents created in daily life are not archived. Some records, however, are retained for future posterity in official archives. Let's look further at archives as a source of documentary and archival data that you can use for research.

What Are Archives?

People frequently associate archives with rare books and dusty documents. There are certainly many aged documents and books in the collections to be found in institutional archives. Yet archival collections include numerous other forms of material culture that are preserved to record people's histories, cultures, and activities. Archives include photos, paintings and artwork, music scores, audio and video recordings, films, and ephemera (i.e., materials created for short range use such as event tickets, advertising brochures) among other items. Some materials are available in formats no longer used (e.g., superseded file formats such as VHS [Video Home System] cassettes or audio cassettes). In order to access these materials, you will need to request that they are digitized so that you can view or listen to them on-site, or access them online. Information now comes to archival collections in digitally native forms (e.g., electronic mail, posts to social media sites, and so forth). Yet, even when we have access to digitized documents and born-digital records warehoused all over the world, only a small fraction of materials are preserved in archives.

How Collections Come to Archives

Archival principles derive from the field of "diplomatics," which examines the creation, preservation, and dissemination of documents. Historically, archives were the preserve of the rich and powerful in terms of what was collected and retained and who had access to materials. Access to archives by members of the public is traced to the French Revolution in the late 1700s, when the archives, including records of property ownership, were burned by protesters (Duranti, 1996). Relationships between archives and marginalized communities have continued to be fraught for a variety of reasons.

Although many contemporary archivists strive to collect materials that better represent the range of diversity existing in societies, historically, opportunities to intentionally preserve materials to do with marginalized communities were frequently missed. Further, when materials and artifacts from colonized communities were retained by early explorers in settler nations, they were sometimes taken and preserved without permission from the owners. In recent years, many museums and archives have initiated policies to repatriate materials to descendants of the original owners. In the United States, the Native American Graves Protection and Repatriation Act (NAGPRA) requires that museums, universities, state agencies, and local government transfer any human remains or cultural items to the appropriate parties. This process is occurring all over the world where First Nations peoples have lobbied to have the human remains and sacred artifacts collected by explorers and now archived in museum collections repatriated.

There are many routes taken for a collection to find its way into an archive. Whereas some documents are preserved because of organizational retention requirements (e.g., state and federal government agencies), other routes to the archives are more haphazard. For example, one of the collections Kathy has examined was donated by a bank after a production company making a documentary film declared bankruptcy prior to project completion. This extensive collection includes information about the interviews conducted for the film as well as production notes. Although a film was produced and is included in the collection, it was not aired extensively. Other collections are donated when people die or retire from public positions (e.g., politicians). In universities, former faculty members frequently donate papers and research libraries that include one-of-a-kind manuscripts and related artifacts. Since archival collections frequently specialize in particular sorts of materials, if researchers are examining a topic related to a person, place, event, or organization, it is useful to search for archival collections that may house other relevant material. For example, extensive archives of an early researcher in the field of gerontology, Belle Boone Beard, are found in the special collections library at Kathy's institution. Other materials are found at the University of Lynchburg where she established the Belle Boone Beard Gerontology Center (now known as the Beard Center on Aging).

Examples of Archives

Across the world, there are archives and special collections pertaining to an infinite variety of topics. Nation-states archive materials that trace the history and culture of a nation, and make these records available to the public. For example, in the United States, the National Archives and Records Administration (NARA) includes numerous collections across the country in addition to the presidential libraries. When visiting the nation's capital, visitors can view the National Archives on Pennsylvania Avenue, a short walk from the U.S. Capitol. Close by the U.S. Capitol building is another extensive archival collection and library, the Library of Congress (LOC). LOC collections are housed in the Thomas Jefferson Building, the James Madison Memorial Building, and the John Adams Buildings. While the NARA preserves records from federal government agencies and Congress and makes these available for research, only 1% to 3% of all records generated are retained. The NARA does not include records from individuals, private businesses, or state or local governments. State and provincial archives preserve materials of regional interest, while universities, corporations, local governments, and nongovernment agencies provide other sources of archives.

Accessing Archives

The process of accessing and entering an archive or special collection is idiosyncratic. The only way to learn what is involved is to study the website of the chosen archive and then visit. While there are some digital archives that are accessible online (e.g., Densho: The Japanese American Legacy Project), accessing other archives involves in-person visits (e.g., The Woodie Guthrie

Center in Tulsa, Oklahoma). Some archives, such as the LOC, have digitized records from larger material collections. Each archive involves a specific process to access materials, with visits typically requiring prior preparation and research. To take the example of the NARA, to explore a collection researchers must first obtain a researcher card after undertaking a short online orientation. Researchers need to explore the online findings aids prior to visiting a collection, as the NARA has facilities across the country. It would not be helpful to find oneself in College Park, Maryland only to find that the collection one wants to examine is in Atlanta, Georgia!

Handling Archives

When visiting an archive, researchers must take precautions to prevent records from being disordered or damaged through handling. At most archives what researchers take into the reading rooms is carefully monitored on entry and exit. At NARA, for example, researchers may take laptops, cell phones, and tablets but are not permitted to take personal belongings such as notebooks, bags, pens, and paper. This is typical for most archives, although each archival collection has specific rules as to how documents are examined (e.g., one might only take out one folder at a time). Permission might also be needed to take photos of materials and use materials for publication. For example, when Kathleen examined documents from anthropologist Margaret Mead's collection at the LOC, she first had to sign a pledge not to use any materials for the purpose of research without first gaining permission from Mead's daughter. And sometimes access to collections is restricted, as Kathy learned when she sought access to records from the American Civil Liberties Union (ACLU) at her institution. Fortunately, in this case, the folder she wanted to review was one of the few open to researchers.

Following Leads

What questions may be asked of documents and material artifacts? The Library of Congress in the United States provides analysis tools for students working with different types of documents, artifacts, and media. See, for example, the teacher's guides and analysis tools made available at http://www.loc.gov/teachers/usingprimarysources/guides.html. Once you have located documents and artifacts related to your research interests, you can easily adapt the questions provided by the LOC. For example, Kathy has used the following questions in working with students:

- Who are the author/s or creator/s of these documents?
- For what audience were these documents created?
- Who are the present audience/s of these documents?
- Who are other potential audience/s?
- What was the purpose of these documents?
- For what occasion were they created?
- What kinds of topics are included in these documents?
- What kinds of identities (and of whom) are produced in these documents?

As one example, Box 7.1 shows questions that could be asked of a collection of epistolary materials (i.e., letters).

Box 7.1. An Activity Using Letters.

1. Describe the "document collection."
2. Who were the writers of the letters?
3. Who were the original readers of the letters?
4. What may be observed about how the letters were originally written? (e.g., typewritten, handwritten)
5. Are there any indications that the authors were writing for audiences other than one another? What evidence do you have for your answer?
6. What can you make of the original purpose and function of the letters?
7. What do you observe about the topic/s of the letters?
8. What was taken for granted by the authors of the letters?
9. What evidence can you locate that writers appeared to take for granted in relation to the intended reader/s?
10. What do readers need to know to understand these letters?
11. Consider the letters as "situated products." What changes have been made to them since the date of writing?
    - How have the documents been transformed from the "original" writing?
    - What has changed as a result?

- Who are the potential audiences for these documents now?
12. What aspects of the letter writer's life are made visible in this particular selection of documents? What aspects are invisible?
13. What "identities" are constructed in this set of documents?

These questions are informed by those provided by Silverman (2011, p. 239) and Prior (2003, 342).

Developing a Research Study Using Archival Records

Archival research follows a different trajectory than library research. This is because collections are idiosyncratic given the ways in which materials come to archives, the collecting policies of an archive, and the archival practices used to catalog and index materials. To make use of archival sources, we suggest that you begin your search with a broad topic.

1. Survey what archival collections might house materials related to your topic of interest.
2. Examine the *finding aids* provided by the archive. Findings aids are archivists' descriptions of the contents and provenance of a collection. Fortunately, these are mostly available in digitized form, although findings aids vary significantly in detail.
3. If your initial search locates materials of interest, schedule a visit to the archives. In preparation for your visit, review the policies of the archive with respect to viewing material. These differ from one archive to the next. To ensure that you make the most of your time at the archive, get in touch with an archivist to let them know about your interest in a collection. Archivists can provide you with suggestions concerning what search terms to use to locate material relevant to your topic. If materials are stored off site, you will also be able to order materials so they are ready for you to examine when you arrive.
4. Once you have traveled to an archive, keep careful track of what you examine and what you learn from review of materials. Depending on the archive, you may be permitted to copy items in the collection or take photos of materials. Carefully note the box numbers and files in which the records that you copy are located.

Introductions to conducting archival research are found in Redman (2013) and Roulston and deMarrais (2021).

Analyzing and Working With Archival Records

Once you have gained an initial understanding of the types of archival records related to your research topic, Liz Stanley (2017) provides an approach to developing and analyzing your "archive of the other archive" (p. 39). This involves surveying what materials exist, generating a bibliography of secondary literature (i.e., work that other researchers have published on the topic and/or collection), exploring the collections systematically using the finding aids, and getting to know the collections through scoping and skimming through materials available. Stanley labels this process "writing the archive," which involves writing and re-writing and reading and re-reading (p. 36). Stanley poses the following questions concerning an archival collection:

1. How is a collection organized, what is included and excluded and how are its boundaries configured?
2. What are its main contents concerned with, its overall themes and concerns? And can guesstimates be made of any glaring absences?
3. What would it be helpful to record now, at first acquaintance with a collection, concerning its organization, overall content and particular aspects (for instance, by writing notes in notebook or computer file or perhaps making an entry in a database?)
4. Should digital photographs of any documents be made, if this is permitted by the archive concerned? If so, of what—and why?
5. Are the contents either in whole or part relevant to your particular research topic? If they are important enough to later carry out more detailed work, what should this consist of? (Stanley, 2017, p. 48)

In our work in the archives, we have encountered both dead ends and interesting detours. Whatever interesting byways you explore, at some point you will need to select a topic that interests you. Once you have located a collection or collections of interest, work to gain a sense of the whole (Stanley, 2017, p. 53). If a collection is very large, you may need to develop a sampling plan to select from the folders and/or boxes. Stanley recommends examining documents and artifacts for place, space, people, events, time, feelings, meanings, while attending to the structure and content of items and how they present aspects of the social world (p. 53)

Prior (2003) and Stanley (2017) remind us that all source materials are produced from a point of view. Therefore, it is important to gain an understanding of the context in which items were created, in addition to the text and its meta-data ("who, when, where from, archive collection"; "to whom, where to") (Stanley, 2017, p. 56). Stanley recommends that researchers "keep it simple," practice even-handedness in their analysis, and ensure that they do not simply focus on content without considering the context in which materials were both created and retained (pp. 58–59). Assertions based on archival records can easily be contested on multiple grounds due to the fragmentary nature of the materials, and how researchers come to understand and interpret these. Let's look more at this issue as it pertains to quality.

Doing Quality Research Using Documents

When using documents as a data source, it is important to establish that the source is what it purports to be. Is the document authentic? Researchers must also determine the representativeness of a source material when compared to the whole collection, as well as materials that exist in other collections. Assessing representativeness based on the collection itself may be difficult if not impossible. You must ask questions about how the source materials came to be in a collection, what other related materials were created contemporaneously, and whether or not they have been preserved. When using documents created in another time period, it is important that you accurately transcribe handwritten materials and gain deep understanding of the context in which source materials were created. This will help you avoid misinterpreting archival data using contemporary concepts ("presentism"). Finally, when using personal documents, you need to consider how authors represent their identities to others. Doing documentary and archival research will certainly lead to understanding, but it would be a mistake to conclude that these understandings are equivalent to "truth" or what "actually happened."

Examples of Archival Research

Although it can be challenging to locate the stories of marginalized populations within archives, if one looks in the right places, stories can be unearthed and represented. Saidiya Hartman (2019), a professor of English and comparative literature, demonstrated how to do this in her book, *Wayward lives, beautiful experiments: Intimate histories of riotous black girls, troublesome women and queer radicals*. Hartman's book introduces readers to the "wayward lives" and "beautiful experiments" of the girls and women who lived in Philadelphia and New York City around the turn of the 20th century. Hartman's study aimed to "convey the sensory experience of the city and to capture the rich landscape of black social life" (p. xiii). The source materials upon which the narratives in the book are based included "The journals of rent collectors; surveys and monographs of sociologists, trial transcripts; slum photographs; reports of vice investigators, social workers, and parole officers; interviews with psychiatrists and psychologists; and prison case files" (p. xiv).

A key challenge for researchers working with archival records is how to represent findings while acknowledging that archival records are always incomplete and fragmentary. All researchers examining archived records must ask questions about whose voices are missing, and whose stories have not been told. Hartman put it this way (p. xiii):

> Every history of the multitude, the dispossessed, the subaltern, and the enslaved is forced to grapple with the power and authority of the archive and the limits it sets on what can be known, whose perspective matters, and who is endowed with the gravity and authority of historical actor. (Hartman, 2019, p. xiii)

Hartman chose to represent real people, although she changed some names for the purposes of preserving the confidentiality of people portrayed. The list of the cast of characters initially disconcerts—since it includes numerous unnamed people, seemingly in no particular order: "Girl #1," "General houseworker," "The Paper Bag Brigade." Other well-known people such as Ida B. Wells, W. E. B. Du Bois, and Billie Holiday have walk-on parts in Hartman's book; however, they are not the book's main characters. The central characters are those whose images, names, and records have found their way into archival collections, sometimes without context. Hartman introduces readers to people whose lives have been marginalized and forgotten.

In another study, anthropologist and art historian Gretchen Stolte (2021) examined the history and contemporary practice of Aboriginal and Torres Strait Islander Art in far north Queensland. Stolte examined archives from the state government in addition to doing ethnographic fieldwork in an art studio specifically for Aboriginal and Torres Strait Islander artists in Cairns, Queensland. Through examining archival records, Stolte traced the history of how works by Indigenous artists from across the state were created and marketed, how the studio in Cairns came into being, and how students represented their identities through artworks. Archival research was accompanied by ethnographic fieldwork in the studio, analysis of artwork, and interviewing students, teachers, and other involved with the creation and dissemination of Aboriginal and Torres Strait Islander art. In this study archival records were used to provide the history and context for how the studio was founded, and what was going on at the studio at a particular point in time.

Conclusion

In this chapter, we examined how you might locate documents and archives to examine your research questions. Exploring the documents that are created as part of everyday life in the social setting you are examining can provide additional insights concerning your research questions. Archival records can also provide historical insights into what people have done in the past, and how things came to be in the present. Because of the haphazard ways in which archival collections are created, however, researchers must take great care in how they interpret evidence of the past from what has been preserved. In the Appendix, you will find two examples of studies using archival data by Edward Muhammad and Amber Neal.

Activities

1. Generate a list of potential places where you could locate documents related to your topic. What permissions would you need to access these documents?

2. Generate a list of institutional sites that house archival collections related to your topics of interest. How might the archives be accessed?

3. Identify and locate one collection that you would like to explore. This may be in either documentary or digital form. Conduct a mapping of the collection using Stanley's 2017 guiding questions (see below). This will generate an in-depth description of the source materials in addition to describing the provenance, information about the creator, and the contents. Address the following questions (adapted from Stanley, 2017, p. 48):

   • How is the collection organized and what is included?
   • What would you expect to find in the collection that is not there?
   • What are the overall themes and concerns of the collection?
   • How might you organize information (e.g., writing notes in a notebook or computer file or creating a database?) Include an example of initial note-taking.
   • Are there items that you might photograph? Is this permitted by the archive? Are there any restrictions in relation to use of materials in the collection (e.g., does permission need to be gained to publish from this collection? If so, who needs to be contacted?)
   • Are their secondary sources that might provide information about the collection? (e.g., articles of publications that use these materials). If so, provide a list of what you have found to date.
   • What kinds of related collections exist? How are these related? How might you expect these other collections to provide insight into the collection examined?
   • What research topic might be examined using this collection? What kind of questions are posed/what questions remain for you about the collection?

4. Create an inventory that lists potential documents that can be explored in relation to a research topic of interest.

5. Analyze documents related to an independent research topic (e.g., websites; personal records etc.)

Further Reading

Resources for Doing Research with Archives and Documents

Grant, A. (2019). *Doing excellent social research with documents: Practical examples and guidance for qualitative researchers.* Routledge.

Kirsch, G., & Rohan, L. (Eds.). (2008). *Beyond the archives: Research as a lived process.* Southern Illinois University Press.

Redman, S. J. (2013). *Historical research in archives: A practical guide.* American Historical Association

Roulston, K., & deMarrais, K. (2021). *Exploring the archives: A beginner's guide for qualitative researchers.* Myers Education Press.

Tinkler, P. (2013). *Using photographs in social and historical research.* SAGE.

Examples of Studies Using Archives

Goodall, H. L. (2006). *A need to know: The clandestine history of a CIA family.* Left Coast Press.

Phillips, P. (2017 [2016]). *Blood at the root: A racial cleansing in America.* W. W. Norton & Company.

Siddle Walker, V. (2018). *The lost education of Horace Tate: Uncovering the hidden heroes who fought for justice in schools.* The New Press.

Stewart, C. A. (2016). *Long past slavery: Representing race in the Federal Writers' Project.* The University of North Carolina Press.

Tamboukou, M. (2016). *Sewing, fighting and writing: Radical practices in work, politics and culture.* Rowman & Littlefield.

References

Chalfen, R. (1998). Interpreting family photography as pictorial communication. In J. Prosser (Ed.), *Image-based research: A sourcebook for qualitative researchers* (pp. 214–234). Falmer Press.

Duranti, L. (1996). Archives as place. *Archives and Manuscripts, 24*(2), 242–255.

Hartman, S. (2019). *Wayward lives, beautiful experiments: Intimate histories of riotous Black girls, troublesome women, and queer radicals.* W. W. Norton & Company.

Prior, L. (2003). *Using document in social research.* SAGE.

Redman, S. J. (2013). *Historical research in archives: A practical guide.* American Historical Association

Roulston, K., & deMarrais, K. (2021). *Exploring the archives: A beginner's guide for qualitative researchers.* Myers Education Press.

Stanley, L. (2017). Archival methodology inside the black box: Noise in the archive! In N. Moore, A. Salter, L. Stanley, & M. Tamboukou (Eds.), *The archive project: Archival research in the social sciences*. Routledge.

Stolte, G. (2021). *Aboriginal and Torres Strait Islander Art: An anthropology of identity production in far North Queensland*. Routledge.

PART III

PUTTING IT ALL TOGETHER: DESIGNING AND ENSURING QUALITY STUDIES

P ART 3, THE FINAL PORTION of the book, transitions to qualitative research traditions that use one or any combination of the three primary
methods of data generation introduced in Part 2 (interviews, observation,
documents, and archives). This last part of the book includes (a) narrative inquiry, (b) autoethnography, and (c) arts-based research followed by a chapter
on designing quality studies. And of course, because qualitative research is
diverse and researchers are creative—these are not the only designs used. For
example, you could design an interview study, an ethnography, or a historical study using the methods discussed in Part 2. And we have not attended
to designs intended to work collaboratively with participant in participatory
action research approaches, or those described as "mixed methods." We selected these three designs given their unique histories in the field of qualitative research and because they are prevalent in recent literature. Throughout
these chapters, we provide the disciplinary backgrounds, theories that inform
the work, the actual practice of that work, and ways researchers approach
data analysis within those designs.

Chapter 8, *Designing and implementing narrative inquiry*, engages you in
thinking about narratives and stories as a way to do qualitative research. What
is narrative? What is story? How do researchers use those terms? The field of
narrative inquiry has a long history and is informed by different theoretical
frameworks. We discuss the "narrative turn" in research and the scholars who
influenced that turn. Next, we look at how different qualitative researchers
have generated narrative data by working with participants who have stories
to share and offer specific suggestions for how to engage in this work. In the
analysis portion of the chapter, we describe the traditions of (a) analysis of
narratives and (b) narrative analysis and how those different processes lead
to different representations of the research. We conclude the chapter with

three distinct representations—composite narratives, counter-stories and counter-narratives, and literary approaches—as well as a discussion of ethical considerations in doing narrative research.

Chapter 9, *Designing autoethnography*, focuses on the relationship between personal experience and culture. Beginning with the disciplinary and theoretical history of autoethnography, we embed discussions of troubling objectivity and present ways to think about reflexivity. The next portion of the chapter engages you in the design of autoethnographic studies, beginning with suggestions for choosing a topic, moving into the work of generating autoethnographic data, and writing about personal experiences. Throughout we share many examples of how researchers have conducted and represented autoethnographic studies. We conclude with ethical considerations researchers within this approach must address including writing about their own families and friends and the implications of publishing autoethnographic studies.

Chapter 10, *Designing studies using arts-based methods*, explores how researchers use artistic forms to generate and analyze qualitative data and employ aesthetic modes of expression to represent research findings. We begin with an introduction to key concepts and explore the origins of arts-based inquiry in qualitative research emerging from the disciplines of anthropology and ethnography. We move to examples of doing arts-based research focusing specifically on poetic, visual, and performative approaches, respectively. Across each of these approaches, we include examples of studies across a variety of disciplinary and theoretical perspectives. We examine the origins of poetic transcription and found poetry and show how researchers use these approaches as modes of analysis and representation in qualitative studies. In our discussion of visual inquiry methods, we begin with a look at visual elicitation methods (e.g., photo elicitation, photo voice, graphic elicitation) used to generate research data. We turn to methods used for analyzing visual data including thematic analysis and approaches that employ visual methods (e.g., collage, painting) as processes of analysis and representation. Lastly, we explore performative approaches focusing primarily on dramatic forms of performance such as performance ethnography and ethnodrama. We discuss processes researchers use to generate scripts from observations, interviews, and documents and adapt their research findings into stage productions. We conclude this chapter with considerations for designing ethical, quality arts-based research and offer some examples of quality criteria from the literature to guide your thinking.

Chapter 11, *Designing quality studies*, is the final, critical chapter to this book that examines how researchers think about and design quality studies in qualitative research studies, no matter what approaches they use. In other words, what is good practice and how do we design for it? We begin with the many terms used to describe quality or goodness in research within the history of the field. We discuss how scholars in the field have defined and debated concepts such as validity and triangulation in qualitative research and the different ways researchers have addressed these issues in research studies. More importantly, we note how scholarly conversations about quality criteria are connected to epistemological assumptions about knowledge production and what counts as evidence in social science research and offer examples from scholars working across different theoretical perspectives. We move to a discussion of how scholars have innovated or offered alternatives to triangulation in qualitative research through approaches such as crystallization. The chapter concludes with guiding questions to help you think about issues of quality in your study.

The book includes an Appendix that provides examples of doctoral studies that have used qualitative methods. You will find a range of theoretical perspectives and research designs employed in these studies, from interpretivist approaches such as symbolic interactionism, ethnomethodology, and phenomenology, to critical approaches such as Critical Race Theory, feminist, and Womanist inquiry, and feminist poststructuralism and new materialist theories. By reviewing the abstracts, research purposes, and research questions posed by these scholars, you will see that qualitative research designs take many shapes. You will also see that scholars represent their work in a variety of ways that span traditional to arts-based approaches.

We hope you will be inspired, as we are, by the creativity demonstrated by the scholars cited in this text. There are many paths to the design and conduct of quality qualitative studies. Enjoy your journey!

EIGHT

Designing and Implementing Narrative Studies

LEARNING OBJECTIVES

After reading this chapter you should be able to:

- Identify key concepts related to the theorization of narratives in the social sciences.
- Understand the epistemological shifts leading to the narrative turn in social science research.
- Distinguish between narrative analysis and analysis of narrative.
- Describe the relationship between narrative and story.
- Explore approaches to generating data, conducting analysis, and representing findings in studies using narrative methods.

IN THIS CHAPTER WE DISCUSS how researchers design studies using narrative inquiry. As you will see, scholars across a range of disciplinary approaches employ narrative methods and draw on specific theorizations of narratives to guide their inquiry. For instance, some researchers are interested in the linguistic and structural elements of stories while others explore themes across narrative accounts or use narrative genres (e.g., vignettes, short stories, speculative fiction) to represent research findings. We begin by defining commonly used terms in the narrative methodological literature and provide a brief history of narrative inquiry in qualitative research. In doing so, we explore questions such as: *What is narrative inquiry? How do narrative scholars describe the relationship between narrative and story? What are the epistemological assumptions surrounding narrative theorizations in the social sciences?* Next, we examine the methods qualitative researchers use to generate and analyze narrative data before turning to a discussion of how researchers use narrative forms of representation in qualitative studies. We conclude with a discussion of the strengths and limitations of narrative inquiry and provide suggestions for further reading.

Narrative Inquiry and Theorizations of Narrative

Narrative inquiry is an approach to research that explores individual or collective stories as a way to understand the nuances of human experience. Narrative qualitative researchers use a range of methods to generate storied data (e.g., interviews, participant observation, archival methods) and may explore substantive as well as methodological and theoretical topics. In short, narrative inquiry refers to a host of topics related to generating, analyzing, and representing stories in qualitative research. Thomas Schwandt (2015) offered a definition that gets at the range of topics included under the umbrella of narrative inquiry. He described narrative inquiry as:

> A broad term encompassing the interdisciplinary study of the activities involved in generating and analyzing stories of life experiences (e.g., life histories, narrative interviews, journals, diaries, memoirs, autobiographies, biographies) and reporting that kind of research. Narrative inquiry or research also includes examining the methodology and aim of research in the form of personal narrative and autoethnography. (p. 211)

Schwandt's description emphasizes the breadth of narrative inquiry. We now look to another definition that examines some of the epistemological assumptions of narrative inquiry. In their early writing on narrative inquiry, Connelly and Clandinin (1990) described narrative inquiry as "both phenomenon and method" (p. 2). They argued narrative inquiry is a way humans make sense of interactions, experiences, and events, rather than simply a mode of communication. Narratives shape our values, perceptions, and interpretations of the world around us. Researchers studying narrative phenomena explore how stories produce particular understandings of the world. Narrative inquiry as method refers to the processes researchers use to generate, analyze, and represent their interpretations of "storied lives" (Connelly & Clandinin, 1990, p. 2).

These definitions of narrative inquiry illustrate the range of potential research topics associated with narrative qualitative research and provide a theoretically informed rationale for why social science researchers investigate narrative phenomena. While later sections of this chapter focus on the nuts and bolts of doing narrative qualitative research (e.g., generating and analyzing narrative data, using narrative modes of representation), in the next

section we examine the theorizations of narrative that led to the rise of narrative approaches in social science research. Although narrative has long been
a topic of inquiry in the humanities (e.g., literary criticism, history), narrative
inquiry in the social sciences has a fairly recent history. We turn now to a discussion of the theories that gave rise to what qualitative scholars have called
the "narrative turn" in social science research (Polkinghorne, 1988).

The phrase *narrative turn* is used to describe a shift in methodological
approaches to research that value narratives as a primary source of data or
inquiry. Methodological literature reveals that scholars approach the evolution of narrative methodologies from different perspectives. Indeed, the story
of narrative inquiry depends on who is telling the story. In her overview of
the narrative turn in the human sciences, Riessman (2008) noted how some
scholars attribute the shift towards narrative research in the early 20th century
with the growth of life history research (e.g., Chase, 2005), while others emphasize the gradual shift from post-positivist epistemologies in the 1960s
(e.g., Langellier, 2001). In their review of studies using narrative approaches to
qualitative research, Pinnegar and Daynes (2007) identified four themes that
described the growing interest in narrative inquiry:

> (1) a change in the relationship between the person conducting the research and
> the person participating as the subject (the relationship between the researcher
> and the researched), (2) a move from the use of number toward the use of
> words as data, (3) a change from a focus on the general and universal toward
> the local and specific, and finally (4) a widening in acceptance of alternative
> epistemologies or ways of knowing. (p. 4)

Rather than a single narrative "turn," life history scholar Matti Hyvärinen
(2010) noted four significant turns in the scholarly evolution of narrative research: "the turn in literary theory in the 1960s; the turn in historiography
following literary narratology; the turn in social sciences from the 1980s onwards; and finally a more broadly cultural and societal turn to narration" (p.
69). As you can see, scholars may begin their history of narrative inquiry in
different time periods or look to different disciplinary influences to account
for the growing interest in narrative methodologies. Regardless of how scholars have mapped the history of the narrative turn, they recognize the importance of narrative inquiry in challenging positivist assumptions surrounding
the production and valuing of knowledge. Although a detailed history of the

narrative turn in qualitative inquiry is beyond scope of this chapter, we focus on exploring theorizations of narrative that influenced the growth of narrative inquiry in the last decades of the 20th century.

Many qualitative scholars acknowledge W. J. Thomas Mitchell's (1981) *On Narrative* as a watershed moment in the turn towards narrative inquiry in social science research (Connelly & Clandinin, 1990). Composed of interdisciplinary essays written by scholars in fields ranging from anthropology, literary criticism, theology, and philosophy, *On Narrative* examined the importance of narrative in human culture. A central tenet in Mitchell's work was the notion that narratives provide both a structure for storytelling and a way for people to interpret experience. In other words, narratives become part of the way people encounter reality. Narratives both shape people's perceptions of the world and are part of the way people communicate those perceptions.

Cognitive psychologist Jerome Bruner offered a similar theorization of narrative. Bruner (1985) theorized how humans organize and make meaning of experiences and events. He described paradigmatic and narrative modes of thought as the primary ways humans make sense of the world. According to Bruner, the *paradigmatic mode of thought* relies on cognitive thinking and organizes experience through classification and categorization. In contrast, the *narrative mode of thought* relies on stories to understand and make sense of the complexities of experiences. Bruner (1986) challenged the concept that the human mind is a passive receptor of information and argued that the mind is an "instrument for producing worlds" (p. 104). He argued that stories are entwined with the ways people encounter and produce worlds. Bruner's conception of narrative thought was informed by his research in the field of cognitive psychology and influential philosophical texts that focused on the role of narrative in shaping and interpreting reality (e.g., Paul Ricoeur's first translated volume of *Time and Narrative* published in 1984). Drawing on Ricoeur (1984), Bruner wrote about the relationship between "lived time" and narrative, noting:

> We seem to have no other way of describing "lived time" save in the form of a narrative. Which is not to say that there are not other temporal forms that can be imposed on the experience of time, but none of them succeeds in capturing the sense of lived time: not clock or calendrical time forms, not serial or cyclical orders, not any of these. (p. 12)

In other words, narrative provides a coherence that imbues interactions, events, and emotions with meaning.

The notion of narrative as a way of understanding and explaining one's reality was taken up by other researchers writing during this time. One notable example can be seen in the work of psychologist and researcher Donald Polkinghorne (1988) who described *narrative knowing* as "the fundamental scheme for linking individual human actions and events into interrelated aspects of an understandable composite" (p. 13). Polkinghorne (1988) drew on examples from his work as a psychotherapist to explore how narratives can be understood as both a process by which someone comes to understand the world *and* a form of representation, arguing that to better understand how people narrate their experiences, we must examine how narrators organize particular details and events into a plot. Polkinghorne described plot as "the organizing theme that identifies the significance and role of individual events" in what we call a narrative (p. 18). He explained:

> The plot functions to transform a chronicle or listing of events into a schematic whole by highlighting and recognizing the contribution that certain events make to the development and outcome of the story. Without the recognition of significance given by the plot, each event would appear as discontinuous and separate, and its meaning would be limited to its categorical identification or its spatiotemporal location. (pp. 18–19)

Polkinghorne used the term *emplotment* to describe the process of selecting and organizing events into a coherent story structure, asserting that examining emplotment was crucial to understanding how people ascribe particular events with meaning.

As philosophers and researchers theorized narrative as a way of knowing and understanding reality, they challenged positivist paradigms that dominated the landscape of social science research at that time. In contrast to positivist perspectives that value objectivity in search of a knowable truth, Bruner (1985, 1986) and Polkinghorne (1988) asserted a constructivist view of knowledge, in which narratives are a fundamental way humans formulate their understandings of the world. Constructivists argue that knowledge is subjective and comprises multiple perspectives in that it is informed by one's background and personal values and experiences. We note the constructivist underpinnings of Bruner and Polkinghorne's theorizations of narrative to remind you that the way researchers value the production of knowledge has implications for the questions they ask and how they use methods to answer those questions.

As social scientists looked to Bruner and Polkinghorne's constructivist theorizations of narratives, they acknowledged the contingent and subjective nature of narrative knowing—that narratives are always socioculturally situated and always partial. Narrative researchers explored questions such as: How do people narrate identities? (McAdams, 1993). How does the researcher participate in the co-construction of narratives during research interviews? (Mishler, 1991 [1986]). During the 1980s and 1990s, narrative research proliferated in disciplines such as education (Connelly & Clandinin, 1990; Cortazzi, 1993), psychology (Crites, 1986; Mishler, 1991 [1986]), psychiatry (Coles, 1989), and communication (Ellis, 1995; Ellis & Bochner, 1996), just to name a few. During this time, peer-reviewed journals were established (e.g., *Journal of Narrative and Life History* and *Qualitative Inquiry*) that provided an outlet for narrative empirical, methodological, and theoretical publications.[1]

As you examine the narrative literature, you will find varied descriptions of narrative inquiry and the narrative turn. We have noted some of these approaches in this section. You may even find that some scholars refrain from using terms like "narrative inquiry" or "narrative turn" altogether, asserting that all human inquiry is narrative (Hendry, 2010). As you consider using narrative methods in your study, think about which definitions of narrative inquiry inform your work. For example, do you define narrative inquiry as both phenomenon and method? Do you consider all human inquiry to be narrative inquiry? How might concepts like "narrative knowing" or "narrative modes of thought" relate to your inquiry? Let's turn now to a deeper look at two fundamental concepts in narrative inquiry—narrative and story.

Narrative and Story

Scholars have noted the ubiquity of stories in our everyday lives (Polkinghorne, 2007; Riessman, 2008). You may recall from an early age, listening to stories told by family elders, hearing stories sung aloud in folk tunes, or gathering on the reading rug for storytime as teachers read aloud from picture books. When a friend or family member asks "How was your day?" your response may include a story about an interesting or unusual thing that happened or an interaction with a friend or coworker. You may even do so without realizing it. As Connelly and Clandinin (1990) argued, "humans are storytelling organisms who, individually and socially, lead storied lives" (p. 2). We hear the words "narrative" and "story" used all the time on the radio, television, and social media. Politicians, journalists, and activists describe "framing the narrative" of political campaigns, social movements, or world events. In instances where celebrities or public figures are involved in scandal, we witness press conferences in which these individuals answer questions to "get ahead of the story." We see #shareyourstory prompts on social media, encouraging people to share experiences ranging from professional and personal success to personal illness, abuse, or loss. In our day-to-day conversations, we may use the terms narrative and story interchangeably without giving much thought to the distinctions between them.

In the narrative methodological literature, some scholars use the terms *narrative* and *story* interchangeably while others distinguish between them. For example, Schwandt (2015) defined story as "a kind of writing that describes a sequence of actions of events with a plot (beginning, middle and end) arranged in a temporal order" (p. 201). Building on Polkinghorne's concept of narrative knowing, Kramp (2004) described the relationship between story and narrative. Kramp wrote, ". . . narrative is a way of knowing. As such, it is natural to us and is part of our cognitive repertoire. Narrative knowing is expressed in a narrative form we call stories" (p. 106). Similarly, narrative scholar Riessman (2008) described stories as informal, conversational ways humans communicate experiences and defined story as something that "connects events into a sequence that is consequential for later action and or the meanings that the speaker wants listeners to take away from the story" (p. 3). In their description of narrative and story, both Riessman and Kramp situate stories within the broader category called *narrative*. Kramp (2004) explained:

> A story is an example of a narrative—a kind of narrative. A story is always a narrative, but narrative structure is not limited to story . . . When I use the word *story*, it is to be understood as a narrative structure that organizes or emplots human events. (p. 106)

In the remainder of this chapter, we draw on the conceptualizations of narrative and story offered by Kramp (2004) and Riessman (2008) as we explore the ways qualitative researchers generate and analyze narrative data and employ narrative genres to represent research. As you survey the literature, you may encounter scholars taking up these terms differently (e.g., Kim, 2016). We encourage you to consider how you distinguish between narrative and story in your own study and which scholars inform how you conceptualize the relationship between them. Now let's explore the methods narrative researchers engage in narrative inquiry.

Generating Narrative Data

As you survey literature on your topic of interest, you might look at whose stories are missing. In their study on the integration experiences of refugee women in the United States, Owino and Weber (2020) noted that although women comprised more than half of the population of displaced people in the United States, there was little research exploring the experiences of women refugees. Drawing on Durkheim (1951) and Merton's (1968) concept of anomie[2] they explored themes of isolation and loneliness in narratives generated from in-depth interviews with 16 women refugees from an Upper Midwest U.S. community. Through this thematic narrative inquiry, Owino and Weber contributed to a growing understanding of the experiences of refugees living in the United States and offered potential implications of their study for improving existing refugee integration programs. If you are considering interview methods for generating narratives, you will want to be sure you are employing sampling methods that ensure your participants have experiences related to your research phenomenon. In the instance of Owino and Weber's study, this required researchers to familiarize themselves with states and communities in their immediate area with a record of participation in the U.S. resettlement program and focus on particular programs serving refugee populations within those communities.

Shelton (2014) noted the importance of recruiting participants with sufficient professional or life experience to offer detailed stories related to the research phenomenon of interest. Lastly, before recruiting participants for your study consider the question: *Will participants feel safe sharing their stories?* Although participants may fit the criteria for your study and have ample life or professional experience, they may be hesitant to share their stories, especially if they are members of vulnerable populations or if you are exploring sensitive topics. In the example of Sefora and Ngubane's (2023) narrative inquiry on career development for students with disabilities, researchers used purposive network sampling[3] to recruit participants with disabilities enrolled in an African online distance learning (ODL) institution. They noted how their sampling decision resulted in a level of comfort around participants' disclosure of disability and willingness to share about their experiences with researchers.

In addition to recruiting participants who have stories to tell and feel safe telling them, you will want to think about the methods you use to generate narrative data. Riessman (2008) described this process as "constructing narratives for inquiry" (p. 21) and noted the importance of the researcher's role producing narrative accounts from interview or focus group studies. Shelton (2014) described this process in her narrative inquiry into teachers' experiences with LGBTQ issues in education. After realizing that her initial interviews did not render the detailed responses she had hoped for, Shelton revisited her research design. She included fewer questions in her interview guide and adopted a phenomenological approach to in-depth interviewing (deMarrais, 2004). Shelton offered tips for researchers new to narrative interviewing through lessons she learned from her own study. We paraphrase some of Shelton's (2014) suggestions below and recommend her case example for further reading:

- Do your participants have stories to tell? Consider the background knowledge or experience that may be needed for participants to provide detailed, rich responses.
- Are you asking too many questions? You may think you need to develop an interview question for any possible scenario or nuance related to your interview topic. This often leads to asking questions that may be unrelated to the research questions and makes interview questions feel more like a checklist and less like a way to guide a conversation.
- Are you asking questions that invite participants to tell, describe experiences, and provide examples? Do not assume that participants will automatically respond to questions with personal stories. Design interview questions that provide opportunities for participants to talk.
- During interviews, are you focused on listening to participant responses? When participants are talking, resist the urge to focus on the next interview question. Focus on what participants are saying and let their narratives guide your follow-up in responses. (pp. 10–12)

Similarly, narrative scholar Jeong-Hee Kim (2016) argued the purpose of narrative interviews is "to let stories be told" (p. 166). Although narrative interviewers should "follow the interviewee's lead" (p. 294), Kim noted that researchers should take time to prepare for the interview and keep the research purpose and questions in mind throughout the interview process. Kim's interview process drew on life story and autobiographical approaches to narrative inquiry. Terms like "life story" and "autobiography" might remind you of studies encountered in a history course. Although both oral history and life story/autobiography are approaches to narrative inquiry and both involve an interest in individuals' recollections of past events, oral history and life history/autobiography differ in purpose, scope, and methodology. Oral history studies typically rely on a combination of archival and interview data and focus on a particular event or time period in a person's life (e.g., Rawicki & Ellis, 2011). Life story and autobiographical narrative inquiry can include data generated from in-depth interviews with others (e.g., Asplund & Pérez Prieto, 2020) or from data generated through memory and/or self-observation in the instance of first-person narratives (e.g., Lieblich, 2013). In contrast with oral history, life story and autobiography focus on a more holistic understanding of a person's entire life.

Drawing on life story and autobiographical approaches to narrative inquiry, Kim (2016) described two phases of narrative interviewing—the narration phase and the conversation phase—to illustrate the balance between following the interviewee and guiding participants' responses. Kim wrote:

> The *narration phase* is an extensive narration by the interviewee/narrator, during which the interviewer restricts his or her interventions to the minimum while keeping the narration going, just as in open-ended interviews. We ask our interviewees to give a full narration of events and experiences from their own life, encouraging their narrative thinking processes. This narrative is not interrupted by questions, but can be encouraged by nonverbal expressions of interest and attention. (p. 167, emphasis in the original)

Goodson and Gill (2011) emphasized keeping "the vow of silence" (p. 39) during life story interviews. Unlike the open approach to interviewing adopted during the narration phase, "the conversation phase is a period of semi-structured, in-depth questioning or interchange when the interviewer wants some clarifications on the issues presented in the first narration" (Kim,

2016, p. 169). Drawing on Goodson and Gill (2011), Spence (1982), and others (Mishler, 1986), Kim described how narratives are co-constructed during the conversation phase through interactions between the researcher and the participant. In this phase of life story interviewing, the researcher might ask a participant to clarify the order of events or provide additional detail about people or encounters mentioned during the narration phase of interviewing. Such details bring cohesion to the life story or "tighten the story." Scholars writing about the benefits of life story or autobiographical interviewing have noted how such approaches honor both a holistic remembering of participants' lived experiences as well as the language participants use to describe those experiences (Atkinson, 2007). Thus, life story or autobiographical interviews construct narratives for inquiry that prioritize the stories participants acknowledge as significant.

While these approaches provide guidance for constructing narratives through interview methods, we want to emphasize that there is no one way to design a narrative interview study. Decisions around how many participants to interview, how many interviews, how to structure interviews, and how to formulate questions depend on your research questions and purpose. Following Kim's approach, you might envision a narrative study that includes multiple interviews with a participant(s) including both narrative and conversational approaches to interviewing. In the example of Janie's dissertation research, she adopted an in-depth, semi-structured approach to interviewing that more closely resembled the example provided in Shelton's narrative interview study and incorporated object elicitation to evoke stories around objects of significance related to her research on mothers preparing children for menstruation (Copple, 2022). In another example, Sheridan and colleagues (2011) used timeline elicitation in combination with multiple in-depth interviews to examine participants' experiences with weight loss. Researchers used timeline elicitation to "encourage narratives and explore the content and dimensions of a participant's memories about being fat and losing weight" (p. 554). These examples highlight the multiple ways researchers "construct narratives for inquiry" through the interview experience. Whether researchers employ a vow of silence, ask open questions inviting participants to tell/ describe, or incorporate elicitation methods, these decisions play a role in the resulting narrative. They become part of the story told. Equally entwined in the process of constructing narratives are decisions related to selecting a research context, determining participant criteria, and recruiting participants for your study. If your research question leads to narrative interview methods, we encourage you to reflect on your decisions throughout this process. In addition to the other questions we offer here, you might ask: How are my questions inviting participants to tell detailed stories? How am I paying attention to the stories participants tell?

Transcription is another way that researchers participate in the practice of generating narrative data. For our purposes here, we briefly discuss the relationship between transcription, theorizations of narrative, and interpretation. First, we emphasize that transcripts, like stories, are always partial. As researchers transcribe talk, they are making decisions about what to include and omit (e.g., utterances, stutters, laughter, pauses). These decisions are informed by theoretical perspectives or disciplinary conventions. James Gee (2014), a sociolinguist, clearly articulated this relationship between theory and transcription when he wrote:

> Such judgments of relevance (what goes into a transcript and what does not) are ultimately theoretical judgments, that is, they are based on the analyst's theories of how language, contexts, and interactions work in general and in the specific context being analyzed. In this sense, a transcript is a theoretical entity. It does not stand outside an analysis, but, rather, is part of it. (p. 112)

Drawing on examples from her research with women in South India, Riessman (2008) pointed to the role of transcription as an interpretive act. In one such example, she featured two transcriptions from a participant narrating her experience of having a miscarriage. In the first transcript, Riessman offered interviewer and respondent interactions, including non-lexical expressions (e.g., mmmm, uh huh) as well as interjecting questions. In the second transcript, Riessman used a structural method of transcription in which she omitted interviewer interactions and organized the narrative into thematic stanzas (for a detailed description of this process, see Gee, 2014). Riessman argued these examples point to the role of interpretation in transcription. The first example offers a co-constructed representation of the narrative occurring through the interaction between the researcher and the participant. The second example offers a representation Riessman described as "highly interpretive" through its use of thematic stanzas. Further, she noted the erasure of interviewer/participant interaction "presents the narrative as if it arose, full blown, from within 'the self' of the speaker" (p. 35). As you consider the role of transcription in constructing narratives for your inquiry, consider how your decision to include or omit utterances, silences, and gestures produce a particular (always partial) version of the interview account. Box 8.1 offers a reflective memo from one of Janie's students writing about the role of transcription in a narrative inquiry into the experiences of Black mothers and daughters.

Box 8.1. Reflective Memo on Transcription and Narrative Inquiry.

> While listening to my interview, I realized that there were so many moments that I felt would never be captured in transcription. The laughter, the non-verbal communication, and the reflective pauses cannot truly be articulated in transcription. I really wanted to try Jeffersonian transcription with this interview. I felt that with that option I might be able to get close to putting into words what I heard during our 45-minute conversation. Given that this was my final interview for this course project, I felt that I finally was coming to terms with the reality of the incompleteness of transcribing. It's somewhat saddening but also understandable given the limitation of words themselves. With that said, I enjoyed going through this transcription and adding the pauses and stammers used during our conversation. It brought me back to our discussion and I envisioned myself being in that space of actively listening to my participant share and trying not to allow my mind to race too much as she detailed her relationships with her mother and daughter.

This reflective memo notes the potential and partiality of transcription in capturing the texture and nuances of language. Further, it provides an example of how writing memos during transcription helps researchers engage with their role in co-creating narratives for inquiry.

Analyzing and Representing Narrative Data

Narrative analysts generate common themes across narratives, explore how narratives are organized, examine how discourses function in narratives, or some combination of these. Regardless of the focus of the inquiry, narratives become the unit of analysis in the data. In this section we introduce you to common approaches used to analyze narrative data. We remind you that the approaches offered here are neither intended as an exhaustive list nor are these approaches prescriptive. As you consider different approaches to narrative analysis, we invite you to play with the data and experiment with some of the approaches offered here. Further examples are found at the end of the chapter.

Analysis of Narrative or Narrative Analysis?

Drawing on Bruner's (1985) concept of paradigmatic and narrative modes of thought, Polkinghorne (1995) argued that analysis in narrative inquiry can be best categorized either as analysis of narrative or narrative analysis. Let's look further.

Analysis of Narrative

Polkinghorne asserted that *analysis of narrative* relies on paradigmatic cognition that recognizes patterns and organizes information categorically. Thus, narrative studies using this approach might explore narratives for salient themes and offer stories from the data as illustrative examples. An example of this approach can be seen in Leavy and Ross's (2006) thematic analysis of oral history interviews from a participant's experiences with an eating disorder. Using a process of inductive coding, Leavy and Ross identified four salient themes across Claire's narratives ("Striving for Perfection," "Yearning for Control," "Autonomy as a Central Value," and "A Web of Pressures: Look at Me, I'm Shrinking") and offered storied excerpts from Claire's interview illustrating each theme.

Other *analysis of narrative* approaches include structural analyses of narratives often associated with sociolinguistic or discourse analysis. Such approaches often rely on focused methods of transcription as in the example described earlier from Riessman's (2008) study of childlessness among women in South India. Another approach to structural analysis of narrative is derived from the work of sociolinguistic scholar William Labov, who examined the temporal sequence oral storytellers use to organize events into a recognizable narrative structure. Labov and Waletzky (1967/1997) argued that spoken stories are organized using a temporal sequence that includes:

1. abstract, which summarizes the upcoming story,
2. orientation, which sets the scene,
3. complicating actions, which propels the story ahead,
4. resolution, which ends of the story,
5. evaluation, which draws attention to the most unusual aspect of the story, and
6. coda, a final comment that connects the story to the "real world" and present moment.

Researchers using this approach identify narrative excerpts or micro-stories from the data and code narrative clauses, according to the temporal sequences identified above.

Literacy scholars have applied Labov's approach to assess students' narrative development (McCabe & Peterson, 1991) and explore the ways individuals narrate social identities (Bamberg, 2010; Delvoye & Tasker, 2016; Ochs & Capps, 2001). In an example from criminology, Weir (2019) used Labovian analysis to explore the relationship between narrative structure and argumentation through an examination of two Canadian documentaries investigating a highly publicized case of the mistreatment and subsequent death of prisoner Ashley Smith. Weir examined patterns of conflicting evaluative statements across both documentaries and explored how particular evaluative statements were interwoven throughout the documentary to create a "through narrative" supporting particular interpretations of the event (p. 143).

Narrative Analysis

In contrast, *narrative analysis* (sometimes referred to as a narrative mode of analysis) focuses on a holistic rather than a categorical approach to examining narratives, where the researcher pulls together actions, events, and other elements into a plot and offers them to the reader in storied form. Following Polkinghorne's definition, Kim (2016) described the purpose of narrative analysis:

> to help the reader understand why and how things happened in the way they did, and why and how our participants acted in the way they did. The final story configured through the narrative mode of analysis has to appeal to readers

in a way that helps them empathize with the protagonist's lived experience as understandable human phenomena. (p. 197)

An example of narrative analysis can be seen in Craig's (2012) ethnographic study of a U.S. middle school during a period of school reform. Through her analysis of fieldwork texts, transcripts, and policy documents, Craig chronicled the narrative of one teacher's experience transitioning from "curriculum maker" to "curriculum implementer" (p. 90). In another example, Madison (1993) drew on Black feminist theories and poetic transcription in her analysis of oral history interviews with Mrs. Alma Kapper, a former domestic worker and sharecropper from Mississippi. Madison recounted Mrs. Kapper's stories using a combination of third-person narrative prose and first-person poetic performance told from the perspective of Mrs. Kapper.

If you are having trouble deciding on what approach to take, paradigmatic and narrative modes of thinking about narrative data are not mutually exclusive. As you play with data, you can employ both paradigmatic and narrative modes of analysis. Although these approaches offer different kinds of questions about the form and function of narratives in research, both are valuable for asking critical questions of your data. In Box 8.2 we offer some questions to guide your thinking about approaches to analyzing narrative data.

Box 8.2. Key Questions for Analyzing Narrative Data.

- What is my interest in narratives/stories as data?
  - Am I interested in ways storytellers compose and sequence events as narratives?
  - Am I interested in patterns or themes across multiple narratives? Within a single narrative?
  - Am I interested in constructing storied accounts from narrative data to represent lived experiences?
- Where am I noticing narratives in the data?
  - How might I bound this data for analysis?
- How are my subjectivities and theoretical perspectives informing my approach to analyzing narrative data?

Let's take a closer look at the ways researchers use narrative forms of representation in qualitative research.

The Appeal of Narrative

Scholars have written about the appeal of narrative inquiry both within and outside the academy to resonate with audiences, increase awareness around social issues, and critique unjust systems to promote more equitable practices (Miller et al., 2020; Stavrou & Murphy, 2021; Stockfelt, 2018). In short, narratives put a face on social issues. Consider political debates where candidates offer constituent narratives as illustrative examples of why a particular issue merits attention or why a particular candidate's policy stance has made a difference in the life of an ordinary citizen. Stories have a way of captivating an audience's attention. Similarly, narrative inquiry can be seductive for researchers as well (Hendry, 2007). You may find yourself more drawn to narrative writing than traditional, academic prose. You might enjoy playing with the narrative elements of plot, character, and setting or using devices such as metaphor or imagery. You may view writing across multiple narrative genres as a way to hone or challenge your creative skills. As we offer some ways researchers have used narrative representations in qualitative research, we invite you to experiment. Consider what different forms of narrative representation offer your inquiry. You might reflect on questions such as: How do different approaches to narrative representation enable you to tell different stories about your topic or participants? How might these approaches resonate with audiences? How do your subjectivities and theoretical perspectives influence the narrative of your research?

Approaches to Representation

Just as there are multiple ways to design and conduct a narrative study, scholars employ a range of approaches to representing narratives. These include composite narratives, counter-stories, and fictional approaches.

Composite Narratives

While some researchers focus on individual accounts in their narrative representation of the findings, others combine accounts from participants into a *composite narrative* (Piper & Sikes, 2010; Wertz et al., 2011; Willis, 2019). Researchers using a composite narrative approach incorporate elements across various participant accounts into a single cohesive story. One example of this approach in qualitative inquiry can be seen in Piper and Sikes' (2010) research with teachers accused and cleared on charges of pupil–teacher sexual abuse. Their decision to use composite narratives stemmed from concerns of protecting participants' identities both due to the sensitive nature of their topic and to the identities of LGBTQ+ teacher participants in their study.[4] Another example can be seen in Willis' (2019) interview study with 14 members of the U.K. Parliament. Willis wrote how she was "drawn to the storytelling by the data . . . they [politicians] had talked to me about their life and work, their aspirations and concerns and the nitty-gritty of how they got through their working day" (p. 473). Although Willis noted she could have chosen a few participants' accounts to focus on in depth or selected particular participants as individual cases in her study, she argued a composite narrative approach provided a way to "investigate how politicians, as (a group of) people, navigate their life and work" (p. 473).

Although researchers' reasons for using composite narratives to represent qualitative data vary, it is important to provide a rationale for doing so. Are you choosing composite narratives to protect participants' identities? Are you choosing composite narratives to present a holistic account of the data? Both? Further, you will want to be explicit about how you incorporate data into composite narratives and consider elements such as dialogue and setting. For example, Willis' (2019) description of the process for constructing composite narratives provides a helpful model:

1. Each composite is based on transcripts from interviews. 3–5 transcripts are condensed into one composite narrative[. . .]
2. All quotations come directly from these interview transcripts.
3. Other details, such as where the interview took place; how the conversation evolved; and any paraphrasing of discussions, are taken directly from one of the source interviews.

4. In the narrative itself, I avoid imposing any judgment on the interviewees' experiences and opinions, and do not assume motivations or feelings. Any comments of this nature in the narrative are taken directly from the interviewees. (pp. 474–475)

Counter-stories and Counter-narratives

In your experiences as a student or consumer of news and entertainment, you may have heard the question: "Who controls the narrative?" The story of the first Thanksgiving in the United States is one that has been widely told from the perspective of white colonists. It is a story that emphasizes a peaceful co-existence among white colonists and Indigenous people and ignores the systematic murder and removal of Indigenous people from their land in the service of white imperialism. Such stories are examples of grand or "metanarratives" (Lyotard, 1979) that provide totalizing accounts of groups, nations, or institutions. Grand or "master" narratives are controlled by the dominant group and work in the service of keeping dominant groups in power. Emerging from the field of critical legal studies and critical race theory, counter-storytelling is a methodological approach that challenges master narratives and dominant or mainstream perspectives. Counter-stories provide nuanced understanding of the social and historical factors that have given rise to systemic issues such as racism, sexism, homophobia, and so forth. While some scholars use the terms counter-narrative and counter-story interchangeably, others draw distinctions between them (see Miller et al., 2020). For our purposes here, we use these terms interchangeably to explore studies that use critical perspectives to challenge dominant narratives about people, groups and institutions.

Testimonios, a narrative methodology with strong ties to feminist Chicana and Latina epistemologies, offer one example of the way counter-stories have been used in qualitative research. Reyes and Curry Rodríguez (2012) defined *testimonio* as "a first person oral or written account, drawing on experiential, self-conscious, narrative practice to articulate an urgent voicing of something to which one bears witness" (p. 525). Although testimonios may take many forms (e.g., memoir, vignette, prose, song, spoken word) they are intentional, political acts meant to "bring to light a wrong, a point of view, or an urgent call for action" (p. 525). Gibbs (2020) used testimonio methodology to provide two narrative accounts of Chicanx[5] social studies teachers' experiences of teaching from a critical lens while fostering a classroom of healing. After conducting life story interviews with participants, Gibbs invited them to participate in the construction of their first-person accounts. In the excerpt below, Gibbs combined narrative third-person prose with a first-person account from a teacher in his study. The line break in the block quote indicates the shift from third-person to first-person perspective:

> Ms. Cortez had long dark hair with long strands of gray on the edges. During our conversation she had a deep undercut, shaved into the back of her hair and one side, causing her hair to fall on her right shoulder. She was speaking about how her Ethnic Studies course was developed.
>
> It's a miracle it came to be. I graduated from my teacher education program, got hired at Patton High School and was happy. Teaching was a struggle . . . but I always knew it would be. Our program [teacher education] talked about that a lot, that to teach for social justice, to build a critical consciousness in your students was going to be hard, the students would struggle with it because it was new and different to them and the system, the school, the curriculum, the administration were likely going to all be opposed to it. So, I knew I was in for a fight. (p. 101).

While some counter-narratives may be generated using interview methods as in the case of Ms. Cortez's testimonio above, others more closely resemble first-person accounts found in autoethnographic studies. In their edited volume, Brewer and deMarrais (2015) feature first-person counter-narratives of teachers' experiences working with the Teach for America (TFA) program. In one example from this collection, Sarah Ishmael (2015) reflected on her experiences as an Afro-Caribbean woman teaching for TFA in Baton Rouge, Louisiana. Drawing on the work of critical race scholars such as Ladson-Billings and Tate (2006), King (1991) and others (e.g., Anzaldúa, 2012), Ishmael's narrative "make(s) visible the ways in which TFA ignores underlying racial and class dynamics and perpetuates institutional racism in classrooms. It challenges the organization's dedication to racial equity and its ability to break down class barriers between corps members and their students" (p. 87). Ishmael's wonderful example of a counter-narrative interweaves historical context, personal story, and theory, offering an example of the ways theory helps us explain how we encounter the world (see Chapter 3 on theory). Taken together, the counter-narratives across this volume challenge grand narratives controlled by the TFA organization and its supporters, offering a space where the "voices of dissenters and critics can be heard" (Brewer & deMarrais, 2015, p. 5).

Although some studies use narrative forms (e.g., vignettes, short story) to represent counter-stories as seen in the example above, others may take a more paradigmatic approach and present counter-stories through discussions of salient themes or categories related to participants' accounts. One example is Kohnen and Lacy's (2018) study of students' reaction to the media coverage of a fight that occurred in their U.S. high school. Drawing on structural discourse analysis and critical race media literacy, Kohnen and Lacy examined how student responses to news coverage resisted the media narrative that framed the fight as an outcome of gang violence. Rather than offer counter-narratives in storied form, Kohnen and Lacy used illustrative examples from students' responses to disprove claims offered in news reports. As you consider the potential of counter-story/counter-narrative approaches, think about the questions and overarching purpose of your inquiry. What dominant narrative does your inquiry challenge? Whose stories provide alternative perspectives to the dominant narrative? Will your research offer intact counter-narratives? Will you explore one or more firsthand accounts that challenge dominant narratives about your phenomenon of interest? Will you explore themes and/or discursive moves across accounts that challenge dominant narratives?

Literary Approaches

In the past two decades there has been growing interest in narrative representations that blur boundaries between fiction and nonfiction (Inckle, 2010; Leavy, 2023; Watson 2022) although both fiction and creative nonfiction has a long history in qualitative research. Inckle (2010) used the term *ethnographic fictions* to describe the process of crafting composite vignettes around particular themes or issues encountered when doing research. Fictional accounts have been generated from ethnographic studies in anthropology (e.g., Angrosino, 1998; Brain, 1977; Hecht, 2006; Wolf, 1992), and other disciplines. Inckle asserted that such fictional approaches "represent the complexities of embodied experience in ways which are ethically salient and which produce manifold possibilities of transformation and change" (p. 39).

Social Fiction. Patricia Leavy has used the terms *social fiction* or *fiction-based research* to describe the process of blending fictional forms of representation with social science research. Drawing from the work of arts-based scholars (e.g., Barone & Eisner, 2012; Cole & Knowles, 2001) and the tradition of ethnographic storytelling, Leavy (2013) similarly noted the "rich history" of blurred genres in social science inquiry (p. 36) and, like Inckle, challenged the rigid binary categories of fact and fiction in social science research. She wrote:

> In the academic world, researchers are storytellers, learning about others and sharing what they have learned. Whether we go into the field in an ethnographic study or conduct oral history interviews, we are charged with telling the stories of others in creative, expressive, dynamic and authentic ways . . . When we represent and share our research, our goal is not simply to expose others to it, but to affect those who read our work. (p. 35)

Researchers using social fiction vary in the ways they incorporate data and methods in their storied accounts. Leavy and Scotti's (2017) *Low-Fat Love Stories* offers an example of social fiction that stays close to participant data. The collection of short stories in this volume is based on interviews with women about their experiences with dissatisfying relationships with partners, family, friends, or with their own bodies. Short story topics were informed by themes generated through analysis of interview transcripts and were constructed from verbatim language of women participants. In another example, Jessica Smartt Gullion's (2014) *October Birds*, which drew on the author's experience as an epidemiologist during national and international health crises (e.g., 2003 anthrax scare in the United States, SARS, H1N1 influenza), used social fiction to represent a small Texas town's response to a pandemic.

In the examples offered here, Leavy and Scotti described methods used to recruit participants, generate data, and conduct analysis. In contrast, Gullion offered a brief description of personal and professional experiences informing the fictionalized account offered in *October Birds*. If you are interested in a social fiction approach to representing research findings, consider how closely you plan to stay to the data in your storied account. Document your process for analyzing data and creating storied accounts. If you are using social fiction for dissertation research, your committee will likely ask you to provide a rationale for using this approach and may require a separate methods chapter in which you describe how you approach data analysis and your process of creating narratives from research data. A research journal is a great place to record your process and write about your relationship to the research process as you go.

Speculative Fiction. More recently, speculative fiction is an approach gaining attention among narrative and arts-based qualitative researchers. Speculative fiction, sometimes called science fiction or fantasy, is a literary genre defined as: "a broad category of fiction encompassing any story that contains imaginative, futuristic, or supernatural elements" (Dictionary.com, n.d.). Book series like *Harry Potter, Maze Runner, A Wrinkle in Time,* or *The Giver* are examples of speculative fiction written for young adult (YA) readers. In recent years, qualitative scholars have taken up concepts explored in the speculative fiction writing of novelists like Octavia Butler and Ursula Le Guin (de Freitas & Truman, 2021) or used speculative fiction prompts as methods for generating research data (e.g., Wilson et al., 2022). Just as social fiction writers challenge boundaries between fact and fiction, qualitative scholars using speculative fiction genres engage temporal and technological boundaries that blur lines between past and present and human–nonhuman.

Stephanie R. Toliver (2022) drew on Black feminist, womanist, and Afrofuturist epistemologies to offer what she called Endarkened storywork in the form of futuristic narratives based on her personal experience and research conducted with six girls attending an Afrofuturist summer writing workshop. Describing her approach to Endarkened storywork, Toliver wrote: "The Endarkened storywork represented in this book highlights the sociopolitical concerns of Black girls while simultaneously featuring Black girls as researchers whose stories utilized the past and present to theorize possibilities for the future" (p. xxxvii). Set in the year 2085 and told from a first-person perspective through a character named Jane, Toliver intertwined storied encounters from her summer Afrofuturist writing workshop. We offer an excerpt from the Introductory chapter entitled "My name is Jane and this is my world" below:

May 1, 2085

The bluer the eyes, the more successful the programming. That's what they tell us anyway. The Dreamers' eyes are brown, amber, green, gray, or hazel. My eyes and the eyes of all the Endarkened are different shades of blue, some as piercing as the color of LED lights and others as bright as the sky on a sunny day . . . In history, we learned that in the early 2000s–2019 to be exact—the experiments started. They'd been experimenting on us for centuries, but that was the first year they started the dream extractions. They used Black women first due to the procedure's scientific infancy. Black women were prime specimens, proud mules ready to bear the burden of scientific progress for the betterment of society. (p. 1)

As you can see in the excerpt above, readers are dropped into the midst of the world Toliver has created. Although the preface and companion chapters situate these narratives within a sociocultural, theoretical, and methodological context, Toliver has skillfully interwoven these pieces within the stories themselves. Toliver's work provides a beautiful example of qualitative research using speculative fiction as a mode of representation. Such innovation and creativity show how qualitative researchers continue to push the boundaries of what constitutes research social science.

Creative Nonfiction. Researchers can also use literature strategies used by fiction writers to represent factual stories. It is important when writing creative nonfiction to accurately represent reality—in other words, events and experiences are represented in chronologically accurate ways and persons are real, rather than invented. Lee Gutkind has worked with science writers to employ literary strategies to represent the "stories" of their research to the public. As one example, Gutkind embedded himself in hospital settings to explore the world of organ transplantation (see Gutkind, 1988). Caulley (2008) has illustrated strategies for how qualitative researchers can use literary tools to write creative nonfiction, making reports "less boring." We paraphrase some of Caulley's suggestions below:

- Use a scene-by-scene approach that puts readers in the research context
- Use realistic, concrete details that conjure emotions and images for readers
- Use conversation and sensory details that show rather than tell
- Use active voice and avoid "to be" verbs (is, are, am, were, was) (pp. 429–435)

Ethical Considerations

As you consider narrative approaches for your research it is important to consider the ethics of storytelling in research. Whether you draw on archival methods, interviews, focus groups, observation, or some combination to generate data, sharing stories of experience is deeply personal and researchers should treat those stories with care. As in the example of Piper and Sikes (2010), researchers used composite narratives to protect the anonymity of participants. If you are considering research with vulnerable populations or minors, you may want to consider using composite narratives or characters. In other chapters, we discuss the importance of member-checking interview transcripts with participants. In some instances, participants may have second thoughts about information they have shared in an interview or focus group. It is important to recognize that the stories we tell with our research are not ours alone and to recognize that the stories we tell have a life beyond our published work (Rosiek & Snyder, 2018).

If you use narrative forms to represent the findings from your study, consider the implications of using literary elements and devices in your work. This may bring up interesting questions for you such as: How do I decide which stories to tell? From whose perspective will I narrate those stories? What point of view (e.g., first person, third person) will I use? How do I develop participants as characters? How do I distill a cohesive plot from data that might enfold multiple possible stories? How do I make decisions about dialogue? As Janie constructed narratives from her dissertation interviews on mothers preparing menstruating children for puberty, she struggled with many of these questions. In addition to member-checking interview transcripts, she found it important to follow up with participants as she constructed and completed narratives from the data. She had ethical questions about writing dialogue in the voice of participants and their children and asked for feedback from participants about how dialogue might best honor the voices of mothers and their children (Copple, 2022). Before submitting her book-length manuscript, Toliver (2022) hired three of the middle school participants from her study as consultants to review her manuscript. Reflecting on this process, she wrote:

> By engaging in this method, the girls were able to read and evaluate the story before anyone else was able to see it. Of course, this work wasn't easy. I had to surrender my storied creation to the wisdom of young Black girls in a society that still refuses to believe in the intellectual expansiveness of Black girlhood. Still, I realized that I wasn't writing this book for traditional academics or an ignorant society. I was writing this book for young Black girls. (p. xxxiii)

This quote from Toliver reminds us that considering the audience for one's research entangles with questions such as: Who is your research for? What do you envision your research doing in the world? How might your published work contribute to the communities with whom you are researching? In addition, the ways we approach ethics in narrative forms of representation are connected with the theoretical and methodological perspectives guiding our inquiry. In this way, honoring participants' input in our creative processes as researchers is a way of "walking the walk" or being "faithful" to the theoretical, philosophical, or spiritual principles guiding our inquiry (Guyotte & Kuntz, 2018; Preissle & deMarrais, 2011).

Connelly and Clandinin (1990) argued that the act of telling and listening to stories is a relational encounter. In other words, as you listen to someone's story you become part of it through the way you respond and communicate it to others. As you consider narrative inquiry through the lens of relational ethics, you might imagine your relationships with participants in each phase of the research process. You might ask: What does it mean to listen to participants' stories carefully and respectfully? What does it mean to transcribe, bound, and analyze narratives carefully and respectfully? What does care and respect look like in the member-checking process? In the publishing process? As we discuss in an earlier chapter of this book, ethics should be considered throughout the process of designing, conducting, and reporting a research study.

As you consider narrative approaches in your study, we encourage you to engage in conversations with participants about how you might use narrative methods to represent your findings should you choose to do so. Should you choose to use storied forms to represent findings, we encourage you to experiment with different genres and points of view. Ask critical questions about the affordances of particular genres and perspectives and be sure to get feedback on your writing from trusted colleagues and participants. An important part of honoring the relational ethics of storytelling is offering a quality narrative representation to your audience. A poorly crafted story runs the risk of readers losing interest. If you incorporate narrative representations in your research, you want readers to be drawn in by your storytelling because doing so bears witness to the stories participants have shared with you. If you do not have a creative writing or literary background, consider enrolling in a creative writing workshop, masterclass, or joining a creative writing group. Doing so offers opportunities for feedback on your writing and will help you be a better critic of your own work as you engage this process with others' work.

Conclusions

In this chapter we explored key concepts related to the theorization of narrative inquiry in qualitative research. We emphasized the epistemological underpinnings of narrative inquiry in social science, focusing specifically on narrative as a way of knowing and making meaning in the world. We provided examples of different ways qualitative researchers generate and analyze data, including structural and storied modes of analysis and representation. We concluded with examples of ways scholars are continuing to innovate and push the boundaries of what is possible in narrative inquiry and offered ethical considerations for novices to this approach. You will also find examples of studies that use narrative inquiry in the Appendix. See the study by Roshaunda Breeden, who used counter-storytelling combined with arts-based inquiry, which we examine in Chapter 10. We close this chapter with recommendations for further reading and exercises to get you thinking about narrative approaches to research.

Activities

1. Working with a partner, create personal narratives of a "first" encounter you have in common (first day of school, first international trip, first graduate course, first day at a new job). Exchange narratives and compare for common themes. Working together, create a composite narrative that combines key elements from each narrative.

2. Conduct an interview with someone about a time when they encountered something challenging or difficult. Transcribe the interview and create a storied account from the interview using one or more of the following approaches:

   a. Reduce the interview to a core story—take out all the words that don't move the plot along or seem extraneous to the story. Add details that enhance the individual's narrative and enrich the story.

   b. Identify themes that run through the interview and incorporate events connected to these themes.

    c. Create a map/table/image to identify story elements (e.g., character, setting, plot, theme, conflict) before constructing the narrative.

3. Look through old family photos or scrapbooks and find an image that stands out to you. Using details from the photo, surrounding photos, and captions, create a story to describe what is happening in the photo.

4. Using the same photo in exercise 6, create a fictional or futuristic narrative to tell the story of what is happening in the photo.

Further Reading

Resources for Using Narrative Methods

Andrews, M., Squire, C., & Tamboukou, M. (Eds.). (2008). *Doing narrative research*. SAGE.

Bold, C. (2011). *Using narrative in research*. SAGE.

Clandinin, D. J., Caine, V., & Lessard, S. (2018). *The relational ethics of narrative inquiry*. Routledge.

De Fina, A., & Georgakopoulou, A. (2015). *The handbook of narrative analysis*. John Wiley & Sons.

Hendry, P. M. (2009). Narrative as inquiry. *Journal of Educational Research, 103*(2), 72–80. https://doi.org/10.1080/00220670903323354

Hendry, P. M., Mitchell, R. W., & Eaton, P. W. (2018). *Troubling method: Narrative research as being*. Peter Lang.

Orr, K., Smith, B., Arbour-Nicitopoulos, K. P., & Wright, F. V. (2021). The café talk: A discussion of the process of developing a creative non-fiction. *Qualitative Research in Sport, Exercise and Health, 13*(6), 887–903. https://doi.org/10.1080/2159676X.2020.1834443

Examples of Narrative Qualitative Research

Gilmore, M., & Miller, M. M. (2013). Writings of lions: Narrative inquiry of a Kenyan couple living in the U.S. *The Qualitative Report, 18*(4), 1–14. https://doi.org/10.46743/2160-3715/2013.1562

Harper, A. B. (2014). *Scars: A lesbian Black experience in rural white New England*. Sense Publishers.

Huber, L. P. (2009). Disrupting apartheid of knowledge: Testimonio as methodology in Latina/o critical race research in education. *International Journal of Qualitative Studies in Education, 22*(6), 639–654. https://doi.org/10.1080/09518390903333863

Johnson Bailey, J. (2001). *Sistahs in college: Making a way out of no way*. Krieger Publishing Company.

Rhee, J. E. (2006). Re/membering (to) shifting alignments: Korean women's transnational narratives in US higher education. *International Journal of Qualitative Studies in Education, 19*(5), 595–615. https://doi.org/10.1080/09518390600886379

Notes

1. In 1998, the title of the *Journal of Narrative and Life History* was changed to *Narrative Inquiry*.

2. Building on Durkheim (1951) and Merton's (1968) concept of anomie, Owino and Weber (2020) noted "anomie is understood as a feeling of disillusionment and despair because society is unable to provide clear boundaries and structures that enable individuals to make meaning out of their lives" (p. 70).

3. Purposive network sampling (sometimes referred to as snowball sampling) refers to the practice of recruiting research participants through a social network of individuals with a shared, common experience (Schwandt, 2015).

4. We recognize that LGBTQIA+ is more inclusive of the ways individuals experience gender identity and sexual orientation. We use LGBTQ+ here to be consistent with the language in the Piper and Sikes (2010) study.

5. Chicanx is used as a gender-neutral alternative to Chicano or Chicana. Researchers can check to see how participants themselves identify, and what descriptors they prefer.

References

Angrosino, M. V. (1998). *Opportunity house: Ethnographic studies of mental retardation*. Altamira Press.

Anzaldúa, G. (2012). *Borderlands/La Frontera: The new mestiza* (4th ed.). Aunt Lute.

Asplund, S.-B., & Pérez Prieto, H. (2020). Approaching life story interviews as sites of interaction: Integrating conversation analysis with a life story approach. *Qualitative Research Journal, 20*(2), 175–187. https://doi.org/10.1108/QRJ-03-2019-0033

Atkinson, R. (2007). The life story interview as a bridge in narrative inquiry. In D. J. Clandinin (Eds.) *Handbook of narrative inquiry: Mapping a methodology* (pp. 224–245). SAGE.

Bamberg, M. (2010). Who am I? Narration and its contribution to self and identity. *Theory and Psychology 21*,1–22. https://doi.org/10.1177/0959354309355852

Barone, T., & Eisner, E. W. (2012). *Arts-based research*. SAGE.

Brain, R. (1977). *Kolonialagent: A novel with an appendix*. Faber.

Brewer, T. J., & deMarrais, K. (2015). *Teach for America counter-narratives: Alumni speak up and speak out*. Peter Lang.

Bruner, J. (1985). Narrative and paradigmatic modes of thought. Teachers College Record, 86(6), 97–115. https://doi.org/10.1177/016146818508600606

Bruner, J. (1986). *Actual minds, possible worlds*. Harvard University Press.

Caulley, D. N. (2008). Making qualitative research reports less boring: The techniques of writing creative nonfiction. *Qualitative Inquiry, 14*(3), 424–449. https://doi.org/10.1177/10778 00407311961

Chase, S. E. (2005). Narrative inquiry: Multiple lenses, approaches, voices. In N. K. Denzin & Y. S. Lincoln (Eds.), *Handbook of Qualitative Research* (3rd ed., pp. 651–679). SAGE.

Coles, R. (1989). *The call of stories: Teaching and the moral imagination*. Houghton Mifflin.

Cole, A. L., & Knowles, J. G. (2001). *Lives in context: The art of life history research*. Altamira.

Connelly, F. M., & Clandinin, D. J. (1990). Stories of experience and narrative inquiry. *Educational Researcher, 19*(5), 2–14. https://doi.org/10.2307/1176100

Copple, J. (2022). *Making menstrual knowledge through multi-genre methodologies: Exploring mothers' encounters with children at menarche* (Publication No. 2685467286) [Doctoral dissertation, University of Georgia]. https://www.proquest.com/dissertations-theses/making-menstrual-knowledge-through-multi-genre/docview/2685467286/se-2

Cortazzi, M. (1993). *Narrative analysis*. The Falmer Press.

Craig, C. (2012). "Butterfly under a pin": An emergent teacher image amid mandated curriculum reform. *Journal of Educational Research, 105*(2), 90–101. https://doi.org/10.1080/00220671.2010.51941

Crites, S. (1986). Storytime: Recollecting the past and projecting the future. In T. Sarbin (Ed.), *Narrative psychology: The storied nature of human conduct* (pp. 152–173). Praeger.

de Freitas, E., & Truman, S. E. (2021). New empiricisms in the Anthropocene: Thinking with speculative fiction about science and social inquiry. *Qualitative Inquiry, 27*(5), 522–533. https://doi.org/10.1177/1077800420943643

Delvoye, M., & Tasker, F. (2016). Narrating self-identity in bisexual motherhood. *Journal of GLBT Family Studies, 12*(1), 5–23. https://doi.org/10.1080/1550428X.2015.1038675

deMarrais, K. (2004). Qualitative interview studies: Learning through experience. In K. deMarrais & S. D. Lapan (Eds.), *Foundations for research: Methods of inquiry in education and the social sciences* (pp. 51–68). Lawrence Erlbaum.

Dictionary.com (n.d.). *Speculative fiction*. In Dictionary.com. Retrieved April 10, 2023.

Durkheim, E. (1951). *Suicide*. The Free Press.

Ellis, C. (1995). *Final negotiations: A story of love, loss, and chronic illness*. Temple University Press.

Ellis, C., & Bochner, A. (1996). *Composing ethnography: Alternative forms of qualitative writing*. AltaMira.

Gee, J. P. (2014). *An introduction to discourse analysis: Theory and method*. Routledge.

Gibbs, B. C. (2020). Critical teaching in classrooms of healing: Struggles and testimonios. *Journal of Curriculum Studies Research, 2*(1), 95–111. https://doi.org/10.46303/jcsr.02.01.6

Goodson, I., & Gill, S. (2011). *Narrative pedagogy: Life history and learning*. Peter Lang.

Gullion, J. S. (2014). *October birds: A novel about pandemic influenza, infection control and first responders*. Springer.

Gutkind, L. (1988). *Many sleepless nights: The world of organ transplantation*. W.W. Norton & Co.

Guyotte, K.W., & Kuntz, A.M. (2018). Becoming openly faithful: Qualitative pedagogy and paradigmatic slippage. *International Review of Qualitative Research, 11*(3), 256–270. https://doi.org/10.1525/irqr.2018.11.3.256

Hecht, T. (2006). *After life: An ethnographic novel*. Duke University Press.

Hendry, P. M. (2007). The future of narrative. *Qualitative inquiry, 13*(4), 487–498. https://doi.org/10.1177/1077800406297673

Hendry, P.M. (2010). Narrative as inquiry. *The Journal of Educational Research, 103*, 72–80. https://doi.org/10.1080/00220670903323354

Hyvärinen, M. (2010) Revisiting the narrative turns. *Life Writing 7*(1), 69–82. https://doi.org/10.1080/14484520903342957

Inckle, K. (2010). Telling tales? Using ethnographic fictions to speak embodied "truth." *Qualitative Research, 10*(1), 27–47. https://doi.org/10.1177/1468794109348681

Ishmael, S. (2015). Dyconscious racism, classism & TFA. In T. J. Brewer & K. deMarrais (Eds.) *Teach for America counter-narratives: Alumni speak up and speak out* (pp. 85–94). Peter Lang.

Kim, J. (2016). *Understanding narrative inquiry.* SAGE.

King, J. (1991). Dysconscious racism: Ideology, identity and the miseducation of teachers. *Journal of Negro Education, 60*(2), 133–146. https://www.jstor.org/stable/2295605

Kohnen, A. M., & Lacy, A. (2018). "They don't see us otherwise": A discourse analysis of marginalized students critiquing the local news. *Linguistics and Education, 46*, 102–112. https://doi.org/10.1016/j.linged.2018.07.002

Kramp, M.K. (2004). Exploring life and experience through narrative inquiry. In K. deMarrais & S. D. Lapan (Eds.), *Foundations for research: Methods of inquiry in education and the social sciences* (pp.103–121). Lawrence Erlbaum.

Labov, W. & Waletzky, J. (1997). Narrative analysis. *Journal of Narrative and Life History 7*(1-4), 3–38. https://doi.org/10.1075/jnlh.7.02nar (Reprinted from *Essays on the verbal and visual arts*, 12–44, by J. Helm, Ed., 1967, University of Washington Press)

Ladson-Billings, G., & Tate, W. F. (2006). Towards a critical race theory of education. In A. Dixson & C. Rousseau (Eds.), *Critical race theory in education: All God's children got a song* (pp. 11–31). Routledge.

Langellier, K.M. (2001). Personal narrative. In M. Jolly (Ed.) *Encyclopedia of life writing: Autobiographical and biographical forms* (pp. 699–701). Fitzroy Dearborn.

Leavy, P. (2013). *Fiction as research practice: Short stories, novellas, and novels.* Routledge.

Leavy, P. (2023). *Re/invention: Methods of social fiction.* Guilford Press.

Leavy, P., & Ross, L. S. (2006). The matrix of eating disorder vulnerability: Oral history and the link between personal and social problems. *The Oral History Review, 33*(1), 65–81. https://www.jstor.org/stable/3675666

Leavy, P., & Scotti, V. (2017). *Low-fat love stories.* Sense Publishers.

Lieblich, A. (2013). Healing plots: Writing and reading in life-stories groups. *Qualitative Inquiry, 19*(1), 46–52. https://doi.org/10.1177/1077800412462982

Lyotard, J. (1979). *The postmodern condition.* Manchester University Press.

Madison, S. (1993). "That was my occupation": Oral narrative, performance, and Black Feminist thought. *Text and Performance Quarterly, 13*(3), 213–232. https://doi.org/10.1080/10462939309366051

McAdams, D. P. (1993). *The stories we live by: Personal myths and the making of the self.* William C. Morrow and Co.

McCabe, A. & Peterson, C. (1991). Getting the story: A longitudinal study of parental styles in eliciting narratives and developing narrative skill. In A. McCabe & C. Peterson (Eds.), *Developing narrative structure* (pp. 217–253). Lawrence Erlbaum.

Merton, K. R. (1968). *Social theory and social structure.* The Free Press.

Miller, R., Liu, K., & Ball, A. F. (2020). Critical counter-narrative as transformative methodology for educational equity. *Review of Research in Education, 44*(1), 269–300. http://dx.doi.org/10.3102/0091732X20908501

Mishler, E. G. (1986). The analysis of interview-narratives. In T. R. Sarbin (Ed.), *Narrative psychology: The storied nature of human conduct* (pp. 233–255). Praeger Publishers/Greenwood Publishing Group.

Mishler, E. G. (1991 [1986]). *Research interviewing: Context and narrative.* Harvard University Press.

Mitchell, W. J. T. (Ed.) (1981). *On narrative.* University of Chicago Press.

Ochs, E., & Capps, L. (2001). *Living narrative: Creating lives in everyday storytelling.* Harvard University Press.

Owino, J., & Weber, C. D. (2020). Explicating anomie in refugee women's integration narratives: A qualitative research study. *International Journal of Intercultural Relations, 74*, 69–79. https://doi.org/10.1016/j.ijintrel.2019.10.011

Pinnegar, S., & Daynes, J. G. (2007). Locating narrative inquiry historically: Thematics in the turn to narrative. In D. J. Clandinin (Ed.), *Handbook of narrative inquiry: Mapping a methodology* (pp. 3–34). SAGE.

Piper, H., and Sikes, P. (2010). All teachers are vulnerable but especially gay teachers: Using composite fictions to protect research participants in pupil–teacher sex-related research. *Qualitative Inquiry 16*(7), 566–574. https://doi.org/10.177/11077800410371923

Polkinghorne, D. E. (1988). *Narrative knowing and the human sciences.* SUNY Press.

Polkinghorne, D. E. (2007). Validity issues in narrative research. *Qualitative Inquiry, 13*(4), 471–486. https://.doi.org/10.1177/1077800406297670

Preissle, J., & deMarrais, K. (2011). Teaching qualitative research responsively. In N. K. Denzin & M. D. Giardina (Eds.), *Qualitative inquiry and global crises* (pp. 31–39). Left Coast Press.

Rawicki, J., & Ellis, C. (2011). Lechem hara (bad bread), lechem tov (good bread): Survival and sacrifice during the holocaust. *Qualitative Inquiry, 17*(2), 155–157. https://doi.org/10.1177/1077800410392337

Reyes, K. B., & Curry Rodríguez, J. E. (2012). Testimonio: Origins, terms, and resources. *Equity & Excellence in Education, 45*(3), 525–538. https://doi.org/10.1080/10665684.2012.698571

Ricoeur, P. (1984). *Time and narrative.* trans. Kathleen McLaughlin and David Pellauer. University of Chicago Press.

Riessman, C. K. (2008). *Narrative methods for the human sciences.* SAGE.

Rosiek, J. L., & Snyder, J. (2018). Narrative inquiry and new materialism: Stories as (not necessarily benign) agents. *Qualitative Inquiry, 26*(10), 1151–1162. https://doi.org/10.1177/1077800418784326

Schwandt, T. (2015). *SAGE dictionary of qualitative inquiry* (4th ed.). SAGE.

Sefora, S., & Ngubane, S. A. (2023). Career development for students with disabilities in an open distance learning institution: A narrative inquiry. *Disability & Society, 38*(3), 445–459. https://doi.org/10.1080/09687599.2021.1946676

Shelton, S. A. (2014). Narrative interviewing: Teachers' experiences with Lesbian, Gay, Bisexual, Transgender, and Queer Issues in education. In *SAGE research methods cases* (pp. 1–20). SAGE.

Sheridan, J., Chamberlain, K., & Dupuis, A. (2011). Timelining: Visualizing experience. *Qualitative Research, 11*(5), 552–569. https://doi.org/10.1177/1468794111413235

Spence, D. P. (1982). *Narrative truth and historical truth.* W. W. Norton.

Stavrou, S., & Murphy, M. S. (2021). Methodological landscapes: Mapping narrative inquiry, critical race theory, and anti-racist education. *Journal of Critical Race Inquiry, 8*(1), 1–21.

Stockfelt, S. (2018). We the minority-of-minorities: A narrative inquiry of black female academics in the United Kingdom. *British Journal of Sociology of Education, 39*(7), 1012–1029. https://doi.org/10.1080/01425692.2018.1454297

Toliver, S. R. (2022). *Recovering Black storytelling in qualitative research: Endarkened storywork.* Routledge.

Watson, A. (2022). Writing sociological fiction. *Qualitative Research, 22*(3), 337–352. https://doi.org/10.1177/1468794120985677

Weir, C. C. (2019). Meaning-making through narrative: Extending narrative analysis for criminological examination of documentary film. *Journal of Qualitative Criminal Justice & Criminology, 7*(3), 123–147. https://doi.org/10.21428/88de04a1.c5fd6e8d

Wertz, M. S., Nosek, M., McNieshm S., & Marlow, E. (2011). The composite first person narrative: Texture, structure, and meaning in writing phenomenological descriptions. *International Journal of Qualitative Studies on Health & Well-Being, 6*(2), 1–10. https://doi.org/10.3402/qhw.v6i2.5882

Willis, R. (2019). The use of composite narratives to present interview findings. *Qualitative Research, 19*(4), 471–480. https://dio.org/10.1177/1468794118787711

Wilson, A., Ross, J., McKie, J., Collier, A., & Lockley, P. (2022). Telling data stories: Developing an online tool for participatory speculative fiction. In *SAGE research methods: Doing research online.* SAGE. https://doi.org/10.4135/9781529603514

Wolf, M. (1992). *A thrice told tale: Feminism, postmodernism and ethnographic responsibility.* Stanford University Press.

NINE

Designing Autoethnography

LEARNING OBJECTIVES

After reading this chapter you should be able to:

- Understand the origins of autoethnography.
- Distinguish between autoethnography and other forms of personal narrative and life writing.
- Identify and select from a range of approaches to autoethnography to design an autoethnographic study.
- Understand ethical considerations and challenges of conducting autoethnographic research.

THIS CHAPTER EXPLORES AUTOETHNOGRAPHIC APPROACHES to qualitative research. While ethnographers explore the interactions of people and communities to better understand cultural norms and practices, autoethnographers examine the relationship between personal experiences and culture. In other words, the question "What is going on here?" is turned on the self. Just as ethnographers create narratives of the communities they study, autoethnographers create personal narratives of particular encounters or events (e.g., grieving, caring for family members, navigating illness). As you will see in the examples across this chapter, autoethnographies cover a wide range of topics and autoethnographers use multiple genres and modalities to represent their findings (e.g., poetic, prose, film, essays, performance). In this chapter we begin by defining terms related to autoethnographic studies. As we define terms, we provide an overview of the origins of autoethnography in qualitative research and distinguish autoethnographic texts from other forms of life writing (e.g., autobiography, memoir). We turn to examples of auto-ethnographic representation and provide suggestions for designing an auto-ethnographic study, including guiding questions for brainstorming potential topics and suggestions for generating autoethnographic data. We conclude with ethical considerations for conducting autoethnographic research and offer recommendations for further reading. Let's begin with an overview of the origins of autoethnography and defining some commonly used terms in autoethnographic inquiry.

Defining Terms

Tony Adams and colleagues (2017), writing in the *International Encyclopedia of Communication Research Methods*, defined autoethnography as "a research method that uses personal experience ("auto") to describe and interpret ("graphy") cultural texts, experiences, beliefs, and practices ("ethno")" (p. 1). Although autoethnography is now widely accepted among qualitative scholars, it has a recent history. The term autoethnography first appeared in a 1975 article written by anthropologist Karl Heider. In his study of the Dani people of Indonesia, Heider used "auto-ethnography" to describe how Dani villagers made sense of their daily activities. He called this process of self-reporting about one's community auto-ethnography. Heider wrote, "auto-ethnography gives some sort of picture of the Dani's own view or knowledge or cognitive map of their world" (p. 9). We can see connections here between Heider's definition of autoethnography and a cognitive understanding of culture as "the acquired knowledge that people use to generate behavior and interpret experience" (Spradley & McCurdy, 2012, p. 16). A few years later, anthropologist David Hayano (1979) used autoethnography to describe his inquiry of the ethnographer as "an indigenous insider" (p. 100). Although Heider employed autoethnography to describe participants' views of themselves and Hayano used autoethnography to describe the researcher's perspective, both examples have to do with the way people understand the relationship between themselves and culture. It is this relationship between personal experience and culture that provides the basis for autoethnographic studies. Writing about the relationship between personal experience and culture, Heewon Chang (2008) noted that autoethnographies are "individual stories . . . framed in the context of the bigger story, a story of the society" (p. 49). We like Chang's definition because of its emphasis on personal experience, culture, and storied representation. Given autoethnography's emphasis on personal narratives, it may not be surprising that the rise of autoethnography in qualitative inquiry can be traced, in part, to the "narrative turn" in qualitative research (Adams & Herrmann, 2020; Denzin & Lincoln, 2000; Douglass & Carless, 2013).[1]

In their introduction to the *Handbook of Autoethnography*, Holman Jones and colleagues (2013) point to four moments in the last decades of the 20th century that contributed to the development of autoethnography:

> (1) *a recognition of the limits of scientific knowledge and growing appreciation for qualitative research; (2) a heightened concern about the ethics and politics of research; (3) a greater recognition of and appreciation for narrative, the literary and aesthetic, emotions and the body; and (4) the increased importance of social identities and identity politics.* (pp. 25–26, italics in the original)

As we consider the four moments offered above, we see that each moment entwines with issues surrounding how knowledge is generated and valued in social science research. Just as our assumptions about epistemology, ontology, and axiology relate to the ways in which we understand reality and how we generate and value particular ways of knowing, Holman Jones and colleagues' four moments point to particular epistemological shifts in the assumptions surrounding the generation of knowledge in social science inquiry and the ethical responsibility of researchers towards particular ways of knowing. We begin with a discussion around objectivity in social science research.

Troubling Objectivity

Holman Jones and colleagues offered four moments to describe how qualitative researchers began questioning the principles of objectivity and neutrality prevalent in social science research (Denzin & Lincoln, 2000; Holman Jones et al., 2013). In *Anthropology as Cultural Critique*, George Marcus and Michael Fischer (1986/1999) coined the phrase *crisis of representation* to describe the "uncertainty about adequate means of describing social realities" (p. 8). They questioned the notion of the researcher as someone who entered the field, set aside personal assumptions,[2] collected data on people and communities, and represented the findings as indisputable reality. As social scientists grappled with questions of representation, they turned the narrative tools of thick description upon themselves to explore the relationship between researcher and research (Richardson, 2000). In your reading you may notice researchers using the term *reflexivity* to describe inquiry that examines the researcher/research relationship.

Reflexivity refers to a "researchers' engagement of continuous examination and explanation of how they have influenced a research project" (Given, 2008, p. 748). As scholars questioned what it meant to represent reality in social science research, they inquired how researchers' subjectivities and personal experiences intertwined with the research itself and incorporated reflexive researcher accounts in their writing. An early example can be seen in Ruth Behar's (1996) book *The Vulnerable Observer: Anthropology that Breaks your Heart*. Sparked by the experience of losing her grandfather while conducting fieldwork in Spain, Behar's writing engaged directly with personal experiences that influenced her research and writing. In this series of personal essays, Behar proposed the concept of the ethnographer as "vulnerable observer"—a concept that challenges the notion of the participant-observer as an innocent bystander. Behar argued that a vulnerable observer engages explicitly with the emotional, personal, and subjective nature of their research. She considered how her theoretical orientations as a feminist ethnographer influenced her observations, relationships, and representations of others:

> As I wrote, the ethnographer in me wanted to know: Who is this woman who is writing about others, making others vulnerable? What does she want from others? What do the others want from her? The feminist in me wanted to know: What kind of fulfillment does she get—or not get—from the power she has? (p. 20)

Although Behar's *The Vulnerable Observer* is not considered autoethnography, autoethnographic researchers point to Behar's work as an early example of narrative self-study in social science research (Adams & Herrmann, 2020; Douglas & Carless, 2013; Ellis & Bochner, 2000).

Another early example of autoethnographic research is Carolyn Ellis's (1995) *Final Negotiations: A Story of Love, Loss and Chronic Illness* (revised and updated in 2018) in which Ellis chronicled her journey losing a spouse to cancer. Like Behar, Ellis (1995) explored personal narratives to "focus on the feeling and thinking self in relationship, narrating particular lived experiences that offer a gateway into understanding social and cultural life" (vxiii). Ellis's work drew widespread attention in the qualitative research community during a time when researchers were becoming increasingly interested in reflexivity, subjectivity, and narrative and poetic representations in qualitative research. In the preface to the 2018 updated edition of *Final Negotiations*,

Art Bochner recalled the influence of Ellis's work. He noted how Ellis "didn't have a covering term she could use that represented the kind of ethnography her research embodied" (p. xiv). In a 1996 chapter for their edited volume *Composing Ethnography*, Ellis and Bochner referred to Ellis's *Final Negotiations* as an "autoethnographic" study.

Norman Denzin's (1997) influential *Interpretive Ethnography* included a chapter on "narratives of the self" in which he explored "sociology's history with experimental narratives" (p. 205). Denzin (1997) noted the importance of reflexive fieldwork texts, personal illness narratives, and autobiographical narratives in changing the landscape of ethnographic inquiry and writing. Although each of these narrative texts recognizes the role of the researcher as a focus of inquiry, their aim and scope vary. *Reflexive fieldwork texts* are ethnographic texts that engage explicitly with the role of the researcher in the production of the text itself. One early example Denzin noted is John Johnson's (1975) *Doing Field Research*, in which Johnson used a first-person perspective in his descriptions of conducting fieldwork on social welfare agencies. Another example is John Van Maanen's (1988) *Tales of the Field: On Writing Ethnography* in which Van Maanen illustrated three approaches for writing up ethnographic studies (realist, confessional, and impressionist tales), underscoring the relationship between researcher voice, subjectivity, and representation in writing ethnographic accounts. Denzin (1997) used the term *autobiographical narratives* in this early writing to refer to personal accounts of ethnographers' experiences in the field or writing ethnography. He pointed to an example from sociologist Laurel Richardson's (1995) work entitled "Writing Stories: Co-authoring 'The Sea Monster', A Writing-story" in which she described the experience of writing an ethnographic drama with her husband, novelist Ernest Lockridge (Richardson & Lockridge, 1991). Although *personal illness narratives* are autobiographical in nature, Denzin distinguished self-narratives of navigating illness and dying from autobiographical narratives of field experiences or writing ethnography. He heralded Ellis's *Final Negotiations* as an innovative, resonant example of a personal illness narrative. Denzin (1997) noted how ethnographers writing reflexive field texts and autobiographical and personal illness narratives exemplified a new age of "social science poets and storytellers" and pointed to the importance of their work in "deploying a parallax view, and recording a constantly changing internal and external world" (p. 202).

The Growth of Autoethnography

Although early critics of self-study as a legitimate form of research argued that autoethnography was "not objective," "too raw," or "too much of the author" (Denzin, 1997, p. 228), autoethnographic texts flourished in the 1990s and early 2000s. Yet, criticisms of narrative and autoethnographic research have lingered. For example, sociologist Paul Atkinson (2015) critiqued Art Bochner's autoethnography (2014) for its "complete absence of analysis" and "absence of interaction" (p. 471). In Atkinson's view, both Bochner and Ellis "share a commitment to narrative reductionism," resulting in a *genre of self-hood*" (p. 472, italics in original). Atkinson's critique of Indigenous, narrative, and autobiographical methods asserts that these approaches represent a "hollowed out" social science, "stripped of the forms of shared social and cultural life" (p. 472). Across disciplines, you will find that there are mixed views of the merits of autoethnography—therefore it is useful to familiarize yourself with debates within your field of study, and how you might develop your argument for the merits of whatever research design you select for your research.

When the second edition of the *Handbook of Autoethnography* was published, Adams and colleagues (2022) commented that Google Scholar listed more than 15,000 sources discussing autoethnography, and a new journal (the *Journal of Autoethnography*) (p. 1). In 2011, Derek Bolen at Wayne State University established the *Doing Autoethnography Conference*, the first conference devoted to autoethnography. Today, conferences such as *The International Conference for Autoethnography* (formerly called the *Bristol Conference of Autoethnography*), the *Critical Autoethnography Conference*, and the *International Symposium for Autoethnography and Narrative* hold annual or bi-annual meetings where scholars from around the world gather to share autoethnographic research. As avenues for presenting and publishing autoethnographic studies continue to grow, so do opportunities for novice autoethnographers to share their work and connect with scholars doing similar work. Let's turn now to some examples of autoethnographic studies.

Designing An Autoethnograhic Study

In the previous section, we explored the origins of autoethnography as a response to qualitative researchers' growing interest in researcher subjectivity and narrative representation. In this section we begin with the question:

What makes a research study autoethnographic? We think it is important to begin with this question because it speaks to the larger purpose of conducting autoethnographic research. If we want to understand what makes a study autoethnographic, we must first consider the question: *What does autoethnography do?* Since autoethnography combines personal experience (auto) to interpret (graphy) culture (ethno), this research approach can help us understand human experiences and interactions (Adams et al., 2017). Although self-inquiry is the focus of autoethnographic research, culture influences how we make sense of our experiences. If the purpose of autoethnography is to deepen our cultural understanding (Chang, 2008), designing and writing autoethnography requires a balance between personal narrative and cultural description (Ellis & Bochner, 2000). However, as you explore examples of autoethnography, you will find that autoethnographic texts vary in their emphasis on culture, personal narrative, and research process.

Some autoethnographers place greater emphasis upon narrative description and storytelling (see for example Boylorn, 2013a; Richardson, 2012) while others combine personal narratives alongside a more traditional literature review and discussion of methods/methodology (Faulkner & Adams, 2021; Yoo, 2020). Regardless of where an autoethnographic text falls on the research process–culture–self continuum, it is this critical ethnographic eye towards personal experience combined with rich descriptive detail that distinguishes autoethnographic texts from other forms of self-writing. And yet, personal experience is vast. You may be wondering, how do autoethnographers decide how to select a research-worthy topic?

Choosing a Topic

Selecting a topic for an autoethnographic study might seem daunting at first. Authors have suggested ways strategies for students to explore autoethnographic topics (Chang, 2008; Pelias, 2019; Tombro, 2016). These include free writing and extended prompts on topics such as: writing about how a particular identity trait (e.g., race, gender, sexual orientation, ability) locates you within a culture; reflecting on religious, family or cultural proverbs; writing about things that trouble you; examining routines and rituals; and considering objects of significance. For instance, as Janie considered potential topics for her autoethnographic study (Copple, 2021), she began her inquiry with loosely connected free writes around memories from her childhood and adulthood. Although many of Janie's initial free writes never made their way into Janie's autoethnographic study, she recognized the thread of mother–daughter interactions running through her writing and situated her self-study within the broader sociocultural context of mother–daughter interactions. From here, Janie paid attention to the way mother–daughter interactions showed up in her personal rituals and routines and objects of significance related to the topic. Additionally, understanding her personal inquiry within a broader sociocultural context led Janie to academic literature on mother–daughter communication and narratives of motherhood and daughterhood. As you consider possible topics for your autoethnographic study, you might look to some of the suggestions in Box 9.1 to begin brainstorming. For more detailed writing exercises, we encourage you to explore the activities found in Chang (2008), Tombro (2016), and Pelias (2019).

Box 9.1. Activities for Brainstorming an Autoethnographic Topic.

- Write about childhood memories that stick or sting
  - Where were you?
  - What happened?
  - Who else was there?
  - What did that encounter look, sound, smell, and feel like?
- Select a valuable object and reflect on its significance
  - How did you acquire this object?
  - What does this object look, sound, smell, and feel like?
  - What people, places, encounters does this object bring up for you?
  - What story(ies) might you tell about this object? Why is it valuable?
- Browse family artifacts and/or photo albums
  - What objects/photos, mementos stand out to you?
  - What people, places, encounters do these artifacts bring up for you?
  - What stories/memories do these artifacts evoke?
- Reflect on a family story
  - Retell the story in as much detail as possible.
  - Why and how has this story been shared among family members?
  - Which family members tell this story? To whom?
  - When do you remember first hearing this story?
    - How old were you?
    - Where were you?

■ Who was the storyteller?
– Has the story changed over time? If so, how?

We suggest experimenting with different brainstorming exercises and caution against narrowing your focus too quickly. As you think with the questions in Box 9.1, be sure to save your response to these questions for future reference. You may find your initial brainstorming and reflective writing useful as you explore questions guiding your inquiry and, even if this writing does not make its way into your final product, early writing may spark ideas for future research.

As you begin to narrow your research topic, an important first step towards developing a critical eye in your self-study is to examine the literature on your phenomenon of interest. Pay attention to cultural, empirical studies published in reputable journals. A review of the scholarly literature will not only help you discern whether your topic of interest merits further investigation it will reveal how researchers are exploring the topic. What issues are researchers exploring related to the topic? How are disciplinary scholars asking critical questions of the topic? How might you ask similar questions of your personal experiences with this topic? Develop a systematic way to review the literature related and begin writing about how research findings may resonate (or not) with your own experiences. Not only will you begin to see how your autoethnographic study may contribute to the scholarly literature on a particular topic, you will begin to see how your personal inquiry is situated within a broader sociocultural context.

Generating and Reflecting on Autoethnographic Data

Most autoethnographic studies begin with memories. The brainstorming activities in Box 9.1. offer exercises to encourage reflection around personal memories. Chang (2008) refers to personal memory data as an important "building block" in autoethnography (p. 71). But, how do autoethnographers make memory data more concrete? In their recommendations for scholars new to autoethnographic research, Robin Cooper and Bruce Lilyea (2022) emphasized the importance of daily journaling, note-taking, and reflective and reflexive writing. They pointed to the example of an autoethnographic dissertation in which the writer explored her experiences being in the World Trade Center during 9/11 (McIntyre, 2016 as cited in Cooper & Lilyea, 2022). Cooper and Lilyea noted how the autoethnographer's commitment to daily writing, even brief thoughts or questions, triggered memories and offered an entry point for further reflection and inquiry around her experience. Just as ethnographers jot observational notes when conducting fieldwork, regular note-taking and reflexive writing are important methods for generating auto-ethnographic data. As you reflect and write about personal experiences, you may find it helpful to create an autobiographical timeline to chronicle these events in relation to other life events. In doing so, you might notice other key moments related to your inquiry and begin to see these moments as part of a cohesive narrative. If your phenomenon of interest focuses on a daily ritual, routine, or interaction, it will be important for you to record observations "in the moment." Chang (2008) suggested creating a time-stamped inventory of daily rituals, much like you might create time-stamped jottings in ethnographic fieldwork. As you analyze personal inventories such as these, be sure to focus not only on patterns and contradictions in the data, but reflect on the observation process as you generate data for your study. What is the process of generating self-data like for you? What is challenging? How are you navigating your role as both researcher and participant in your self-study?

In addition to reflective and observational memoing on memories, rituals, or interactions, autoethnographers may rely on external data such as diaries, photos, archival documents, or letters to name a few. In recent years, cultural anthropologists have explored the possibilities of incorporating digital self-tracking in social science research (Fors et al., 2020). Depending on your topic, data related to the time and duration of physical activities, heart rate, or hours of sleep might be interesting external sources of self-data. One example of incorporating external sources in self-study can be seen in Bud Goodall's (2006) *A Need to Know: The Clandestine History of a CIA Family*. In this inquiry, Goodall looked to archival sources from the 1950s on CIA agents to provide historical context for understanding his personal experience growing up as the child in a family with secrets. Government archival records including internal memos, case assignments, and agent narratives helped Goodall construct a cohesive narrative of his father's life as a secret agent, mapping these moments onto his recollections from this childhood. In this way, Goodall's archival research both corroborated and, in some instances, challenged Goodall's remembrance of childhood events. Another example can be seen in Robin Boylorn's (2016) *On Being at Home with Myself: Blackgirl Autoethnography as Research Praxis* in which Boylorn incorporates reflective sensory data and interview data from women with whom she has shared homeplaces over the years. In this account, Boylorn offers an autoethnographic narrative of how she came to blackgirl autoethnography as an approach that:

> ... centers and makes claims about particular, but shared, experiences of women of color, but it also troubles traditional (white, male, heterosexual) ways of knowing and being in the world by embracing the tenets of autoethnography (Ellis, Adams, & Bochner, 2011), which resist singular representations of experience or research. Blackgirl autoethnography also embraces the impulse to critique, theorize, and analyze our lives as we live and reflect on them. (pp. 49–50)

To understand her methodological journey towards blackgirl autoethnography, Boylorn drew on interviews and research notes from her ethnographic study conducted in her hometown in North Carolina (Boylorn, 2013b). Drawing on external data from her ethnographic study allowed Boylorn to not only reflect on her emerging blackgirl research praxis, it situated Boylorn's journey in relation to "shared experiences of women of color." Thus, Boylorn's decision to incorporate external data from interviews and research notes aligns with the broader aims of blackgirl autoethnography.

As you embark on your autoethnographic inquiry, be open to multiple approaches for generating data. Remember to maintain a critical eye as you collect and reflect on self-data. Be systematic in your approach to self-observation and be sure to reflect on your observational data just as you might generate reflective or analytic memos following participant observations (see Chapter 6). If you include external data such as archival documents, photos, letters or diaries, you may find it helpful to look to resources for asking questions of documents (see Chapter 7). If you choose to interview family or friends about a shared memory or significant event (see Chapter 5), you might consider techniques to elicit detailed descriptions or narratives (see Chapter 8). We offer these suggestions to help you maintain a critical eye and to build quality in your study. As you generate and analyze autoethnographic data, we encourage you to write reflectively and reflexively about your process. For instance, if you develop themes to describe patterns across the data, how did you generate those themes? If you coded data, how did you develop codes? Which scholars guided your approach? How are you incorporating data from your study into a cohesive narrative? We turn now to a discussion of writing autoethnographic texts and explore some of the creative ways autoethnographers interweave self, others, and culture in creative narrative writing.

Writing Personal Experiences

How do autoethnographers compose autoethnographic texts? Some autoethnographers rely exclusively on creative genres (e.g., narrative vignette, poetry, script, list) to communicate personal experiences, while others combine creative representations with traditional academic prose. In this section we provide examples of autoethnographies that use performance texts (Luckett, 2018), poetry (Tillmann, 2014), and lists (Faulkner & Adams, 2021) to communicate personal experiences. Autoethnographers must make intentional decisions about the genre and/or style that capture the narrator's voice and convey the nuances of a lived experience. As we move through these examples, consider how each approach offers something different. How does the narrator's voice come through in each piece? How do the writers rely on literary devices (e.g., imagery, metaphor, allusion) to provide rich, resonant description?

Sharrell Luckett (2018) described her critical autoethnography *YoungGifted andFat: An Autoethnography of Size, Sexuality, and Privilege*, as "expansive" in that it enabled her to tell her stories via messy texts (p. 15) based on journal entries, food diaries, feel-notes (descriptions of feelings as a Black transweight actress), photos, video recordings, and interviews. Luckett recounted her experiences of extreme weight loss via multiple literary strategies, including narratives, monologues, poetry, journal entries, and testimony. Chapters are interspersed with critical reflexive texts labelled "Talk 'Fat' sessions" in which Luckett reflected on the narratives. Luckett concluded the book with the script of a solo performance, *YoungGiftedandFat*, which serves as an example of a performance autoethnography.

Throughout the text, readers see conversations between three Sharrells expressing different responses to weight loss and dieting, for example:

> *Liminal Sharrell:* I think about my size every time I look in the mirror. I want so badly to be smaller.

Skinny Sharrell:	My arms irk me. They don't fit. They are the one indication that I'm not normal. That something used to be wrong with me. The fat on my arms is like smudges on a new car. I want it gone. I am trying to put the thought in Sharrell's mind to consider having the skin on her arms removed, but she won't hear it.
Liminal Sharrell:	I won't hear it. I'm scared of surgery.
Fat Sharrell:	Cutting the skin off would mean that I would never be welcomed back.
Liminal Sharrell:	I can't cut the skin off. It's a part of me. It reminds me of someone lost. Someone who I wish I could talk to.
Fat Sharrell:	I will love you even harder when I come back. It will be just me and you. Just like old times. (p. 105)

Luckett's autoethnography demonstrates how performance texts can be used to represent autoethnography, in addition to a variety of literary strategies.

In another example, Lisa Tillman (2014) intertwined personal and historic moments into a series of poetic stanzas advocating for marriage equality in the United States. She explored her complicated relationship with marriage and divorce, interspersing these accounts between stanzas on topics including President Clinton's 1996 Defense of Marriage (DOMA) legislation[3] and *Loving vs. Virginia*.[4] In the following stanza, Tillmann (2014) wrote about attending a friend's wedding shortly after her own divorce.

The law that once undergirded my marriage
blasts the foundation and scatters the wreckage.
In preparation to attend a postapocalypse wedding,
I bear arms of a date, dapper, dashing, and handsome.
"Stunning,"
say I with a playful tug to his tie.
This old friend, a gay man, barred from the institution
I just escaped.
We make quite a pair:
a divorcee with a sensibility queer
and a man who will fall for an international partner,
a legal stranger. (p. 305)

In the poetic narrative excerpt provided here, Tillman conveyed the poignancy of attending the celebration of an institution she has "escaped" and from which her gay friend is "barred." The juxtaposition of these experiences in a single poetic stanza illustrates Tillman's increasingly complicated relationship with the institution of marriage and situated her experience within the broader social discourse regarding marriage equality. Tillmann concluded her autoethnography with a section entitled "Coda'" that provided an overview of federal policy and public opinion regarding marriage equality in the United States in the 21st century.

Lastly, we point to a recent example from Sandra Faulkner and Tony Adams' (2021) collaborative autoethnography of sexual harassment and assault in the academy. Collaborative or collective autoethnography (see Holman Jones, 2021) combines personal narratives of two or more individuals around a shared or common experience. In your reading, you might come across the term "duoethnography" to describe autoethnographies that combine narratives of two individuals (see Norris et al., 2012). For our purposes, we look to Faulkner and Adams' (2021) use of an enumerated list of personal notes to chronicle observations and experiences of sexual harassment and assault in higher education. The authors derived this autoethnographic approach from Susan Sontag's 1964 *Notes on Camp*, in which Sontag used notes and jottings to describe aesthetic encounters with the natural world. Faulkner and Adams argued that notes capture "a multitude of disparate, yet sometimes related, acts and traits" and conveys the "often complicated and incoherent" ways sexual harassment and assault operate within academic contexts (p. 267). Faulkner's and Adams' notes described personal encounters and observations of sexual harassment and assault experienced as undergraduate students, graduate students, and early career, tenure-track professors. The following excerpt recounts two early career experiences:

11. Keeping your office door locked when you are inside because of post-traumatic stress flashbacks of your colleague fake knocking as he struts into your office to press his penis against the back of your desk chair as he reads over your shoulder. He tells you how to spell his name as you type the report you feel forced to write for him.

12. Being asked by a male colleague if you are a rabid feminist when you accept a position as Director of Women's Studies. You are pissed you didn't think

of a response—feminists bite back—until he was gone from your office with his tainted congratulations. (p. 270)

Faulkner and Adams situated their collective autoethnography within recent academic literature on sexual harassment and assault in the academy fueled by the #MeToo movement. The text begins with an overview of the academic literature, an explanation of the notes approach, and moves to an enumerated, descriptive list of 26 moments of sexual harassment and assault. Faulkner and Adams (2021) wrote their accounts in second person ("you") to engage readers (mainly academics) as potential witnesses or bystanders of sexual harassment and assault "in the hopes of challenging the normalized behavior" (p. 266).

Luckett (2018), Tillman (2014), and Faulkner and Adams (2021) provide three unique approaches to writing autoethnography. Luckett showcased a variety of narrative strategies along with a performance text. Although the introduction nods to academic prose and citations from academic literature, the book as a whole takes a performative approach to representation. Tillman, on the other hand, began with narrative poetic stanzas and concluded with academic-style prose to situate her experiences with the broader context of marriage equity legislation in the United States. Like Tillmann, Faulkner and Adams (2021) included academic prose and citation along with creative narrative in the form of notes. In each of these examples, we witness autoethnographers navigating what Chang (2008) called the complex "web of self and others" to understand cultural experience (p. 15). We offer these examples to give you a sense of different stylistic approaches to composing an autoethnographic text. And yet, these examples only begin to scratch the surface of the creative possibilities when crafting an autoethnographic text. As you consider potential genres for your autoethnographic writing, you might look to resources on life writing and autobiography for inspiration.

There is no one way to write autoethnography. Autoethnographic research and writing is a deeply personal endeavor. Researching and writing about personal encounters entangles with the stories of other people and may engage emotional, sensitive topics. In the following section, we discuss the ethical considerations of writing about colleagues, friends, and family. How researchers engage the process of writing and represent research through writing is a critical exercise. We advise writing early and often in your autoethnographic inquiry and experimenting with different styles and genres. As you do so, think about the affordances and constraints of different approaches. In Box 9.2 below, we offer some guiding questions to consider when writing an autoethnographic text.

Box 9.2. Guiding Questions for Writing an Autoethnographic Text.

- What story(ies) do I want to tell?
  – Why this story(ies) and not others?
- Who is the audience for this story(ies)?
- Who are the other characters in the story(ies) I want to tell?
  – How will I describe these characters to readers?
- What genre(s) help me narrate my personal experience?
  – How does this genre help me paint a picture for readers?
  – Why this genre and not others?
- How will my text connect personal experience with culture?
- Will I include a traditional academic literature review?
- Will I reference current or historical events related to my topic?
- How will I communicate methods of data collection and analysis?
  – Will I include sections for methods and analysis?
  – Will I intersperse data collection and analysis throughout?
  – Will I use academic prose? Narrative?

We encourage you to experiment with writing and representation throughout the research process. Read examples of autoethnographic texts as you compose your study. Which texts resonate with you as a reader and why? How might you apply the questions in Box 9.2 to these texts? As you question autoethnographic texts on issues of style and structure, you will want to examine how autoethnographers write about ethical issues that arise in their autoethnographic study as well. In the final section of this chapter, we turn explicitly to ethical considerations in autoethnography.

Considering Ethics in Autoethnography

Although we conclude this chapter with considerations for designing ethical autoethnography, ethics should not be an afterthought. Far from it. Engaging ethical questions should be an iterative, ongoing process. In this section, we take up the ethical issues of writing about associated others and offer some suggestions for negotiating consent and asking critical questions about how we represent others in our writing. We conclude the chapter with a discussion of the personal and professional implications of doing autoethnography and provide a list of activities and recommendations for further reading.

Writing About Friends and Family

One of the most complicated issues in conducting autoethnographic research entails the ethics of writing about friends and family. The degree to which autoethnographers write explicitly about other people and personal relationships varies and depends largely on the kinds of questions guiding one's study. Some autoethnographic studies explore topics related to personal interactions among colleagues (e.g., Bhattacharya & Gillen, 2016; Faulkner & Adams, 2021) or family members (e.g., Goodall, 2006; Tamas & Tamas, 2021). And yet, even autoethnographic studies focused intently on the self and deeply personal encounters such as experiencing depression (Jago, 2002) or illness (Tillmann, 2009) often include information about family, friends, or acquaintances. In sum, any autoethnographic inquiry, either directly or indirectly, engages the stories and experiences of others and researchers have an ethical responsibility to account for the decisions they make as they write personal experiences that may implicate others. As we stated in Chapter 2 on ethics and qualitative research, ethical considerations are often complex and solutions to ethical quandaries in qualitative research are rarely clear-cut. The guiding questions and suggestions in this section are offered not as a recipe or ethical checklist, but rather as a starting point to get you thinking about the kinds of ethical decisions you may encounter when conducting an autoethnographic study.

To get started, we offer guiding questions from Jillian Tullis (2022) that ask autoethnographers to think about whose stories they have the right to tell. Tullis, paraphrasing Ellis (2009) asked:

- Do you have the right to write about others without their consent?
- What effect do these stories have on individuals and your relationship with them?
- How much detail and which difficulties, traumas, or challenges are necessary to include to successfully articulate the story's moral or goal?

- Are you making a case to write (or not to write) because it is more or less convenient for you?
- Should you and will you allow participants to read and approve all of the stories about them? Or just those stories that you think are problematic or potentially hurtful? (p. 109)

As you generate data for your study, you may encounter ethical questions about memory data involving associated others. As we noted earlier in the chapter, autoethnography usually begins with memories that stand out as salient or significant. And yet, memories that are significant for you, might not be significant to others. You may remember different details or perhaps have entirely different recollections of events. Corroborating personal memory through external data such as archival sources (Goodall, 2006) or interviews with family or friends (Boylorn, 2016) not only offers a way to check the accuracy of events, conversations with others around shared memories may reveal ethical blind spots in the way you represent events and people in your personal narrative. As you begin to craft your personal narrative, you might offer drafts for others to read. Member-checking your representations of people and events is an important way to ensure that your narrative does no harm. Many autoethnographers advocate for member-checking throughout the research process as researchers remember, interpret, and write about personal experience (e.g., Tullis, 2022).

In addition to member-checking, it is important to consider processes of consent in the early stages of developing your autoethnographic study. As you consider the story or stories you want to tell, make a list of people who might be associated with or implicated in your story and think about how and whom you should contact to obtain consent. Tullis (2022) advised researchers to check with the Institutional Review Board (IRB) at their institution to discern the processes required for gaining approval for autoethnographic studies. Your IRB may have specific requirements for gaining consent from people connected with your inquiry. Even if your institution considers autoethnography exempt from review, we encourage you to develop processes for gaining consent from associated others and member-checking manuscripts before publication.

In *Searching for an Autoethnographic Ethic*, Stephen Andrew (2017) offered guiding questions for reading your autoethnographic writing with "ethical eyes" (p. 53). We find these questions helpful in identifying potential ethical pitfalls when writing about friends and family. We offer Andrew's questions here as provocations for you to think with in the drafting stages of your writing and as you move towards a final manuscript:

- Does anything in the text leap out as being potentially harmful to others (or myself) if published?
- Was I venting, boasting, scoring points, maliciously undermining or attacking people or organisations named in the text?
- Was I projecting my own neuroses onto the descriptions I had created on the page?
- Did I want revenge, to hurt and injure those that have in some way hurt me?
- What is my gut response if I imagine this particular piece of writing being out in the world and read by the people mentioned in my writing and by those known to them? (p. 53)

You might use these questions as reflective prompts to critically examine your representation of others in your writing and consider possible responses to ethical quandaries. Again, we note that ethical issues are often complex and most fall outside the purview of IRB protocols. Ultimately, your decisions about whose stories to tell and how you choose to tell them are yours to make. As you grapple with ethical questions about how to write autoethnographies that "do no harm," we encourage you to consider potential harm for autoethnographers as they reveal personal and sometimes painful encounters in their studies.

Implications of Publishing Autoethnographic Studies

As you consider possible topics for your autoethnographic study, we remind you to think about potential implications for your life and career. For instance, you might be considering a tenure-track career in a discipline within which autoethnography is not widely known or accepted. If you are considering an academic career in which publications count towards your eligibility for tenure and promotion, we advise you to explore journals publishing qualitative studies in your discipline. Are these journals publishing autoethnography? Are leading qualitative scholars in your discipline publishing autoethnographies or supporting students who use autoethnographic methods in their dissertation research?

We have noted some examples in this chapter of autoethnographies that deal with workplace culture. If your autoethnographic inquiry touches on relationships with workplace colleagues, how might colleagues react to your representation of them in your writing? How might they remember events differently? How might publishing or presenting your manuscript affect working relationships? If you are a new assistant professor, how might presenting or publishing this work impact tenure and promotion? Just as you might offer family members or friends the opportunity to review your manuscript or reflect with them on the details of particular events related to your autoethnographic inquiry, you might use a similar approach with colleagues who are implicated in your study. Although you may use pseudonyms and anonymize the names of places in your study, publications typically include the author's institutional affiliation and determining the identities of institutions or colleagues might be as simple as an internet search. Again, we direct your attention to Andrew's (2017) questions above as you think about the ethics of writing about colleagues or professional experiences. Similarly, you might use pseudonyms for friends and family members and we strongly encourage this practice! And yet, if you have a publicly accessible digital footprint and post images and information about family and friends on social media, this may simplify the process for readers who wish to find out the identities of people associated with or implicated in your study.

Lastly, we ask you to "not underestimate the afterlife of a published narrative" (Tullis, 2022, p. 110). In some instances, autoethnographers have revisited previous publications to address the implications of their writing. One such example is Carol Rambo's chapter (2022) "Remixing/reliving/revisioning 'My mother is mentally retarded'" in which Rambo returned to her autoethnographic account of being the daughter of an intellectually disabled parent (Ronai, 1997). In this piece, Rambo included sections from her original article alongside stories that narrate the consequences of writing about her mother and herself. Publications have a life of their own as audiences encounter them years, decades, and perhaps even generations after publication. Furthermore, our representations of ourselves and others become part of the discourse surrounding our work. While no one can foretell the future, it's worth considering how representations might stand the test of time. For instance, if you are writing an autoethnographic study that explores issues related to parenting small children, how might your children encounter these accounts as teenagers or adults? If you are writing about conflict among friends or family members, how might publishing these accounts foreclose possibilities for reconciliation?

Conclusions

In this chapter, we provided a brief overview of the origins and key terms associated with autoethnographic approaches to qualitative research. We distinguished between autoethnography and other forms of life writing and provided suggestions for selecting a topic and generating autoethnographic data. Lastly, we noted some of the ethical considerations and implications of doing autoethnography and posed some guiding questions from autoethnographic scholars to help you grapple with these issues. Although there are risks to doing autoethnography, we encourage you to consider how you might join others who "write their narratives despite the risks to themselves in the interest of challenging narratives that render so many marginalized and stigmatized identities and experiences voiceless" (Tullis, 2022, p. 111). For an example of a study that intersperses autoethnographic writing within a narrative study, see Janie Copple's work in the Appendix.

Activities

1. Examine a personal diary or photo album as self-study data. Make a list of people, places, and events that show up diary entries or photos. Note recurring topics or possible themes. What stories do these diary entries or photos bring up for you? Generate a list of possible autoethnographic research topics from this data.

2. Find a "junk drawer," box, or closet in your home. Photograph the items as they are assembled in the drawer, box, or closet. What do you notice about how these items are arranged? Are they sorted? Piled together? Create an inventory of the items. Do you notice any patterns across types of items? Select one or two items of interest. Describe them in detail and explain why they are interesting to you.

3. Generate a list of personal and professional milestones, accomplishments, or future goals. Select an item from your list and create a timeline of events related to this moment. Next, generate a list of instrumental

people (e.g., mentors, friends, family) who offered encouragement or support. Expand your timeline to include events related to these individuals. Select an event from your expanded timeline and write a creative narrative vignette of this event.

4. From a list of potential autoethnographic topics you would like to explore further, select one topic from your list and do a deep dive into the autoethnographic literature on that topic. How are scholars conducting self-studies related to this topic? In what disciplinary journals are scholars publishing autoethnographies on this topic? What ethical issues arise for scholars conducting self-studies on this topic? How do autoethnographers theorize their research? What issues or perspectives have been unexplored? How might your self-study contribute to the autoethnographic literature on this topic?

Further Reading

Resources for Doing Autoethnography and Life Writing

Chawla, D., & Atay, A. (2018). Introduction: Decolonizing autoethnography. *Cultural Studies ↔ Critical Methodologies, 18*(1), 3–8. https://doi.org/10.1177/1532708617728955

Denzin, N. K. (Ed.) (2018). *Performance autoethnography: Critical pedagogy and the politics of culture* (2nd ed.). Routledge.

Norris, J., Sawyer, R. D., & Lund, D. (Eds.). (2012). *Duoethnography: Dialogic methods for social, health, and educational research*. Left Coast Press.

Smith, S., & Watson, J. (2010). *Reading autobiography: A guide for interpreting life narratives* (2nd ed.). University of Minnesota Press.

Spry, T. (2016). *Autoethnography and the other: Unsettling power through utopian performatives*. Routledge.

Examples of Autoethnographic Texts

Anderson, P. (2017). *Autobiography of a disease*. Routledge.

Ferdinand, R. H. (2021). *An autoethnography of African American motherhood: Things I tell my daughter*. Routledge.

Pelias, R. J. (2021). *Lessons on aging and dying: A poetic autoethnography*. Routledge.

Richardson, L. (2016). *Seven minutes from home: An American daughter's story*. Sense Publishing.

Notes

1. For a more detailed discussion of the "narrative turn" in qualitative research, see Chapter 8.

2. In the phenomenological literature the process of setting aside one's assumptions is commonly referred to as "bracketing." In some studies, researchers may write about participating in bracketing interviews (see for example Rolls & Relf, 2006) in which a colleague asks questions of the researcher related to their topic of interest to identify implicit assumptions about their inquiry. In their book *Reflective Lifeworld Research*, Karin Dahlberg and colleagues (2008) critiqued the notion of bracketing, arguing that researchers are never fully able to set aside their assumptions. Rather than bracketing, they offer the metaphor of "bridling" one's assumptions when conducting research. Just as you might bridle a horse to keep them on a particular path, researchers bridle their assumptions. In this way, researchers remain aware of their assumptions and can reflect upon the ways they influence their inquiry.

3. The Defense of Marriage Act (DOMA) prevented same-sex couples from receiving federal benefits even if the marriage was recognized in the couples' home state.

4. *Loving vs Virginia* refers to the 1967 Supreme Court ruling that struck down state laws banning interracial marriage in the United States.

References

Adams, T. E., Ellis, C., and Jones, S. H. (2017). Autoethnography. In J. Matthes, C. S. Davis, & R. F. Potter (Eds.), *The International Encyclopedia of Communication Research Methods*. https://doi.org/10.1002/9781118901731.iecrm0011

Adams, T. E., & Herrmann, A. F. (2020). Expanding our autoethnographic future. *Journal of Autoethnography, 1*(1), 1–8. https://doi.org/10.1525/joae.2020.1.1.1

Adams, T. E., Holman Jones, S., & Ellis, C. (2022). Introduction. Making sense and taking action: Creating a caring community of autoethnographers. In T. E. Adams, S. Holman Jones, & C. Ellis (Eds.), *Handbook of autoethnography* (2nd ed., pp. 1–19). Routledge.

Andrew, S. (2017). *Searching for an autoethnographic ethic*. Routledge.

Atkinson, P. (2015). Rescuing interactionism from qualitative research. *Symbolic Interaction, 38*(4), 467–474. https://doi.org/10.1002/symb.183

Behar, R. (1996). *The vulnerable observer: Anthropology that breaks your heart*. Beacon Press.

Bhattacharya, K., & Gillen, N. K. (2016). *Power, race, and higher education: A cross-cultural parallel narrative*. Sense Publishers.

Bochner, A. (2014). *Coming to narrative: A personal history of paradigm change in the human sciences*. Left Coast Press.

Boylorn, R. M. (2013a). "Sit with your legs closed!" and other sayin's from my childhood. In S. Holman Jones, T. E. Adams, & C. Ellis (Eds.), *Handbook of Autoethnography* (pp. 173–185). Routledge.

Boylorn, R. M. (2013b). *Sweetwater: Black women and narratives of resilience.* Peter Lang.

Boylorn, R. M. (2016). On being at home with myself: Blackgirl autoethnography as research praxis. *International Review of Qualitative Research, 9*(1), 44–58. https://doi.org/10.1525/irqr. 2016.9.1.44

Chang, H. (2008). *Autoethnography as method.* Routledge.

Cooper, R., & Lilyea, B. V. (2022). I'm interested in autoethnography, but how do I do it? *The Qualitative Report, 27*(1), 197–208. https://doi.org/10.46743/2160-3715/2022.5288

Copple, J. (2021). Earnin' your raising: Autoethnographic remembrance of mother-daughter stories and reflections on parenting. *Qualitative Inquiry, 27*(3/4), 346–352. https://doi.org/10. 1177/1077800420917425.

Dahlberg, K., Dahlberg, H., & Nyström, M. (2008). *Reflective lifeworld research* (2nd ed.). Studentlitteratur.

Denzin, N. K. (1997). *Interpretive ethnography: Ethnographic practices for the 21st century.* SAGE.

Denzin, N. K., & Lincoln, Y. S. (2000). Introduction: The discipline and practice of qualitative research. In N. K. Denzin & Y. S. Lincoln (Eds.), *The SAGE handbook of qualitative research* (2nd ed., pp. 1–28). SAGE.

Douglass, K., & Carless, D. (2013). A history of autoethnography. In S. Holman Jones, E. Adams, & C. Ellis (Eds.), *Handbook of Autoethnography* (pp. 84–106). Routledge.

Ellis, C. (1995). *Final negotiations: A story of love, loss, and chronic illness.* Temple University Press.

Ellis, C., & Bochner, A. P. (2000). Autoethnography, personal narrative and reflexivity. In N. Denzin & Y. Lincoln (Eds.), *The handbook of qualitative research* (2nd ed., pp. 733–768). SAGE.

Ellis, C. (2009). Telling tales on neighbors: Ethics in two voices. *International Review of Qualitative Research 2*(1), 3–27. https://doi.org/10.1525/irqr.2009.2.1.3

Ellis, C., Adams, T. E., & Bochner, A. P. (2011). Autoethnography: An overview. *Historical Social Research / Historische Sozialforschung, 36*(4), 273–290. http://www.jstor.org/stable/23032294

Faulkner, S. L., & Adams, T. E. (2021). #YouToo: Notes on sexual harassment and assault in the academy. *International Review of Qualitative Research, 14*(2), 266–273. https://doi.org/10.11 77/1940844721991085.

Fors, V., Pink, S., Berg, M. & O'Dell, T. (2020). *Imagining personal data: Experiences of self-tracking.* Routledge.

Goodall, H. L. (2006). *A need to know: The clandestine history of a CIA family.* Routledge.

Given, L. M. (2008). Reflexivity. In *The SAGE encyclopedia of qualitative research methods* (p. 748). SAGE Online. https://dx.doi.org/10.4135/9781412963909.n377

Hayano, D. M. (1979). Auto-ethnography: Paradigms, problems and prospects. *Human Organization, 38*(1), 99–104. https://www.jstor.org/stable/44125560

Heider, K. G. (1975). What do people do? Dani auto-ethnography. *Journal of Anthropological Research 31*, 3–17. https://doi:10.1177/1541344608326899

Holman Jones, S., Adams, T.E., & Ellis, C. (2013). *Handbook of autoethnography*. Routledge.

Holman Jones, S. (2021). Autoethnography and the importance of working collectively. *International Review of Qualitative Research, 14*(2), 217–220. https://doi.org/10.1177/1940844720978765

Jago, B. J. (2002). Chronicling an academic depression. *Journal of Contemporary Ethnography, 31*(6), 729–757.

Johnson, J. M. (1975). *Doing field research*. Free Press.

Luckett, S. D. (2018). *YoungGiftedandFat: An autoethnogrpahy of size, sexuality, and privilege*. Routledge.

Marcus, C., & Fischer, M. (1999). *Anthropology as cultural critique* (2nd ed.). University of Chicago Press. (Original work published in 1986).

McIntyre, S. (2016). Plummeting into chaos: Rising from the ashes of 9/11. [Doctoral dissertation, Nova Southeastern University].

Norris, J., Sawyer, R. D., & Lund, D. (Eds.). (2012). *Duoethnography: Dialogic methods for social, health, and educational research*. Left Coast Press.

Pelias, R. (2019). *The creative qualitative researcher: Writing that makes readers want to read* Routledge.

Rambo, C. (2022). Remixing/reliving/revisioning "My mother is mentally retarded". In T. E. Adams, S. Holman Jones, & C. Ellis (Eds.), *Handbook of autoethnography* (2nd ed., pp. 401–410). Routledge.

Richardson, L. (1995). Writing-stories: Co-authoring "The Sea Monster," a writing-story. *Qualitative Inquiry, 1*(2), 189–203. https://doi.org/10.1177/107780049500100203

Richardson, L. (2000). Evaluating ethnography. *Qualitative Inquiry, 6*(2), 253–255. https://doi.org/10.1177/107780040000600207

Richardson, L. (2012). Sentimental journey. *International Review of Qualitative Research, 5*(2), 251–270. https://doi.org/10.1525/irqr.2012.5.2.251

Richardson, L., & Lockridge, E. (1991). The sea monster: An ethnographic drama. *Symbolic Interaction, 14*, 335–340.

Rolls, J., & Relf, M. (2006). Bracketing interviews: Addressing methodological challenges in qualitative interviewing in bereavement and palliative care. *Mortality, 11*(3), 286–305. https://doi.org/10/1080/13576270600774893

Ronai, C. R. (1997). On loving and hating my mentally retarded mother. *Mental Retardation, 35*(6), 417–432. https://doi.org./10.132/0047-6765(1997)035<0417:OLAHMM>2.0CO;2

Spradley, J. P., & McCurdy, D. W. (2012). *Conformity and conflict: Readings in cultural anthropology* (14th ed.). Jill Potash.

Tamas, S., & Tamas, R. (2021). Conscripted collaborators: Family matters in autoethnography. *International Review of Qualitative Research, 14*(2), 296–301. https://doi.org/10.1177/1940844720974108

Tillmann, L. M. (2009). Body and bulimia revisited: Reflections on "A Secret Life". *Journal of Applied Communication Research, 37*(1), 98–112. https://doi.org/10.1080/00909880802592615

Tillmann, L. M. (2014). Wedding album: An antiheterosexist performance text. *International Review of Qualitative Research, 7*(3), 302–311. https://doi.org/10.1525/irqr.2014.7.3.302

Tombro, M. (2016). *Teaching autoethnography: Personal writing in the classroom*. Open SUNY textbooks.

Tullis, J. A. (2022). Self and others: Ethics in autoethnographic research. In T. E. Adams, S. Holman Jones, & C. Ellis (Eds.), *Handbook of autoethnography* (2nd ed., pp. 101–113). Routledge.

Van Maanen, J. (1988). *Tales of the field: On writing ethnography*. University of Chicago Press.

Yoo, J. (2020). An autoethnography of mothering in the academy. *The Qualitative Report, 25*(8), 3173–3184. https://nsuworks.nova.edu/tqr/vol25/iss8/20

Designing Studies Using Arts-based Methods

ARTS-BASED RESEARCH (ABR) IS AN approach to qualitative research that uses artistic methods as a means of inquiry, data collection, and representation. Barone and Eisner (2012) described one of the aims of arts-based research as "an effort to extend beyond the limiting constraints of discursive communication in order to express meanings that otherwise would be ineffable" (p. 1). Similarly, Savin-Baden and Wimpenny (2014) defined arts-based research as "research that uses the arts, in the broadest sense, to explore, understand, represent and even challenge human action and experience" (p. 1). Researchers may use arts-based approaches to explore sensitive or complex topics that might be difficult to represent using traditional, text-based methods. For example, researchers might incorporate images, collage-making, or drawing in interviews or focus groups (e.g., Bailey & Woodall-Greene, 2022; Vacchelli, 2018), represent research findings using music or sound compilations (e.g., Springgay & Truman, 2017), or employ visual or poetic methods in data analysis (Gerstenblatt, 2013).

In this chapter, we examine ABR in qualitative inquiry, focusing specifically on poetic, visual, and performative approaches. Following a brief overview of the origins and epistemological underpinnings of ABR, we move to a discussion of poetic, visual, and performative approaches to ABR with examples of studies using these approaches. We conclude with an examination of criteria for judging quality in ABR and provide recommendations for further reading. Although this chapter focuses on studies that use poetic, visual, and performative ABR, by no means is ABR limited to these approaches. Rather, we offer these examples as an entry point for understanding how qualitative researchers engage the arts as a way of doing research. We encourage you to explore the readings at the end of this chapter to further your understanding of the possibilities of ABR. Let's turn now to the origins of ABR in qualitative inquiry.

Origins and Epistemological Assumptions of ABR

Elliot Eisner, an education researcher and visual artist, coined the term "arts-based research" in 1993 at an American Educational Research Association (AERA) research institute he organized consisting of a series of sessions for 25 academic and applied researchers to showcase examples of artistic approaches to qualitative research and underscore the potential of arts-centered methods (Barone & Eisner, 2012). Although Eisner introduced the term arts-based research there, other researchers in anthropology and those who used ethnography (Geertz, 1980; Lawrence-Lightfoot, 1983) had been writing about the value of artistic forms of research for over a decade. In 1981, Eisner published an article in *Educational Researcher* entitled "On the Differences Between Scientific and Artistic Approaches to Qualitative Research," in which he argued for expansive approaches to qualitative inquiry in education that included both scientific and artistic methods in efforts to "avoid methodological monism" (p. 9). He pointed to the need for methodological diversity to engage both scientific questions related to generalizability and truth as well as artistic questions "which are less concerned with the discovery of truth than with the creation of meaning" (p. 9). Eisner argued that arts-based researchers operate from a basis of knowing that values the role of emotions in research and acknowledges the relationship between the representational form and the audience. He wrote:

Thus, when the content to be conveyed requires that the reader vicariously participates in a social situation context, the writer or filmmaker attempts to create a form that makes such participation possible . . . It rejects the view that affect and cognition are independent spheres of human experience. (pp. 8–9)

Eisner drew examples from films and literature (e.g., Mario Puzo's *The Godfather*, Ken Kesey's *One Flew Over the Cuckoo's Nest*) to demonstrate the value of artistic forms that invite multiple interpretations and evoke emotional or visceral responses.

Think about movies, films, songs, and so forth that have resonated with you. How have these works of art informed or challenged your understanding of an event, emotion, or experience? Recall a time when you encountered a new song that captured your attention. Were you struck by the lyrics? The melody? The vocalist's range? The instrumental composition? You might have been unable to name what it was that specifically struck you about the song the first time you encountered it. This feeling of being struck or moved when making or encountering art is the "affective" quality described in Eisner's quote above. ABR centers such encounters as valued ways to know and make meaning of experience. Although arts-based approaches to research were considered controversial by some in the educational research community, others embraced arts-based methodologies. One such example can be seen in Sara Lawrence-Lightfoot's (1983) development of *portraiture* methodology in which Lawrence-Lightfoot combined empirical description with aesthetically crafted narratives to explore learning communities across six U.S. high schools. While Lawrence-Lightfoot and other researchers using arts-informed approaches (Edelsky, 1981; Foster, 1989) might not have used terms like "arts-based research" or "artistic research" to describe their work, their work was instrumental in shaping what we have come to call arts-based qualitative research.

In 1997, Eisner in collaboration with Barone offered a framework for an aesthetic approach to educational research in a chapter entitled "Arts-based educational research." Building on the "dimensions" of artistic research outlined in Eisner's earlier work, Barone and Eisner described the value of *blurred genre texts*—texts that blur the genres of science and art (see also Denzin, 1997). They showcased examples of scholars using literary and poetic forms to represent anthropological and ethnographic research (Geertz,

1980; Lawrence-Lightfoot, 1983) and refused the premise held by many in the educational research community that "legitimate" social science research offered provable, generalizable truths. They asserted that scientific and artistic texts alike are open to interpretation and underscored the affordance of literary and poetic texts that encourage multiple interpretations and value ambiguity. They argued that hybrid, blurred-genre texts have the potential to provide new insights into data, leading researchers and connoisseurs of research to different questions. Barone and Eisner noted one of the primary aims of arts-based educational research was its prioritization of questioning over closure. They argued research texts that blended vernacular language and images with academic prose provoked critical questions around complex issues in education and made social science research more accessible to non-academic audiences.

As qualitative researchers in the 1990s and early 2000s built on the work of pioneers like Eisner, Barone, and Lawrence-Lightfoot, they incorporated forms such as dance (Bagley & Cancienne, 2001), visual art (Irwin & de Cosson, 2004), poetry (Cahnmann, 2003), and drama (Saldaña, 2005) into the repertoire of arts-based methods. Since the early 2000s, there have been a number of qualitative handbooks with chapters dedicated to arts-based approaches (Butler-Kisber, 2010; Denzin & Lincoln, 2011) as well as handbooks and edited collections (Burnard et al., 2022; Cahnmann-Taylor & Siegesmund, 2018; Knowles & Cole, 2008; Leavy, 2017) devoted entirely to arts-based qualitative research. Although histories of arts-based methods in qualitative research attribute the emergence and popularity of ABR to the postmodern turn in qualitative inquiry (Barone, 1995; Cahnmann-Taylor & Siegesmund, 2018), researchers draw on a variety of theoretical perspectives including postmodern/poststructural/posthuman theories (e.g., Clark/Keefe, 2020) as well as decolonizing (e.g., Bhattacharya, 2009), and critical theories (e.g., Travis, 2020).

In one recent example, Khanolainen and Semenova (2020) combined comics with a symbolic interactionist framework to explore how teenage students in a Western Russian school inscribe and interpret signs and symbols of bullying through the use of student-created comics. Researchers asked students to generate comics related to different forms of social interactions at school, and students participated in follow-up interviews in which researchers incorporated students' comics to elicit further details about personal experiences reflected in students' drawings. Drawing on a social behaviorist approach to symbolic interactionism, Khanolainen and Semenova explored how students combined language with images to attribute meaning to particular interactions. Today, we see arts-based research taken up in fields such as public health (Archibald & Blines, 2021), psychology (Chamberlain et al., 2018), social work (Furman et al., 2006), sports (Forde, 2022), and organizational studies (Biehl-Missal, 2015). Let's take a closer look at the way researchers design arts-based research.

Doing Arts-Based Research

As you can see in the examples discussed thus far, there is much variation in the ways researchers design studies using arts-based methods. Perhaps overwhelmed by the possibilities and wondering which arts-based methods are best suited for your study, you might be asking: *How do I know if my study qualifies as arts-based research?* In our discussion of the epistemological underpinnings of ABR, we drew your attention to Eisner's (1981) concept of art as a way of knowing—a thread running through the examples of poetic, visual, and performative ABR we provide in this section.

Although you might be appreciative of art on a personal level and the cultural and critical contributions of film, literature, dance, painting, or poetry, you may have questions about how to incorporate such approaches in your work. Drawing on Savin-Baden and Major's (2013) categories, Wang and colleagues' (2017) review of studies using ABR described three "families" of ABR in qualitative inquiry: research about art, art as research, and art in research. They defined these families in the following way:

- Research about art: The researcher explores topics related to art but does not employ artistic processes or forms as modes of analysis or representation.
- Art as research: The researcher-artist actively engages artistic processes and forms to explore the role of art-creation as part of the research process.
- Art in research: The researcher guides participants and/or participates in art-making or artistic processes as part of the research process. (pp. 14–16)

We emphasize that while we find these categories useful in conceptualizing research designs, there is often overlap across categories. You may find some combination of these approaches useful as you design your study. In considering Wang and colleagues' (2017) categories, think about how these approaches map onto the research questions and theories guiding your study. The questions in Box 10.1 are offered to guide your thinking about possibilities for designing an arts-based qualitative study.

Box 10.1. Guiding Questions for Designing an Arts-based Study.

- How are artistic forms and processes connected to my research questions?
  - Am I interested in artists' experiences?
  - Am I interested in experiences with art forms or art processes (e.g., art-making, crafting)?
  - Am I interested in art as a way to represent research findings?
- How might creative processes be used to generate data (e.g., collage, drawing, photography)?
  - How will I describe creative processes to participants?
  - What methods might be useful to analyze creative data?
- What would an artistic installation of my inquiry look like?
  - What form would it take? (e.g., sculpture, painting, sound, film, multimedia)
  - What does this installation reveal about my research topic?
  - Who is the audience for this installation?

Let's turn now to some specific examples of art-based qualitative research, beginning with poetic inquiry.

Poetic Approaches to ABR

Carl Leggo (2008) described poetic inquiry as "a way of knowing, being and becoming in the world . . . Poetry invites researchers to experiment with language, to create, to know, to engage creatively and imaginatively with experience" (p. 168). In her meta-analysis of poetic inquiry, Monica Prendergast (2009) listed 40 terms used to describe poetic inquiry in qualitative research. Based on reviews of over 230 social science studies using poetic inquiry, Prendergast identified three salient categories to describe how researchers employed poetic methods across multiple disciplines in social science research: a) researcher-voiced poems, b) participant-voiced poems, and c) literature-voiced poems. She described *researcher-voiced poems* as autoethnographic or autobiographical poems derived from researcher diaries, field notes, and reflections. Researcher-voiced poems often take up issues related to the researcher's role in the research process and may examine topics such as reflexivity, subjectivity, or ethics. In contrast to researcher-voiced poems, Prendergast described *participant-voiced poems* as poems constructed from interview transcripts, elicited from participants during interviews or focus groups, or even co-created with the researcher. Lastly, Prendergast described *literature-voiced poems*, in which researchers craft poetic responses to disciplinary, literary, or theoretical texts or write about the process of poetic inquiry itself. Examples of literature-voiced poems can be seen in Clough's (2000) poem about the relationship between poetry and the unconscious or in poems Leggo (2002) referred to as poetic "ruminations" in which he explored poetic thinking and expression as a way of living and being in the world. For our purposes here, we focus on participant-voiced poems. Although it may seem like poetic inquiry centers on poetry as representation, we remind you of Leggo's quote at the beginning of this section. Poetic inquiry is both process and product—it is a way of making sense of your data and a way of representing findings to others. Let's look at some examples.

Poetic transcription is widely used in qualitative research studies. Glesne (1997) defined poetic transcription as "poemlike compositions from the words of interviewees" and demonstrated this approach using interview data from a participant named Doña Juana in her study with educators from Puerto Rico (p. 202). Glesne began by coding Doña Juana's data for broad themes, then sorting data according to those themes. Rather than moving to additional rounds of coding, the way one might do in a grounded theory analysis, Glesne read the interview data sorted under each theme trying to "make sense of the data" and "convey the emotions the interview evoked in me" (p. 206). Although Glesne's poetic transcriptions stayed close to the participant's actual words, in some instances she repeated words for emphasis, dropped or added word endings (-ing, -ly, -ed), or changed tenses. Glesne used brackets [ ] around words or phrases not used in the original transcript, but included these to provide necessary context for readers. Below, we offer an excerpt from one of Glesne's (1997) poetic transcriptions entitled "A Century of Reading":

At the beginning of the century
when the Americans came,
the old people would hire teachers
who went to the home and taught them to read.
So my mother learned and became a teacher.

At the beginning of the century,
the chief of the barrio system
hired people to work the sugar fields.
He was forty years [old]
but didn't know how to write.
My mother taught him.
And that was the reason, I think,
I became a teacher. (p. 208)

In later work, Glesne (2010) explored how poetic pedagogies might be adapted to public school settings to enhance students' ability to listen and learn from one another. She suggested approaches such as creating poetic summaries of class discussions or inviting students to create poetry from personal narrative writing.

Similar to poetic transcription, found poetry is another approach to poetic analysis and representation in qualitative research. Like poetic transcription, found poems are typically created from observational field notes or interview data. However, researchers creating found poems may adhere less strictly to the word order or syntax found in original transcripts or field notes, focusing on the lyrical rather than narrative characteristics in the data. For instance, Lynn Butler-Kisber (2002) described how she clustered words and phrases from a particular participant's data and "experimented with the words to create rhythms, pauses, emphasis, breath-points, syntax, and diction" and "played with order and breaks in an attempt to portray the essence of her story'" (p. 233). Using a similar approach, Miller et al. (2015) created found poems from their study on aging people's experiences of living in residential facilities in Australia. We offer a found poem from their study below to illustrate the lyrical quality of this approach. As you read this example, consider how it compares to the narrative example offered in Glesne's example above.

You could scream the place down

My family said
I was too old
to be on my own,
that I needed organizing.

You lose everything
you lose everything
to come in here.
You only have the barest minimum
there's not much here.

It is not nice,
not nice at all.
It is not good for me.
I can't get out.
That's what you lose, when you come in.

All your independence is taken away from you.
I'm not able to do it myself.
That's very hard to take, you get so frustrated at times you could scream the
   place down
Joy, Age 85 (Miller et al., 2015, p. 410)

While the examples offered here use different stylistic approaches, they underscore the importance of voice. It is important to note that poetic transcription and found poetry are modes of analysis as well as modes of representation. As researchers categorize and organize data they are guided by theoretical perspectives and overarching research questions to make sense of data. Although these examples focus on researchers creating poems from interviews and observational data, there are numerous examples of researchers innovating these methods in their own studies. In Burdick's (2011) action research study, teacher participants were asked to generate poems from transcripts from their own interviews. In other examples, researchers have explored poetic transcription with archival sources (Lahman & Richard, 2014) or combined poetry with other artistic forms of expression (Faulkner, 2014). We turn next to visual approaches to arts-based research.

Visual Approaches to ABR

The use of visual methods in research is not new. In the early 20th century, anthropologists used photographs and film as part of the documentary process of fieldwork.[1] By the 1950s, anthropologists used photographs to elicit responses from participants during interviews (Collier, 1957). Today, researchers refer to this technique as photo-elicitation. Researchers have continued to adapt visual elicitation methods to include drawing, collage, and other art-making practices. In addition to visual methods for generating data, arts-based researchers use visual methods of analysis and take up visual forms of expression to represent findings. A key assumption here is that visual images have the potential to open new ways of knowing for participants, researchers, and audiences (Mulvihill & Swaminanthan, 2019). Let's look at the way researchers design studies using visual approaches.

Visual Methods in Data Generation. Researchers use visual methods to generate data on their topic. In studies using *photo-elicitation*, researchers use images to "elicit" responses from participants about their experiences. Harper (2002) offered a detailed history of photo elicitation methods in anthropology, sociology, and ethnography with examples of various ways photo methods have been used in these disciplines. In one such example, Harper noted how he used aerial photographs of farmland in a phenomenological interview study about the experiences of farming. He described how aerial photos "led farmers to reflect upon farm strategies, structural differences between farms and the patterns of change" (p. 20). When using visual elicitation methods, researchers may provide images or invite participants to take photos or bring personal images related to a particular topic. In these studies, images serve primarily as external stimuli to provoke or "elicit" information, although photos themselves might be considered a source of data as well.

Building on photo-elicitation methods, *photovoice* is an approach used in participatory and community-based research in which participants use photos to chronicle particular activities or experiences over a period of time (Wang & Burris, 1997). In photovoice studies, participants engage as co-researchers in the data collection process as they capture experience through photographs. Clark-Ibáñez's (2004) ethnographic study of schoolchildren in South Central Los Angeles is an early example of a researcher using participant-generated photos in research. Clark-Ibáñez (2004) invited children to take photos of important people and things and conducted interviews in which she asked children to reflect on these photos to better understand their everyday lives outside of school. In a recent example, Suárez and colleagues (2021) used photovoice methods to understand experiences of grief among a group of university students in response to a mass shooting at an LGBTQ+[2] nightclub in the southeastern United States. Participants took photos chronicling daily events in the aftermath of the shooting and participated in follow-up focus groups and interviews to reflect on collective and individual processes of grief.

For decades, scholars have explored the use of creative practices in social science research (Gauntlett, 2007) and have noted the value of such methods in biographical research as well as studies with vulnerable populations. In Vacchelli's (2018) study with refugee women seeking asylum in London, women participants were asked to create collages illustrating their journey to the United Kingdom. Vacchelli noted that collage-making afforded participants time to consider how they represented their personal stories and argued that this process offered a "less intrusive" approach to discussing sensitive topics (p. 186). Other researchers described the transformative potential of collage in focus group and participatory research (Bailey & Woodall-Greene, 2022; Plamondon & Caxaj, 2018) while still others explored how drawing and collage help participants express complex or abstract concepts (Guillemin, 2004).

Visual methods can stimulate conversation or build rapport in focus groups or interview studies, but it is important to remember that drawings, collages, and photos are also data. Just as excerpts from fieldnotes or interview transcripts are included as evidence in research reports or publications, so are visual artifacts.

Visual Data in Analysis and Representation. Researchers using visual methods use different approaches to analyze visual data. Bagnoli (2009) described her process of moving between visual and textual analysis in her analysis of participants' drawings from two qualitative studies conducted with young people in the United Kingdom. Using qualitative data analysis software, Bagnoli examined participant-created timelines, self-portraits, and relational maps alongside transcript data from interviews where participants described and reflected on their drawings. She described how drawings and interview data, taken together, deepened her understanding of the complex ways young people narrated their identities over time. Bagnoli (2009) asserted that visual data was not merely "an add-on to text-based analyses" but rather was integral to "making sense at all different stages in the analytical process" (p. 567). Like Bagnoli, Bartlett (2012) used a thematic approach to analyze photo and audio diaries and postdiary interviews in her ethnographic study of people living with dementia. Rather than using data analysis software, Bartlett used a manual approach to coding and cataloging visual, audio, and textual data. She argued that manual methods of analysis provided "an intuitive sense of the data" and provided flexibility to "determine my own approach to managing and coding data, rather than have it defined by software" (p. 1720). While these examples focus on images or drawings, a growing number of studies are incorporating videos (Blazek & Hraňová, 2012) and social media content (Volpe, 2019) in participatory approaches. As Mulvihill and Swaminathan (2019) noted, it is important to examine how analysis of visual data is approached across different disciplines. If you come from disciplines such as anthropology or sociology, sources on visual ethnography (Pink, 2021) or visual methods (Banks & Zeitlyn, 2015) might be helpful for thinking about analysis. Consider how your theoretical perspective and research purpose inform your analysis. For instance, if you are using decolonizing theories, how does your analysis of visual data center non-Western perspectives and ways of knowing (e.g., Yuen, 2016)? If you are drawing on critical theories, how are you thinking about issues related to equity and power in your analysis (e.g., Skinner & Masuda, 2013)?[3]

Arts-based researchers may engage visual methods as part of the process of data analysis. For instance, Clark/Keefe (2020) interspersed her own drawings and paintings with participant-created pieces to explore encounters during a multimedia participatory project on student identity. For Clark/Keefe, painting and drawing in response to participants' pieces functioned as a way to make sense of creative data, but a way to reflect on the research process. Balmer (2021) described "painting with data" as a creative participatory approach to analysis in which participants paint images or patterns of their interpretations of the data. Others have explored collage as an approach to data analysis (Butler-Kisber, 2007). In one example combining collage methods with Lawrence-Lightfoot's (1983) portraiture, Gerstenblatt (2013) outlined the following steps to create what she called "collage portraits" from interviews:

1. Listening to the interview, taking notes by hand, and highlighting portions of the text;
2. Typing the notes and printing them out in large font;
3. Cutting portions of the text to place on the collage;
4. Selecting images;
5. Arranging text, photographic images, and archival documents;

6. Identifying the themes as they emerge;

7. Applying colour, texture, hand drawn imagery, and words; and

8. Continually referring back to notes and transcripts, making additions of text and images to the collage as needed. (p. 300)

Gerstenblatt offered collage portraits for participant feedback as part of the member checking process and noted the potential of collage portraits as an alternative way for participants and audiences to engage with research beyond the limits of published articles. Drawing on Deleuze and Guattari's concept of the fold, Holbrook and Pourchier (2014) interrogated their processes of using collage as analysis. They noted how collaging extends the boundaries of data analysis beyond a list of recorded steps or procedures as researchers assemble and layer previously disconnected data fragments (e.g., visual and written research memos, artifacts, transcripts). For example, in Janie's research on mothers' experiences of preparing menstruating children for puberty, she created collages from menstrual materials, instructional literature, and other items mothers mentioned in stories of preparing children for puberty. Drawing on new materialist theories that value the relationship among humans and nonhumans (Barad, 2007), Janie engaged collaging to explore such human/nonhuman relationships as part of her analysis (Copple, 2022). Figure 10.1 shows an example of collage analysis from Janie's dissertation research.

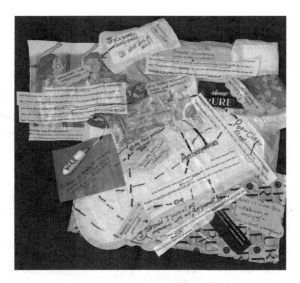

Figure 10.1. Collage Analysis.

As you consider using visual approaches in your research, think about which methods might contribute to your understanding of the research topic. Develop a plan for using visual methods used to generate data for your study using the guiding questions in Box 10.2.

Box 10.2. Guiding Questions for Using Visual Methods in ABR.

- If you are using photographs or images in interviews or focus group settings, will you provide images or will you ask participants to bring personal images or take photos?
- If you select images as elicitation device, what criteria will inform your selection of images?
- If you use approaches such as photo voice or digital diaries, what criteria will guide participants as they chronicle experiences using photo data?
- If you ask participants to create drawings or collages, how might this data inform your approach to analysis?
- How might you use visual approaches to data analysis or to represent findings from your study?

We turn now to performative approaches to arts-based research.

Performative Approaches to Arts-based Research

As the name implies, performative arts–based research involves methodological approaches that draw on disciplines associated with the performing arts (e.g., drama, dance, music). And yet, many forms of arts-based research are performative in that they are created to resonate with audiences. Consider the performative quality of many forms of creative writing discussed in this chapter (poetry) and in the narrative and autoethnographic chapters of this book. Have you ever attended a poetry, fiction, or creative nonfiction reading? As authors read or "perform" such texts aloud, words move from the page to the stage. Listeners may come away from such encounters with completely different understandings or reactions to poems or short stories read aloud. Just as performances resonate with audiences, the act of performance or using performative methods offers something unique for the researcher as well. Douglas and Carless (2013) described the relationship between performative methods and the performer (researcher) this way:

Performative methods depend upon the *doing* of creative, artistic, performative practice for insights and understandings to emerge. Embodiment is core to the process and knowing is seeded in, and depends upon, the *act* of performing (whether in private rehearsal or public display). (p. 55, emphasis in original)

They described five characteristics of performance-based research including:

- A different way of "coming to know"
- Inclusive form of representation
- Provides an experience
- Blurring self-other divide
- Provide an alternative vision. (p. 54)

Researchers using performative approaches may use creative forms such as drama, dance, or music to represent findings from a research study. As with the poetic and visual arts–based approaches discussed thus far, researchers using performative methods may incorporate these approaches in studies using interviews, focus groups or ethnographic methods for generating data. Ethnodrama and ethnotheatre describe methods researchers use to create scripts and dramatized performances based on ethnographic research (Saldaña, 2005). Participatory approaches like *playbuilding* bring participants into the process of generating a script and performing scenes based on research topics of interest (Norris, 2009). The landscape of performative arts–based research is ever-expanding and, while a comprehensive overview of performative research is beyond the scope of this section, we hope the dramatic approaches described here pique your interest in the possibilities of performative arts–based research.

Generating Performative Data. In relation to Turner's (1986) call for performance in the 1980s, Mienczakowski (2001) asserted that it took some time before cultural anthropologists employed this approach. Mienczakowski asserted that ethnodrama and ethnographic performances

are about *the present moment* and seek to give the text back to the readers and informants in the recognition that we are all co-performers in each other's lives. . . . ethnodrama is explicitly concerned with decoding and rendering accessible the culturally specific signs, symbols, aesthetics, behaviours, language and experiences of health informants using accepted theatrical practices. It seeks to perform research findings in a language and code accessible to its wide audiences. (p. 468, italics in original)

Whereas Mienczakowski defined a specific participant group (participants of projects to do with mental health), ethnodrama and performative ethnography have been applied in numerous disciplines.

Performance, in Denzin's (1997) view, "is a public act, a way of knowing, and a form of embodied interpretation," and he distinguished between three types of performance: those of (a) "natural" or staged performances of recorded interactions, (b) dramatic performances that draw on existing texts or literature that are performed (e.g., reader's theater), and (c) performances that enact rituals and stories from fieldwork (p. 97). Denzin listed multiple types of performance text—dramatics texts, natural texts, performance science texts, and improvisational, critical ethnodramas (p. 99). Performances can range from involving audience members in readings, to the performance of dramatic texts based on fieldnotes, to improvisational performances involving audiences such as those used in *Theatre of the Oppressed* developed by Brazilian activist Augusto Boal (1931–2009). As but one example of reader's theater, Donmoyer and Yennie-Donmoyer (1995) described how scholars can engage audiences in reading scripts based on data. As Kathy learned, this is not without hazards if audience members' focus on performing obscures the purpose of delivery (see Roulston et al., 2008).

Performance has been taken up across disciplines, including anthropology, education, the health sciences, and communications, and you will come across a variety of terms such as performance art, performance science texts, ethnodrama, performed ethnography, performance ethnography, and ethnographic performance to describe variations. For example, ethnographer Soyini Madison (2020) used "perform*ed* ethnography" to

emphasize the dramatic scenarios, public staging, crafted theatricality, and improvisational enactments of fieldwork and ethnographic data that will *be*, that have *been*, and that are *being* perform*ed*. In denoting perform*ed* ethnography, we also deliberately acknowledge performances that occur during fieldwork. These grounded fieldwork performances are then translated and adapted for the stage to be performed. In addition, this vision of future performances, which will move forward from the time and place of the fieldwork, also emphasizes the aesthetics and critical process of adaptation, representation, and embodiment. (p. 169)

In order to move from ethnographic data to dramatization, researchers draw on sources used to generate data for the study (e.g., newspapers, archives, fieldnotes, or interview transcripts). For example, in an ethnographic study exploring the cultural identity of swimmers, McMahon et al. (2017) created a script using a combination of personal images, social media posts, media statements, and personal reflections. In contrast, O'Connell and Lynch (2020) drew on interview data to create an ethnodrama exploring the experiences of deaf interpreters living in Ireland. Researchers using participatory approaches to performance-based research may involve participant-researchers directly in the process of data generation, script development, and performance (e.g., Kazubowski-Houston, 2010).

Drawing from theater pedagogies, the term *playbuilding* refers to a process in which students participate in the creation of a performative work. Norris (2009) adapted the term *playbuilding* to describe participatory approaches to performance-based research. He described the initial stages of generating data as follows:

- Participant focus groups discuss a topic of shared concern
- Participants share beliefs and experiences related to the topic
- Participants individually write a recap of the group conversation
- Participants generate themes from individual summaries of the group conversation to frame dramatic scenes (pp. 21–23)

Once you have determined an approach for generating data you will need a process for creating a script. This will require deep reflection about the story you want to tell with your data, who (which characters/participants) will tell that story, and how you will use the elements of playwrighting to connect your story with audiences. Let's turn to some examples.

Representing Performance-based Research. The creation of a performance script is likely to look very different depending on one's discipline and familiarity with conventions and theories from performance studies. For example, Conrad's (2012) fictionalized ethnodrama about incarcerated youth drew on a participatory arts-based study conducted in an Alberta youth detention center. Conrad drew on fieldnotes and journals recording her observations and reflections from 3 years working with youth in the jail using applied theater. Data included youth-devised scripts, transcribed stories, poems, photos, drawings, and video recordings and so forth (p. xii). After performances of *Athabasca's Going Unmanned*, talkback periods with audiences were convened. As another example, Kazubowski-Houston's performance ethnography with Polish Roma women drew on her expertise as a theater professional to use an acting methodology called Illustrative Performing Technique "that relied heavily on grotesque, abstract, and physical (over verbal) means of expression and aimed at politicizing the audience" (p. 9) to work with Roma and Polish women in the writing and staging of a performance. Although Kazubowski-Houston's aims were critical, and she intended to raise community awareness concerning violence and racism toward Roma women in Poland, her efforts at a collaborative performance were plagued by strife. Ironically, Kazubowski-Houston found her research moving from "studying the hegemonic forces that supported violence against Roma women in Poland," to the "power relations" within her own work (p. 179). *Staging Strife: Lessons from Performing Ethnography with Polish Roma Women* demonstrates that although researchers may enter a context with the best intentions, working collaboratively with others can move a project in unintended directions. This applies to all research with humans, whatever methods used.

Nevertheless, if you want to create a quality script adaptation based on research findings, you will need to understand the tools playwrights use as well as how performances come together on a stage. In a narrative reflection on using ethnodrama in her dissertation research, Bhattacharya (Bhattacharya & Gillen, 2016) emphasized the importance of attending theatrical performances. She described how attending these performances helped her "balance creativity and scholarly work in one space that could appear as an engaging and entertaining play" (p. 74). Drawing on Goffman's (1959) concept of front and backstage,[4] Bhattacharya presented findings through a series of front and backstage plays to show how transnational Indian graduate students "show up in the different spaces we occupy based on who else is present in that space, who we trust, and how safe we feel" (Bhattacharya writing in Bhattacharya & Gillen, 2016, p. 74). Below we provide an excerpt from a front stage scene Bhattacharya (2009) created from her performative ethnographic dissertation project:

Neerada's Informal Academia (front stage)

What kind of Asian/Indian are you?

Act 1, Scene 1 (Time: Late August 2004)

Scenography: Neerada is completing paperwork in a secretary's office in a university setting in the United States. The secretary is a White female, a heavyset woman in her late 40s or early 50s with blonde hair, and speaks with an accent that Neerada doesn't understand very well at times.

Neerada: There you go, Mary. All finished.

Mary (looking at the completed form): Honey, this ain't right. You checked off Asian for your race. You need to check off Other.

Neerada: But I am Asian. India is in Asia!

Mary: I don't know about that, but as far as the form goes, only people from China, Japan, you know, like those countries, they can say they are Asians. (Neerada takes the form and corrects it appropriately.)
(p. 1067, emphasis and formatting in the original)

Another example of the use of a critical approach to explore the potential of performative ethnography to examine power relations is that of professional actress and scholar Deveare Smith (2019). Smith's (2019) ethnodramas created from interview studies with community members across four geographic regions in the United States show a range of American perspectives on the school-to-prison pipeline. Created from interviews with 19 participants ranging from prisoners, elected officials, school administrators, parents, counselors, and clergy, Smith's ethnodramatic performances took the format of a one-woman show. Smith described her ultimate goal for this project was "to inspire action, to suggest to the youngest person in the crowd that they have agency" (p. xvii). Both Bhattacharya's and Smith's examples underscore the role of theory in designing studies that use performative approaches to research.

While the examples noted here highlight dramatic approaches to performance-based research, we reiterate that these examples serve as an entry point to performative arts–based research. There is no one way to do performative qualitative research, and as you adapt a performative approach informed by your theoretical perspective and research questions, you may find yourself adapting or innovating some of the dramatic approaches offered here. You might find yourself drawn to using performative writing strategies (Pelias, 2019), or you might gravitate towards processes that engage participants (Norris, 2009), such as developing collaborative theatrical performances (Kazubowski-Houston, 2010) or working with audiences (e.g., Prentki & Preston, 2013) in these processes. In the example from Smith (2019) above, she described particular performances in which the audience became "act two" of the performance. With the assistance of trained facilitators, Smith divided the audience into groups to visit unfamiliar locales in the surrounding community and engage conversations with one another about experiences with inequity and injustice (pp. xvi–xvii). Although the audience did not contribute explicitly to Smith's individual performance, audience members became part of the performance event through this interactive experience. Engaging the audience in this way aligned with Smith's justice-oriented goals for the project. As you consider performative approaches, think about how methods of generating and representing data align with the goals of your study.

Quality in ABR

You might wonder whether nonartists can engage in artistic practice as researchers. You might also wonder, given disparities in how different people judge artistic merit, how the quality of research using arts-based approaches be judged. These are important questions to ask, and there are no easy answers. Cahnmann-Taylor (2018), who is both a published poet and educational researcher, outlined four guiding principles in relation to the conduct of ABR, those of (a) subjectivity and public good, (b) attribution and ethical good, (c) impact and aesthetic good, and (d) translation to scientific good. These principles intertwine the significance of a study, ethics, aesthetics, and how researchers communicate with audiences.

As we have noted across this chapter, a key consideration in conducting ethical studies in ABR has to do with the issue of representation and voice. While one of the advantages of ABR is its ability to extend beyond the boundaries of academic publications and open multiple possible interpretations, as a researcher you are instrumental in this process. In each of the approaches discussed in this chapter, representations of research using poetry, visual images, or drama/performance involve processes that distill or descriptions representing participants' experiences. For instance, how might selecting and ordering particular words and phrases into poetic stanzas or performative dialogue have unintended consequences for audiences' interpretations of research participants? Before rushing to poetic, visual, or performative representations of your research findings, explain your process to participants and provide a rationale for your approach. As with many examples noted across this chapter, engage participants in member-checking your representations or responses to their data.

There is debate among scholars when it comes to what constitutes quality in arts-based research. While some scholars point to artistic knowing as an invitation for researchers to experiment with arts-based methods in their research, others insist that arts-based research, particularly when using artistic forms of representation, requires aesthetic expertise or commitment to learning the "tools of the trade." For instance, Freeman (2017) described how although she was not trained as a poet, thinking poetically and experimenting with poetic forms opened new ways of seeing research data. Similarly, Janie is not trained as a collage artist or painter but used these artistic approaches as processes to think with data and analysis in her dissertation research (Copple, 2022). However, Janie's choice to use multi-genre narratives to represent her research findings was informed by her experience with these creative approaches to writing. If you are using an arts-based approach to represent your findings, immerse yourself in this art form, especially if it is an approach with which you are unfamiliar. Take a poetry or painting class. Attend theatrical performances. Visit art installations at your institution or local museum. We agree with Barone and Eisner (2012) who argued that arts-based research must succeed as both art and research. They offered six criteria for judging arts-based research including. We paraphrase these criteria here:

- Incisiveness: Research gets to the heart of a social issue
- Concision: The work uses minimal space/verbiage to convey a clear, straightforward message to an audience
- Coherence: The work holds complex pieces together in a strong form (e.g., Does the piece hold together? Can the audience follow the story or message?)

- Generativity: The work enables one to see or act on the research issue or phenomenon studied
- Social significance: The work or issue examined matters for the lives of people in society
- Evocation and illumination: The work stirs feelings that lead to new ways of seeing, understanding or responding to the phenomenon or issue (pp. 148–154)

Barone and Eisner recognized that criteria as outlined above do not function in the same capacity as standards. While the term 'standards' connotes measures used to quantify a work's merit, criteria are more flexible, situational, and unique to the characteristics of the particular work itself. For example, using the list of criteria above, you would not apply the criterion of "Concision" to a performative ethnodrama in the same way that you would apply it to a painting or drawing. "Concision" varies across contexts and may be more or less applicable for different arts-based methods. As you design your study, use Barone and Eisner's criteria as provocations to think with along your research journey. For example, you might offer in-process work to trusted peers or colleagues and ask for feedback related to these criteria. You might use these criteria with exemplars of arts-based research you find in the literature. Use these criteria with your favorite examples of arts-based research. Which of these criteria do those pieces embody?

Conclusions

In this chapter we provided an introduction to designing qualitative research studies using arts-based approaches. We discussed key concepts and epistemological assumptions related to the growth of arts-based approaches in qualitative research, specifically focusing on art as a way of experiencing, knowing, and making meaning in the social world. We moved to a discussion of poetic, visual and performative approaches to arts-based research and how qualitative researchers ask questions, generate data, conduct analysis, and represent findings using these approaches. As we conclude this chapter, we include activities and recommendations for further reading as you experiment with arts-based methods in your own work. To examine examples of doctoral studies that used arts-based inquiry, see the dissertations in the Appendix by Roshaunda Breeden (performance), Janie Copple (poetry), and Maureen Flint (collage).

Activities

1. Conduct an interview with someone in which you ask them to draw, create a concept map, or make a collage illustrating their educational journey. Ask participants to explain their drawing, map, or collage. How do the images or drawings contribute to a participant's story about their educational journey?
2. Using a transcript of the interview from activity #1 or using another interview transcript, identify an interesting portion of the talk. Create a poetic transcript or found poem from this section of the interview.
3. Recall a time when something unexpected occurred at a family gathering (e.g., holiday, birthday, wedding). Create a script of this event.
4. Member-check your script from activity #3 with a family member(s). How might you change your script based on their recollections of the event? After making any needed changes to the script, practice performing the script.

Further Reading

Resources for Doing Arts-based Research

Faulkner, S. L. (2020). *Poetic inquiry: Craft, method and practice* (2nd ed.). Routledge.

Knowles, J. G., & Cole, A. L. (2008). *Handbook of the arts in qualitative research: Perspectives, methodologies, examples, and issues.* SAGE.

O'Donoghue, D. (2011). *Doing and disseminating visual research: Visual arts-based approaches.* SAGE.

Pelias, R. (2019). *The creative qualitative researcher: Writing that makes readers want to read.* Routledge.

Smith, K. (2008). *How to be an explorer of the world: Portable life museum.* Penguin Books.

Examples of Arts-based Qualitative Research

Chambers, L. A. (2022). Listen to her: Re-finding culturally responsive poetic inquiry as home knowing for women of African descent. *Qualitative Research, 23*(2).

CohenMiller, A. (2018). Creating a participatory arts-based online focus group: Highlighting the transition from DocMama to Motherscholar. *The Qualitative Report 23*(7), 1720–1735. https://doi.org/10.46743/2160-3715/2018.2895

Faulkner, S. L. (2014). *Family stories, poetry and women's work: Knit four, frog one (poems).* Springer.

Forde, S. D. (2022). Drawing your way into ethnographic research: Comics and drawing as arts-based methodology. *Qualitative Research in Sport, Exercise and Health, 14*(4), 648–667. https://doi.org/10.1080/2159676X.2021.1974929

Jackson Foster, L. J., Deafenbaugh, L., & Miller, E. (2018). Group metaphor map making: Application to integrated arts-based focus groups. *Qualitative Social Work, 17*(2), 305–322. https://doi.org/10.1177/1473325016667475

Spray, J., Fetchel, H., & Hunleth, J. (2022). What do arts-based methods do? A story of (what is) art and online research with children during a pandemic. *Sociological Research Online, 27*(3), 574–586. https://doi.org/10.1177/13607804211055492

Warr, D., Taylor, G., & Jacobs, K. (2021). You can't eat art! But can arts-based research challenge neighbourhood stigma? *Qualitative Research, 21*(2), 268–287. https://doi.org/10.1177/1468794120927683

Notes

1. Scholars have long examined visual culture and analyzed video and images in work that is not arts based. For more on image-based research, visual methodologies, and visual ethnography, see Jordanova (2016), Prosser (2011), Rose (2007), Stanczak (2007), and Pink (2021).

2. We use LGBTQ+ rather than LGBTQIA+ to be consistent with the language used in the Suárez et al. (2021) study.

3. Use of visual (and other) methods must be situated within the context of inquiry. For example, we have learned from our colleague Giovanni Dazzo how he learned that in an Indigenous community he worked with, adults viewed drawing as an activity for children. This means that researchers must seek to learn about participants' preferred methods for generating data. See Dazzo et al. (2023).

4. Drawing a symbolic interactionist theorization of the social world, Goffman's (1959) concept of front and back stage describes the role of performance in everyday interactions. The idea is predicated on the assumption that humans perform differently for different audiences, where front stage describes spaces for behaviors that have been rehearsed, practiced, and curated while back stage describes spaces where people practice or rehearse those behaviors. For a detailed explanation, see Goffman's (1959) *The presentation of self in everyday life.*

References

Archibald, M., & Blines, J. (2021). Metaphors in the making: Illuminating the process of arts-based health research through a case exemplar linking arts-based, qualitative and quantitative research data. *International Journal of Qualitative Methods, 20*(1). https://doi.org/1609406920987954

Bagley, C., & Cancienne, M. B. (2001). Educational research and intertextual forms of (re) presentation: The case for dancing the data. *Qualitative Inquiry, 7*(2), 221–237. https://doi. org/10.1177/107780040100700205

Bagnoli, A. (2009). Beyond the standard interview: The use of graphic elicitation and arts-based methods. *Qualitative Research, 9*(5), 547–570. https://doi.org/10.1177/1468794109343625

Bailey, L. E., & Woodall-Greene, T. L. (2022). Collaging as embodied method: The use of collage in a study of American Sign Language (ASL) interpreters' experiences. *Qualitative Report, 27*(9), 1958–1974. https://doi.org/10.46743/2160-3715/2022.5588

Balmer, A. (2021). Painting with data: Alternative aesthetics of qualitative research. *The Sociological Review, 69*(6), 1143–1161. https://doi.org/10.1177/0038026121991787

Banks, M., & Zeitlyn, D. (2015). *Visual methods in social research* (2nd edition). SAGE.

Barad, K. (2007). *Meeting the universe halfway: Quantum physics and the entanglement of matter and meaning.* Duke University Press.

Barone, T. (1995). The purposes of arts-based educational research. *International Journal of Educational Research, 23*(2), 169–180. https://doi.org/10.1016/0883-0355(95)91500-G

Barone, T., & Eisner, E. W. (1997). Arts-based educational research. In R.M. Jaegar (Ed.), *Complementary methods for research in education* (2nd ed., pp. 75–116). American Educational Research Association.

Barone, T., & Eisner, E.W. (2012). *Arts-based research.* SAGE.

Bartlett, R. (2012). Modifying the diary interview method to research the lives of people with dementia. *Qualitative Health Research, 22*(12), 1717–1726. https://doi.org/10.1177/104973 2312462240

Bhattacharya, K. (2009). Negotiating shuttling between transnational experiences: A de/colonizing performance ethnography. *Qualitative Inquiry, 15*(6), 1061–1083. http://dx.doi.org/ 10.1177/1077800409332746

Bhattacharya, K., & Gillen, N. K. (2016). Finding self in ethnodrama. In K. Bhattacharya & N. K. Gillen (Eds.), *Power, race, and higher education: A cross-cultural parallel narrative* (pp. 73–103). Brill.

Biehl-Missal, B. (2015). 'I write like a painter': Feminine creation with arts-based methods in organizational research. *Gender, Work & Organization, 22*(2), 179–196. https://doi.org/10. 1111/gwao.12055

Blazek, M., & Hraňová, P. (2012). Emerging relationships and diverse motivations and benefits in participatory video with young people. *Children's Geographies 10*(2), 151–168. https://doi. org/ https://doi.org/10.1080/14733285.2012.667917

Burdick, M. (2011). Researcher and teacher-participant found poetry: Collaboration in poetic transcription. *International Journal of Education & the Arts, 12*(1), 1–12. http://www.ijea. org/v12si1/

Burnard, P., Mackinlay, E., Rousell, D., & Dragovic, T. (Eds.). (2022). *Doing rebellious research: In and beyond the academy.* Brill.

Butler-Kisber, L. (2002). Artful portrayals in qualitative inquiry: The road to found poetry and beyond. *Alberta Journal of Educational Research, 48*(3). https://doi.org/10.11575/ajer.v48i3. 54930

Butler-Kisber, L (2007). Collage in qualitative inquiry. In G. Knowles & A. Cole (Eds.), *Handbook of the arts in social science research* (pp. 265–278). SAGE.

Butler-Kisber, L. (2010). *Qualitative inquiry: Thematic, narrative and arts-informed perspectives.* SAGE.

Cahnmann, M. (2003). The craft, practice, and possibility of poetry in educational research. *Educational Researcher, 32*(3), 29–36.

Cahnmann-Taylor, M. (2018). Four guiding principles of arts-based research. In M. Cahnmann-Taylor & R. Siegesmund (Eds.), *Arts-based research in education* (2nd ed., pp. 247–258). Routledge.

Cahnmann-Taylor, M., & Siegesmund, R. (2018). *Arts-based research in education: Foundations for practice* (2nd ed.). Routledge.

Chamberlain, K., McGuigan, K., Anstiss, D., & Marshall, K. (2018). A change of view: Arts-based research and psychology. *Qualitative Research in Psychology, 15*(2–3), 131–139. https://doi.org/10.1080/14780887.2018.1456590

Clark-Ibáñez, M. (2004). Framing the social world with photo-elicitation interviews. *American Behavioral Scientist, 47*(12), 1507–1527. https://doi.org/10.1177/0002764204266236

Clark/Keefe, K. (2020). Becoming backpack: Towards a counter-inscription of young adult collegian identity work. *Art/Research International: A Transdisciplinary Journal, 5*(1), 158-179. https://doi.org/10.18432/ari29495

Clough, P. T. (2000). A familial unconscious. *Qualitative Inquiry, 6*(3), 318–336. https://doi.org/10.1177/107780040000600302

Collier, J. (1957). Photography in anthropology: A report on two experiments. *American Anthropologist 59*, 843–859. https://www.jstor.org/stable/665849

Conrad, D. (2012). *Athabasca's going unmanned: An ethnodrama about incarcerated youth.* Sense Publishers.

Copple, J. (2022). *Making menstrual knowledge through multi-genre methodologies: Exploring mothers' encounters with children at menarche* (Publication No. 2685467286) [Doctoral dissertation, University of Georgia]. https://www.proquest.com/dissertations-theses/making-menstrual-knowledge-through-multi-genre/docview/2685467286/se-2

Dazzo, G. P., Cúmez, C., Henderson, E., & Peccerelli, F. (2023). Restorative validity and healing through inquiry: A visual ethnographic case study in Guatemala. *Conflict Resolution Quarterly, 40*(4), 383–404. https://doi.org/10.1002/crq.21376

Denzin, N. K. (1997). *Interpretive ethnography: Ethnographic practices for the 21st century.* SAGE.

Denzin, N. K., & Lincoln, Y. S. (Eds.). (2011). *The SAGE handbook of qualitative research* (3rd ed.). SAGE.

Donmoyer, R., & Yennie-Donmoyer, J. (1995). Data as drama: Reflections on the use of reader's theater as a mode of qualitative data display. *Qualitative Inquiry 1*(4), 402–428. https://doi.org/10.1177/1077800495001004

Douglas, K., & Carless, D. (2013). An invitation to performative research. *Methodological Innovations Online, 8*(1), 53–64. https://doi.org/10.4256/mio.2013.0004

Edelsky, C. (1981). Who's got the floor? *Language in Society, 10*(3) 383–421. https://www.jstor.org/stable/4167262

Eisner, E. W. (1981). On the differences between scientific and artistic approaches to qualitative research. *Educational Researcher, 10*(4), 5–9. https://doi.org/10.3102/0013189X010004005

Faulkner, S. L. (2014). *Family stories, poetry and women's work: Knit four, frog one (poems).* Springer.

Foster, M. (1989). It's cookin' now: A performance analysis of the speech events of a Black teacher in an urban community college. *Language in Society, 18,* 1–29. https://www.jstor.org/stable/4167999

Freeman, M. (2017). *Modes of thinking in qualitative data analysis.* Routledge.

Furman, R., Lietz, C., & Langer, C. L. (2006). The research poem in international social work: Innovations in qualitative methodology. *International Journal of Qualitative Methods, 5*(3), 1–8. https://doi.org/10.1177/160940690600500305

Gauntlett, D. (2007). *Creative explorations: New approaches to identities and audiences.* Routledge.

Geertz, C. (1980). Blurred genres: The refiguration of social thought. *The American Scholar, 49*(2), 165–179. https://www.jstor.org/stable/41210607

Gerstenblatt, P. (2013). Collage portraits as a method of analysis in qualitative research. *International Journal of Qualitative Methods, 12*(1), 294–309. https://doi.org/10.1177/160940691301200114

Glesne, C. (1997). That rare feeling: Re-presenting research through poetic transcription. *Qualitative Inquiry, 3*(2), 202–221. https://doi.org/10.1177/107780049700300204

Glesne, C. (2010). Commentary: Disappearing into another's words through poetry in research and education. *Learning Landscapes, 4*(1), 29–37. https://doi.org/10.36510/learnland.v4i1.358

Goffman, E. (1959). *The presentation of self in everyday life.* Doubleday.

Guillemin, M. (2004). Understanding illness: Using drawings as a research method. *Qualitative Health Research, 14*(2), 272–289. https://doi.org/10.1177/1049732303260445

Harper, D. (2002). Talking about pictures: A case for photo elicitation. *Visual Studies 17*(1), 13–26. https://doi.org/10.1080/14725860220137345

Holbrook, T., & Pourchier, N. M. (2014). Collage as analysis: Remixing in the crisis of doubt. *Qualitative Inquiry, 20*(6), 754–763. https://doi.org/10.1177/1077800414530260

Jordanova, L. (2016). Approaching visual materials. In S. Gunn & L. Faire (Eds.) *Research methods for history* (2nd edition) (pp. 30-47). Edinburgh University Press.

Irwin, R., & de Cosson, A. (2004). *A/r/tography: Rendering self through arts based living inquiry.* Pacific Educational Press.

Kazubowski-Houston, M. (2010). *Staging strife: Lessons from performing ethnography with Polish Roma women.* McGill-Queen's University Press.

Khanolainen, D., & Semenova, E. (2020). School bullying through graphic vignettes: Developing a new arts-based method to study a sensitive topic. *International Journal of Qualitative Methods, 19*(3). https://doi.org/10.1177/1609406920922765

Knowles, J. G., & Cole, A. L. (2008). *Handbook of the arts in qualitative research: Perspectives, methodologies, examples, and issues.* SAGE.

Lahman, M. K., & Richard, V. M. (2014). Appropriated poetry: Archival poetry in research. *Qualitative inquiry, 20*(3), 344–355. https://doi.org/10.1177/1077800413489272

Lawrence-Lightfoot, S. (1983). *The good high school: Portraits of character and culture*. Basic Books.

Leavy, P. (Ed.). (2017). *Handbook of arts-based research*. Guilford Publications.

Leggo, C. (2008). Astonishing silence. In J. G. Knowles and A. L Cole (Eds.), *Handbook of the arts in qualitative research: Perspectives, methodologies, examples, and issues* (pp. 165–174). SAGE.

Madison, D. (2020). Performance and performed ethnography. In D. Madison (Ed.) *Critical ethnography: Method, ethics and performance* (3rd ed., pp. 145–178). SAGE.

McMahon, J., Zehntner, C., & McGannon, K. R. (2017). Fleshy, female and forty: A docudrama of a former elite swimmer who re-immersed herself into elite swimming culture. *Qualitative Research in Sport, Exercise and Health, 9*(5), 546–553. https://doi.org/10.1080/2159676X.2017.1340328

Mienczakowski, J. (2001). Ethnodrama: Performed research: Limitations and potential. In P. Atkinson, A. Coffey, S. Delamont, J. Lofland, & L. Lofland (Eds.), *Handbook of Ethnography* (pp. 468–476). SAGE.

Miller, E., Donoghue, G., & Holland-Batt, S. (2015). "You could scream the place down": Five poems on the experience of aged care. *Qualitative Inquiry, 21*(5), 410–417. https://doi.org/10.1177/1077800415572396

Mulvihill, T. M., & Swaminathan, R. (2019). *Arts-based educational research and qualitative inquiry: Walking the path*. Routledge.

Norris, J. (2009). *Playbuilding as qualitative research: A participatory arts-based approach*. Routledge.

O'Connell, N. P., & Lynch, T. (2020). Translating deaf culture: An ethnodrama. *Qualitative Inquiry, 26*(3–4), 411–421. https://doi.org/10.1177/107780041984394

Pelias, R. (2019). *The creative qualitative researcher: Writing that makes readers want to read*. Routledge.

Pink, S. (2021). *Doing visual ethnography* (4th edition). SAGE.

Plamondon, K., & Caxaj, S. (2018). Toward relational practices for enabling knowledge-to-action in health systems: The example of deliberative dialogue. *Advances in Nursing Science, 41*, 18–29. https://doi/org/10.1097/ANS.0000000000000168

Prendergast, M. (2009). "Poem is what?" Poetic inquiry in qualitative social science research. *International Review of Qualitative Research, 1*(4), 541–568. https://doi.org/10.1525/irqr.2009.1.4.541

Prentki, T., & Preston, S. (Eds.). (2013). *The applied theatre reader*. Routledge.

Prosser, J. (2011). Visual methodology: Toward a more seeing researching. In N. K. Denzin & Y. S. Lincoln (Eds.), *The SAGE handbook of qualitative research* (4th ed., pp. 479–496). SAGE.

Rose, G. (2007). *Visual methodologies: An introduction to the interpretation of visual materials* (2nd ed.). SAGE.

Roulston, K., Legette, R., DeLoach, M., & Buckhalter, C. (2008). Troubling certainty: Readers' theatre in music education research. In M. Cahnmann-Taylor & R. Siegesmund (Eds.), *Arts-based inquiry in diverse learning communities: Foundations for practice* (pp. 208–219). Routledge.

Savin-Baden, M., & Major, C. H. (2013). *Qualitative Research: The essential guide to theory and practice*. Routledge.

Savin-Baden, M., & Wimpenny, K. (2014). *A practical guide to arts-related research*. Sense Publishers.

Saldaña, J. (Ed.). (2005). *Ethnodrama: An anthology of reality theatre*. AltaMira Press.

Skinner, E., & Masuda, J. R. (2013). Right to a healthy city? Examining the relationship between urban space and health inequity by Aboriginal youth artist-activists in Winnipeg. *Social Science & Medicine, 91*, 210–218. https://doi.org/10.1016/j.socscimed.2013.02.020

Smith, A. D. (2019). *Notes from the field*. Anchor Books.

Springgay, S., & Truman, S. E. (2017). A transmaterial approach to walking methodologies: Embodiment, affect, and a sonic art performance. *Body & Society, 23*(4), 27–58. https://doi.org/10.1177/1357034X17732626

Stanczak, G. C. (Ed.). (2007). *Visual research methods: Image, society, and representation*. SAGE.

Suárez, M. I., Asadi, L., Scaramuzzo, P., Slattery, P., & Mandala, C. R. (2021). Using photovoice as an arts-based method for grieving: LGBTQ+ students and the *pulse* nightclub shooting. *International Journal of Qualitative Studies in Education, 34*(5), 412–428. https://doi.org/10.1080/09518398.2020.1762255

Travis, S. (2020). Portrait of a methodology: Portraiture as critical arts-based research. *Visual Arts Research, 46*(2), 100–114. https://doi.org/10.5406/visuartsrese.46.2.0100

Turner, V. (1986). *The anthropology of performance*. Performing Arts Journal Publications.

Vacchelli, E. (2018). Embodiment in qualitative research: Collage making with migrant, refugee and asylum seeking women. *Qualitative Research, 18*(2), 171–190. https://doi.org/10.1177/1468794117708008

Volpe, C. R. (2019). Digital diaries: New uses of photovoice in participatory research with young people. *Children's Geographies, 17*(3), 361–370. https://doi.org/10.1080/14733285.2018.1543852

Wang, C., & Burris, M. A. (1997). Photovoice: Concept, methodology, and use for participatory needs assessment. *Health Education & Behavior, 24*(3), 369–387. https://doi.org/10.1177/109019819702400309

Wang, Q., Coemans, S., Siegesmund, R., & Hannes, K. (2017). Arts-based methods in socially engaged research practice: A classification framework. *Art/Research International: A Transdisciplinary Journal, 2*(2), 5–39. https://doi.org/10.18432/R26G8P

Yuen, F. (2016). Collage: An arts-based method for analysis, representation, and social justice. *Journal of Leisure Research, 48*, 338–346. https://doi.org/10.18666/JLR-2016-V48-I4-6922

Designing Quality Studies

IN THIS CHAPTER WE DISCUSS the criteria that researchers use to describe and assess quality in qualitative research. A wide range of terms relevant to how the quality of qualitative research might be assessed are found in literature dating from the 1960s. We examine where these terms come from and how scholars have defined them before reviewing strategies that you can use to demonstrate that you have conducted quality studies and readers can trust reports of findings.

Defining Terms

When qualitative researchers talk about adequacy, authenticity, confirmability, consistency, credibility, dependability, integrity, plausibility, reliability, rigor, transferability, trustworthiness, and validity—among others—they are discussing the "quality" of a study and why you should believe the findings reported. For example, credibility—typically defined as believability or trustworthiness—is accepted as a crucial benchmark that qualitative researchers must meet in their research. Some scholars have deemed some of these concepts inappropriate for qualitative inquiry. As but one of numerous examples,

Arminio and Hultgren (2002), after defining rigor as related to "internal and external validity, reliability, [and] objectivity" (p. 449), suggested the alternative term "goodness." They related goodness to how researchers explain the dimensions of (a) epistemology and theory, (b) methodology, (c) method, (d) researcher and participants as multicultural subjects, (e) interpretation and presentation, and (f) recommendations in their reports. In other words, the "goodness" or "quality" of a study pertains to how researchers explain how they designed and conducted research and represented findings to others. Similarly, we take discussions of goodness or quality as relating to how researchers *design* their studies, what they *do* during a study (i.e., practice and procedures), how they *represent* what they have learned to readers, and how readers *interpret* a study and *apply* the findings to theory and practice. When researchers select and apply strategies to show that readers should trust the findings of their studies, they consider not only how they situate the design of a study within a community of scholarship, but the theories they use and how they intend to conduct inquiry and work with participants in ethical ways throughout the research process.

The originators of grounded theory, Glaser and Strauss (1967), wrote about this when they talked about the process by which the *credibility* of a grounded theory study might be established. Glaser and Strauss discussed establishing the credibility of a grounded theory through a three-part process in which a researcher became convinced of the accuracy of the theory they had developed, how they conveyed that to readers, and how other researchers subjected the theory to further verification. The process of developing a grounded theory described by Glaser and Strauss (1967) involved systematic generation and analysis of data in contexts in which the researcher had been "sufficiently immersed" to understand what was going on while demonstrating the appropriate detachment to "protect him [sic] from 'going native'" (p. 226). Glaser and Strauss reminded researchers to explain the theoretical framework for a study and vividly described findings so that readers could "almost literally see and hear" those represented (p. 228). Readers, in turn, were thought to judge the credibility of researchers' narratives by how "caught up" in the description they became, and whether or not assertions were based on sufficient evidence. Other researchers would then verify the adequacy of a grounded theory through further research (pp. 230–235). This approach to establishing the quality of a grounded theory demonstrates the complex interplay of practice involved in conducting research and the norms of conduct that scholars working in a particular theoretical tradition and/or discipline accept (Freeman et al., 2007).

What is accepted as "good" practice in research is constantly in tension with the press towards innovation that the research enterprise encourages. Yet while some qualitative scholars continue to revise our understandings of terms used when discussing quality, others continue to apply concepts suggested decades ago. This is partly due to both the ways in which discussions of quality in qualitative research first drew on concepts used in experimental research, and the interdisciplinary nature of methodological writing in which cross-pollination of ideas occurs and proliferates new approaches to qualitative inquiry (Lather, 2006).

Historical Discussions of Quality in Qualitative Research

Numerous scholars have written countless articles, chapters, and books on how to ensure and assess the quality of qualitative research (e.g., for books, see Cho, 2018; Flick, 2018; Seale, 1999). Rather than reprise reviews found in these books, we first highlight key texts that discussed quality criteria before suggesting pathways that you might take as you design your own studies.

As more qualitative researchers began to publish methodological texts in the second half of the 20th century, they discussed how to assess the quality of research. Sociologist Norman Denzin (1970) outlined an approach to establishing the validity of assertions generated from multi-method naturalistic research (revised as Denzin, 1978 and 1989). Denzin's approach to triangulation in naturalistic inquiry contrasted with social psychologists Campbell and Fiske's (1959) argument for applying a multi-trait multi-method matrix approach to validating tests used to measure traits. Writing from a positivist perspective, Campbell and Fiske called their approach a "*methodological triangulation*" and "*convergent validation*" (p. 101, italics in original). The idea that using multiple measures of a phenomenon, or completing triangulation of data, would lead to more "persuasive evidence" to validate findings was asserted by other social scientists in the 1960s, who assumed that by using multiple measures, researchers could eliminate other plausible explanations (Webb et al., 1966, p. 174).

Asserting that "no *single* method will ever meet the requirements of interaction theory," Denzin (1978, p. 28) proposed "triangulation" as an approach to study one object using naturalistic methods for qualitative inquiry. In Denzin's (1978) formulation, triangulation encompassed four forms:

- Data triangulation (i.e., examining multiple concrete situations of phenomenon in order to check emerging propositions);
- Methodological triangulation (i.e., using multiple methods, such as various forms of interviews, observations, or demographic methods);
- Researcher triangulation (i.e., involving multiple observers to examine the object of study); and
- Theoretical triangulation (i.e., employing multiple theoretical perspectives) (pp. 101–102)

Similar to Webb et al. (1966), by combining methods Denzin (1978) argued that the researcher would be able to "forge valid propositions that carefully consider relevant rival causal factors" (p. 29). Since Denzin's initial explanations of triangulation in qualitative inquiry, scholars have pointed out that multiple data sources, methods, researchers, and theoretical orientations will not necessarily lead to convergence on a single point or unitary conclusions (Hammersley & Atkinson, 1995; Lincoln & Guba, 1985; Mathison, 1988; Seale, 1999). Hammersley (2008), for example, has troubled the application of the metaphor of triangulation derived from navigation and surveying to social research. Whereas in navigation and surveying the purpose of triangulation is to identify a specific location, applications in social research frequently involve support for the validity of claims. Yet, assertions that triangulation lends support to the validation of claims is complicated when evidence leads to contradictory claims.

Other scholars took up strategies such as triangulation in relation to the larger criteria that scholars formulated to assess the quality of empirical studies. In an influential article, LeCompte and Goetz (1982) began with the concepts of internal and external reliability and internal and external validity used in experimental research and outlined how these might be applied in ethnographic research, asserting that when research is reliable, other researchers are able to generate the same sorts of findings and constructs using similar methods. When applied to qualitative inquiry, validity relates to whether findings accurately represent the phenomenon examined. LeCompte and Goetz discussed strategies that ethnographers could use to conduct credible research, as well as "threats" and how these might be mitigated (see also Maxwell, 2013, pp. 124–125 and LeCompte & Preissle, 1993).

Another educational ethnographer, Harry Wolcott (1994), wrote about working to not to "get it all wrong" via the following practices:

- Talk little, listen a lot
- Record accurately, in their words, immediately after or during events
- Begin writing early, share drafts with others knowledgeable about the setting
- Let readers see for themselves, include primary data in final accounts
- Report fully, deal with discrepant cases
- Be candid, see subjectivity as a strength of qualitative research
- Seek feedback
- Try to achieve a balance—return to site or field notes to reread the data, then reread the draft
- Write accurately—write for technical accuracy, internal consistency with generalizations grounded in what is seen/heard (paraphrased from pp. 347–356)

LeCompte and Preissle[1] (1993) commented that one of the challenges with questions of goodness that qualitative researchers must navigate is that different communities of practice hold varying philosophical assumptions about "truth" and the criteria by which quality should be assessed. LeCompte and Preissle (1993) remind us that "[g]etting it all is impossible, but getting it right is tougher" (p. 317), and that the standards that scholars use are "constructed" (p. 318). We would add that they are also subject to continuous revision. Let's look further at some of these revisions.

Lincoln and Guba (1985) began their discussion of quality by defining "trustworthiness"—that is, how do researchers and audiences answer questions concerning truth, applicability, consistency, and neutrality in relation to a study's findings (p. 290)? They responded to each of these questions by offering four criteria, those of credibility, transferability, dependability, and confirmability as replacements for the ideas of internal and external validity and internal and external reliability as discussed in LeCompte and Goetz (1982) (see Table 11.1).

Table 11.1. Summary of Techniques for Establishing Trustworthiness

Criterion area	Technique

Credibility	(1) Activities increasing the probability that credible findings will be produced
	   a. Prolonged engagement
	   b. Persistent observation
	   c. Triangulation (sources, methods, and investigators)
	(2) Peer debriefing
	(3) Negative case analysis
	(4) Referential adequacy
	(5) Member checks

Transferability	(6) Provide sufficient description for readers to judge whether findings are transferable to other contexts ("thick description")
Dependability	(7a) Audit trail
Confirmability	(7b) Audit trail (establish adequate records throughout the research process to understand what the researcher did); a sample of findings are traced back to the data upon which assertions are based.
All of the above	(7) The reflexive journal

Source: Lincoln & Guba (1985, p. 328)
Used with permission of SAGE College from *Naturalistic Inquiry*, Y. S. Lincoln and E. G. Guba (1985); permission conveyed through Copyright Clearance Center, Inc.

Table 11.1 discusses strategies that qualitative researchers have long relied on to demonstrate that their work is of quality. In relation to demonstrating that a study is credible, *prolonged engagement* is used as an indicator that researchers have spent sufficient time working with participants or conducting observations to develop in-depth understandings of what is going on. *Persistent observation* suggests that one or a few observations are unlikely to provide sufficient warrant that what a researcher saw is typical of what occurs in a field setting. Through repeated observations over time, however, researchers can assert that their fieldnotes provide insight into the typical and atypical events that occurred over a particular time period. *Triangulation*, as mentioned previously, suggested that multiple data sources, methods, and investigators will yield additional insights concerning the phenomenon examined. *Peer debriefing* as a technique refers to spending time with peers discussing ongoing research to access others' points of view. This strategy is thought to help prevent researchers from getting too close to a topic, overlooking issues with which they may have become too familiar, or ignoring relevant issues that might stand out to outside observers. *Negative case analysis* is a strategy that can be used during the analysis phase. Here, researchers deliberately look for disconfirming data, or "negative cases" that would disprove emergent ideas or support an interpretation. *Referential adequacy* refers to archiving or recording materials (audio/video) for future reference by other scholars who can check a researcher's assertions with original data sources. *Member checking* or *member validation* can range from weak to strong (Seale, 1999, p. 62). Weak forms might include return of transcripts of interviews to participants to allow participants to make edits prior to analysis. Strong forms involve returning drafts of findings sections, discussing how findings might be most effectively represented with participants, or members of a community applying the findings of a study in practice. More recently, there have been calls to archive qualitative data. This allows other researchers to access original data sets for secondary analysis (Corti et al., 2020).

Whereas scholars who use quantitative methods strive to accomplish statistical generalizability in their studies—that is, sample sizes and data generated are representative of larger populations—qualitative researchers are more likely to aim for transferability. *Transferability* is achieved through effective reporting of findings. That is, a report from a research study is sufficiently detailed and compelling for readers to apply what they learn to the contexts with which they themselves are familiar. For transferability to be possible for readers, not only must the findings be described in detail, but the methods that researchers used and how they analyzed data must be included. This relates to what is known as an *audit trail.* That is, given access to how a study was conducted, could other researchers follow how a researcher arrived at the findings? Finally, qualitative researchers are encouraged to keep track of their decision-making and thought processes by way of a *reflexive journal.* The journal also becomes a potential data source, in that researchers track the process of conducting a study while they conduct it.

As Seale (1999) pointed out, the criteria offered by Lincoln and Guba have proven exceptionally resilient over time, even though these authors later offered alternative "authenticity criteria" for constructivist inquiry founded in relativist ontological assumptions (fairness, along with ontological, educative, catalytic, and tactical authenticity) (Lincoln, 1995; Lincoln & Guba, 2013, pp. 70–71). Alongside the widespread application of the concepts of credibility, transferability, dependability, and confirmability to assess the quality of interpretivist inquiry, scholars have also suggested new criteria. For example, let's look at Tracy's (2010) "Big-Tent criteria" found in Table 11.2. Traces of Lincoln and Guba's (1985) criteria noted in Table 11.1 linger in Tracy's (2010) proposal for eight "Big-Tent" markers of quality in qualitative research (see Table 11.2).

Table 11.2. Eight Big-Tent Criteria for Excellent Qualitative Research

Criteria for quality (end goal)	Various means, practices, and methods through which to achieve
Worthy topic	The topic of the research is • Relevant • Timely • Significant • Interesting
Rich rigor	The study uses sufficient, abundant, appropriate, and complex • Theoretical constructs • Data and time in the field • Sample(s) • Context(s) • Data collection, and analysis processes
Sincerity	The study is characterized by • Self-reflexivity about subjective values, biases, and inclinations of the researcher(s) • Transparency about the methods and challenges
Credibility	The research is marked by • Thick description, concrete detail, explication of tacit (nontextual) knowledge, and showing rather than telling • Triangulation or crystallization • Multivocality • Member reflections
Resonance	The research influences, affects, or moves particular readers or a variety of audiences through • Aesthetic, evocative representation • Naturalistic generalizations • Transferable findings
Significant contribution	The research provides a significant contribution • Conceptually/theoretically • Practically • Morally • Methodologically • Heuristically
Ethical	The research considers Procedural ethics (such as human subjects) Situational and culturally specific ethics Relational ethics Exiting ethics (leaving the scene and sharing the research)

Criteria for quality (end goal)	Various means, practices, and methods through which to achieve
Meaningful coherence	The study Achieves what it purports to be about Uses methods and procedures that fit its stated goals Meaningfully interconnects literature, research questions/foci, findings, and interpretations with each other

Source: Tracy (2010, p. 840).
Used with permission of SAGE Publications Inc. Journals from S. J. Tracy (2010) "Qualitative quality: Eight 'Big-Tent' criteria for excellent qualitative research", *Qualitative Inquiry, 16*(10); permission conveyed through Copyright Clearance Center, Inc.

Although the ideas of reliability and validity as espoused by scholars such as Merriam (Merriam & Grenier, 2019) and Silverman (2017) are absent from Tracy's list of criteria, vestiges remain in the practices recommended (e.g., "thick description," "time in the field," "triangulation"). What is clear from the criteria for the assessment of quality in qualitative research discussed by methodologists and the strategies proposed to meet those, is that these underlying ideas remain constant: that (a) researchers must clearly convey their research process to others; (b) others can logically follow a researcher's reasoning from data source to interpretation; (c) a study must be designed in a way to accurately examine what it purports to; and (d) a study be judged as making a significant contribution to a field of study. Thus, it is no surprise that the criteria of reliability and validity as applied to qualitative research by LeCompte and Goetz (also published as Preissle) and credibility, transferability, dependability, and confirmability offered by Lincoln and Guba (1985) continue to be conveyed in countless textbooks, and in some disciplines are accepted, if not expected, in publications of qualitative studies.

Meanwhile, other scholars have forwarded quality criteria related to specific theoretical approaches. For example, in relation to values-based research such as critical and feminist work, Lather (1986) argued for the use of multiple forms of triangulation, reflexive subjectivity, face validity (in which preliminary findings are shared with participants), and catalytic validity (in which researchers and/or participants have been spurred to acts of self-determination through their engagement in research) (p. 78). Lather (1993) later argued for a "transgressive validity" after poststructuralism (validity as simulacra/ironic validity; Lyotardian paralogy/neo-pragmatic validity; Derridean rigour/rhizomatic validity; and voluptuous/situated validity). The strategies that Lather outlined played with the impossibilities of science after poststructuralism in an effort to explore the "not yet." In addition to discussing how to think about validity in the conduct of qualitative inquiry (Dennis, 2018; Freeman, 2011; Li & Ross, 2021), numerous scholars have proposed criteria, questions, strategies, and frameworks for promoting and/or evaluating the quality of qualitative inquiry. These relate to:

1. Methods, such as interviewing (Lavee & Itzchakov, 2023; Roulston, 2010);
2. Aspects of research, such as place (Tuck & McKenzie, 2015); and
3. Methodological approaches, including
   a. autoethnography (Sparkes, 2022; Watson, 2009);
   b. constructivist grounded theory (Charmaz, 2014);
   c. narrative inquiry (Polkinghorne, 2007; Riessman, 2008);
   d. performative research (Cho & Trent, 2009);
   e. arts-based research (Barone & Eisner, 2012; Cahnmann-Taylor, 2018);
   f. fiction (Gibson, 2021; Leavy, 2013);
   g. poetic inquiry (Faulkner, 2020);
   h. participatory inquiry (Call-Cummings, 2016; Howard & Thomas-Hughes, 2021; Mosher, 2013); and
   i. qualitative research that takes risks (Denzin, 2024).

And just as scholars innovating with these different methodologies have revised ways to think about quality criteria and strategies related to different approaches to qualitative research, other scholars have continued to reconceptualize strategies outlined decades ago. This state of flux in criteria by which quality is judged represents the tensions that exist between normative standards accepted by a community of scholars, and the press for engaging with new ways of doing things. By way of one example, let's look at the concept of "triangulation."

Innovations on "Triangulation"

With the rise in popularity of mixed methods research encompassing qualitative and quantitative methods, some scholars now use triangulation as a *synonym* for mixed methods research. Scholars have debated this transformation in how the term is applied and whether the concept is still useful. Denzin (2012) has even claimed that "The term [triangulation] has been used, abused, and misinterpreted" (p. 85). Still, triangulation is a well-used concept, and scholars continue to innovate.

Torrance (2012), for example, has suggested that "member validation" be included in the larger idea of triangulation to support democratic practices in mixed methods research. As another example, Flick et al. (2012) proposed the idea of "systematic triangulation" and used an example of a study of sleep disorders in nursing homes to illustrate how this can be done. Flick et al. (2012) discussed how investigator, theoretical, methodological, and data triangulations could be applied in various phases of a study to build on prior understandings. The object in using multiple forms of triangulation in this application is to pursue different perspectives on the phenomenon of interest (p. 102).

In 2012, Denzin called on researchers to reconsider triangulation to fit a postmodern epistemology, stating "hopefully, in the next decade there will be renewed efforts to embed all our interpretive methodologies in expanded social justice discourses" (p. 86). Some scholars have taken up Denzin's call for considering multiple subjective realities (Ellingson, 2009). Let's look at one alternative.

An Alternative to Triangulation

Based on an earlier reference to crystallization by sociologist Richardson (1994, 2000), Ellingson (2009) elaborated on the idea of crystallization:

> Crystallization combines multiple forms of analysis and multiple genres of representation into a coherent text or series of related texts, building a rich and openly partial account of a phenomenon that problematizes its own construction, highlights researchers' vulnerabilities and positionality, makes claims about socially constructed meanings, and reveals the indeterminacy of knowledge claims even as it makes them. (p. 4)

Ellingson (2009) offered principles for how to apply crystallization in qualitive inquiry. This is exemplified by Barbosa Neves et al. (2023) in a study in which they used two forms of narrative representation—sociological and creative narratives—to evoke elderly people's experiences of loneliness in care facilities in Australia. The changing ways in which the concept of triangulation has been applied illustrates how understandings of the concepts and strategies related to establishing the quality of qualitative research develop over time.

What Should You Do In Your Research?

Given the diversity of positions on quality in qualitative research, we suggest thinking through these initial questions:

- How do <u>scholars in the discipline</u> to which you speak discuss goodness and quality in relation to research broadly, and qualitative research in particular?
- How do <u>scholars who use the theoretical perspectives and methodological approaches</u> that you plan to use for a study discuss quality? What concepts and strategies do these scholars use that you might apply in your work?
- How do you define the concepts you plan to use?
- What are the critiques and limitations of the concepts and strategies you plan to use?

As in any aspect of qualitative inquiry, when you explore how different scholars define and use a concept in their work, you will come to more nuanced applications in your research.

Here, we have not provided a template of how to engage with questions of quality in qualitative inquiry. This is because we see qualitative research design as a process that provides researchers with enormous latitude for creativity. That said, we understand that simply being innovative does not necessarily mean that a study is "good." Rather, the goodness of qualitative inquiry is judged by scholars in a particular research area based on current norms of practice that are in tension with the impetus to create new ways of creating knowledge.

Conclusions

Rather than apply strategies in a prescriptive way, we recommend that researchers exercise "responsibility" throughout the research process. As Koro-Ljungberg (2010) put it,

In the context of qualitative inquiry, "responsible" researchers could possibly be seen as methodologically uncertain and responsive by revising and reconceptualizing the research purposes, processes, techniques, and approaches, as well as interactions with participants and data based on changing social circumstances and rapid shifts in power. (p. 605)

As Koro-Ljungberg discussed, this is an ethical endeavor in which researchers engage fully with the messiness and ambiguities involved in conducting qualitative studies with humans.

In this chapter, we have discussed some of the history in how the quality of qualitative research has been assessed. Although the terminology related to quality in qualitative research has changed over time, you should be aware that

1. qualitative researchers have done extensive work to offer quality criteria by which research informed by interpretivist, critical and poststructural theories might be judged. More recently, critical materialist scholars such as Rosi Braidotti (2019) have offered criteria that could potentially be applied by researchers conducting post qualitative inquiry.
2. although generalized criteria are a starting point to thinking about the assessment of quality (Tracy, 2010), new scholars are well served to explore how scholars have discussed quality with relation to specific methodological approaches (e.g., arts-based, narrative, performative, new materialist). There is value in reading deeply in methodological literature throughout the design process to include strategies consonant with one's axiological, ontological, epistemological, and theoretical assumptions about qualitative inquiry.

Finally, both new and experienced scholars profit from sitting with contradictions and ambiguities and exploring discomfort and uncertainty as part of the research process. And as you design, conduct, and complete your study, be aware that even the best prepared researchers encounter surprises along the way and make mistakes. You will learn by doing, just as we have. Enjoy the process!

Activities

1. Identify examples of what you view as high-quality qualitative empirical studies in your disciplinary field. In your view, what did the researchers do that qualify this study as one of quality?

2. Create a plan for ensuring quality in all phases of your research design.
3. Assess a peer's plans for ensuring quality in qualitative research and provide constructive feedback.

Further Reading

Cho, J. (2018). *Evaluating qualitative research*. Oxford University Press.
Flick, U. (2018). *Managing quality in qualitative research*. SAGE.
Seale, C. (1999). *The quality of qualitative research*. SAGE.

Note

1. Judith Goetz later published under the name Judith Preissle.

References

Arminio, J. L., & Hultgren, F. H. (2002). Breaking out from the shadow: The question of criteria in qualitative research. *Journal of College Student Development, 43*(4), 446–460.
Barbosa Neves, B., Wilson, J., Sanders, A., & Kokanović, R. (2023). Using crystallization to understand loneliness in later life: Integrating social science and creative narratives in sensitive qualitative research. *Qualitative Research, 23*(1), 38–54. https://doi.org/10.1177/1468 7941211005943
Barone, T., & Eisner, E. W. (2012). *Arts based research*. SAGE.
Braidotti, R. (2019). *Posthuman knowledge*. Polity.
Cahnmann-Taylor, M. (2018). Four guiding principles of arts-based research. In M. Cahnmann-Taylor & R. Siegesmund (Eds.), *Arts-based research in education* (2nd ed., pp. 247–258). Routledge.
Call-Cummings, M. (2016). Establishing communicative validity: Discovering theory through practice. *Qualitative Inquiry, 23*(3), 192–200. https://doi.org/10.1177/1077800416657101
Campbell, D. T., & Fiske, D. W. (1959). Convergent and discriminant validation by the multitrait-multimethod matrix. *Psychological Bulletin, 56*(2), 81–105. https://doi.org/10.1037/h0046016
Charmaz, K. (2014). *Constructing grounded theory* (2nd ed.). SAGE.
Cho, J. (2018). *Evaluating qualitative research*. Oxford University Press.
Cho, J., & Trent, A. (2009). Validity criteria for performance-related qualitative work: Toward a reflexive, evaluative, and coconstructive framework for performance in/as qualitative inquiry. *Qualitative Inquiry, 15*(6), 1–29.
Corti, L., Van den Eynden, V., Bishop, L., & Woollard, M. (2020). *Managing and sharing research data: A guide to good practice* (2nd ed.). SAGE.
Dennis, B. (2018). Validity as research praxis: A study of self-reflection and engagement in qualitative inquiry. *Qualitative Inquiry, 24*(2), 109–118. https://doi.org/10.1177/1077800416686371

Denzin, N. K. (1970). *The research act in sociology: A theoretical introduction to sociological methods.* Butterworths.

Denzin, N. K. (1978). *The research act: A theoretical introduction to sociological methods* (2nd ed.). McGraw-Hill.

Denzin, N. K. (1989). *The research act: A theoretical introduction to sociological methods* (3rd ed.). Prentice Hall.

Denzin, N. K. (2012). Triangulation 2.0. *Journal of Mixed Methods Research, 6*(2), 80–88. https://doi.org/10.1177/1558689812437186

Denzin, N. K. (2024). The elephant in the living room, or extending the conversation about the politics of evidence, Part 2. In N. K. Denzin, Y. S. Lincoln, M. D. Giardina, & G. S. Cannella (Eds.), *The SAGE handbook of qualitative research* (6th ed., pp. 549–566). SAGE.

Ellingson, L. L. (2009). *Engaging crystallization in qualitative research: An introduction.* SAGE.

Faulkner, S. L. (2020). *Poetic inquiry: Craft, method and practice* (2nd ed.). Routledge.

Flick, U. (2018). *Managing quality in qualitative research.* SAGE.

Flick, U., Garms-Homolová, V., Herrmann, W. J., Kuck, J., & Röhnsch, G. (2012). "I can't prescribe something just because someone asks for it . . .": Using mixed methods in the framework of triangulation. *Journal of Mixed Methods Research, 6*(2), 97–110. https://doi.org/10.1177/1558689812437183

Freeman, M. (2011). Validity in dialogic encounters with hermeneutic truths. *Qualitative Inquiry, 17*(6), 543–551. https://doi.org/10.1177/1077800411409887

Freeman, M., deMarrais, K., Preissle, J., Roulston, K., & St. Pierre, E. A. (2007). Standards of evidence in qualitative research: An incitement to discourse. *Educational Researcher, 36*(1), 25–32. https://doi.org/10.3102/0013189x06298009

Gibson, W. (2021). Aesthetics, verisimilitude and user engagement: Reporting findings through fictional accounts in qualitative inquiry. *Qualitative Research, 21*(5), 650–666. https://doi.org/10.1177/1468794120925769

Glaser, B. G., & Strauss, A. (1967). *The discovery of grounded theory: Strategies for qualitative research.* Aldine de Gruyter.

Hammersley, M. (2008). Troubles with triangulation. In M. M. Bergman (Ed.), *Advances in mixed methods research* (pp. 22–36). SAGE.

Hammersley, M., & Atkinson, P. (1995). *Ethnography: Principles in practice* (2nd ed.). Routledge.

Howard, M., & Thomas-Hughes, H. (2021). Conceptualising quality in co-produced research. *Qualitative Research, 21*(5), 788–805. https://doi.org/10.1177/1468794120919092

Koro-Ljungberg, M. (2010). Validity, responsibility, and aporia. *Qualitative Inquiry, 16*(8), 603–610.

Lather, P. A. (1986). Issues of validity in openly ideological research: Between a rock and a soft place. *Interchange, 17*(4), 63–84.

Lather, P. (1993). Fertile obsession: Validity after poststructuralism. *The Sociological Quarterly, 34*(4), 673–693. https://doi.org/10.1111/j.1533-8525.1993.tb00112.x

Lather, P. (2006). Paradigm proliferation as a good thing to think with: Teaching research in education as a wild profusion. *International Journal of Qualitative Studies in Education, 19*(1), 35–57.

Lavee, E., & Itzchakov, G. (2023). Good listening: A key element in establishing quality in qualitative research. *Qualitative Research, 23*(3), 614–631. https://doi.org/10.1177/14687941211039402

Leavy, P. (2013). *Fiction as research practice*. Left Coast Press.

LeCompte, M. D., & Goetz, J. P. (1982). Problems of reliability and validity in ethnographic research. *Review of Educational Research, 52*(1), 31–60. https://doi.org/10.3102/00346543052001031

LeCompte, M. D., & Preissle, J. (1993). *Ethnography and qualitative design in educational research* (2nd ed.). Academic Press.

Li, P., & Ross, K. (2021). Validity of transformative experiences: An unfolding. *Qualitative Inquiry, 27*(3–4), 385–396. https://doi.org/10.1177/1077800420918905

Lincoln, Y. S. (1995). Emerging criteria for quality in qualitative and interpretive research. *Qualitative Inquiry, 1*(3), 275–289. https://doi.org/10.1177/107780049500100301

Lincoln, Y. S., & Guba, E. G. (1985). *Naturalistic inquiry*. SAGE.

Lincoln, Y. S., & Guba, E. G. (2013). *The constructivist credo*. Left Coast Press.

Mathison, S. (1988). Why triangulate? *Educational Researcher, 17*(2), 13–17.

Maxwell, J. A. (2013). *Qualitative research design: An interactive approach* (3rd ed.). SAGE.

Merriam, S. B., & Grenier, R. S. (2019). *Qualitative research in practice: Examples for discussion and analysis*. John Wiley & Sons, Inc.

Mosher, H. (2013). A question of quality: The art/science of doing collaborative public ethnography. *Qualitative Research, 13*(4), 428–441. https://doi.org/doi:10.1177/1468794113488131

Polkinghorne, D. E. (2007). Validity issues in narrative research. *Qualitative Inquiry, 13*(4), 471–486.

Richardson, L. (1994). Writing: A method of inquiry. In N. K. Denzin & Y. S. Lincoln (Eds.), *Handbook of qualitative research* (pp. 516–529). SAGE.

Richardson, L. (2000). Writing: A method of inquiry. In N. K. Denzin & Y. S. Lincoln (Eds.), *Handbook of qualitative research* (pp. 923–948). SAGE.

Riessman, C. K. (2008). *Narrative methods for the human sciences*. SAGE.

Roulston, K. (2010). Considering quality in qualitative interviewing. *Qualitative Research, 10*(2), 199–228. https://doi.org/10.1177/1468794109356739

Seale, C. (1999). *The quality of qualitative research*. SAGE.

Silverman, D. (2017). *Doing qualitative research* (5th ed.). SAGE.

Sparkes, A. C. (2022). When judgment calls: Making sense of criteria for evaluating different forms of autoethnography. In T. E. Adams, S. Holman Jones, & C. Ellis (Eds.), *Handbook of Autoethnography* (pp. 263–276). Routledge.

Torrance, H. (2012). Triangulation, respondent validation, and democratic participation in mixed methods research. *Journal of Mixed Methods Research, 6*(2), 111–123. https://doi.org/10.1177/1558689812437185

Tracy, S. J. (2010). Qualitative quality: Eight "Big-Tent" criteria for excellent qualitative research. *Qualitative Inquiry, 16*(10), 837–851. https://doi.org/10.1177/1077800410383121

Tuck, E., & McKenzie, M. (2015). Relational validity and the "where" of inquiry: Place and land in qualitative research. *Qualitative Inquiry, 21*(7), 633–638. https://doi.org/10.1177/1077800414563809

Watson, C. (2009). Picturing validity: Autoethnography and the representation of self? *Qualitative Inquiry, 15*(3), 526–544. https://doi.org/10.1177/1077800408318426

Webb, E. J., Campbell, D. T., Schwartz, R. D., & Sechrest, L. (1966). *Unobtrusive measures: Nonreactive research in the social sciences.* Rand McNally College Publishing Company.

Wolcott, H. (1994). On seeking—and rejecting—validity in qualitative research. In H. Wolcott (Ed.), *Transforming qualitative data: Description, analysis, and interpretation* (pp. 337–373). SAGE.

∾ Examples of Dissertation Designs

D ISSERTATIONS TAKE MANY FORMS. In this appendix, we have in-cluded the Tables of Contents for different approaches to dissertations, including (1) a traditional format; (2) a three-article dissertation; and (3) experimental dissertations.

Examples of Traditional Dissertations

The four dissertations shown in this section are all modeled on the "traditional" five-chapter dissertation. Nevertheless, readers will note variations in how dissertations might be presented—with additional findings chapters (Example 1) and a participant portrait chapter (Example 2). One dissertation includes a coda.

Example 1

Parylo, O. (2012). *Connecting principal succession and professional learning: A cross-case analysis.* [Doctoral dissertation, University of Georgia]. http://getd.libs.uga.edu/pdfs/parylo_oksana_201208_phd.pdf

Abstract

The purpose of this interpretative qualitative study was to explore the connections between principal succession and professional learning through the analysis of the current practices in leader identification, development, support, and retention in two Georgia (USA) school districts. The findings of the cross-case analysis were summarized in five major themes: (1) A key component to the overall success of principal professional learning and succession is a visionary superintendent; (2) Planning for principal succession, school districts strongly favor the local applicants; (3) In light of the anticipated principal turnover, growing leaders from within the district is an effective way to ensure leader continuity; (4) In the process of growing future principals, school districts express strong preference for the non-university leader preparation programs, tailored to the needs of their districts; and (5) Leader professional development and succession are tightly connected, as demonstrated by the school districts practices in the preparation, support, and retention of principals. This study also explored how the central office leaders conceptualized principal effectiveness. The membership categorization analysis revealed that central office leaders believed that an effective principal was an instructional leader, who: (1) had a track record of being an effective leader; (2) was a perfect fit to the school; (3) was able to address the needs of the school; (4) was identified as leader by others; (5) was a team player; (6) was the data leader in the school; (7) was a technology leader; (8) was a community leader; (9) was focused on results; and (10) had a passion for education, and for working with teachers and students. These findings support the major trends in the leadership literature about the changes that occurred in educational administration in the accountability era. The findings of this study contribute to the literature on educational administration by exploring the practitioners' beliefs about the principalship and offer implications for principal preparation, socialization, and professional development. Overall, this study enriches the body of research on principal succession and professional learning and suggests implications for redesign of the university leaders preparation and district-based professional development and leader succession planning.

Table of contents	Comments
1. Introduction 2. Review of the related literature 3. Research design and methodology 4. Illustrious County School system—A case study 5. Remote County School system—A case study 6. Cross-case analysis 7. Membership categorization: Describing an "effective" principal 8. Discussion, implications, and conclusions	This dissertation used the basic form of the traditional five-chapter dissertation, with findings presented in four, rather than one chapter (chapters 4–7). Chapters 4, 5 and 6 present two cases and a cross-case analysis. Chapter 7 provides an additional and contrasting analysis of interview accounts using membership categorization analysis, while Chapter 8 completes the dissertation with conclusions and implications.

Research purpose
The purpose of this study was to explore the connections between principal succession and professional learning through the analysis of the current practices in leader identification, development, support, and retention in two Georgia school districts. (p. 3)

Research questions

1. How do current leader identification, development, support, and retention practices foster principal professional growth and build leadership pipeline?

2. How do the district leaders describe an "effective" principal in conversations on leader professional development and succession planning?

3. In the context of participating districts and school leaders, what is the relationship between principal succession and professional learning? (pp. 9–10)

Publications

Parylo, O., & Zepeda, S. J. (2014). Describing an 'effective' principal: Perceptions of the central office leaders. *School Leadership & Management, 34*(5), 518–537. https://doi.org/10.1080/13632434.2014.928684

Zepeda, S. J., Bengtson, E., & Parylo, O. (2012). Examining the planning and management of principal succession. *Journal of Educational Administration, 50*(2), 136–158. https://doi.org/10.1108/09578231211210512

Zepeda, S. J., Parylo, O., & Bengtson, E. (2014). Analyzing principal professional development practices through the lens of adult learning theory. *Professional Development in Education, 40*(2), 295–315. https://doi.org/10.1080/19415257.2013.821667

Example 2

Herron, B. A. (2019). *Teaching our shared world: Women educators using feminist pedagogy in transnational adult education settings.* [Doctoral dissertation, University of Georgia]. http://getd.libs.uga.edu/pdfs/herron_brigette_a_201908_phd.pdf

Abstract

The purpose of this study was to explore how women adult educators use feminist pedagogy in transnational adult education settings. Three research questions guided this study: 1. What are the teaching philosophies, personal beliefs, feminist strategies, and sources of wisdom (practices) that feminist adult educators report in their teaching? 2. What feminist topics or issues (episodes) have feminist adult educators described as occurring? 3. What kinds of feminist classroom activities (encounters) do feminist adult educators describe and how do these connect to their previously described feminist practices? Feminist qualitative interviews were conducted with eight women adult educators using feminist pedagogy in transnational adult education settings.

The researcher identified three conclusions. First, the women adult educators in this study embraced a political intersectional and transnational feminist teaching philosophy that was influenced by their individual ethics, their social justice-based activist practices, and an understanding grounded in feminist consciousness. Next, the women in this study constructed practices that were learner-centered, responsive to the context, and strategic in mining current events and the students' lived experiences for teachable moments that guided the discussions and learning. Finally, the women in this study negotiated their tense, politically charged learning environments by selecting seemingly neutral activities that, when enacted, contained implicit and explicit components promoting critical thinking. This study has implications for literature on feminist pedagogy in adult and higher education by addressing the impact of educators' ability and attempts to use feminist pedagogy despite pervasive neoliberal and postfeminist constraints in transnational adult education settings. This study has implications for practice in its illumination of multiple pathways for using feminist pedagogy with adults and the politics of claiming and naming feminism in transnational adult education practice.

Table of contents	Comments
1. Introduction 2. Review of the literature 3. Methodology 4. Participant profiles 5. Research findings 6. Discussion and conclusions	This dissertation also uses the traditional form for a dissertation, with a chapter providing participant profiles prior to the presentation of findings. The dissertation ends with discussion and conclusions.

Research purpose

The purpose of this study was to explore how women adult educators use feminist pedagogy in transnational adult education settings. (p. 12)

Research questions

1. What are the teaching philosophies, personal beliefs, feminist strategies, and sources of wisdom (practices) that feminist adult educators report in their teaching?

2. What feminist topics or issues (episodes) have feminist adult educators described as occurring?

3. What kinds of feminist classroom activities (encounters) do feminist adult educators describe and how do these connect to their previously described feminist practices? (p. 13)

Publication

Herron, B. A. (2022). 40 years of qualitative feminist interviewing: Conceptual moments and cultivating ecosystems of care. *Qualitative Inquiry, 29*(6). https://doi.org/10.1177/10778004221139611

Example 3

Pate, J. A. (2012). *A space for connection: A phenomenological inquiry on music listening as leisure.* [Doctoral dissertation, University of Georgia]. http://getd.libs.uga.edu/pdfs/pate_joseph_a_201205_phd.pdf

This polyvocal text leveraged Post-Intentional Phenomenology (Vagle, 2010) to trouble, open up, and complexify understanding of the lived leisure experience (Parry & Johnson, 2006) of connection with and through music listening. Music listening was foregrounded as one horizon within the aural soundscape that affords deeply meaningful and significant experiences for many. Past scholarship within the Leisure Studies literature has primarily attended to the impact and relevancy of music in the lives of adolescents. This study focused on engagement with music of five adults, accessing phenomenology as both a philosophical and methodological lens to look along (Lewis, 1990) this lived-experience. Using multiple voices and styles of representation, this polyvocal work challenged traditional ways of knowing by inviting listening, music, and voice to serve as additional data embedded throughout its discursive representation. Accessing Bachelard's (1990) phenomenology of the resonation-reverberation doublet revealed five partial, fleeting, and tentative manifestations (Vagle, 2010) of this lived leisure experience, which included: Getting Lost: Felt Resonation and Embodiment; I'm Open: Openness, Receptivity, and Enchantment; Serendipitous Moments; The Found Mirror: Oh There You Are; and Cairns and Echoes: The Lustering Potency of Song. Ultimately, music appeared to *speak to* so as to *speak for* participants, providing musical affirmation and sustenance throughout their lives.

Table of contents	Comments
1. The inescapability of music 2. Philosophy of methodology: Tracings of one's *taking up* of phenomenology 3. On methods: An improvisational-infused phenomenological jam	This dissertation, which was a phenomenological exploration of the experience of music listening, was represented in five chapters with an added musical track and liner notes.

4. The experiential soundscape of music listening: Aural horizons and the foregrounding of depth and significance of connection 5. From resonation to reverberation: Manifestations of music connection *speaking to* so as to *speak for* 6. Coda on musical sustenance	

Research purpose

The purpose of this study was to phenomenologically explore adults' engagement and connection with music.

Research questions

1. What is it to find oneself connected/connecting with music?
2. What does it mean for one to connect with music?
3. What does a connection with music afford, or make possible, for individuals? (p. 46)

Publication

Pate, J. A., & Johnson, C. W. (2013). Sympathetic chords: Reverberating connection through the lived leisure experiences of music listening. *International Journal of Community Music, 6*(2), 189–203. https://doi.org/10.1386/ijcm.6.2.189_1

Example 4

Kim, S.-J. (2011). *Voices in career transitions: A qualitative study to understand Korean adults' career construction in post-retirement.* [Doctoral dissertation, University of Georgia]. http://getd.libs.uga.edu/pdfs/kim_seon-joo_201108_phd.pdf
A rapidly changing society, shaped by demographic changes and a global economy, has created different employment trends and work lives, which in turn require adults to adapt to changes in their careers. This is particularly the case for Korean middle-aged professionals. The combination of the demographic change and socio-economic development has created unprecedented social phenomena, denoting the extension of the working period. For many adults in Korea, this retirement transition presents permeable boundaries between cessation of full-time work and continuous commitment to the workforce. Retirement has become a career transition moving them to another career cycle in which individuals interact with different factors. The purpose of the study was to examine the career transition experiences of Korean

middle-aged professionals—who have retired from their primary career and in their post-retirement employment—by investigating their perspectives of the processes involved in their career transition and construction. This interpretative study was guided by the following research questions: (1) What is the process of career transition for Korean middle-aged adults? (2) What contextual factors shape their career construction? (3) How do professionals interpret their career transition processes? Criterion-based sampling was used to select participants for the study. Two female and five male Korean adults in their second careers who had already retired from their primary careers were interviewed for this study; their ages ranged from 48 to 65. Semi-structured, in-depth interviews were used to collect the data. The constructivist grounded theory method was used to analyze and interpret data. Three broad categories of themes emerged from the data to address the research questions: (a) the career transition process, (b) contextual factors shaping career transition and construction, and (c) interpretation of career transitions and construction. The findings resulted in two major conclusions. First, career transition and construction was a process which entailed an appraisal of the threads linking person and context. Second, personal values created a balance between personal situations and societal environments and in turn enabled them to employ career adaptability. These conclusions led to implications for research and practice.

Table of contents	Comments
1. Introduction 2. Review of the literature 3. Research methodology 4. Findings 5. Summary, conclusions, and implications	This dissertation is formatted in the traditional five-chapter dissertation.

Research purpose
The purpose of the study was to examine the career transition experiences of Korean middle-aged professionals.

Research questions
1. What is the process of career transition for Korean middle-aged adults?
2. What contextual factors shape their career construction?
3. How do professionals interpret their career transition processes?

Publication

Kim, S.-J. (2014). The career transition process: A qualitative exploration of Korean middle-aged workers in postretirement employment. *Adult Education Quarterly, 64*(1), 3–19. https://doi.org/10.1177/0741713613513491

Examples of 3-Article Dissertations

All four of these three-article dissertations use a similar format. Authors introduce the topic of the research and the articles, and after a presentation of three discrete articles, authors provide a conclusion discussing the contribution of their work to their fields of inquiry.

Example 5

Halpin, S. (2021). *A framework for iterative integration of qualitatively-driven mixed methods in formative evaluation.* [Doctoral dissertation, University of Georgia]. https://esploro.libs.uga.edu/esploro/outputs/9949374969702959

Abstract

Creating evidence-based interventions (EBIs) is difficult and time-consuming, involving many iterative improvements that are rarely documented. An articulated process for integrating improvements could increase transparency and trust in reported results thus improving the success of adapting EBIs to other contexts. In this three-article dissertation, I introduce a framework for iteratively integrating qualitatively-driven mixed methods (QDMM) in formative evaluation (FE). In the first chapter, I outline and define FE, QDMM, and the Ready 4 Transplant (R4T) example study. The R4T study, highlighted in chapter two, involved the 18-month design of supplemental education videos for multiple myeloma patients receiving autologous stem cell transplant (ASCT). Ethnographic observations, audio recordings of naturally occurring data, informal and semi-structured interviews, and document review were employed to explore the patients' (n=70), caregivers' (n=70), and clinicians' (n=7) video engagement from their first "evaluation day" visit until their ASCT months later. The videos were improved iteratively during the study based on stakeholder feedback. Chapter three represents a study using conversation analysis of how patients, caregivers, and nurses referenced the videos during in-person education. Results revealed unanticipated ways the video impacted the visits; patients often discussed the videos to demonstrate their knowledge (n=15, 88%) and less often to clarify details they learned from the videos (n=2, 12%). Nurses responded by praising the patient's diligence but also relegating the patient to the role of "student" and reinforcing the nurse's role as teacher. Likewise, nurses initiated a dialogue about the video using positive (n=14; 39%), negative (n=13= 36%), or neutral appraisals (n=9; 25%), all used to re-orient the discourse back toward the script the nurse intended to discuss. In chapter four, I provide a review of the proposed framework for integrating QDMM into FE with questions to ask while creating EBIs including those about method choice (i.e., pertinent questions, restrictions, emergent findings) and integrating findings. Last, in chapter five, I summarize findings and consider opportunities for expanding the framework to include other components of evaluation, and future directions using data from the example study.

Table of contents	Comments
1. Introduction 2. An iterative formative evaluation of medical education for multiple myeloma patients receiving autologous stem cell transplant. 3. Using conversation analysis to appraise how novel educational videos impact patient medical education 4. A framework for iterative integration of qualitatively-driven mixed methods in formative evaluation 5. Overview and conclusion	This dissertation demonstrates how the findings from a study can be represented in a "three-article" format. These articles are prefaced by an intro-duction, and the dissertation closes with an overview of the research project. The first article describes the larger evaluation project, the second article brings the lens of conversation analysis to examine patient medical education, and the third article makes a methodological case for the use of qualitatively-driven mixed methods in formative evaluation.

Research purpose

In this study we[1] sought to identify how proprietary video-based education (VBE) impacted the communication between patients, caregivers, and nurses during in-person patient medical education (PME). (p. 77)

Research questions

In what ways, if any, do patients, caregivers, and nurses orient toward the videos during in-person education? (p. 77)

Publications

Halpin, S. N., Konomos, M., & Jowers, I. (2021). Interrupted identities: Autologous stem cell transplant in patients with multiple myeloma. *Journal of Patient Experience, 8*, 1–7. https://doi.org/10.1177/2374373521998864

Halpin, S. N., Konomos, M., & Roulston, K. (2021). Using applied conversation analysis in patient education. *Global Qualitative Nursing Research, 8*, 1–11. https://doi.org/10.1177/23333936211012990

Halpin, S., Konomos, M. & Roulston, K. (2022). Using conversation analysis to appraise how novel educational videos impact patient medical education. *Patient Education & Counseling, 105*(7) 2027–2032. https://doi.org/10.1016/j.pec.2021.11.012

Example 6

Guthrie, K. H. (2019). *Exploring the experiences of gifted adolescent girls through qualitative inquiry, with methodological implications for future research.* [Doctoral dissertation, University of Georgia]. http://getd.libs.uga.edu/pdfs/guthrie_kate_h_201905_phd.pdf

Abstract

The purpose of this dissertation was to explore the lives and experiences of gifted adolescent girls through qualitative inquiry. Qualitative inquiry with adolescents is challenging, especially in educational research in which they see adults as the gatekeepers of 'right' and 'wrong' answers. To help diminish power dynamics, group interviews are a common method for inquiry; however, the intense desire to fit in with a group of peers (Erickson, 1980) and the risks associated with confidentiality can influence how adolescents respond in a group setting. The first study summarizes common obstacles to group interviews with adolescents followed by strategies qualitative researchers can employ to foster richer meaning making among adolescent participants. Implications for researchers and teachers of qualitative research methods are addressed. For many gifted and high ability adolescent girls, navigating the social terrain of peer acceptance in classrooms can be challenging. The second study employed some of the suggested strategies discussed in the first study to understand the influence of an all-girls advanced math class from the perspectives of a class of gifted adolescent girls and their teacher. Data included student written reflections, two group interviews with students, two interviews with the teacher, and two small group follow-up discussions with the students. Through deductive and inductive analyses, I identified four key themes of influence. The findings indicate that single-sex classes may benefit gifted girls, especially in STEM classes, by supporting meaningful engagement in the classroom. The chapter begins with a poetic transcription that I composed, based on the work of Glesne (1997), representing the participants' collective voice. Inspired by narrative inquiry methodology, the purpose of the third study was to explore how gifted adolescent girls experience giftedness and belonging through the perspectives of their mothers. Participants were three mothers who were invited to be shared narrative inquirers and co-negotiators of their daughters' narratives. Their perspectives provided unique insight that can be difficult to capture through direct inquiry with adolescents. Three narratives are presented that demonstrate the complexity of how giftedness can influence a girls' sense of belonging, focusing primarily on the social landscapes of adolescence and school.

Table of contents	Comments
1. Introduction 2. Qualitative inquiry with adolescents: Strategies for fostering rich meaning making in group interviews 3. "I have my confidence . . . which I didn't have before": The influence of an all-girls advanced math class on gifted adolescent girls 4. Stories of giftedness and belonging: A shared narrative inquiry with three mothers of gifted adolescent girls 5. Conclusion Appendices	This dissertation uses a similar format to introduce three articles and again ends with a conclusion. Chapter 1 is a methodological review of relevant research on the topic. The author used the review to situate the study methodologically, since the dissertation contributes to both methodological literature and the substantive topic. Chapter 2 represents a methodological article concerning the use of group interviewing with adolescents as a method. The chapter also contributes to literature on qualitative pedagogy, maintaining a focus on methodological issues. Chapter 3 presents the findings of the study with gifted adolescent girls in an all-girls math classroom using poetic transcription; and Chapter 4 uses narrative inquiry to explore gifted adolescent girls' sense of belonging.

Research purpose
The purpose of this dissertation was to explore the lives and experiences of gifted adolescent girls through qualitative inquiry.

Research questions
- What does being gifted mean to gifted adolescent girls? What messages do they receive? How do their interpretations of their giftedness influence their sense of self? In what way does their giftedness influence the ways in which they experience and make meaning of their world?
- How do adolescent participants engage and respond to qualitative inquiry? How can group interviews and group interaction support efforts of qualitative inquiry and meaning-making? How can we encourage rich meaning-making among adolescents in group interviews? In what ways might group interviews benefit gifted adolescent girls in their search for meaning and understanding?

Publications

Guthrie, K. H. (2020). The weight of expectations: A thematic narrative of gifted adolescent girls' reflections of being gifted. *Roeper Review, 42*(1), 25–37. https://doi.org/10.1080/02783193.2019.1690080

Guthrie, K. (2020). Qualitative inquiry with adolescents: Strategies for fostering rich meaning making in group interviews. *American Journal of Qualitative Research, 4*(3), 92–110. https://doi.org/10.29333/ajqr/8586

Guthrie, K. (2022). (Re)fractional narrative inquiry: A methodological adaptation for exploring stories. *Methodological Innovations, 15*(1), 3–15. https://doi.org/10.1177/20597991221077902

Example 7

Muhammad, E. (2019). *"The Strangeness of the Other": A Critical Qualitative Analysis of Racialized Alterity in Two "Sacred" Encounters.* [Doctoral dissertation, University of Georgia]. https://esploro.libs.uga.edu/esploro/outputs/9949365552502959

Abstract

The concept of alterity has a long history in the Western philosophical tradition. Commonly articulated as recognition of an "other" or of "difference", the meaning and usage of alterity in the social sciences and humanities have varied. In this dissertation, I offer a discussion of alterity in three separate articles. Article one addresses alterity directly by defining it, analyzing its use historically, troubling the western philosophic portrayal of it, and discussing the more modern reconceptualization of it. Articles two and three provide two separate analyses of a racialized form of alterity in evocative, real-world, religious encounters. By enlisting various methodological approaches to the "self/Other" relationship, articles two and three make a meaningful contribution to the literature on alterity through the use of multiple qualitative methods. Through the lens of critical qualitative inquiry, I emphasize in this dissertation the necessity of respect and of care within the self/Other dichotomy in an era where racial, national, and religious alterity is again rupturing and dividing the nation.

Table of contents	Comments
1. Introduction 2. The concept of alterity: Its usage and its relevance for critical qualitative researchers in the era of Trump 3. Weaponizing religion: A document analysis of the religious indoctrination of slaves in service of white labor elites 4. Racialized alterity: The Nation of Islam's phenomenology of Blackness 5. Coda Appendix	This dissertation is structured in three articles, with an introduction and coda. The first article introduces the concept of alterity. The second article uses this concept in a document analysis of two 19th century catechisms of the Protestant Episcopal Church of the Confederacy. The third article analyzes doctrine of The Nation of Islam (NOI) using hermeneutic phenomenology.

Research purpose
In this dissertation study on alterity, I intend to explore its meaning, usage, and manifestations in the real world and to creatively fashion theoretical and methodological traditions around the central themes of race, religion, and alterity.

Research questions
How was religious indoctrination through the catechisms used to enslave black bodies? (p. 6)
What does a phenomenological analysis reveal about the Nation of Islam's doctrine? (p. 6)

Publications
Muhammad, E. A. (2020). Weaponizing religion: A document analysis of the religious indoctrination of slaves in service of White labor elites. In S. Finley & L. Martin (Eds.), *The religion of White rage: White workers, religious fervor, and the myth of racial progress* (pp. 192–212). Edinburgh University Press.

Muhammad, E. A. (2021). Countering the "phenomenology of whiteness": The Nation of Islam's phenomenology of blackness. *Journal of Critical Phenomenology, 4*(1). DOI: https://doi.org/10.5399/PJCP.v4i1.2

Muhammad, E. A. (2023). The concept of alterity: Its usage and its relevance for critical qualitative researchers. *Cultural Studies of Science Education, 18*, 309–325.

Example 8

Neal, A. (2022). *Black women abolitionist teachers and the spirit of our work.* [Doctoral dissertation, University of Georgia].

Abstract

This dissertation utilized digital archival methods to establish the significance of 19th and early 20th century Black women teachers in the fight for abolition. Historical Black women were not only active participants in the fight to abolish slavery but broadened the scope of the movement to include education. They expanded the role and responsibility of a teacher by providing instruction to pupils in the pulpit, podium, prisons, and the press, in home schools, churches, in quiet nooks, and in secret. More importantly, they injected their work with deeper meaning—namely, that freedom and education were not only human and civil rights but God-given rights. Grounded in womanist theology, this dissertation is presented in a three-paper format in order to ask distinctive research questions and engage interdisciplinary bodies of literature. In the first paper, I explored the spiritual underpinnings of historical Black women teachers' radical abolitionist work. I theorized a theo-ethic of abolition to demonstrate how historical Black women teachers were guided by and rooted in deep moral, ethical, and spiritual values, igniting them into radical action. In the second paper, I established how historical Black women teachers contended with staunch antiblackness, white supremacy, and racialized terror in their educational strivings, specifically by constructing sacred, hush harbors spaces of healing for Black students, even in the midst of it. In the final paper, I explored how the historical struggles for freedom and education are inextricably linked to the contemporary demands for abolition and equitable education. Extending the abolitionist trajectory of historical Black women teachers, I examined how they responded after the abolition of slavery through an examination of the Reconstruction era. In conclusion, my dissertation study suggested that there exists a radical womanist tradition of Black women teachers subverting oppressive structures to ensure educational justice and Black liberation, through radical faith. Abolition persisted in slavery and freedom; it was a way of knowing, being, and believing. This conceptualization highlights that if true educational justice is to take place under our contemporary social conditions, abolition must become a way of life and must be guided by something deeper, the Spirit.

Table of contents	Comments
Preface: Deeper than doctrine: He knows my name Introduction: Becoming an abolitionist (teacher) 1. "God meant I should be free": Historical Black women teachers and the theo-ethical imperative of abolition 2. The fugitive spirit of historical Black women teachers theorizing hush harbors as praxis 3. To be an abolitionist teacher: (Re) constructing education in the afterlife of abolition Appendix: Art-of-facts in the colour of Amber	This three-article dissertation includes a preface and introduction to introduce the organization of the dissertation, followed by three independent articles related to Black women abolitionist teachers.

Research purpose

To establish the significance of 19th and early 20th century Black women teachers in the fight for abolition.

Research questions

1. Why did historical Black women teachers engage in the fight for educational equity and abolition?
2. How did historical Black women abolitionist teachers contend with incessant antiblackness and racialized terror?
3. How did Black women teachers respond after the abolition of slavery? What can it teach us about education now?

Publications

Neal, A. M. & Dunn, D. C. (2020). Our ancestors' wildest dreams: (Re)membering the freedom dreams of Black women abolitionist teachers. *Journal of Curriculum Theorizing, 35*(4), 59–73.

Dillard, C. B. & Neal, A. M. (2020). I am because we are: (Re)membering Ubuntu in the pedagogy of Black woman teachers from Africa to America and back again. *Theory into Practice, 59*(4), 370–378.

Experimental dissertations

Experimental dissertations take many forms. Each of the four below makes use of arts-based inquiry methods.

Example 9

Berbary, L. (2008). *Subject to sorority: Women's negotiations of competing discourses of femininity.* [Doctoral dissertation, University of Georgia]. http://getd.libs.uga.edu/pdfs/berbary_lisbeth_a_200808_phd.pdf

Abstract

Based on the need to expand literature on sorority women and explore all women's negotiations of gendered discourses, this dissertation details the process and findings of an ethnographic study of a southern sorority. This ethnography was grounded in a priori theories of Michel Foucault and Judith Butler and their notions of discourse, discipline, subjectivity, and performativity and was guided by the following research questions: 1) What discourses of femininity are enabled within Zeta Chi sorority culture? 2) How are such discourses of femininity disseminated and disciplined within Zeta Chi culture? and 3) How do women in Zeta Chi negotiate the gendered expectations disciplined within such discourse? The findings of this study were presented through a creative analytic "pseudo" screenplay that illuminates the ways sorority women learned gendered expectations, were disciplined towards compliance, and sometimes resisted or reinterpreted expectations of the dominant discourse of "ladylike." The fact that some women resisted and re-interpreted expectations even within this strictly disciplined discourse of gender reinforces the possibility for us all to potentially "see" ways that we are disciplined, to challenge that discipline, and to open new possibilities for our own gendered selves.

Table of contents	Comments
1. Reflections of culture: I'm not a typical sorority girl 2. Theoretical foundations of the gendered self 3. Methodology 4. Dominant discourses of femininity 5. Discipline of ladylikeness 6. Negotiations of ladylike subjectivity 7. Conclusions and final reflections	This dissertation uses creative analytic practices as an experimental mode of presenting a dissertation study. The first chapter is represented as diary entries alongside a fictional email dialogue between a participant and the researcher. Chapter 2 explores the poststructural theories informing

the study, and Chapter 3 outlines the methods used. Findings are presented as a script with director's comments across Chapters 4, 5 and 6. The director's comments offer initial engagements with thinking through the data. The final chapter presents conclusions and reflections.

Research purpose

The purpose of this study was to explore how sorority women understand and negotiate the meaning of femininity among competing and complex societal messages. (p. 65)

Research questions

- What discourses of femininity are enabled within Zeta Chi sorority culture?
- How are such discourses of femininity disseminated and disciplined within Zeta Chi culture?
- How do women in Zeta Chi negotiate the gendered expectations disciplined within such discourse? (p. 65)

Publications

Berbary, L. A. (2011). Poststructural writerly representation: Screenplay as creative analytic practice. *Qualitative Inquiry, 17*(2), 186–196. https://doi.org/10.1177/1077800410393887

Berbary, L. A. (2012). "Don't be a whore, That's not ladylike": Discursive discipline and sorority women's gendered subjectivity. *Qualitative Inquiry, 18*(7), 606–625. https://doi.org/10.1080/14927713.2012.746072

Berbary, L. A. (2013). Reflections of culture: A diary of a sorority girl. *Creative Approaches to Research, 6*(1), 6–43.

Berbary, L. A. (2014). Too good at fitting in: Methodological consequences and ethical adjustments. *International Journal of Qualitative Studies in Education, 27*(10), 1205–1225. https://doi.org/10.1080/09518398.2013.820856

Berbary, L. A., & Johnson, C. W. (2012). The American sorority girl recast: An ethnographic screenplay of leisure in context. *Leisure/Loisir, 36*(3–4), 243–268.

Example 10

Copple, J. (2022). *Making menstrual knowledge through multi-genre methodologies: Exploring mothers' encounters with children at menarche.* [Doctoral dissertation, University of Georgia]. https://esploro.libs.uga.edu/esploro/outputs/9949450622702959

Abstract

This inquiry draws on concepts from Karen Barad's agential realism theory and uses multi-genre creative modalities to explore mothers' encounters preparing menstruating/soon-to-be menstruating children for menarche. Specifically, I examine how mothers navigate the complexities of being supportive of children during this developmental milestone and how this entangles with mothers' personal experiences with menstruation as well as sociocultural narratives of taboo and empowerment surrounding menstruating bodies. The extant literature on children at menarche suggests maternal support fosters a positive self-concept for children around changes associated with coming of age, yet few studies examine mothers' experiences directly. This inquiry speaks to this gap in the literature through an explicit focus on mothers' encounters preparing children for menarche using multi-genre creative formats (e.g., short story, letter, journal, email, data poetry, narrative poetry, autoethnography). Through these multi-genre forms, I explore supportive motherhood as subjectivity in motion produced as mothers navigate encounters with their children—considering these encounters always already entangled with personal experiences and sociocultural narratives of menstruating bodies. In doing so, I think with the tensions and contradictions of supportive motherhood in its ongoing becoming. I explore how becoming supportive both acknowledges and resists shame narratives, both reproduces and disrupts taboos. As I think with Barad's concepts, I explore the entanglement of being and knowing in mothers' encounters as I consider supportive motherhood—its complexities and contradictions—part of menstrual knowledge in the making. Further, I examine my entanglements in this inquiry as a mother-researcher, consider my own subjectivities in motion and explore the methodological implications of thinking with Barad and mothers' data through multiple creative genres. Substantively, this inquiry provides an entry point for considering how mothers' encounters with children at menarche make visible the complexities and possibilities of disrupting stigma surrounding menstruation. Methodologically, this inquiry explores the possibilities of thinking with Baradian concepts across multi-genre modalities and examines the ethical implications of boundary-making practices that both resist and reproduce traditional forms of representation in qualitative research.

Table of contents	Comments
I. Unruly, messy contradictions: Three tales Autoethnographic tangling with entanglements Methodological cut: The never-not (enough!) research with friends II. Surviving clutch moments: Stories of making do with menstruation Autoethnographic ramblings on intra-active sensemaking Methodological cut: Considering objects becoming material III. Getting it right, wrong and in-between: Encounters that make, break and remake us Autoethnographic meanderings in narrative apparatuses Methodological cut: Inquiry with multi-genre apparatuses IV. More than a pad in a purse, more than 'just stories' Towards a closing letter to the reader Coda References Appendices	This experimental dissertation is structured in four parts, each with a "methodological cut" that discusses methodological issues—making the contribution of the study both substantive and methodological. The author first presents an introduction (Part I), before discussing findings (Parts II, III, and IV). The findings are represented using multiple genres, including short narratives, letters, journal entries, poetry, images, an audio-file, and autoethnographic vignettes. The dissertation's conclusion is staged in the form of a letter to readers, followed by a coda.

Research purpose

The purpose of this study was to examine how mothers navigate the complexities of supporting menstruating/soon-to-be menstruating children for menarche.

Research questions
- What are the experiences of mothers preparing menstruating children for puberty?
- How do mothers' narratives of preparing children for puberty materialize through human and object encounters?

Publication

Copple, J. (2021). Earnin' your raising: An autoethnographic remembrance of mother–daughter stories and reflections on parenting. *Qualitative Inquiry, 27*(3–4), 346–352. https://doi.org/10.1177/1077800420917425

Example 11

Flint, M. (2019). *Methodological orientations: College student navigations of race and place in higher education.* [Doctoral dissertation, University of Alabama]. http://ir.ua.edu/handle/123456789/6135

Abstract

This inquiry explores how college students navigate the sociohistorical context of race on campus, guided by critical material and spatial theories. Specifically, I explore how students navigate the tangle of discourses surrounding race on a college campus from the history of buildings and monuments, the perceptions and stereotypes of the campus before arriving, and how they navigate, resist, and reproduce those discourses and rhetoric. This inquiry is informed by research from higher education, which has demonstrated not only a gap in experiences between historically marginalized students and their majority peers but a persistent culture of white supremacy that is reified through formal and informal policies and systems. Specifically, I take up the idea of belongingness in relation to White supremacy and higher education to explore how higher education outcomes that are often positioned as neutral are historically situated and hegemonic concepts that are reproduced through institutional practices. In other words, this research explores and works the tensions between the idea of belongingness as an achievable, boundable, and predictable outcome, and the persistent reproduction of racism and White supremacy in higher education that works against belonging. I explore the contradictions between what institutions say they do (with regards to diversity, equity, and inclusion) and how those values are experienced and encountered in higher education by students. This inquiry creates conversations between the experiences and navigations of students and the productions of place and space and race in higher education, moving between slippages in discourses between the South and Alabama, how the South is produced as racist, and how racism and White supremacy produce the South. This is followed by an exploration of disruptions in these slippages, moments where these slippages became visible, and the possibility for conspiratorial resistance, intervention, and reclamation of space. This inquiry suggests possibilities for higher education practitioners to consider the specifics of place, the context of our coeval becomings, even as we understand and take the global in perspective to inform how we make the place of higher education differently.

Table of contents	Comments
1. On maps 2. The boulder 3. Happenings 4. Encounters and intersections 5. Higher education, race, and belonging 6. Spatial/material haeccities 7. Compass 8. Methodological practices 9. The wall 10. Returning to the boulder 11. More maps 12. Slippages 13. Theoretically faithful 14. Disruptions 15. Still more maps 16. For whom 17. Not a secret 18. Before 19. Interventions, becoming here 20. Implications 21. Coda 22. Un/faithful, not/enough References Appendices	The table of contents from this experimental dissertation provides fewer clues as to what aspects of a study are included in each section. Like Example 8, this dissertation contributes both methodological and substantive findings. In the former, the researcher explores theoretical and methodological innovations; in the latter, the researcher contributes to studies in higher education. Findings are represented in artful representations across short chapters that include poetic transcriptions, collages, images, maps, and methodological wonderings.

Research purpose
This study used critical material and feminist spatial theories to examine how college students navigate the sociohistorical context of race on campus.

Research questions
How do college students navigate the space/place of higher education?
What role does the socio-historical context of race play in students' navigations of space?

Publications

Flint, M. A. (2019). Hawks, robots, and challkings: Unexpected object encounters during walking interviews on a college campus. *Educational Research for Social Change, 8*(1), 120–137. https://doi.org/https://doi.org/10.17159/2221-4070/2018/v8i1a8

Flint, M. A. (2019). Ruptures and reproductions: A walking encounter with a campus tour and a Confederate monument. *Cultural Studies ↔ Critical Methodologies, 19*(2), 91–104. https://doi.org/10.1177/1532708618809136

Flint, M. A. (2021). More-than-human methodologies in qualitative research: Listening to the leafblower. *Qualitative Research, 22*(4), 521–541. https://doi.org/10.1177/1468794121999028

Flint, M. A. (2021). Racialized retellings: (Un)ma(r)king space and place on college campuses. *Critical Studies in Education, 62*(5), 559–574. https://doi.org/10.1080/17508487.2021.1877756

Flint, M. (2021). Sounded histor-futurit-ies: Imagining posthuman possibilities of race and place in qualitative research. *International Journal of Qualitative Studies in Education, 36*(4), 672–688. https://doi.org/10.1080/09518398.2021.1885071

Example 12

Breeden, R. L. (2021). *"Miles away, but in our own backyard": A participatory action study examining relationships between historically white institutions and Black communities.* [Doctoral dissertation, University of Georgia].

Abstract

This study explored the relationships between historically white institutions (HWIs) and their local Black communities. Using participatory action research (PAR) methodology, grounded in a Critical Race Theoretical (CRT) framework, undergirded by endarkened feminist epistemology, research questions included: (a) How do Black communities experience and make meaning of their local HWI? and (b) How does history intersect between Black communities and the University? Rooted in PAR methodology, this study included two Black undergraduate co-researchers from Athens, Georgia. Together, we used an intergenerational approach for data collection, centering the voices of Black undergraduate students, community leaders, and families from the Athens-Clarke County community. Collectively, Black participants in this study reported strained relationships, intentional erasure of their history, and a legacy of institutional racism from their local HWI, the University of Georgia (UGA). Using participants' voices, study findings were contextualized through performative counter-storytelling, shared in one stage-play over three vignettes. The findings shed light on how the historical and current contexts of institutions lead to economic and educational injustices in Black communities. While this study took place in Athens, Georgia, study implications can be applied to institutions with similar contexts. HWIs across the United States can improve their relationships with Black communities by naming racial histories and complexities, atoning for what was lost, and making amends through systemic changes for generations of Black families and communities.

Table of contents	Comments
1. Introduction 2. Literature Review 3. Methodology 4. Findings 5. Participation Action Research 6. Discussion, Implications, and Future Research	On the face of it, this dissertation is a traditional one with the usual five chapters (introduction, literature, methodology, findings, and discussion/implications). Two things make this work distinct. First, the findings are presented as a script to a stage play, centering the participants' voices. Second, this dissertation has an extra chapter. Chapter 5 is a detailed account of how to complete an action research project with a research team of undergraduate students.

Research purpose

The purpose of the study was threefold. First, I sought to understand the significance of historical and current events which impact educational and economic opportunities for Black communities. Second, I explored the role of participatory action research (PAR) methodology to center the voices of Black families and communities. Third, I used the implications from this study to inform higher education practices and policies.

Research questions

The following questions guided this qualitative research study:

1. How do Black communities experience and make meaning of their local HWI?
2. How does history intersect between Black communities and the University?

Publication

Breeden, R. L., Smith, T. L., & Willis, A. L. (2023). "Strained relationships": A participatory action research study examining relationships between Black communities and historically White institutions. *Journal of Diversity in Higher Education.* Advance online publication. https://doi.org/10.1037/dhe0000482

Note

1. Although this dissertation represented individual work, Dr. Halpin worked with several others at the hospital where this study was conducted to complete the evaluation study, hence the use of "we."

✏ About the Authors

Janie Copple is an Assistant Professor in the Department of Educational Policy Studies at Georgia State University. Her research explores qualitative research methodologies and pedagogies, specifically feminist critical materialist approaches to narrative, autoethnographic, and arts-based research as well as topics on motherhood and puberty education. Janie has published works in *Qualitative Inquiry* and *The Qualitative Report* as well as book chapters and essays on qualitative research methods. She is also co-editor and contributing author of *Conservative Philanthropies and Organizations Shaping U.S. Educational Policy and Practice* (with K. deMarrais & B. Herron, 2020).

Kathleen deMarrais is Professor, Emerita, of Qualitative Research in the Mary Frances Early College of Education at the University of Georgia. Her research interests include qualitative research methods, critical qualitative research, and archival methods. In addition to numerous articles and book chapters, her recent books include *Exploring the Archives: A Beginner's Guide for Qualitative Researchers* (with K. Roulston, 2021), *Conservative Philanthropies and Organizations Shaping U.S. Educational Policy and Practice* (with B. Herron & J. Copple, 2020), and *Philanthropy, Hidden Strategy, and Collective Resistance: A Primer for Concerned Educators* (with T. J. Brewer, J. C. Atkinson, B. Herron, and J. Lewis, 2019). In her spare time, she enjoys gardening, raising chickens, baking pies, and exploring local community history.

Kathryn Roulston is Professor of Qualitative Research in the Mary Frances Early College of Education at the University of Georgia. Her research interests include qualitative research methods, qualitative interviewing, and analyses of talk-in-interaction. She is the editor of *Quests for Questioners: Inventive Approaches to Qualitative Interviews* (2023) and *Exploring the Archives: A Beginner's Guide for Qualitative Researchers* (with K. deMarrais, 2021), and editor of *Interactional Studies of Qualitative Research Interviews* (2019). She has contributed chapters to handbooks of qualitative research as well as articles to *Qualitative Research, Qualitative Inquiry*, the *International Journal of Research and Method in Education*, and the *International Journal of Qualitative Methods*, among other journals. In her spare time, she enjoys textile arts, including hand-dyeing, spinning, and weaving.

Index